3 1842 02657 2105

Y0-BZY-060

CADOGANguides

BILBAO & THE BASQUE LANDS

*'The main street is a river, and it is one of the most
delightful centrepieces a city could ask for,
lined with busy quays and old tall houses
painted in bright Basque red and green.'*

Dana Facaros & Michael Pauls

About the Guide

The full-colour introduction gives the authors' overview of the region, together with suggested itineraries and a regional 'where to go' map and feature to help you plan your trip.

Illuminating and entertaining cultural chapters on local history, food, wine and everyday life give you a rich flavour of the region.

Planning Your Trip starts with the basics of when to go, getting there and getting around, coupled with other useful information, including a section for disabled travellers. The Practical A–Z deals with all the essential information and contact details that you may need while you are away.

The regional chapters are arranged in a loose touring order, with plenty of public transport and driving information. The author's top 'Don't Miss' ⭐ sights are highlighted at the start of each chapter.

A language and pronunciation guide, a glossary of cultural terms, a chronology, ideas for further reading and a comprehensive index can be found at the end of the book.

Although everything we list in this guide is personally recommended, our authors inevitably have their own favourite places to eat and stay. Whenever you see this Author's Choice ⭐ icon beside a listing, you will know that it is a little bit out of the ordinary.

Hotel Price Guide

Luxury	€€€€€	over €200 and above
Very Expensive	€€€€	€160–200
Expensive	€€€	€120–160
Moderate	€€	€80–120
Inexpensive	€	under €80

Restaurant Price Guide

Expensive	€€€€	over €45
Moderate	€€	€25–45
Inexpensive	€	under €25

About the Authors

Dana Facaros and Michael Pauls have written over 30 books for Cadogan Guides. They have lived all over Europe with their son and daughter, and are currently ensconced in a old farmhouse in southwestern France with a large collection of tame and wild animals.

5th Edition published 2012

01 INTRODUCING BILBAO & THE BASQUE LANDS

While we were writing the first edition of this book, the news broke that scientists, much to their wonder, had discovered traces of tobacco and cocaine in the mummy of an ancient pharaoh, and our first thought was that it was probably the Basques who supplied the Egyptians with the stuff from America. Well, on second thoughts, perhaps they didn't – but the Basques were around at the time, and an air of mystery and improbability hangs about them. Above all, they are full of surprises. They eat red-hot peppers; they play the world's fastest ball game, run in front of bulls and dance on goblets; they have bards who improvise poetry at the drop of a hat; they founded one of the world's first multinationals, the Real Compañia Guipúzcoana de Caracas, in the 18th century. Conjuring up the Guggenheim Museum in old Bilbao is only their most recent feat, and surely not the last.

There is something almost magical about their very existence. The 2.9 million Basques, a taciturn though likeable lot, are Europe's great survivors, as old as the hills they inhabit, speaking the same language for thousands of years – maybe 10,000, maybe more; no one knows. Since Roman times they've been squeezed into a 20,864 square kilometre elbow of rugged land between France and Spain on the Bay of Biscay, and in spite of their bossy neighbours they have held on tight to their identity. After long decades of suppression, their culture, festivals, music, sports, cuisine, literature and so on – among the great attractions of the Basque country – are thriving, thanks in part to the work of ardent nationalists. Nationalism isn't that popular a concept in Europe these days (although if you read a bit of Basque history you may understand their point of view), but you should not confuse it with terrorism

Previous page: Traditional street in Hondarribia

This page, from top: Pyrenean landscape; Peppers hung out to dry

*Above: Windmill,
Aixerrota, near Getxo
Right: Surfing near
Donostia-San Sebastián*

and ETA, which started out as the only armed resistance to Franco's regime but has been carried on and on by a handful of die-hards. But the vast majority of Basques are in favour of negotiated solutions. There is, in general, a much higher political awareness here than in most places, and certainly a lot more volunteers ready to go out and paint every highway underpass with their message.

The Basques may be nationalistic, but their global outlook pre-dates most European nation states, and the role they've played in Spanish and French affairs is far out of proportion to their numbers. They were great sailors and explorers, shipbuilders and whalers, *conquistadores* and pirates, early capitalists and industrialists, and nowadays they run most of Spain's banks and insurance agencies plus Mondragón, one of the world's most successful co-operative ventures. Basque sailors helped the English conquer Wales, built the

Spanish Armada and founded a number of colonies, including the
Philippines, as well as cities like Buenos Aires. The *conquistadores*
Lope de Aguirre and Pedro de Ursúa were Basques, and so was Juan
Sebastián de Elcano, the first man to sail around the world. So were
two of Spain's most important saints, Ignatius of Loyola and Francis
Xavier, and, in more recent times, the great philosopher Miguel de
Unamuno, politician Dolores Ibarruri ('La Pasionaria' of the Spanish
Republic), and Eduardo Chillida, one of Spain's best-known sculptors.

Although the world-famous Guggenheim Museum may well be
the shiny lure that brings you to the Basque country in the first
place, it would be a shame to stop there. The rest of Bilbao has been
in the throes of one of the most dramatic makeovers of any city in
Europe; and the smaller cities of Pamplona, Bayonne and Vitoria-
Gasteiz are vibrant and full of surprises. The dramatic coast is dotted
with glittering *belle époque* beach resorts – Donostia-San Sebastián,
Zarautz, Hondarribia, Biarritz and St-Jean-de-Luz – once famous for
collecting the crowned heads of Europe, now renowned for surfing.

Neat-as-a-pin villages and sloping-roofed farmhouses dot emerald
landscapes that have been tended by the same people for millennia
(and well they should be emerald – the Basque country gets as much
rain as the west of Ireland), and are filled with quiet wonders – deep
primordial forests, caves (some with Palaeolithic art), megalithic
monuments, and strange and beautiful Romanesque churches,
especially in Navarra along the pilgrims' road to Santiago. The
Pyrenean and the Cantabrian mountain ranges keep the rain from
the plain of southern Navarra and Álava, the fief of Rioja wine and
perhaps the last thing you'd expect: a desert, the Bárdenas Reales.

The Basques' own integrity has made their home one of those rare
places where the word 'authentic' has no meaning, because it's
never been anything but. As Victor Hugo wrote, 'Everyone who has
visited the Basque country longs to return; it is a blessed land.'

Where to Go

This book starts with **Bilbao**, the industrial dynamo of the Basque country, and now a role model for other cities of how to recreate themselves with a new image. The Guggenheim Museum is the showpiece, of course, and merits a trip to Bilbao on its own. But it's worth taking a look at the rest of Bilbao, a city of no little character, with a dazzling new infrastructure, excellent older museums, the largest covered market in Spain and the Siete Calles, a great neighbourhood for exploring the city's vibrant bar culture. You may even like to spend an afternoon by the sea at Bilbao's beach resort, Getxo.

After Bilbao comes the rest of **Euskadi**, the Spanish Basque country. Vitoria-Gasteiz, south of Bilbao, is the regional capital and a fine city in its own right, although relatively little known outside of Spain. To the east lie Gaceo and Alaiza, with stunning Gothic frescoes in the former, and bizarre, primitive and belligerent 14th-century frescoes in the latter. South of Vitoria, towards the Ebro, are the vineyards of La Rioja Alavesa and fascinating wine villages, especially Laguardia. The next section heads east of Bilbao, first taking an inland route through typical Basque villages. The coast is probably the biggest draw, though: the islet of San Juan de Gaztelugatxa, the sacred town of Gernika and Upper Palaeolithic painted cave of Santimamiñe; and the beach resorts of Lekeitio, Deba, Zumaia, Getaria, and the biggest of them all, lovely Donostia-San Sebastián. Inland from Donostia-San Sebastián, the province of Guipúzcoa is home to the attractive and scholarly towns of Oñati and Bergara, as well as the modern Sanctuary of Aránzazu and Loyola, birthplace of St Ignatius, the founder of the Jesuits.

Navarra, the next chapter, begins with Pamplona, once the capital of the Basque kingdom and now the capital of *Los Sanfermines*, the bull-running in July. But there's plenty to see at other times, and Pamplona makes a convenient base for excursions into the countryside. To the northwest is Aralar, Navarra's magic mountain; southwest lie Estella and other sites along the pilgrims' road to Santiago; while directly south, where the landscapes are more arid, is the fairytale town of Olite, historic Tafalla, Tudela, more Rioja vineyards and the spectacular desert of the Bárdenas Reales. To the east of Pamplona, Sangüesa, Yesa, Javier and Leyre offer great days out for fans of funny old churches, while the nearby Foz de Arbayún is Navarra's version of the Grand Canyon. Farther to the east wait the beautiful Basque valleys of the Pyrenees, Roncal and Salazar, and northeast of Pamplona is the famous pass of Roncesvalles. Northwest are the startlingly lush valleys of Baztán and Bidasoa, where you'll find Zugarramurdi, scene of a 17th-century witch hunt.

From here it's over the border into France's **Pays Basque**, beginning along the coast, and its resorts, which, like Donostia-San Sebastián, enjoyed a vogue among the aristocracy in the mid-19th century

Above, from top: Plaza Sagrado Corazón, Bilbao; grapes in La Rioja; Cathedral, Donostia-San Sebastián. Opposite page: Port, Saint-Jean-de-Luz

and now find themselves invaded by surfers as well as more genteel holidaymakers. The picturesque fishing town of St-Jean-de-Luz is a seductive place to stay and eat, or there are smaller resorts such as Bidart and Guéthary, and Urrugne with its castle and gardens. Biarritz, of course, is the star of the Côte Basque, a stylish old resort with a huge beach, full of memories of the Empress Eugénie, who first made it popular. Bayonne, adjacent, was an old whaling port and remains a city that works for its living, with unspoiled old neighbourhoods along the river Nive; it also boasts a pair of El Grecos, a Botticelli and several chocolate-makers. Just in from the coast, the Labourd interior contains archetypal Basque scenery and villages such as Sare, St-Pée and Espelette, where red peppers come from. The valley of the Nive follows, where remarkable prehistoric art was discovered in the Istaritz caves and delicious cherries grow in Itxassou. Here, too, is handsome St-Jean-Pied-de-Port, centre for exploring the lush Basque Pyrenees and the secretive little region of Soule.

Chapter Divisions

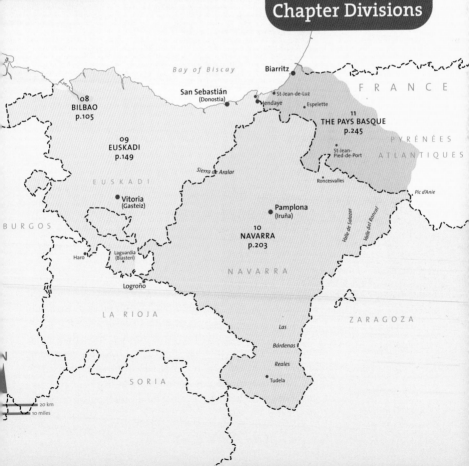

Where Old Means Old

They say here that when God created the first man, he got the bones from a Basque graveyard. This is a land full of ancient forests, Palaeolithic painted caves and Neolithic dolmens – built by giants according to the old tales. But the most astounding thing, according to recent research, is that it may have been the Basques themselves who were doing all that long-ago stone-carrying.

By any measure, they're the oldest people of Europe, the real natives. Visiting their little corner not only provides a window on an unimaginably distant past, but a vision of settled contentment and serenity. This is true nowhere more than in the lovely green Pyrenean foothills south of Biarritz, with the perfect little farmhouses with shutters invariably painted Basque red or green. Some of these houses, and their predecessors on the same foundations, have been in the same family for hundreds of years.

Above, from top:
Traditional Basque
farmhouse;
Dolmen, near Oiz

Opposite page:
San Juan de
Gazteluatxe

*Above: Guggenheim
Museum, Bilbaoo, at
night
Right: Bridge over the
Nervión, Bilbao*

Above, from top:
Arriaga Theatre, Bilbao;
Donostia-San Sebastián
at night

Cities with an Edge

A peculiar place, Bilbao is, with a topography so unreasonable that steel mills perch atop hilltops, and getting from one part of town to another occasionally requires riding an elevator. Not so long ago, they'd have laughed if you had suggested that this rusty old industrial centre could turn itself into a tourist destination. But with a lot of money, a lot of nerve, some creative ideas and a little help from Frank Gehry and the Guggenheims, they pulled it off.

There are other cities in the region worthy of your attention, too: the thoroughly gorgeous resort towns of Donostia-San Sebastián and St-Jean-de-Luz, Bayonne, with its ornate cathedral and colourful, half-timbered medieval centre, and one place few people have ever heard of: Vitoria-Gasteiz, the modest and amiable capital of Basque Euskadi.

Beyond the Titanium

Ever since the Guggenheim opened, tourists have been flocking to Bilbao, making this old steel town one of the art meccas of the galaxy. Is there anything else to look at? The Basques, in their quiet way, have produced quite a bit; there are celebrated modern figures such as the sculptor Eduardo Chillida, and many others whose works you can inspect in the fine museums of Bilbao, Vitoria-Gasteiz and Bayonne.

But, as in much of this part of Europe, the best of the heritage is medieval. When pilgrims were pouring over the pass at Roncesvalles on their way to Compostela, this was a busy place, and that age has left us great monuments such as Bayonne's Gothic cathedral and lovely medieval towns like Estella in Navarra.

Clockwise from top: Church of San Sebastián, Donostia-San Sebastián; Castle, Olite; Bridge over the Irati River, Navarra

The Best Cooks in Spain

The archaeologists have dug up evidence that the Basques were cooking up seafood here 10,000 years ago. So they've had a lot of practice, and it should be no surprise that this little nation has one of the finest cuisines on the globe. Right now the little corner around Donostia-San Sebastián boasts more Michelin-starred restaurants than anywhere outside France.

After all those years, seafood still rules: a Basque chef can conjure up a marvellously complex *ttoro* (fish soup) or make simple *bacalao* (salt cod) into something transcendent. Beyond that you'll enjoy the best tapas in Spain, Bayonne hams, rustic *charcuterie*, lots of hot peppers from Espelette and famous wines from the Basque side of La Rioja.

Above, from top: Wine casks; pintxos *laid out in a Basque bar*

*Clockwise from top left:
Biarritz; Ondarreta beach,
Donostia-San Sebastián;
Dusk view of Donostia-
San Sebastián*

Come and Play on the Bay of Biscay

The Basques may seem like a people rooted to the land, cosy as
hobbits in their emerald-green hills. But they've always felt just as
much at home on the sea. Basques were the first to venture out on
it chasing whales. Columbus's pilot was a Basque, and so was the
first man to sail around the world. They haven't been doing much
exploring lately, but Basque life still keeps its ties to the sea.
Nowadays it's mostly for fun: the Bay of Biscay's big waves have
made it the European centre for surfing. A century ago, this short
but lavishly appointed stretch of coast made a perfect setting for
some of Europe's first fashionable beach resorts, Biarritz and
Donostia-San Sebastián. These retain their *belle époque* elegance
today, and there are scores of quieter beaches all around; you can
even ride the metro to some nice ones from the centre of Bilbao.

Itineraries

The Best of Euskadi and Navarra in Eleven Days

Days 1–2 Start the tour in the place most unlike the rest of the Basque lands, **Bilbao**. There's the Guggenheim and all the other recent embellishments, shopping in the Casco Viejo and grand-scale urbanism in the Ensanche, and maybe an afternoon on the beach at Plentzia, just down the metro line.

Day 3 Depart for the south and **Vitoria-Gasteiz**, the Spanish Basque capital: elegant monuments and streetscapes, and museums of art and armour and playing cards. If there's time, make a side trip to **Gaceo** and its unique medieval frescoes.

Day 4 From Vitoria, head southwest to the River Ebro, then eastwards into the Basque part of the **La Rioja wine region**. There are plenty of vineyards to inspect along the way, and also the artistocratic wine town of **Haro**. Finish in **Laguardia**.

Day 5 Now, head eastwards into a very refined corner of Navarra, and spend the day in the lovely medieval town of **Estella**; in the afternoon, climb up to the Monasterio de Irache.

Day 6 From Estella, continue eastwards, with a look at the Templar church at **Obanos**, before arriving at **Pamplona**, where there's a wealth of medieval art to see if the bulls aren't running.

Day 7 Heading back towards Euskadi, to the northwest, there is Navarra's holy mountain of **Aralar**. Visit the weird sanctuary of St Michael, and stay at **Lekunberri** or **Leitza** – or continue northwards all the way to Donostia-San Sebastián.

Days 8–9 **Donostia-San Sebastián** is worth at least two days. Between all the tapas and lolling on the beach, save some time for a tour of the old town and the Museo San Telmo.

Day 10 Take a short loop inland, through **Tolosa**, **Loyola** with its great Basilica of St Ignatius, and maybe **Oñati**, returning to the coast at the delightful fishing village/resort of **Getaria**.

Day 11 West of Getaria, take in the paintings at the Villa Zuloaga in **Zumaia**. Continue westwards along the pretty coastal road, stopping at whatever beach or restaurant catches your fancy, and by evening you'll be back in Bilbao.

Above, from top: Cathedral, Vitoria-Gasteiz; Pamplona; Vineyard, La Rioja

A Tour through the Basque Pyrenees in Eight Days

Day 1 Starting from Biarritz or Donostia-San Sebastián, head down the coast to **St-Jean-de-Luz** and then head inland through the most cultivated landscapes the Basques have to offer, through **Ascain** and **Sare**, finishing in **Cambo-les-Bains**.

Day 2 Spend the morning touring more of this tiny region: **Espelette** for the hot peppers, and the **Grottes d'Isturits** for the stalactites, then head south for **St-Jean-Pied-du-Port**.

Days 3–4 You're deep enough in the mountains here to spend a while enjoying the scenery around St-Jean: the trail through the **Gorges de Kakouetta** or **Holcarte**, the villages of the **Haute-Soule**, and the ancient church at **Ste-Engrâce**.

Day 5 Now it's time to cross over into Spain, into Navarra, on the back roads past the **Pic d'Orhi** or the **Pic d'Anie**. Spend the day touring the lovely **Valle de Salazar** or the primeval **Forest of Irati**, ending in **Ochagavia**.

Day 6 This day is devoted mostly to **Roncesvalles**, with pilgrimage monuments and walks in the surrounding mountains.

Day 7–8 The last two days are spent in **Valle de Baztán** and **Valle de Bidasoa** to the west, for a look at the witches' caves, the **Cuevas de Zugarramurdi** and the stalactite **Cuevas de Urdax**, and the **Parque de Señorio de Bértiz**. There are easy and beautiful hikes here on the ancient smugglers' paths into France. Spend a night in **Elizondo** or another of the small mountain villages; from there it will be a short hop over the mountains back to your starting point.

Above: Traditional Basque architecture, Espelette
Below: Pilgrim cross, Roncesvalles; Village of Sare, Pays Basque

CONTENTS

Reference

Maps and Plans

History

02

100,000–218 BC

European aborigines

'The Basques are like good women; they have no history.' So runs the old Basque saying. Another of their jokes is that, when God created the first man, he got the bones from a Basque graveyard. No one knows for sure just how far back the Basque people go – only that someone, incredibly, was around even before them. For the area around the Pyrenees is one of the oldest inhabited places on earth, one of the cradles of human culture. The first European discovered so far, '**Tautavel Man**', parked his carcass in a cave at the western end of the chain some 400,000 years ago. Traces of habitation in the Basque lands go back at least 100,000 years, and somebody was painting pictures on cave walls as early as 35,000 BC. The **Cro-Magnons** living in what is now the Basque country formed an integral part of the Franco-Cantabrian civilization of reindeer hunters, who painted the famous caves of Lascaux and Altamira and elsewhere. The prize examples in the Basque provinces are the rupestrian art in the caves at Santimamiñe (near Gernika), Isturits (near Bayonne), and others usually not open to the public: Camou-Cihigue in the Soule; Venta de Laperra, Arenaza and Berriatúa in Vizcaya; Deba and Aya in Guipúzcoa; and Urdax in Navarre.

When did the inhabitants of the Basque lands become Basques? They are rare, if not unique, in the annals of western Europe for having no migration stories and no ancestral memory of ever having been anywhere else, and recent scholarship seems to confirm that the Basques are direct descendants of Cro-Magnon hunter-gatherers and painters, having survived in their secluded valleys during the great Indo-European migrations of peoples from the east thousands of years ago. This theory has had a big boost from studies showing that the Basques have the highest proportion of type O blood in the world, along with other ancient peoples shoved long ago into Europe's nooks and crannies – the Irish, the Scots and the Cretans. Even more peculiarly, the Basques also have the world's highest incidence of Rhesus negative blood anywhere, a factor characteristic of the indigenous prehistoric Europeans. Another clue may be in their physique. Basques have slight but telling physical differences from their neighbours. Not only are they bigger and stronger, but they have long noses and long earlobes, and the distinct shape of their skulls is matched by the shape of the oldest skulls found on the territory, in the Upper Palaeolithic deposit at Urtiaga, as well as in Bronze Age finds.

In the 1990s, genetic research confirmed a unique persistence of European Palaeolithic DNA markers in the ethnic Basque population (the only other people who come close are the Irish of Connacht). The French and Spanish have similar DNA markers, although they are fainter, having become more mixed over time. In the meagre 0.1 per cent of genetic differences between every human on the planet, the Basque and Lapps have the greatest distance between Europeans; Basques and New Guineans have the greatest distance on earth. Being unusual also has its drawbacks: Basques have the highest incidence in the world of the mutant gene associated with cystic fibrosis.

The Basques may be as old as their steep green hills, but their constant companions there, the sheep, only arrived in the Pyrenees around 5000 BC, followed by horses and cattle, part of the **Neolithic** agricultural and cultural revolution that spread across Europe. One theory has it that those with the farming know-how migrated west from the Middle East, and hunter-gatherer traditions slowly disappeared through intermarriage. This is when the Basques remained aloof. Still, if they didn't mingle, they did learn agriculture, the domestication of animals and building: their lasting monuments include dolmens (especially on the Álava plain by the Ebro), cromlechs (most famously at Aralar) and menhirs. They began to travel, herding their flocks up into the mountains in summer and into the lowlands between the Garonne and the Ebro in the winter – the extent of so-called 'Pyrenean culture'. Neolithic peoples were great traders and liked to live near the sea or important rivers; one of Europe's oldest known roads, the 'Salt Road', linked their lands with the Mediterranean. Most of the outlandish place names in the Pyrenees as far east as the Mediterranean can be traced to these proto-Basques. Still, if the *gaztelulaks* are any evidence, the various Aquitanian tribes didn't always get along; the remains of these hilltop earthen forts are still a feature of the Basque country, which counts 242 of them.

Around 800 BC, **Celtic** tribes started moving through the region, probably inter-marrying with the people as often as conquering them. Again, the ancestors of the Basques, for whatever reason, remained unassimilated while learning new skills from the newcomers, in this case metalworking and cultivating wheat.

218 BC–AD 407
Carthaginians and Romans

Modern Basques find grave fault with their ancestors for letting others write their history, since the first to put stylus to tablet were the **Romans**. Their influence was first felt in the Basque country in 218–201 BC, during the **Second Punic War** with the Carthaginians. The latter were probably already a familiar fixture in Biarritz and other Atlantic harbours where they would call, along the sea trading route to Cornwall and its tin mines, and Basque mercenaries were listed in Hannibal's army. But the first mention of Romans we have in the present-day Basque country is not until 75 BC, when Pompey campaigned against rebels in Spain and founded the city that still bears his name, Pompaelo (Pamplona), near the Basque village of Iruña.

When Caesar finally conquered Gaul in 51 BC, he wrote that it was occupied by three different peoples. Two were Celtic, but the third, occupying southwestern Gaul from the Pyrenees to the Garonne, were a people who were entirely distinct from their neighbours. The Romans called them **Aquitani** (or Aquitanians), and they spoke a language linguists call Aquitanian, an ancestral form of Basque and the only pre-Indo-European language surviving in Gaul. The conquest north of the Pyrenees was made by Caesar's partner Crassus without much fuss in 56 BC. Many Aquitanians escaped over the Pyrenees into the rugged country of northern Spain, where they joined up with their cousins already there, the **Vascones**, and took their name. There was little the Romans could do, or even wanted to: the Romans coveted Aquitania and the fertile Ebro valley; the aborigines could have the hills.

While the Aquitanians who stayed put in Aquitania adopted Gallo-Roman ways, the Vascones carried on in the Pyrenees, preserving their language, culture and religion. Yet their live-and-let-live relations with the Romans were so cordial that the Basques still hold them up as a model for the larger powers that surround them today. The Romans' primary interest was transport over the mountains, and they built some useful roads which the Vascones were glad to have. They also learned to cultivate olives and grapes, and traded them with the Romans in Pamplona and Bayonne. Pliny wrote that the Vascones of Vizcaya possessed a mountain 'made entirely of iron', but a lack of fertile land led many to hire themselves out as Roman mercenaries, and they were valued warriors. By the 4th century AD, the Romanized Gauls and Iberians had converted to Christianity. However, with the exception of a few communities by the Ebro, this new religion was one foreign novelty the Basques didn't care to emulate.

407–1000
In the Dark Ages, the Basques defend their homeland

The fatal invasions came after 407. Both **Vandals** and **Visigoths** passed through the Basque country, and after 420 Aquitania found itself part of the new Visigothic kingdom, with its capital at Toulouse. But this was not to last. The Franks whipped the Visigoths at the Battle of Vouillé in 507, and gained, if not control of Aquitania, at least the right to try to collect a little tribute from it. The Visigoths retreated into Spain, where their kingdom was to last two centuries until the Arab conquest.

As Teutonic barbarians go, the Visigoths were a cut above the rest. They were Christian, and did not drink out of skulls like the Lombards or smear bear fat all over their bodies like the Franks. However, they weren't as cordial as the Romans. The Visigoth kings launched campaign after campaign against the pagan Vascones, and they managed to extend Christianity as far as Pamplona. But on the whole the Visigoth agenda backfired: rather than subdue the Vascones, their persistent attacks united formerly disparate tribes (whose names and dialects survive today as the various Basque provinces) into a nation dedicated to resisting the Visigoths.

Many of the Vascones who had fled the Romans generations before and settled in Spain were either pushed by the Visigoths back over the Pyrenees, or decided on their own to retake their old homeland in Aquitaine, by then largely a wasteland. Whatever the case, they reappeared in the 580s, and people began calling the area as far north as the Garonne **Wasconia**, which later got turned into Gascony. Those Vascones who remained in the western Pyrenees, fierce enough to put up a good fight whenever it was necessary to defend their homes, became specialists in guerrilla warfare and mountain ambush, and lapsed into *de facto* independence. They have been there ever since, and are the people we call the Basques.

As if the Visigoths were not enough, in 602, the king of the Franks appointed a 'duke of Aquitaine' and 'duke of Wasconia', military overlords charged with bringing the entire area under closer control. The chronicles of the next two centuries tell a tale of continuous and spirited resistance on the part of the Basques. A big surprise for all parties concerned came when the **Moors** roared through the Pyrenees in the early 8th century after their rapid conquest of Spain, only to be defeated and driven back by the **Franks** at Poitiers in 732. What kept them from consolidating their hold over northern Spain was a short but intense revolt by the Muslim Berber troops in 740 against their Arab leaders. Pamplona took advantage of the revolt to free itself from its Arab governor and the Basques were independent once again.

Once again, however, they had to fight to stay that way. After beating the Moors at Poitiers, the self-confident Franks came over the Pyrenees looking for new lands to conquer. One of their raids on Pamplona gave birth to the legend of Roland and Oliver, the famous knights of Charlemagne who perished at the hands of the furious Basques in an ambush at the pass of Roncesvalles in 778 (see pp.238–40).

The troubles of the Franks gave the Basques south of the Pyrenees a chance to assert themselves. At the beginning of the 9th century, the kingdom of Pamplona was founded under King Iñigo de Arista, a unique Basque experiment with monarchy that would grow into the **kingdom of Navarra** (Nafarroa). At first this embraced the three provinces known as the Vascongadas (Gipuzkoa, Bizkaia and Araba), the French Basque country and neighbouring areas in Spain. It would remain a major actor in the region's history for centuries to come.

North of the mountains, the Basques weren't so lucky. Aquitaine and Gascony suffered the visitations of the most destructive barbarians of them all, the **Vikings**, or **Normans**. From the 840s onwards they came raiding nearly every year, completely wrecking Bayonne in 862. Not until 982 did Duke Guilhem of Gascony finally convince them they weren't wanted – but not before the Basques, who were already messing about in boats in the Bay of Biscay, had had a chance to study and imitate the well-built ocean-going hulls of the Viking ships. By this time, the Basques had mostly converted to **Christianity**, thanks, according to legend, to the efforts of Léon, the bishop of Rouen, who resigned his post to preach to the Basques before he was killed by Norman pirates in Bayonne. It was also around this time that the feudal pattern was set. The king of the Franks was just a bad dream somewhere up north, and the lesser vassals the **Carolingians** had created drifted into near-total independence. The arrangement makes history messy and complex, but it gave the region stability and some breathing space. After almost six centuries of terror, towns were growing again and churches began to spring up everywhere. By the magic year 1000, which many expected to bring the end of the world, medieval civilization was in fact well on its way.

1000–1492
Medieval prosperity, and the founding of a Basque kingdom

The new millennium got off to an auspicious start for Christian Spain, and for a while it looked as if the big victor among the Christian states would be little Navarra. Still Basque, but becoming increasingly Hispanicized in its southern half, Navarra reached its zenith under Sancho III 'the Great' (c. 1000–35), capturing all of La Rioja and even much of Castile. But, like so many of the transient empires formed in the free-for-all of the Reconquista, Sancho's proved to be only a house of cards, and Alfonso VI of Castile cut Navarra down to size in the 1070s.

With prosperity came increasing power for the growing towns, and nearly all of them in this period were able to organize themselves into *comunes* and gain a high degree of independence from the kings, bishops or nobles who had formerly bossed them around. Some were new creations altogether, such as Vitoria (Gasteiz), founded by Alfonso VI in 1081, soon after he had captured the territory. Alfonso wanted a loyal town to consolidate his hold, and to keep the new settlers' loyalty he granted Vitoria a charter of liberties, or **fueros** (*see* box, below). *Fueros* such as these would give medieval Spain a less oppressive government than most countries, and they were made possible by the good example of the Basques.

The Middle Ages were a prosperous time for the industrious Basques as they began to turn their talents to the sea. In winter, the Bay of Biscay was full of whales, where they had long been hunted from shore. Copying the Viking ships and their methods of provisioning for long journeys (basically living off wind-dried cod) enabled Basque sailors to follow the whales north to their summer quarters in the North Atlantic, and they had reached the Faroe islands by 875.

At home, Basque shipbuilders, using oak from the Pyrenees and iron from the Vizcayan mother lode, gained a reputation as the best in the world. In 1296,

The *Fueros*

... after studying the customary laws of Europe, I place the Basque Foral Laws above the Swiss laws, also endorsed by their centuries-long existence. For their virtues, their union and above all the local freedoms they enjoy, the Basques provide us with an example that one scarcely knows how to praise enough, maintaining their allegiance to the best social constitution in Europe.
L'Organisation de la Famille, Frédéric Le Play (1806–82)

Fueros (*fors* in French, *foruak* in Basque) are municipal charters or privileges, whether you derive the word from the Latin *forum*, the public square where municipal business was conducted, or from *fuera* (outside), as exceptions to royal authority. During the early Middle Ages, cities and towns, and sometimes entire provinces, were granted *fueros* by the kings of France and Spain.

As any Basque nationalist will hasten to remind you, however, the word *fueros* has over time been distorted in an important way. Basque *fueros* were not privileges and favours conceded or taken away by the will of a king, but were the Basques' own ancestral laws. It was the Basques of the three Vascongada provinces who consented to be ruled by a king (of Castile after 1200, when they broke away from Navarra), but only if the king swore to abide by their *fueros*, not the other way around. This was done under the sacred tree in Gernika, where the main Basque council, or *junta general*, met for two or three weeks to legislate on foral matters. There were obviously proper *fueros*, too, granted by the king when he wanted to curry favour with the Basques, but in general, when Basques wax nostalgic about their old *fueros*, they mean their ancient laws.

And in many ways these ancient laws were remarkable. Thanks to their *fueros*, the Basques remained free of the depredations of a nobility that ravaged the rest of Spain and France; the Basques with their egalitarian ethos had no nobles, and the only Basques with titles, besides the king of Navarre, were those like the Loyolas, who were ennobled by the Castilians for services rendered. Tax demands (and demands for military conscripts) were negotiated through Basque authorities, who kept both far below the levels of money and men demanded elsewhere in Spain. Nor were Basque soldiers expected to serve outside their province.

Women were granted more rights than in most medieval codes; for example, the family's first born, whether male or female, inherited the family house. The *fueros* also made the Basque provinces into a duty-free zone: Spanish customs were located at the Ebro, so the Basques paid considerably less for imports than their French and Spanish neighbours. When the *fueros* were revised in Gernika in 1526, they went even further, abolishing torture and eliminating debtors' prisons – nothing less than the first human rights legislation in Europe, well in advance of any other government.

a kind of Hanseatic League of Basque ports was founded, the **Hermandad de las Marismas**; shipping whale oil and Castile's wool northwards, the Hermandad grew to control a disproportionate share of the Atlantic trade. In 1351, an innovative peace treaty was signed between Vizcaya, Guipúzcoa and Edward III of England, guaranteeing the freedom of the seas. In 1482 another one signed with Edward IV guaranteed that, even if England and Castile went to war, it would not affect relations between England and Guipúzcoa.

The Basques remained feistily independent, but, as the medieval states surrounding Basque property – Asturias-Castile, Catalunya-Aragón, England (through its duchy of Aquitaine), Béarn and France – grew in wealth and power, there was increasingly little chance that an event like Roncesvalles could ever be repeated. This was a world dominated by a feudal aristocracy, and with such bossy neighbours it is not surprising that the Basques never coalesced into a nation-state. All through the Middle Ages, Basque boundaries shrank gradually but inexorably, as the natives were either pushed out, diluted or assimilated by Spaniards, Gascons and Catalans. By the 14th century the Basque lands had contracted roughly to the boundaries they retain today. Navarra, condemned by geography to lose out in the Reconquista land grab, was in full decline.

French involvement in the kingdom dated from the blazing of the main pilgrimage route to Santiago through its confines (*see* pp.49–51) and became official after 1284, when an heiress to the kingdom, **Juana I**, married the future King Philip the Fair of France. Afterwards, members of the Capetian dynasty would rule Navarra as a quaint Pyrenean Ruritania.

1492–1792
Reconquista to revolution

Throughout the 14th and 15th centuries, the Spanish kingdoms occupied themselves with consolidating the gains of the Reconquista. On the whole, the experience coarsened the life of Castile, creating a pirate ethos where honest labour was scorned and wealth and honour were things to be snatched from one's neighbours. The climax came in 1469 with the marriage of los Reyes Católicos, **Ferdinand of Aragón and Isabella of Castile**, during whose reign Spain's borders were rounded out. Not only did they finally conquer the kingdom of Granada, the last remnant of Moorish al-Andalus, but Spain was also embarking on its career as a grand imperialist, invading Italy and colonizing the Americas (often, as in the case of Columbus, taking along experienced Basque pilots to guide the way). The religious bigotry of the 'Catholic Kings', Isabella in particular, put a perverse twist on Spanish life that was to last a long time. Under their rule, the Inquisition was reintroduced, and Jews expelled from Spain. The kings of Navarra took them under their wing – at least until 1514, when Navarra itself was slyly gobbled up by Ferdinand, who got permission to march through and stayed. He kept the peace, however, by swearing to respect its sovereignty and *fueros* in an arrangement identical to that of the other Basque provinces of the peninsula.

North of the Pyrenees, the end of the Hundred Years War and departure of the English in the 1450s allowed France to extend its control over all of the southwest – only this time, the French kings were not content with being mere feudal overlords; the heavy-handed authoritarianism of Paris brought with it economic stagnation that was to last for centuries, especially in Gascony. The 1539 **Decree of Villars-Cotterets**, mandating the use of the French language in all matters of law and government, was a preview of coming events. French Navarre enjoyed its last 15 minutes of fame in 1589 when its king became one of the very best rulers of France, **Henri IV**.

Still, of all the peoples of the south the Basques adapted best to French rule, primarily because they retained a substantial degree of self-government up until the French Revolution. In Labourd a kind of parliament called the *biltzar*, with elected representatives (but no nobles or clergy), met regularly to set tax rates and look after local business; and each small region or town possessed its *fors*, which the French usually respected. In return, the Basques remained stalwartly loyal to the French Crown and performed important services for it in time of war, especially on the seas, thanks to the feared privateers of Bayonne.

In Spain, whatever wealth remained was soon sucked out by Ferdinand and Isabella's grandson, the Habsburg Charles I, better known to history as Holy Roman Emperor **Charles V**. As the country embarked on a remarkable and ultimately successful attempt to destroy its own economy, the Basques, safeguarded by their *fueros*, got by. A golden moment occurred when their own Juan Sebastián de Elcano, lieutenant of Magellan's fleet, became the first man to sail around the world in 1522 (*see* p.177). Their aptitude for learning from outsiders made the Basques more open to innovations than most Europeans: they were among the first to appreciate tobacco, chilli peppers and especially corn, brought back by Columbus in 1492. It was one of the few crops to do well in the meagre soil of the Basque lands. Within three decades the Basques had marketed it as far as China.

Under Charles' neurotic son **Philip II** (r. 1556–98), Spain reached the height of its book- and heretic-burning frenzy, while the economy stayed wrecked and military defeats piled up on every side. The heretic-free Basques made their own special contribution to the age: the Jesuits, founded by St Ignatius of Loyola with his right-hand man, the Basque Francis Xavier. A particular blow to Bilbao and other northern ports, motivated by corrupt ministers, was Philip's decision in 1573 to allow Seville to monopolize trade with the New World. The northern ports dwindled, and all the poor souls whose prospects had been ruined even had to find their way to the south to catch a boat just to emigrate. The majority of the crew of the Spanish Armada of 1588 were Basques, whose whaling fleet had been requisitioned for the effort and sank with the rest. But the greatest setback to the Basque whaling industry was the Basques' own willingness to teach others their secrets, in spite of (or perhaps to spite) the Spanish Crown's rule that they were to use their seafaring skills only in the service of Spain. Defiantly they taught the English and the Dutch, and, as these states claimed the high seas and fishing grounds, the Basques were increasingly muscled out.

The early 17th century witnessed a series of dust-ups between France and Spain. The intermission set by the **Treaty of the Pyrenees** in 1659 fixed the current international border through the Basque country; peace was cemented in that year by the betrothal and eventual marriage of Louis XIV and the Spanish infanta, María Teresa, in St-Jean-de-Luz. In the next round, the War of the Spanish Succession, the Basque provinces and Navarra were smart enough to back the right horse for the throne of Spain, Louis XIV's grandson, and as a reward got to keep their *fueros* (unlike the Catalans, who backed the Habsburg one and lost theirs).

Under Spain's new Bourbon king, **Philip V** (1700–46), the semi-autonomous Basques regained the right to trade with the New World, and they soon found ways to wring a penny from the Americas. In 1730, the **Real Compañía Guipuzcoana de Caracas** broke the Dutch monopoly over the chocolate trade in the West Indies and brought a lot of money home to the Basque country. From cocoa it expanded into tobacco, coffee and beans, while shipping iron, sardines and wine to Venezuela. The other regions of northern Spain, as well as France, Germany and the Netherlands, soon began to deal with the Compañía Guipúzcona, exporting their own goods to the New World. By the late 18th century, Bilbao was the busiest port in Spain.

1792–1876
Revolution, Carlism and steel mills

The **French Revolution** marked a turning point for the Basques, and brought with it the irony of this most democratic of peoples ranging themselves solidly on the side of reaction. It wasn't their fault. In the name of equality for all, the Jacobins up in Paris abolished the last foral rights, self-government and traditional liberties north of the Pyrenees, but even more resented than the Revolution's push for centralization and Frenchification were its attacks on the Church.

In 1793, the Convention sent a large army down to the Pyrenees. Four thousand Basques from Labourd were deported for refusing to fight in the southern Basque country. On the Spanish side, however, urban Basques were fascinated by the Revolution, and the French army occupied the Basque provinces with hardly a fight; Guipúzcoa's assembly even welcomed them. In Madrid, the nervous Bourbon cousins of Louis XVI, who had counted on the Basques to defend their frontier homeland, blamed them for the humiliation and got the French to retreat in 1795, in exchange for rights over Santo Domingo.

They were soon back, however, under **Napoleon**. Basque guerrilla resistance this time was impressive enough to lead him to seek their support by promising to safeguard their *fueros* in the constitution he imposed on Spain, even suggesting the creation of a Basque state that would be controlled by France. The Navarrese, especially around French-occupied Pamplona, didn't believe a word of it and fought all the harder. French reprisals and executions in Pamplona further hardened positions; it took a four-month siege in 1813 by the Spanish-British allies to finally dislodge the French. If Navarra would later become the most intransigent and conservative of Basque provinces, the roots of its position are there.

In the end, the only real fruit of the Revolution and Napoleon for the three French Basque provinces was a lasting economic depression, helped along by the British blockade and Wellington's siege of Bayonne. All remnants of self-rule were stripped away, and in spite of protests from both the Basques and Béarn, they were made to share the same *département* of the Pyrénées-Atlantiques. Paris-appointed prefects replaced Paris-appointed *intendants*, but few of the ephemeral governments of the 19th-century Gallic banana republic/monarchy/empire ever stirred themselves much to help the Pays Basque. Nor did the region ever show much energy of its own. The railway arrived at Bayonne in the 1850s, but this served mainly to help make it easier for young people to leave, and for imported goods to flow in and ruin the region's already hard-pressed farmers and manufacturers. The only positive thing the train brought was tourists, as 19th-century Biarritz found its vocation as a resort, promoted by Napoleon's nephew, Napoléon III.

Like 19th-century France, Spain too seemed the very image of the banana republics that had just gained their independence from it in Latin America. But unlike their French counterparts, Spanish Basques played a major role in keeping the pot boiling. The first sign of trouble came in 1812, during the war with Napoleon, when the newly formed Liberal Party in Cádiz produced a constitution for Spain, citing the Basques as the model for the freedom they intended for everybody in Spain, but without offering much hope that traditional Basque rights would be respected. Although the absolutist king **Ferdinand VII** snuffed Liberal yearnings in the so-called 'nefarious decade' (1823–33) and even brought back the Inquisition, his death and the succession of his infant daughter Isabella II to the throne under the regency of her mother María Cristina rekindled Liberal hopes across Spain, for a weak queen would enable them to realize their secular anticlerical agenda in a modern centralized nation-state.

This suited the capitalists of Vizcaya and Guipúzcoa just fine. They were beginning to find the traditional *fueros* a hindrance: the duty-free status they gave the Basque provinces were a serious obstacle when they needed custom barriers to develop their own industry. Furthermore, the *fueros* protected Vizcaya's iron mountains as the Basques' greatest asset and forbade the sale of ore abroad, when it was precisely the money-spinner the new industrialists needed to start up their own mills.

Rural Basques, however, looked down on Bilbao and San Sebastián from their mountains in growing anger. Their priests had warned that the anticlerical Liberals meant to banish God from Spain and expropriate Church property and rights, threatening not only the religious but the poor, who depended on the Church's charity. The Liberals, they feared, meant to abolish the *fueros* which kept prices low. The abolition of common pastures, sold at auction and bought by the rich, had already forced shepherds to pay rent for what used to be free. The Bilbao bourgeoisie began to purchase farms as investments, and rents for farmers rose.

In 1833, the Liberals – the military, the bourgeoisie, capitalists and upper aristocracy – hoisted **Isabella II** onto the throne. The Vatican refused to recognize her. The Church's privileges were rescinded and the Inquisition abolished. The country was divided into artificial, uniform provinces; even Navarra, until then still nominally a kingdom, was reduced to provincial status. For the rural conservatives, the peasants and the priests, this meant war, and they rallied around Ferdinand's brother, the pretender Don Carlos, who vowed to restore the status quo for the Church and maintain the Basques' *fueros*.

Although all Spain took sides, the brunt of the **first Carlist War** of 1833–9 was borne in the Basque country, where it became a civil war pitting city Basque against country Basque. Bilbao's leading families sent Isabella II 33 million *reales* for the war effort. The underdog Carlists, in their romantic costumes, long hair and red berets, were led by the brilliant guerrilla tactician **Zumalacárregui** until he died during the siege of Bilbao in 1835. Fighting, atrocities and church burnings continued for four years until the Carlists surrendered, on the promise that their *fueros* would be maintained.

But Madrid was just fooling, and stripped away much of Basque autonomy in a law of 16 August 1841. Spanish Customs were moved to Hendaye from the Ebro. The big loan to Isabella II by Bilbao's financiers was no hindrance to the founding of the **Banco de Bilbao** in 1857, soon to be followed by the **Banco de San Sebastián** and **Banco de Vizcaya**. Vizcaya's iron mountain turned out to have the perfect ore for making steel according to the new Bessemer process. Easily transported to the port of Bilbao, huge quantities could now be exported to England. The three banks financed new rail links, shipyards, hydroelectric plants and the first steel mills and blast furnaces, knowing they would have a monopoly in Spain thanks to the new customs arrangements. Bilbao became a noisy boom town, but its new shipyards, factories, mills, mines, blast furnaces, chemical works and refineries required something the Basques were not prepared for: an influx of poor Spanish workers, who were willing to work in appalling conditions for abysmal wages because the alternatives in Andalucía were even worse. The Basques were not particularly kind to the *maketos*, as they called the new arrivals, regarding them as sowers of revolution, unrest and bad habits.

The **second Carlist War** (1872–6), spurred by new legislation on civil marriages and freedom of religion, led again to an unsuccessful siege of Bilbao, bitter defeat and the **Law of Abolition** of the *fueros* in July 1876. From now on, Basques would have to do compulsory service in the Spanish army and pay taxes to the State (to soften the blow in prosperous Vizcaya, this was done through the new provincial parliament, the Diputación, which soon came under the control of Bilbao's big industrialists). After all, Spain needed the Basque country more than the Basque country needed Spain.

1876–1923
The birth of Basque nationalism

Throughout history the Basques have wanted only to be left alone to run their own affairs, and they nearly always support any sort of politics that promises to uphold their ancient rights and liberties; in modern times, this has meant adventures with both the far right and the far left. Now that the *fueros* were dismantled and industrialization was rapidly changing almost every aspect of what had been a relatively isolated and balanced society (in the most radically changed province, Vizcaya, the population nearly doubled between 1850 and 1900), local historians began to define what had been lost, and polish it up to fit the spirit of the age.

Nationalism was hardly a recent phenomenon. In the 18th century, Enlightenment thinkers such as **Manuel de Larramendi** had already developed a

The Basque Diaspora

Leaving is hard: the peasants' name for places outside of the Basque country is 'wolf's land'. Yet the Basque country has always had a hard time supporting its population; in spite of appearances, it isn't very fertile. According to traditional Basque property laws, only one child would inherit the *exte* (house) and estate, leaving the others the choice of a career in the Church or at sea, or the option of moving elsewhere. In the 19th century, rural poverty, combined with the loss of Basque *fueros* in the Carlist Wars, drove many young Basques from their mountain uplands to the Americas, especially to Argentina, Chile and the USA, where the Basque connection goes back to the 1,500 sailors, many of them veteran corsairs, who came to join Lafayette and fight for American independence. In the bayous of Louisiana and east Texas, as well as on the Argentine pampas, Basques became some of the New World's first shepherds and cowboys in the 1840s, setting the model and contributing much to the image (*lariat, chaparral* and *honcho* are derived from Basque words). The centre for Basque studies today in the USA is the University of Nevada at Reno. There are scores of Basque place names in Mexico and South America; in Chile, many of the vineyards have Basque names. Some Basques opened restaurants, and often as not, in the middle of an American Nowheresville in Idaho or Utah, what will you find? A decent Basque restaurant.

concept of Basque nationhood based on language and tradition. The French Basque historian **Augustin Chaho** (1811–58) was the first to popularize the idea of the Basques as an oppressed nation, spurring a renewed interest in Basque things. Navarra's intellectuals led a minor Basque Renaissance, forming the **Asociación Euskara** to study and propagate Basque studies. Journalist and politician **Arturo Campion** (1854–1937) became a leader in the movement, linking language to independence and organizing poetry contests with traditional Basque games. By the end of the century, the Basque country reverberated with choral societies belting out arrangements of traditional songs.

Basque nationalism, however, owes nearly everything else to a one-man band named **Sabino de Arana y Goiri** (1865–1903). Arana's family owned a shipbuilding firm in Vizcaya, building wooden ships (which were quickly becoming obsolete), and as supporters of the Carlists, they had been forced into exile in France. The bitterness of the experience convinced Arana that what the Basques needed most was their own country. In 1890 he wrote *Bizkaya por su Independencia*, in which he inflated four historic battles between Basques and Castilians into an epic struggle for Basque independence. He invented all the national elements that were lacking: a name for the country, **Euskadi** (formerly, to talk about themselves, the Basques would say Euskal Herria, 'the land of Euskera speakers'), and a flag, the red, green and white *ikurriña*, modelled on the Union Jack (like many Basques, he admired the feisty island nation as a role model). The day of his political conversion, Easter Sunday 1882, became the Basque national holiday, **Aberri Eguna** (the Day of the Fatherland). In 1895 Arana founded the first Basque nationalist party, **Eusko Alderdi Jeltzalea**, or the **Partido Nacional Vasco (PNV)**, with the motto *Jaungoikua eta Lagizarra* ('God and the old laws'), and in prison he composed what would become the words of Euskadi's national anthem, *Gora ta Gora*. As a humourless ideologue, however, Arana was also an embarrassment. Many of his other ideas have been discarded – among them, the requirement that PNV members have at least one pure Basque grandparent and at least four Basque surnames in their ancestry, and that they be practising Catholics. The racism has been explained by sympathizers as a method of instilling a sense of separate destiny in the Basques, while the Catholicism was a sincerely held conviction of Arana, who detested the immorality of the new secular state in Bilbao: 'All of us know that today the poor are inhumanely exploited and treated like beasts by industrialists and businessmen, mine owners and property owners.' In 1890, 20,000 workers in Bilbao underlined his point by leading Spain's first general strike. Another aspect of Arana's Catholicism was a policy of seeking nationalist goals through non-violence, which remains PNV doctrine to this day.

Arana, who suffered from Addison's disease, died in 1903 aged 38. In his lifetime the PNV's political victories had been minor (he himself had been elected to Vizcaya's provincial assembly), but his more pragmatic heirs would make it a force to be reckoned with as the PNV attracted voters from across the political spectrum: former Carlists and priests, but also former Liberals, intellectuals and professionals, disillusioned by the nepotism and corruption in Madrid. Even bankers, industrialists and shipping magnates, who would have had little voice in Spain's larger national parties, found in the PNV a ready-made power base and ideology.

Although Arana's Euskadi was to include all seven Basque provinces under the slogan *Zazpiak-bat* ('seven in one') or '**4+3=1**', his addition ran into a brick wall in the more repressive climate of France; the French, after all, knew better than to leave economic power in the hands of ethnic minorities, and could safely ignore the Basques, along with the Bretons and Corsicans. The seven Basque provinces would undergo dramatically different experiences in the **First World War**. In France, the war contributed mightily to the already existing trend towards abandonment and depopulation; many villages lost a third or even half of their young men. For Basques in neutral Spain, these were boom years as Bilbao pumped out armaments to supply the belligerents; by the end of the war, Bilbao's banks controlled a third of the investments in Spain. From 1917 on, the PNV controlled a majority of the region's parliamentary seats. Under their rule, the first Basque-language elementary schools, *ikastola*, were opened, and the Academy of Basque Studies was founded in Oñati, with the goal of distilling the very diverse Basque dialects into a **Standard Euskera** all could understand, a project that would take half a century.

The deep depression that followed the war brought social problems to a head. Increased immigration of Castilians and others to Basque industrial centres exacerbated labour troubles, urban crowding and pollution, and attracted many migrants to socialism, whose internationalism was anathema to the PNV. Its concern for social justice, however, attracted a fair number of Basques; one was the eloquent **Dolores Ibarruri**, who became famous as 'La Pasionaria', the voice of the Second Republic.

1923–75
Autonomy, Civil War and Franco

Political and cultural repression under dictator **Primo de Rivera** (1923–30) only broadened support for the PNV and, after the creation of the Second Republic in 1931, it won a huge electoral victory under the moderate **José Antonio Aguirre**, who began the difficult negotiations with Madrid for autonomy, despite reservations about the new Second Republic's secularism. The **Statutes of Basque Autonomy** were hastily granted shortly after Franco and his fellows revolted in July 1936. The Navarrese, whose politics still revolved around Carlism and who wanted nothing to do with the 'church burners', supported Franco's right-hand man **General Mola**, who took Pamplona to widespread acclaim on the day of the coup.

In the other three Basque provinces, the vote for an autonomous Euskadi topped 80 per cent and was hugely supported, even by the socialists. The 32-year-old Aguirre was made president, or *lehendakari*, and chose the equally young aristocrat **Telesforo de Monzón** to run the new Basque police, which he did with aplomb. The Basques, even the priests, sided enthusiastically with the Republic in the war against the rebels. Unlike Catalunya, where anarchists murdered priests and nuns before the Communists murdered the anarchists, the Basque country under Aguirre and Monzón was well run. To break their spirit, the German Condor Legion practised the world's first saturation bombing of civilian targets at Durango and Gernika in early 1937. The Basques fought on; then Bilbao, for the third time in a century, was besieged. As food ran out, 20,000 children were sent abroad on refugee ships, including 4,000 who went to England. Unfortunately, the architect of Bilbao's defences gave the plans to the enemy, and the city surrendered. After only nine months in existence, autonomous Euskadi ceased to exist. Aguirre, who escaped on foot into France, formed the Basque government in exile in New York.

Franco's rule was a catastrophe for the Basques: over 100,000 prisoners were taken, 200,000 Basques went into exile and thousands (21,780 according to Basque nationalists) were executed after the Civil War, including the entire intelligentsia and political leadership. Franco took special pains to single out the Basques for reprisals of all kinds, suppressing even casual use of their language, and forbidding most festivals and cultural events. State industrial schemes were consciously planned in a way to bring in large numbers of Spanish job-seekers to dilute the Basque population (by 1975, 40 per cent of the population had no Basque parents at all). But, just as the Visigoths had long ago oppressed the Basques into uniting, so did Franco; even the thousands of Castilians who emigrated to Euskadi to work in the factories felt oppressed enough in the years of hunger, stagnation and police brutality to sympathize with Basque nationalist goals. In contrast, plenty of Navarrese Carlists found posts in Franco's army and government; the Spanish fascists even borrowed the Carlists' yoke-and-arrows symbol for their own party, and the province was allowed to keep a number of its traditional *fueros* in exchange for good behaviour.

The mass exodus of Basques and other republicans into France after the Civil War added new blood and new energy to many towns and villages in the southwest. No one thought Franco would last for long, especially as the Spanish Civil War turned out to be only a warm-up for the atrocities of the **Second World War**. Although less destructive for France than the First World War, it was still a miserable and dangerous time. From the beginning, the Germans seized a strip along the entire Atlantic coast as part of the occupied zone. The 'border' with Vichy-controlled territory was heavily guarded, and locals needed special papers to cross it. The Basques, including many former republican soldiers and civilians, did good work smuggling escapees over into Spain, and helping Allied agents coming the other way. The Basque Gernika Battalion fought alongside the forces of liberation, and the *ikurriña* flew proudly among the Allies' flags as De Gaulle entered Paris. At the end of the war, in Bordeaux (the last French city to be liberated), De Gaulle promised the Basques that the Allies would not stop at the Pyrenees but would carry on to rid Europe of fascists once and for all.

Only they didn't. The Basques were frustrated with the Allies, and frustrated with their beloved Church for supporting Franco. Aguirre and the PNV in exile sat on their hands, waiting for Franco to wither away, ostracized from the world community. They didn't count on the Cold War, and Franco playing the anti-Communist card. Feelings of frustration soon turned into feelings of betrayal. In 1953, Spain signed a bilateral treaty with the United States and received millions of dollars in exchange for the right to establish military bases. In 1955, in spite of heated protests from the Basque government in exile, Spain, still run by the same men who had condoned the bombing of Gernika, was admitted to the United Nations.

Disillusioned with the fossilized PNV, the first student resistance groups formed in 1952. The grim atmosphere of Francoist repression and American 'betrayal' determined the equally poisonous nature of the antidote. **ETA (Euskadi Ta Askatsuna**, or Basque Homeland and Liberty) was founded by seven young intellectuals in 1959 as a study group. Its first action was painting 'Our Euskadi' and the Basque flag on walls (daring enough back then, when such things meant extended prison sentences). In 1967, radical members, inspired by Cuba, Algeria and Vietnam, took over ETA and formulated the means it would use to achieve an independent Euskadi: taking action to provoke the State into overreacting, so that its oppression would mobilize the majority of people in the Basque country; race, religion and language, all that was so precious to Arana, no longer counted. The violence began haphazardly, in 1968, when the first Guardia Civil was killed after pulling over a car carrying ETA leader **Txabi Etxeberrieta**. Etxeberrieta was tracked down and killed at the next roadblock. The next death, of Manzanas, a notorious police torturer, was ETA's first planned assassination, and led to just the kind of reaction the group sought: the infamous Burgos trial of 16 *etarristas* in 1970, which showed Franco's regime in the worst light and lead to an international uproar that persuaded Franco, much against his will, to commute the four death sentences to life imprisonment.

As the only active resistance to the dictatorship, ETA attracted widespread sympathy within Spain and elsewhere. In 1973, ETA could take credit for changing history when it blew the car of Franco's hand-picked successor, Admiral Carrero Blanco, over the roof of a Madrid church. With Carrero Blanco gone, Spaniards for the first time began to see a light at the end of the tunnel. But the repression in Euskadi worsened, and it became a battleground between ETA (whose new slogan was 'Actions Unite, Words Divide') and the Guardia Civil, whose state violence was enough to convince many Basques that nationalist violence was legitimate. Every ETA action defiantly confirmed that the Basques still existed, in spite of Franco's boast that he had unified the State and rid it of ethnic minorities forever. By the time Franco finally performed his long-awaited exit from the stage in 1975, the Spanish State in the eyes of many Basques had lost all right to govern their land.

1975–the Present
Big changes, but not big enough for everyone

After 40 years of Franco, the Basques were ready to explode. No region had suffered more, but during the delicate transition period Madrid did little to encourage the notion that change was imminent. The king proclaimed a general amnesty of political prisoners, but it included fewer than 10 per cent of Basque prisoners, leading to the formation of the **Gestoría Pro-Amnistía**, a Basque human rights organization that brought their plight to the attention of the rest of Europe. Because of the need to appease the numerous Francoists and right-wingers still in power ('the bunker', as Spaniards called them), the Basques were the chosen target for a stringent law and order campaign. Demonstrations were brutally broken up, while ETA continued its campaign against Francoist politicians and the Guardia Civil.

In 1977, the first elections in the new Spain brought back exiles such as Telesforo Monzón and Dolores Ibarruri. Parties in favour of autonomy, led by the PNV, won the majority. The following year, voters were presented with a referendum on the new Spanish constitution. The mass demonstrations in Catalunya and Euskadi had pushed its authors to adopt a regional form of government – in fact regionalism for all of Spain, whether a region wanted it or not. These **Comunidades Autónomas** would have the right to their Basque, Catalan or Gallego language and culture, but the constitution insisted that Castilian was the official language of the State and that 'The Constitution is based on the indivisible unity of the Spanish Nation, common and indivisible fatherland of all the Spaniards.'

It was to this that the majority of Basques objected; in fact, they no longer considered themselves Spaniards at all. They remembered their *fueros* and wanted autonomy from Madrid as before, on their terms, as a right, not as a favour from a government they mistrusted. The PNV refused to vote for the constitution in the Spanish parliament, and called on Basques to abstain from voting in protest. Over 40 per cent followed their lead; in Guipúzcoa and Vizcaya 56 per cent of voters abstained. The majority of Basques who did actually vote, voted against it. To this day, it remains a major nationalist complaint that the constitution was imposed on them against their will. They were next asked to approve the statutes of autonomy, which the PNV did support, and 53 per cent voted in favour, despite anger over the fact that Navarra was left out and never offered the chance to vote on whether or not it wanted to remain with the other three Basque provinces (this, too, remains a very bitter bone of contention). The Basque government in exile returned after 43 years. Vitoria (Gasteiz) was chosen to be the capital of the autonomous Basque Community of Euskadi, and in 1980 a new PNV *lehendakari* was sworn in under the oak tree in Gernika.

But most Basques were not satisfied. One Basque in particular, old Telesforo Monzón, an ex-member of the government in exile, broke with the PNV in 1978 in disgust at the constitutional referendum and founded a new radical party called **Herri Batasuna**, or Popular Unity. He was imprisoned as an apologist for terrorism, and went on a hunger strike, then was elected to the Cortes, where he refused to take his seat. As the party's main stance is opposition, pure and simple, Herri

Batasuna soon became one of the most unorthodox parties in Europe, attracting a heterogeneous group from radical priests to gay rights activists, feminists, ecologists, students, Marxists, and so on. It also openly supported ETA, although it always denies being its political wing.

Reflecting the Basque opinion that the State had railroaded them into accepting an imposed autonomous solution, 1978–80 was ETA's most murderous period, with some 80 killings a year. Its operatives waged an intractable campaign against the Lemoiz nuclear power plant, planned by Franco only 16km from Bilbao, until it was finally shut down in 1982 (*see* pp.168–9). In the 1970s, drug addiction among young Basques was well above the national norms; sensing a conspiracy from Madrid, ETA started knocking off drug-dealers. The situation became so polarized that no Basque would talk to a Guardia Civil or the police. Ostracized with their families from normal life, the police began to be infected with what has been dubbed the 'northern syndrome'. They hated the Basques and pleaded to be relocated. Suicide rates among the Guardia Civil soared. They often took out their miseries on Basque demonstrators.

If in the new Spain ETA seemed like a relic of the bad old days, Basque sympathizers countered that the government was still rife with Francoists and torturers, not one of whom had ever been brought to justice. The Spanish call this the *pacto de olvido*, the pact of forgetfulness. The attempted coup in 1981 in the Cortes by the Guardia Civil Lieutenant Tejero was a bitter reminder of the nightmare Spain wanted to forget. To keep the peace, no one would be blamed. To placate 'the bunker', each party would vie to prove it was the toughest on ETA. Spain would remain the only country in western Europe where prisoners were routinely tortured. As documented by Amnesty International, most of the victims were Basques, so they didn't care to forget.

In 1982, the country overwhelmingly voted in the **Socialist Party (PSOE)** of **Felipe González** on the promise of change. One change was a new anti-terrorist law that allowed police to detain suspects for up to 10 days incommunicado. Many detainees were bullied or tortured, then released without ever being accused or tried; nationalist journalists were a favourite target. Basque conspiracy theories about Madrid's intentions were not totally loony: the Socialist government was secretly waging a 'dirty war' through the **Anti-terrorist Liberation Group (GAL)**, passing it off as an extreme right-wing death squad unrelated to the government. By extending its activities into the French Basque country, it finally spurred Paris to act against suspected ETA members, who always used France as a safe haven, and to extradite them for the first time in 1984, even though the old reason for not doing so – reasonable suspicion that they would be tortured in Spain – had not changed. In 1989, slip-ups by its mercenaries traced GAL back to its mastermind, González's law enforcement chief.

González himself managed to survive this scandal, but not the host of other corruption scandals that plagued his government, and in 1996 the Socialists lost the election to the right-wing **Partido Popular (PP)** and **José María Aznar**. Aznar (who had survived an ETA assassination attempt the year before) claimed that González hadn't been tough enough on the Basques, and, to show that he was, he imprisoned all 23 members of the directorate of Herri Batasuna for showing an ETA film during their 15 minutes of free air time during the election.

The autonomous community of **Navarra**, as ever, stands apart. Some have called it the Basque Ulster and, similarly to Northern Ireland, its union with the rest of Euskadi is a chief ETA demand. North of Pamplona live a majority of Basques; to the south of Pamplona the majority is Spanish. Between the two of them, Navarra remains the most reactionary part of Spain, maybe of all Europe; it still has a strong Carlist streak, even though the current pretender, Prince Hugo de Borbón, has tacitly acknowledged King Juan Carlos by paying him a social visit. Pamplona, its bright and prosperous capital, is the mecca of Opus Dei, the shadowy Catholic organization that in Franco's later years attempted to gain control of the Spanish government by insinuating its members into high positions. In a recent poll, a higher percentage of Navarrese claim to feel 'Navarrese' as opposed to Basque or Spanish. No one is really sure how they would vote in a referendum to join Euskadi, but, according to the Spanish constitution, even a referendum is illegal.

In the French **Pays Basque**, or North Euskadi as the Basques prefer to call it, the biggest political change since the Second World War has been the creation of regional governments under the Socialists' decentralization programme in 1981. So far it isn't much, but as the first reversal in five centuries of Parisian centralism it at least gives provinces a start in reclaiming some control over their own destinies. Mitterrand actually promised a separate Basque *département*, but in spite of repeated reminders over his 14 years in office, he reneged. The French Basques constitute a mere 0.4 per cent of the national population but, jealous of the autonomy their countrymen have won over the border in Spain (where they comprise 7.5 per cent of the population), they continue to be quietly assertive in trying to push decentralization even further. An informal council of mayors, heir to the old *biltzar*, meets regularly. In the 1990s, when the French government started cracking down on ETA operatives and sympathizers, the organization responded by bombing Renault dealerships around Spain. Then suddenly they stopped, which suggests that somewhere a deal had been cut.

Although most French Basques decided long ago that being French wasn't so bad, there are still plenty of nationalists. The police watch over them and manipulate them silently and skilfully. This is something at which the French have had centuries of practice – all over the Midi, as well as in Brittany, Corsica and the colonies – and they're extremely good at it, probably the best in the world.

In Spain, widespread disgust with terror tactics has made ETA fall out of favour. Three-quarters of all Spaniards regard Basque terrorism as the country's worst problem (among the Basques themselves the percentage may even be higher). Support for an independent Euskadi remains considerable, but Basques today recognize that the political situation has changed and would rather independence was brought about peacefully and through constitutional amendments. Some 70 per cent of Basques vote for nationalist parties, mostly for the moderate PNV and the more nationalist but still peaceful Bildu (*see* p.38).

The two Basque regions, Euskadi and Navarra, have the highest level of **self-government** in Spain. Taxes are collected by local governments, and local rule covers education, culture, industry, health services, police, agriculture, fishing, and so on. Many parents choose to have their children educated bilingually. The Basque government in Vitoria-Gasteiz is held up in Spain as a model of efficiency and progressiveness, more supportive than any of new technologies and ways of doing business.

Financed by bank robberies, kidnappings and 'revolutionary taxes' imposed on Basque businesses, ETA die-hards have continued their murders and bombing campaigns in the name of the Basque people, although the organization's logic of violence now seems to be its only logic. The surprise truce declared in September 1998 brought 15 months of peace, during which Aznar's government held talks with the PNV, but refused to budge on the general Basque demand of amending the constitution. Unfortunately, ETA found its marginalization in peace worse than the disgust it inspired when it was active, and in December 1999 the organization resumed the terror. The following summer it conducted a particularly fierce campaign of murders throughout the country. Successive raids in September 2000 in both the French and Spanish Basque territories whittled ETA down, but the issue was far from settled – rather like the Hydra, when one head is lopped off, another one springs up.

In 2002, tourism became ETA's target when, during the height of the summer season, two car bombs exploded in Fuengirola on the Costa del Sol and a few weeks later in a resort near Alicante, resulting in the death of a child. The Spanish government responded decisively by applying the newly devised *Ley de Partidos* to Batasuna, the political wing of ETA, effectively making the party illegal. The group's offices were closed by the Basque police and its accounts frozen. In a further development three months later, the president of the (recognized) Basque government, **Juan José Ibarretxe**, put his cards on the table and proposed that the EU grant the Basque country the status of free state, associated to Spain with shared sovereignty, a plan that no one but the Basques takes seriously.

Aznar and his hardline Partido Popular were ousted from government in the general election of 2004, after a clumsy attempt to blame ETA for the Madrid train bombings in March of that year. In October, the new Socialist goverment under **José Luís Rodríguez Zapatero** got some unexpected presents when the French police nabbed **Mikel Albizu Iriarte**, political leader and chief ideologue of ETA, in the town of Salies-de-Béarn, along with his girlfriend (a suspect in over a dozen murders) and 15 henchmen. In the same week, the *gendarmes* uncovered huge caches of weapons in several villages, including some Soviet anti-aircraft missiles.

Greater autonomy was still a key issue in the Basque elections of April 2005, which Ibarretxe's party won – but only just. They lost their majority and much of their bargaining power with it. ETA is down but not completely out. Madrid promised to open peace talks with the group if it laid down its arms, but the terrorists replied with a series of car bombings in Madrid and northern tourist centres. These were interpreted as a gesture of defiance, or perhaps desperation, and the government responded by arresting **Arnaldo Otegi**, the leader of the (still outlawed) Batasuna party, and threatened to limit the Basques' autonomy. Fragile hopes for peace were raised when ETA declared a 'permanent' ceasefire on March 2006, and a few months later Zapatero's government showed signs that it was prepared to sit and talk with the armed separatists. But the sceptics were proven right when, on December 30th, ETA detonated a van bomb in a car park building at Madrid Barajas international airport, killing two men. Although Zapatero discontinued talks immediately, it wasn't until June 2007 that ETA formally announced the end of the 'permanent' ceasefire. In 2008 and 2009, ETA attempted to put a popular spin on its ongoing struggle, drawing comparisons with independence movements in other parts of Europe such as Scotland and Kosovo, but the organisation was badly damaged by a series of high-profile arrests of some of its most senior members.

With its leadership in disarray, and links with political parties severed, ETA finally declared a new ceasefire on 5 September 2010. This was followed in January 2011 with a statement promising that the ceasefire would be 'permanent, general and verifiable'. However, most Spaniards remain sceptical that this third ceasefire will endure and some fear that it will split ETA into two groups, with hardliners continuing to use armed struggle along the lines of the Real IRA. The Spanish Supreme Court banned Sortu, a Basque nationalist political party, soon after it was established in February 2011, even though Sortu's manifesto specifically condemned politically motivated violence. The Basque reaction was mixed: some felt that Sortu was only the latest incarnation of Batasuna, but most believed that a political party that promoted non-violent strategies should be supported. Indeed, the new party, **Bildu** ('gather' in Basque), which was quickly founded in 2011 in the wake of Sortu's demise, and made an impressive showing at the Basque elections in the same year, gaining 27 per cent of the vote in local elections. On the whole they lean to the left on most issues and are strongly anti-nuclear and anti-NATO.

As Euskadi looks to the future, however, the most promising story is not this relic of a troubled past, but the surprising rebirth of Bilbao as a symbol of the Basques' prosperity. Long known only for industrial obsolescence and rust, the city has pulled itself up with such projects as Frank Gehry's Guggenheim Museum, Philippe Starck's arts centre (the Alhóndiga), and a huge riverfront redevelopment plan; in just a couple of decades Bilbao has emerged from nowhere to become one of the most exciting cities in Spain, and the showcase for a small, ancient nation that in the past has always been able to absorb new ideas, innovate and prosper. The Basques, in spite of their troubles, seem poised to do it again.

Basque Culture

03

The Language that Defeated the Devil Himself

Want to impress your hosts with a few words of Basque? Go ahead and try it! The Basques point out with great pride that their language, which they call Euskera, is not only Europe's oldest, but the most difficult: an old story tells how the Devil came to the Basque country to learn Euskera and tempt the Basques, but could only manage to learn 'yes' and 'no' (*bai* and *ez*) before he gave up and returned to hell.

As a general rule, the more declensions a language has, the older it is: Euskera shoots the moon with 20. Verbs can vary according to the gender of the person you are addressing (pluri-personal). Nouns are described in a three-number system (singular, plural and indefinite). The vast number of grammatical moods and tenses includes not only a subjunctive, but two different potentials, an eventual and a hypothetical. Euskera is also maddeningly, spectacularly indirect, in what linguists call ergative constructions. For example, to say 'I am spinning', comes out *Iruten ari nuzu*, or literally, 'In the act of spinning doing you have me'! Or try out this proverb: *Izan gabe eman dezakegun gauza bakarra da zoriona.* 'Having without, give (*Izan gabe eman*), we can (*dezakegun*), one thing only is (*gauza bakarra da*), happiness (*zoriona*)' – 'happiness is the only thing we can give without having it'. But such grammatical complexity permits beauty and economy; you can express anything in Euskera in far fewer words than in most other languages. Other advantages are its regular spelling, no grammatical gender, no irregular nouns and hardly any irregular verbs. Pronunciation is not a problem either. Euskera is phonetic, and there are only a few letters you need to know: **e** as long 'a', **u** as 'oo', **j** as 'ee', **s** as halfway between 's' and 'sh', **tz** or **z** as 's' and **x** as 'sh'.

Like the Inuit, who know no generic word for 'ice', the Basques, at least originally, had no word for 'tree' or 'animal'. And being the democratic folk they are, there is no word for 'king' either – they had to borrow one from the French and Spanish potentates to whom they were forced to pay taxes.

Some important Basque words and phrases you might want to try on your trip:

Ongi-etorri!	Welcome!
kontuz, lanak	danger, roadworks
hondartza	beach
zuzen	straight ahead
turismo bulegoa	tourist office
itxita	closed
tren geltokia	train station
atzerapena	delay
Kaixo, zer moduz?	Hello, how are you?
zuritoa	a small beer
garagardoa	a large beer
Sardinak, mesedez	Some sardines, please
gizonak	men's
emakumiak	ladies
Zer du hau?	What is this?
xipirolak	squid

bai	yes
ez	no
Nik ez dut ulurtzen	I don't understand
Gero arte	See you later

Language and Identity

One is born Basque, one speaks Basque, one lives Basque, one dies Basque. The Basque language is a country, I almost said a religion. Say a word in Basque to a mountaineer, and although before you were scarcely a man to him, you suddenly become a brother.

Victor Hugo, *Alpes et Pyrénées*, 1843

Language remains the crux of Basque identity, and for many its survival is a major concern. In Euskera, a Basque is an *Euskaldun*, one 'who speaks Euskera'. The Basque country is *Euskal Herria*, 'the land of Euskera speakers'. Or at least it was until Sabino Arana, the founder of Basque nationalism, conjured up the neologism *Euskadi* as the name of a country. After all, 'everything with a name exists' (*Izena duen guztiak izatea ere badauke*), according to the most famous of Basque proverbs, although another, lesser-known bit of wisdom adds, *Izenak ez du egiten izana* ('a name doesn't make something true').

Existing in name but not in truth sums up the current status of Euskadi for nationalists, but it also defines many an Euskaldun: so many, in fact, don't speak their own language that another neologism, *Euskotar*, was invented for an ethnic Basque with the O-negative blood, but without the tongue. 'To lose your language is to lose your soul,' warn the Sards, another of Europe's linguistic minorities. The Catalans to the east have had tremendous success in revitalizing their language in the New Spain. The Basques are having a much harder time of it.

Euskera's very strangeness weighs against it. No one has yet found another language related to Basque, although linguists have put forth scores of candidates over the past two centuries (the most convincing is the most recent one, Ainu, the language of the Caucasian Ainu people of Japan, proposed by Edo Nyland). Some linguists believe Euskera has been spoken in the Basque lands since 7000 BC (thus predating the invasions that carried Indo-European languages west), and they could be right: practically every word for common tools, for instance, comes from the ancient root *haiz*, meaning stone – even *haiztur*, scissors. Writing, unfortunately, came late. Although the names of people and places (with useful Latin translations) were recorded in Roman times, written Euskera hibernated until the 9th century, when a few words and phrases were jotted down by missionaries. On the other hand, the Basque oral tradition was exceptionally strong, and continues even today with the *bertsolari*, the bards, often scarcely literate shepherds, who have memorized a vast repertoire of traditional pieces and are dazzlingly skilled at improvization. Another oral legacy in Euskera are the plays known as *pastorales*, descended from medieval mystery plays (you can still see them produced at festival times, especially in the villages of Soule).

The first book in Euskera, *Lingua Vasconum Primitiae*, a collection of poems, was published in 1545 by the French Basque priest Benat Etxepare (or Detchepare,

A Basque Outline

Very few Basque words have made it into English, although one is 'silhouette', derived in a most roundabout way from the Basque word for 'many holes', *zuleta*. The surname Zulueta or Zuloeta was probably given to a family who lived among the holes, or caves. One branch of the Zulueta family in France adopted the spelling Silhouette. Their most famous member, Etienne de Silhouette (1709–67), was a writer and politician who held the powerful post of controller-general. He wasn't very good at it and didn't keep his office long, and his meagre policies cast but a shadow (according to one explanation), although others say Silhouette himself liked to draw portraits in outlines and hang them on the walls of his château.

among other spellings); one of his desires, he stated, was to show that 'this language is as good a written language as any other'. In 1729, the Jesuit university professor Manuel Larramendi followed with the first Euskera grammar book, *El Imposible Vencido* (*The Impossible Overcome*). In the same century, Pierre de Agerre, or 'Axular', wrote *Gero*, a literary version of his own sermons, which may not sound like something you'd curl up with for a good read, but nevertheless is considered the first masterpiece of Euskaldun literature.

Most Basque authors, however, including the most famous, Miguel de Unamuno, wanted to reach the widest possible audience and wrote in Spanish or French. One deterrent was the sheer number of dialects in Euskera, one for each of the seven provinces, with variations in every valley; a Bilbaíno, for instance, can only with great difficulty make out a farmer from Soule. Perhaps an even greater deterrent was the abandonment of Euskera by the 18th-century Basque bourgeoisie, who stigmatized it as lower-class hick talk and eliminated it from the schools, the government and their new university at Bergara.

Some fought back, especially Ignacio Iztueta de Zaldibia (1767–1845), a man of humble origins who wrote about Basque music, dance and folklore, fearing they were in danger of extinction. His fears spread after the loss of Basque political autonomy in the Carlist Wars, and with the industrialization that brought in a huge influx of immigrants from across Spain. As the language began to die out in the street, a 19th-century cultural flowering, a Basque Renaissance, arose to preserve it. Plays, poems, novels, grammatical works and dictionaries appeared, many designed to rally the Basques to a sense of themselves as a nation. Among the classics of the period were Augustin Chaho's creation of the myth of Aïtor, the father of all Basques, in 1848, a story that has become a part of Basque culture.

In 1914, the nationalist community founded the first *ikastola* (private Euskera-language elementary school) and they soon became widespread under the Republic. Although some *ikastolas* survived underground during the severe cultural oppression under Franco, his 38 years in power left a huge generational gap in transmitting Euskera; for a while, the fascist campaign to 'Speak Christian!' was so fierce that older Basques who couldn't speak Spanish feared to even leave their homes. Combined with the French-only policies in the north, and the fact that now even the most remote Basque farmhouse is bombarded with radio and TV broadcasts in Spanish and French, the oldest spoken language in Europe was in danger of becoming a museum piece until recently. In Victor Hugo's day, half the inhabitants in all the Basque country spoke fluent Euskera. Today about a third do, some 665,000 people altogether. Owing to the severe cultural oppression under Franco, the percentage of Basque speakers is higher on the French side, according to a 2001 survey: 64 per cent in Basse-Navarre, 55.5 per cent in the Soule and Labourd, as opposed to 49 per cent in Guipúzcoa, 31 per cent in Vizcaya, 11 per cent in Navarra, and 14 per cent in Álava. However, for the first time, the numbers are rising on the Spanish side in a revival that has touched all aspects of Basque culture.

One reason for the revival of Basque is the completion of Modern Standard Basque (*Euskera Batua*) by Bilbao's Academy of Language, a task begun in 1911 but only completed in the 1960s; now, for the first time, in theory at least, there exists an Euskera comprehensible to speakers of all dialects. Banned under Franco, *Batua* was at first taught on the sly in the *ikastolas* and at nationalist cultural events; Gabriel Aresti's *Harri eta Herri* (*Rock and People*) in 1964, boldly published in the face of government opposition, became the inspiration for a whole new generation of Basque writers.

Today, both Euskera and Spanish are the official languages of the three provinces of Euskadi and the valleys of northern Navarra. In the past decade some 100,000 adults, mostly middle-aged people denied the chance under Franco, have learned to speak it; the recently coined *Eskaldunberri* ('new speaker of Basque') embraces them, whatever their ethnic origin. Euskera-language TV and radio are broadcast on both sides of the border, encouraging interest among French Basques, where the language still has no official status and very few children are in *ikastolas*.

For all that, the explosion in print inspired by the creation of *Batua* is nothing short of amazing. The Basque country had its own daily Euskera newspaper, the *Egunkaria*, until its closure in 2003 after being suspected of ETA links (it was subsequently exonerated, but not until 2010), and more than 1,000 books of all kinds are published annually, all for a population of 665,000 potential readers. One Basque novel, *Obabakoak*, by Bernardo Atxaga (1989), was the first ever to be translated from Euskera into English. Equally encouraging is the continuing popularity of the *bertsolari*, the Basque bards, who, like rappers, improvise at festivals, where they compete: given a theme, each must immediately compose and sing an original song about it, sometimes singing alternate verses, each trying to get the upper hand. One is the hero of a Basque cartoon series for children – or what few children there are: the Basque birth rate is the lowest in western Europe, with only 9.9 births per thousand according to a 2008 survey.

Giants, Shaggy Men and a Not-so-Virgin Mari

The Basques are not alone. In fact, their long intimacy with their land has forced them to share it with an unreasonably large number of gods, demons, spirits and fairies – creatures of one of the richest mythologies in Europe. There is no element in the Basque landscape, no chapter of Basque history and legend, that is not suffused with the otherworldly and the divine. Christianity, after all, didn't take a firm hold in this isolated region until the 10th century (the Arabs, during their lightning strike through in the 8th century, called the Basques *majus* – pagans or wizards), and the old gods and spirits who lingered were still lively enough to bedevil Basque children in their catechism classes well into the 20th century. When they questioned the priests – themselves inevitably Basque, because they had to speak Euskera – what was real and what wasn't, the standard reply was: 'Everything that has a name exists in the world... but it's best to keep that a secret!'

One myth the Basques don't have is a migration myth. They were always there, and paradise, where the rivers ran with milk, was deep in the bowels of the Basque country. **Ortzi** or **Ost**, god of the heavens, and the sun, **Eguzi**, were the bright forces of the day and the earth, since the sun was the earth's daughter, reborn every day in the east. Solar symbols decorated the Basques' pre-Christian tombs, and old houses are nearly always orientated towards the east. The moon, **Ilargi**, the 'light of the dead', had to do with all that was hidden, with souls and the spirit world. The fact that old people familiarly called both the sun and moon 'Grandma' suggests that they were once two aspects of the same deity. There are vague hints – curiously, very similarly to the Ainu (see p.41) – that the Basques believed themselves to be descended from bears, as in the ancient carnival figure **Artza**, whose emergence from hibernation in spring is also a symbol of renewal.

One possible origin of the name Pyrenees is 'mountains of fire', after the ritual bonfires that shone from their peaks on the great holidays of the year. Every Basque mountain had its attendant deity; some of these live on in folklore, such as **Jauna Gorri**, the 'Red Lord', who lives atop the Pic d'Anie (Ahunamendi in Basque) and sends the storms down to the valleys. Jauna Gorri tends a garden on the mountain-top where the flowers of immortality grow, and he keeps his treasures there, guarded by hairy black giants called the *pelutlak*. Beneath the mountains are the caves, sites of worship from the Palaeolithic era.

The dolmens were built by the *jentillak*, the race of giants that once lived side by side with the Basques. The *jentillak*, often a great help to their neighbours, invented metallurgy and the saw, and introduced the growing of wheat. One day, a strange storm cloud appeared from the east, and the wisest of the *jentillak* recognized it as an omen and interpreted it as the end of their age. The giants marched off into the earth, under a dolmen (still visible in the Arratzaran valley in Navarra). One was left behind, **Olentzero** the charcoal burner, and he explained to the Basques: 'Kixmi [Jesus] is born and this means the end of our race.' Olentzero lives on today (after nearly vanishing after Franco, he has made a dramatic comeback in all seven Basque provinces) as the jolly, fat doll in a hundred different guises, the leader of all the processions, his ancient association with the winter solstice making him a prominent participant in celebrations of Christmas and New Year's Day; the Basque yule log is 'Olentzero's trunk'. You will find Olentzero in Basque homes and even in the churches, often bearing an uncommon resemblance to the Michelin man, puffing a pipe; he'll probably be surrounded by food and wine because, being one of the *jentillak*, Olentzero likes to eat all day. In many places, straw effigies of Olentzero are paraded through the streets, distributing sweets, before going up in a midnight bonfire.

Then there are the strong, shaggy lords of the wood, the *basajaunak*, who worked the land but kept agriculture secret from the Basques, until St Martin (a Christianization of the original hero) won a bet with them, with their seeds as the wager. Today, when the sheep suddenly start and weird cries echo in the mountains, Basque shepherds say the *basajaunak* are warning of a storm. Other creatures include the ***lamiak***, small female fairies with webbed bird feet and fish bodies who live by the shore and rivers and comb their hair with golden combs, and have a capacity to help or harm; in modern times they have become a bit like leprechauns and get blamed for everything that goes wrong. They often have little goblin assistants, the ***prakagorris***, or 'red pants' (the Devil in Basque, **Galtzagorri**, dresses in a similar fashion).

And where mythology fades off into nursery-lore, we have the 'man with the sack' who comes to carry off naughty children, and a large bestiary with jokes like the elusive ***dahu***, a kind of lizard with legs that are shorter on one side – the better to walk the mountain slopes. Along with the myths goes a remarkable body of pre-Christian religious survivals, including rituals that lasted well into the 20th century; many old Basques in isolated villages can remember festivals with midsummer bonfires in their childhood, and in some villages the custom is coming back (any excuse for a party).

Springtime and Carnival in the Basque country are as atavistic as any ethnographer's heart could desire; besides the aforementioned Artza, or bear, a whole range of primordial characters are unleashed, especially in rural villages in Navarra and Álava. There's Artza's grotesque sidekick, **Ziripot**, who comes covered with old sacks and is attacked by the **Zaldiko**, a malicious man-horse, until he is caught and shod by the ***txatxoak***, young men completely covered with hairy pelts. **Mielotxin**, who is 10ft tall, stuffed with straw and covered with boar skins, is burned at the end of Carnival, as is **Marquitos**, covered with ferns and wearing a beret and necklace of feathers and eggshells. Alarming ***momotxorroak***, 'cow men' in horns and bloody aprons, attack onlookers, while the shaggy but more peaceful ***joaldunak*** awaken spring with pairs of giant bells, symbolic of testicles, strapped to their backs.

All the wealth of folk- and fairytales give only teasing hints of the ancient rites and beliefs from which they are descended. Without much in the way of written records, trying to reconstruct the details is difficult indeed. A large number of inscribed votive altars from Roman times have been dug up around the Pyrenees and, just to tease (or so it seems), nearly each one bears the name of a different god: religion for the proto-Basques may have been a local affair; the same deities, more or less, might go under a different name and carry different attributes in every valley or village.

But concerning the most important deity in the Basque pantheon there is no confusion. Her name is **Mari**, of all things, and she is the Pyrenees' version of the transcendent Great Goddess that ruled the old religion throughout Europe before the coming of the Indo-European peoples. At once the queen of heaven and of the underworld (she dwells in caves, with direct links to the Basques' underworld paradise), she sent thunder and storms down from the mountain-tops, the places where her rites were always observed (favourite abodes were Gorbea, Anboto, Aketegi and Aralar), and she travelled from peak to peak in a blazing fireball. All the other goddesses, spirits and fairies created by the pantheistic mind are just aspects of her, manifest in various forms.

This Mari is no virgin; her consort, shocking as it must have seemed to the ears of the Christian proselytizers, was a great serpent named **Sugaar** or **Maju** – the prototype for all the Pyrenees' many dragons and, according to legend, the founding father of many of the oldest Basque families.

Like many mountain regions, the Basque country has always been fantastically conservative in terms of religion; today it's the last corner of the world that will ever keep the pope up at night worrying. Mari and Mary may bear the same name only by coincidence, but 1,200 years ago, when Christian missionaries began to expropriate the sacred sites, holidays and processions of the old Basque religion to wean people away from it, they probably didn't realize they were helping to maintain a religious continuity that goes back to the beginnings of time.

Basque Accessories

Typically for the mystery people of Europe, no one has a clue how they came by their most beloved and widespread symbol, the *lauburu*, or 'four heads' (*see* box, opposite). Fashion is a bit less mysterious. No old Basque gentleman would be complete without a *txapela*, or beret, and a walking stick, or *makila*. The Basques may have been the first to wear berets. The first recorded ones are the red Jesuit *birettas*, which went on to become the symbol of the Carlists in the 19th century and have never fallen out of fashion since; both men and women don them for festive occasions, along with a red neck scarf and sash. For everyday wear, Basques prefer berets in black or dark blue. In bardic or other competitions, the prize is nearly always a beret, hence *txapeldun*, or 'champion', is 'one with the beret'. Occasionally, even the beret itself is the object of a competition.

Makilas, likewise, are taken very seriously. Descended from the Basque shepherd's staff, they represent authority, justice and respect. The reliefs on the wood originate from incising the wild medlar in the forest, causing the sap to swerve around the cuts and form designs. The branch is cut in winter, peeled, stained with quicklime and heat-straightened. The bottom is then fitted in brass or silver and hand-engraved with Basque motifs. The other end is topped with a horn grip and covered with plaited leather. Traditionally, there is always a coin built into the *makila*, and each one will usually carry an inscribed motto, such as *hitza hitz* – 'one's word is one's word'. The Basques customarily offer a *makila* to anybody they wish to honour: Churchill, General de Gaulle and Pope John Paul II were all beneficiaries.

On festive occasions, at least, many Basques of all ages still wear **espadrilles**, their traditional black-cloth, hemp-soled shoes that lace up around the ankle. They've been around at least since the 13th century, and are still hand-sewn today in Mauléon. They are worth looking out for, although the majority of the cheaper espadrilles you find in the shops these days are machine-sewn in China.

The real monument of Euskadi is the *etxe*, a word that means much more than just 'house'. Set on its own on the velvet hillsides, the traditional Basque farmhouse, usually called a *baserri* (or *borda*, in the French Basque country), is one of the most distinctive characteristics of the whole region: pretty, simple, functional and

The *Lauburu*

Nothing except the relatively recently invented Basque flag, the *ikurriña*, better conveys the message that Here Be Basques. Known sometimes as the pre-Christian Basque cross, the *lauburu* resembles four commas joined at their points, contained in a circle. Some say it represents the four elements, while others find it a variation of the swastika, a solar symbol of ancient China, India, Egypt and America before the Nazis got their hands on it. Modern Basques consider it a sign of good luck. And that's all anyone knows.

nearly always painted white, they are usually two storeys high, with a distinctive long, low gable along the façade and a built-in shelter for animals or other farm business on the ground floor. The upper section often has half-timbering and shutters – trimmed, of course, with green and *rouge basque* (really more of a maroon 'ox blood', which was, in fact, used before the invention of paint).

Most *etxes* face east, towards the rising sun; older houses have carved lintels over the main door, with the year and name of the builder, accompanied by a *lauburu* or two and a sententious inscription.

A Basque house is not only a place to live, but the symbol of the clan, its identifying tartan, its Shinto-style shrine to its ancestors. All Basque houses have names (always bestowed by neighbours, not by the residents) that still serve as the postal address in most cases. Older Basques, when meeting other Basques, will identify themselves by the name of their ancestral *etxe*, even if the house no longer physically exists. The **etxekojaun**, 'master of the house', and the **etxekoandrea**, 'lady of the house', make all the decisions affecting the clan. In the old days, the *etxekojaun* also attended the communal assemblies where the Basques made their laws, while the *etxekoandrea* took charge of more spiritual matters, thwarting evil spirits with a fire in the hearth, gathering laurel, ash leaves or thistle heads (*eguzkilorea*, 'flower of the sun'), and keeping the memory of departed family members alive. One way they do this is by lighting *argizaiolaks*, thin candles wrapped around wood. After the arrival of Christianity, much of this was transferred to the church, where every family has in perpetuity its special place, the *yarleku*. When the master and mistress grow old, the titles are formally handed over to the most suitable child (son or daughter) and to that child's spouse. It is common to find Basque families that have kept their home on the same site for over a thousand years.

The cemeteries have been around even longer, and here, too, each family has its special tomb or area set aside. The Basques have their own distinctive 'discoidal' or round-headed tombstones. Archaeologists have dug up some models 4,500 years old, and the same style has been in use ever since. The earliest ones often had human figures, sun symbols or other symbols carved on them; since the coming of Christianity, the stones usually show crosses. You will see them in any churchyard, usually turned south so that the sun shines on the carved face all day.

Music, Dance and the Basque Yodel

Basques, considered rather taciturn by their French and Spanish neighbours, lose all their inhibitions when it comes to music. 'To sing like a Basque' is a nice compliment in French, and they do do it well, with passion, whether it's choral music, traditional tunes played by village bands, or Basque rock (rare, fortunately, although as one of the few things that Franco couldn't be bothered to suppress, it became a popular vehicle of national solidarity in the 1960s and '70s). Several Basques have enjoyed international success, including Maurice Ravel (who had a Basque mother), Juan Crisóstomo de Arriaga, the great child prodigy composer from Bilbao who died at the age of 19, and the 19th-century opera tenor Julián Gayarre.

The Basques have their share of traditional **musical instruments**, which are played in both the traditional and classic Basque repertoire; special quartets and so on have been composed for them since the 16th century. One of the most widespread instruments is the **txistu**, a three-holed flute (the word, rather distressingly, also means 'saliva', although we've stood near one, safe and dry). One was discovered among the Upper Palaeolithic finds at Istaritz cave, making it the oldest known musical instrument in the world. The *txistu* is usually played with one hand, while the other hand beats out the rhythm on a tambour. Rhythms can also be supplied by the *txalaparta*, a long wooden plank suspended across padded barrels and struck with sticks. Other ancient instruments are the **dultzaina**, a clarinet-like flute, and the **alboka**, a pipe made of straw, wood and horn. A more recent addition is the **trikitixa**, a small diatonic accordion. In Navarra, the archetypal instrument is the **gaïta**, a trumpet that plays an essential part in any fiesta.

Dozens of **traditional dances** are still current, and small groups in many villages keep them up; you'll have a chance to see them at any village fête – and especially in Guipúzcoa, where you can tour the villages on a Sunday morning and usually find at least one or two with traditional dances going on in the square. When they're in the mood, the Basques perform some of the most furiously athletic dances in the world, such as the *Bolant Dantza* ('flying dance'), the *Espata Dantza* ('sword dance') and the impossible *Godalet Dantza* ('goblet dance') of Soule, performed by four men in elaborate costumes, one wearing a large paper horse around his waist so he cannot see his own feet as he leaps on and off a glass of wine without spilling a drop. Many dances are descended from ancient war dances, pitting one set of dancers against another in choreographed battles using swords or poles. There are social dances as well, where men and women hold hands or each other's handkerchiefs in a circle, while the experts, the *dantzari*, do the fancy footwork in the centre.

In a different category altogether is the **irrintizi**, the uncanny Basque yodel, descended from shouts made by the worshippers of Mari (*see* pp.45–6) as they approached her mountain shrines. Basque linguist Larry Trask described it as 'a ululation characterized by a rising pitch and concluded with a kind of demented laugh'. The shepherds later adopted the *irrintizi* to communicate across mountains, and they still occasionally let rip a joyful one when they're feeling good. Perhaps the best place to hear it is at Urcuray's *irrintizi* contest, generally held the first weekend in August, when both male and female *irrintzinari* compete for the prize.

Surviving the Pilgrimage to Santiago

Although the medieval Basques, who chased whales up to the Arctic Circle back in the 10th century, were never as insular as most people think, they laboured under the bad press they received (and this is a bit embarrassing) from a travel guide. A millennium before there were pilgrims to Bilbao's Guggenheim, pilgrims to Santiago tramped through the Basque country, and a French monk, writing a guide for them, slammed the Basques so hard that it took them centuries to recover, if they ever have, from the aspersions he cast.

What made it such a rotten deal is that the pilgrimage was cooked up by the French to begin with, without ever once asking the Basques if they wanted the equivalent of an international highway going through their lands, with all the riff-raff of Europe piling through. The story was far-fetched from the beginning. Santiago, or James the Greater, the fisherman, was one of the first disciples chosen by Jesus, who nicknamed him Boanerges, 'the son of thunder', after his booming voice. After the Crucifixion, he seems to have been a rather ineffectual proselytizer for the faith; in the year 44, Herod Agrippa in Caesarea beheaded him and threw his body to the dogs. End of story, or so it seemed for about 800 years, until Spain found him another task: nothing less than posthumously leading a 700-year-old crusade against the infidels.

All the evidence suggests that it was really the French who put him up to it: the first mention of the Apostle's relics in Spain appears in an 830 appendix to the *Martirologio de Florus*, written in 806 in Lyon. After the fright of 732, when the Arabs invaded as far as Poitiers, the French were ready to pull out all the stops to encourage their old Christian neighbours to rally and defeat the heathen, and a new history of James emerged. First, before his martyrdom he went to Zaragoza to convert the Spaniards and failed. Second, after his martyrdom two of his disciples piously gathered his remains and sailed off with them in a stone boat. The destination was remote Galicia, where the disciples buried Boanerges. In 814, a shower of shooting stars guided a hermit shepherd to the site of James's tomb at Compostela, 'the field of stars'. Another legend identifies Charlemagne (who died in 814) with the discovery of the relics: in the emperor's tomb at Aachen you can see the *Vision of Charlemagne*, with a scene of the Milky Way, the *Via Lactea*, a common name for the pilgrims' road.

In 844, not long after the discovery of the tomb, James was called into active duty at the Battle of Clavijo, appearing on a white horse to help Ramiro of Asturias defeat the Moors. This new role as Santiago Matamoros, the 'Moor-Slayer', was a great morale-booster for the forces of the Reconquista, who made '*Santiago!*' their battle cry. Ramiro was so pleased by his divine assistance that he made a pledge, the *voto de Santiago*, that ordained an annual property tax for St James's church at Compostela. Never mind that the bones, the battle and the *voto* were as bogus as each other; the story struck deep spiritual, poetic and political chords that fitted in perfectly with the great cultural awakening of the 10th and 11th centuries. The medieval belief that a few holy bones or teeth could serve as a hotline to heaven made the discovery essential. After all, the Moors had some powerful juju of their own: an arm of the Prophet Muhammad in the Great Mosque of Córdoba. Another factor in the early 9th century was the Church's need for a focal point to assert its doctrinal control over the newborn kingdoms of Spain, especially over the Celts in Galicia and the very recently converted Basques. A third factor must have been the desire to reintegrate Spain into Europe – and what better way to do it than to increase human, commercial and cultural traffic over the Pyrenees? Pilgrimages to Jerusalem and Rome were already in vogue; after the long centuries of the Dark Ages, the Church was keen on re-establishing its contacts for Christianity across the old Roman empire.

The French were the great promoters of the road to Santiago – so great, in fact, that the most commonly tramped route through the pass at Roncesvalles became known as the *camino francés*. The first official pilgrim was Gotescalco, bishop of Le Puy, in 950. In the next century, the French monks of the reforming Abbey of Cluny did more than anyone to popularize the pilgrimage, setting up sister houses and hospitals along the way. Nor were the early kings in Spain slow to pick up on the commercial potential of the road; the Basque king Sancho the Great of Navarra and Alfonso VI of Castile founded a number of religious houses and institutions along the way and invited French settlers to help run them. It was at this time, too, that the French stuck another oar in with their *Chanson de Roland*, which made Charlemagne something of a proto-pilgrim, although his adventure into Pamplona happened decades before the discovery of James's relics. The 12th century witnessed a veritable boom along the *camino francés*, and the arrival of new monastic and military orders, including the Templars, the Hospitallers and the Knights of Santiago, which all vowed to defend the pilgrim from dangers en route. The final bonus came in 1189, when Pope Alexander III declared Santiago de Compostela a Holy City on equal footing with Jerusalem and Rome, offering a plenary indulgence – a full remission from Purgatory – to pilgrims on Holy Years (when St James's Day falls on a Sunday; the next will be 2021, 2027 and 2032; other years only offer half-time off).

The Tour de Saint-Jacques in Paris was a traditional rallying point for groups of pilgrims (there was more safety in numbers); from there, the return journey was 800 miles and took a minimum of four months on foot. It was not something to go into lightly, but for many it was more than an act of faith: it was a chance to get out and see the world. Many who went were ill (hence the large number of hospitals), hoping to complete the pilgrimage before they died. Not a few were thieves, murderers and delinquents condemned by the judge to make the journey as punishment. Sometimes dangerous cons had to do it in chains. To keep them from cheating or stealing someone else's indulgence (the Compostellana certificate), pilgrims had to have their documents stamped by the clergy along the route, just as they do today.

In 1130, the Abbey of Cluny commissioned Aymery Picaud, a priest from Poitou, to write Book V of the *Codex Calixtinus*. The world's first travel guide, it is chock-full of prejudices and practical advice for pilgrims: he describes the four main roads through France and gives tips on where not to drink the water, where to find the best lodging and where to be on guard against 'false pilgrims' who come not to atone for crimes but to commit them. Aymery was also the first to write extensively about the Basques, and they come in for a sound thrashing, 'expert in all deeds of violence, fierce and savage, dishonest and false, imperious and rude, cruel and quarrelsome'. In fact, according to Aymery, they were the biggest menace on the road. The Basques serve bad food and overcharge at the inn; they are more than likely to ambush the unwary pilgrim (shades of Charlemagne's rearguard) and demand his clothes, money or even his life. 'A Basque or a Navarrese would kill a Frenchman for a copper,' warns the *Codex Calixtinus*. 'The Navarrese fornicate shamelessly with animals.' No one can ever know how much, if any of it, was true; perhaps one or two bad experiences or misunderstandings (needless to say, Aymery didn't speak Euskera) were enough for the monk to condemn the whole race as barbaric. An estimated half-million pilgrims a year made the trek in the Middle Ages (out of a European population of about 60 million). Thousands read the *Codex*, and it made such an impression that, not long after it was written, the Church in France petitioned to have all Basques excommunicated as heretics. Basques today feel the same way when people who don't know any better stigmatize them all as terrorists.

The Sporting Life

The real national sport, of course, is smuggling, or it was until the EU took the fun out of it. But the Basques do love to play, and over the millennia they have evolved a number of outlandish games that are unique in the world. Many of these are based on pure brute strength, the celebrated **force basque** that is a major element of the national mystique. Even today, particularly strong, tall people are said to be descendants of the *jentillak* (*see* p.44). One can imagine them, back in the mists of time, impressing each other by carrying around boulders – because that's what they do today, in a number of events generally called the *harri altxatzea*, literally 'stone-lifting'. In one, contestants see how many times they can lift a 500lb stone in five minutes; in others, they roll round boulders around their shoulders. Related to this is the *untziketariak*, in which we see how fast a Basque can run with 100lb weights in each hand. They're fond of the tug-of-war (*sokatira*) too; they probably invented it. Besides these, you will see them at village festivals pulling loaded wagons (or making teams of oxen do it), or lifting them (*orgo joko*), or racing with 200lb sacks of grain on their shoulders, or chopping tree trunks against the clock. Shepherds indulge in sheep-fighting, or *aharitalka*. Don't fool with these people.

The miracle is that at the same time they could develop a sport like **pelota** (*pelote basque* in France), the fastest ball game in the world. Few sports can offer an image as beautiful and memorable as the *pelotari* in his traditional loose, pure-white costume, chasing down the ball with a long, curving *chistera*. *Pelota* takes a wide variety of forms, but the basic element is always the ball: a hard core, wrapped tightly with woollen string (which was replaced with rubber after its discovery in America) and covered with hide – like a baseball, only smaller and with much more bounce. In a serious match, this ball can reach speeds of 150mph. The oldest form of the game is *rebot*, played bare-handed without a wall. Other versions soon evolved, played in an outdoor *frontón* (court) with a leather glove (*pasaka* or *joko garbi*), a racket, or the *chistera*, a basket made of leather and osier, which enables a player to scoop up the ball and fling it back in the same motion. This last game is *cesta punta*, the fastest and most furious form of *pelota*. Thanks to Basque emigrants, this has become a popular sport around the Caribbean and Florida, where it is known as *jaï-alaï* (the 'festival game'), which curiously enough is a Basque expression not used in the Basque country (don't ask us why!). Whatever the game, it usually requires teams of two players each. The ground in front of the wall is marked off in *cuadros* every 13 feet from it; to be in, a ball bounced off the wall must usually hit between the 4th and 7th *cuadros*, if it is not returned on the fly. Games are usually to 35 points.

Every Basque village has a *frontón* as its principal monument, usually right in the centre. On some village churches from as far back as the 17th century you can see how the architects left one smooth blank wall to accommodate the game. Besides the *frontón*, the game may be played in a covered court (*trinquete*). If you want to get in a little action yourself, you might try to talk your way into it at any village *frontón* when they're practising (they'd be charmed), or see p.103. As for getting in on the gambling aspect of *pelota* – go ahead and throw your money away if you want to. Each tourist office has schedules of matches; they are usually played at the same time every week.

The **zezenketa** or **encierro** (bull-running) requires agility similar to that required for *pelota*. The Basques make no great claims to have invented the sport, although they may well have; they painted the beasts on their caves 15,000 years ago and were probably being chased by them even back then. The goddess Mari is guarded by a fierce red bull who lives in caves. Whatever the case, the Navarrese have perfected the sport, culminating in the greatest *zezenketa* of all, the *Sanfermines* at Pamplona (*see* pp.211–12). The casualties are almost always tourists. The *sokamutur*, on the other hand, offers many of the thrills but fewer chills; the bull is held by ropes attached to a ring in its nose, which allows its handlers to pull it back (in theory) if it looks as if someone is about to be seriously injured.

The Basques have their own very lively and exciting card game, too, called **mus**, with rules as inscrutable as Philadelphia pinochle. In most *tabernas* you'll find a game going, especially at weekends. There are any number of variations on the rules – with only four kings and four aces in Navarra, or with '10 kings' in Eibar (Guipúzcoa), or the Juego Real. If you want to have a go, the rules in this chapter should be enough to get started, but you can find more details online.

The Rules of Mus

Along with fish soup and structural iron, one of the great contributions of the Basques to Spanish life is the popular card game of *mus*. Like most things Basque, it is a game that outsiders might find inscrutable, perhaps unfathomable. The most endearing feature is institutionalized cheating, which will occasionally cause the player to stick his tongue out at his partner, perhaps even twice.

Mus works best with four players in two partnerships, seated as in bridge, with a deck of Spanish cards (which has 40 cards in it). The suits are swords, staffs, cups and coins (which correspond respectively to spades, clubs, hearts and diamonds), and each suit consists of *Rey* (R), *Caballo* (C), *Sota* (S), 7, 6, 5, 4, 3, 2, ace. The *Rey* (king) is numbered 12 on the card, the *Caballo* (a knight on a horse; in this macho country there are no females in the deck) is numbered 11; the

Sota (jack) is numbered 10. Note well that a 3 is the equal of a king and a 2 is the same as an ace (1). Don't ask why. You will also need 22 pebbles or beans, in a saucer in the centre of the table.

Mus is like poker, in that you do not play the cards, but hold them and make bets on their value. But, while poker is a game for the avaricious and simple-minded, *mus* is not usually played for money. What's more, it offers all the complexity you could ask for and probably more; opportunities for creative bluffing are endless. You have to bet on your hand four times, in four different ways.

Dealing

First, the dealer hands out four cards to each player, dealing backwards (to the right). All the betting goes backwards too, and always starts with the *mano*, the player to the right of the dealer. If you don't like your cards, you may have a chance to get rid of some or all of them, for the first thing that happens is the discard. Starting with the *mano*, each player in turn says either '*mus*' (call for new cards) or '*no hay mus*' (or, for Basques, '*hasi*' or '*mintza*': 'start the game'). One 'no' vote is an absolute veto, and the game begins immediately. Otherwise, all players can discard as many as they like after the fourth '*mus*', and the dealer replaces them in turn; then the *mano* says '*mus*' or '*no hay mus*', and so on. If everyone keeps saying '*mus*', you might conceivably go through the whole deck; if so, shuffle all the discards and keep going.

Cheating

This business of the *mus* is accompanied by the start of the cheating, which consists of a series of signals (*kenuak*) to let your partner know what you've got. The signals in accepted use are:

- Biting your lower lip means you have two kings (doing this twice shows four kings).
- Showing the tip of your tongue means you have two aces (twice for four aces).
- Raising both eyebrows means you have *duples* (two pairs).
- Twisting your mouth to one side means you have *medias* (three of a kind).
- A wink means you have a *Juego* of 31, the best *Juego* you can get (*see* below).
- Closing (or lowering) both eyes (*ciego*) means you have a bum hand.

No other signals are permitted; that would be cheating. Of course you want to try and do it when your opponents aren't looking, at the same time peeking to catch their signals while pretending to look the other way. Shifty eyes are a definite advantage; another is keeping your opponents' glasses full at all times.

The Game

Now come the four stages of the game, in each of which there may or may not be betting (*see* below).

First is **Grande**, or *Haundia*, where the highest hand wins – the highest card, and in case of a tie, the next highest, and so on. Thus R-3-4-4 beats R-C-C-7 (remember a 3 is as good as a king).

Next comes the **Chica**, or *Txikia*, which is like the *Grande* only backwards: the lowest hand wins (note that in the example given above the first hand wins this too, because the 4 is lower than the 7).

In the **Pares**, or *Pareak*, the best hand is the one with *duples* (*dobleak* in Basque) – two pairs of anything (in case of a tie the highest pair wins). Four of a kind counts simply as two pairs. If no one has *duples*, three of a kind wins (*medias*, or *mediak*), and again, the highest threesome rules. If no one has three of a kind, the highest *par simple* (or *parea*) is tops.

It gets trickier in the last stage, the **Juego**, or *Jokoa*. Here you need to learn another system of values for the cards. R, 3, C and S are worth 10 each; 7, 6, 5 and 4 are worth their face value, and ace and 2 count as 1. If your hand totals exactly 31 points (R-3-7-4, for example), then you have the best *Juego*. The next best is 32. Then come in descending order 40, 37, 36, 35, 34 and 33. Anything with 30 or under is no *Juego* at all (and 38 and 39 are impossible to get). If no one has a *Juego*, then you compete instead for the best **Punto**, or *Puntuak*, which is a hand totalling 30 or fewer points. The highest *Punto* is a hand with 30 points, then 29, 28 and so on, down to 4 (the lowest).

Betting

In each of the four stages there is a separate round of betting, though no one shows their cards until all four are completed. The betting is where the saucer and the 22 pebbles come in. In *mus*, you do not bet your own stake of money or counters, but simply the amount of points each stage will be worth. The pebbles are used for keeping score. A round of betting starts with the *mano*, who may pass (*paso*), or bet (*envido*, or *enbido*) an amount of 2 or more. If all four players pass the chance to bet, the betting is over and the stake for that stage is one.

After a bet, is made the opposing team may fold (*no quiero*, or *tira*), see (*quiero*, or *edoki*) or raise (*reenvido*, or *beste hiru*) any amount. To do this, either player may speak – the two might disagree, in which case one partner can overrule the other by saying 'we fold' or 'we see' ('*no queremos*' or '*queremos*'). Then, if the bet has been raised, the other team must answer. When one side folds, the other wins the previous amount staked (not the raise that caused the fold). When one side sees, the betting is done, though settling the bet is put off until the end of the game when the cards are revealed.

In the *Pares*, before the betting, each player in turn must say whether or not he has at least a pair (say just '*si*' or '*no*'). If neither side has a player who does, there is no betting and no score. If only one side does, they score one. If both sides do, there is a round of betting. Before the *Juego*, each player must say whether or not he has a *Juego* (31 points or more). Then, as in the *Pares*, if both sides have one there is a round of betting. If there is no betting in the *Pares*, the best *Pares* scores 3 points for *duples*, 2 for *medias*, and 1 for a *par simple* from both hands (if there is betting, at the end of the game these points are scored in addition to any bets). If there is no betting on the *Juego*, the winning side scores 3 points for a *Juego* of 31, 2 for any other *Juego*, or 1 for any *Punto*; as in the *Pares*, the winning side scores these points from both hands, in addition to any betting.

There is a special bet called **Hordago** that any player may make at any time in the four stages (when it's his or her turn). *Hor dago* means 'here it is' in Basque, and it's an immediate showdown, a bet to stake the whole game on whatever stage it is in at the moment. If the opponents fold, they concede that stage at whatever level the betting has reached (1 point only if no previous bets were made). If they see it, the cards are shown and the best hand wins the game.

Note that in any of the four stages there can be ties – hands of absolutely equal value (for example, in the *Pares*, if both sides have pairs of the same rank). If this happens, the *mano*, or the player closest to him on the right, wins.

Scoring

A game of *mus* is 40 points, and this usually requires several hands. The deal alternates, naturally, since being the *mano* is such a big advantage. The play of *mus* is really more simple and straightforward than it looks, once you get the hang of it, but the method of keeping score is something that could only have been dreamt up by Basques. Remember the 22 pebbles? Instead of using them like poker chips, they are simply markers to keep score. One member of the partnership keeps 'ones' (*piedras*) and the other keeps 'fives' (*amarracos*, or *hammarekos* in Basque). So if a team has 4 points, the keeper of *piedras* will have four pebbles taken from the dish in front of him. If they then score 3 more, he will give one to his partner, where it becomes a *hammareko*, keep two and put one back in the dish. You'll never need more than 22 of them – if both sides are on the threshold of winning at 39 points, each will have seven *hamarrekos* (35 points) and four *piedras*.

Scoring after a hand is always done in precise order of the stages, because the first side to hit 40 wins, even if their opponents racked up big scores in later stages that would have beaten them.

Food and Drink

04

Nomansland, the territory of the Basques, in a region called Cornucopia, where the vines are tied up with sausages. And in those parts there was a mountain made entirely of grated parmesan cheese on whose slopes there were people who spent their whole time making macaroni and ravioli.

Boccaccio, *The Decameron*, VIII

Boccaccio may have got the recipes all wrong, but even in the 14th century his antennae caught culinary signals emanating from the Basques. By popular acclaim they are the champion cooks of Spain, and they come out fairly well in the gourmet stakes in France, too. It is one of their great sorrows, however, that the Basque country isn't quite the cornucopia of the Florentine's imagination. There were mountains made of iron, but not of Parmesan. In the steep hill country, cow pastureland is rare.

Basque cuisine is not elaborate, but is based on high-quality ingredients from the sea or small Basque farms. Much of its theory lies in the timing, in *el punto*, knowing during preparation precisely when a dish has achieved perfection. Although the ingredients are often few in number, the knack can be maddeningly elusive, as anyone who has tried to prepare *bacalao pil-pil* at home can attest. Sauces are simple, and come in two basic hues: gastronomes say forget all that mumbo jumbo about the green of their hills and the blood of their warriors; the colours of the Basque flag represent green sauce and red sauce.

One peculiarly Basque institution is those freemasons of food, the **txokos**: exclusively male gastronomic clubs formed in the middle of the 19th century 'to eat and sing'. Donostia-San Sebastián alone has 75 of them; to join, one must be sponsored by at least two members, and the waiting lists are long. They take turns cooking lavish meals for each other, although according to their wives they would never touch a saucepan at home. A few *txokos* allow women in to eat, but they are never allowed to cook.

Traditional Basque Cuisine

Not surprisingly, Basque cooks exert most of their talent on seafood, the one thing the region has always had in abundance. They have had plenty of practice – a 12,000-year-old painting of sea bream decorates the walls of one ancient cave and the remains of sea urchins have been found in settlements 10,000 years old. The bounty of the sea finds expression in famous fish soups and stews, and there are any number of prized delicacies – surprising things like *kokotxas*, normally translated as 'cheeks' but really the jowls of the hake or spider crab.

Marseille has its *bouillabaisse*, among a score of other treasured fish soups of southern Europe, but the French Basques stoutly maintain that their version, called **ttoro** (pronounced 'tioro'), is the king of them all. Naturally, as in Marseille, there is a solemn confraternity of the finest *ttoro* chefs dedicated to maintaining standards, although there are as many variations of *ttoro* as there are cooks. A proper one requires a pound of mussels and a mess of crayfish and congers, as well as three different kinds of other fish. The dish was invented by fishermen of St-Jean-de-Luz and the other small ports at the mouth of the Nivelle river, and it's there that you'll find the best versions. St-Jean-de-Luz holds a *ttoro* festival with a competition and *dégustation* in early September; this may be your last chance on the coast to try it, as *ttoro* runs out of popularity west of here.

Tuna, **bonito** (a more streamlined, bullet-shaped tuna) and **cod** are caught on the high seas. *Thon basquaise* is fresh tuna cooked with tomatoes, garlic, aubergine and spices; bonito goes into a popular fisherman's stew called *marmitako*, cooked with potatoes, tomatoes, garlic and a red pepper. Salt cod, once a cheap staple and increasingly a rare delicacy, achieves a kind of epiphany in **bacalao pil-pil** (originally named for the sound it made while frying), where somehow olive oil, garlic and chillies magically meld with the cooking juices of salt cod to form a sauce with the consistency of a soft mayonnaise. There are at least a dozen other Basque recipes for *bacalao*, including *a la bizkaina*, with a red sauce of tomatoes, onions and roasted peppers, and crumbled and baked with potatoes or bread in a *zurrukutuna* (wood oven) that gives the dish its name. You can even find it stuffed in red pepper. Another variation is *ajoarriero*, a succulent dish prepared with cod, tomatoes and red peppers.

Other favourites from the sea are **scallops**, big **eels** (served with parsley and garlic) and the unusual *chipirones* or *txipirones* (baby squid served fried or stuffed, or in a casserole in their own ink) – reputedly the only dish in the world that's all black, and better than it sounds. Basques also have an insatiable passion for tiny worm-like **elvers** (known as *angulas*, *pibales*, *civelles* or *txitxardin*) that arrive in January on the Basque coast straight from the Sargasso Sea, only to be drawn by the lights of night fishermen and tossed in the hot oil of a frying pan with garlic and chilli peppers. The fact that they are increasingly rare is a cause for great dismay and quests for substitutes; if your bowl of *angulas* doesn't cost a kingly sum, you can bet they're not the real McCoy. Another Basque classic is **txangurro** – spider crab, which is flaked, seasoned, stuffed and served in its own shell; order it with a side dish of *kiskillas* (prawns), *nécoras* (small crabs) or *txirlas* (baby white clams). In summer, the ports have tempting stands of barbecued fresh sardines. Gourmets particularly recommend **hake**, a delicate white fish, in green sauce (*merluza a la koskera*) or as *kokotxas a la Donostiarra*, hake cheeks with a garlic and parsley green sauce, clams and slightly piquant red Basque peppers. Or with cider, *a la ondarresa*. The important thing is that the hake in question has to be a large (and expensive) one, weighing at least three kilos.

In a country of shepherds, **lamb** grazed in mountain pastures is, not surprisingly, the favourite meat, especially lamb chops, sweetbreads and roast leg of lamb. In landlocked Navarra, look for *chuletas de cordero a la navarra* (lamb chops), *chilindron* (lamb stew with peppers), *trucha con jamón* (trout stuffed with ham), *estofado de toro* (beef stew, especially after a *corrida*) or, for something out of the ordinary, *liebre con chocolate* (hare with chocolate), washed down by the strong wines from Tudela and Estella. The Basques are also known for their *charcuterie*, such as *tripotcha*, a kind of pudding made from sheep's tripe, *pâté basque*, spicy chorizo sausage (try it with a *talo*, a cornmeal pancake, a mainstay in the countryside in the 17th century) and *loukinkos* (also spelled *lukenques*), little garlic

Hot Stuff

Espelette is synonymous with *Capsicum annuum L*, or *piments d'Espelette* (*Ezpeletako Biperra*), and it's a great source of local pride that these hot red peppers were made an AOC in 2000. Brought back from America by Columbus's Basque pilot, the peppers are grown in Espelette and nine surrounding *communes*; they are planted in February and produce until the first frost. You can see them in the late summer hanging everywhere, drying on houses, on walls, on roofs; and you can buy a string of them, or you can buy them reduced to a powder like paprika, or mushed up in a paste in a jar. According to locals, a pinch improves just about every dish, while gracing it with hidden virtues – as a stimulant, aphrodisiac and cure for hangovers.

The Espelette *mairie* sells a book entirely devoted to them, with a selection of recipes; and the last Sunday in October is given over to a gastronomic knees-up, in which the peppers appear where you might not expect them, even in chocolate. One highlight of the festival is the election of Madame or Monsieur Piment, a local who wins their weight in local food products.

In Europe, the hot pepper was one of the very few items brought back from America that didn't catch on, and in both Spain and France the only regional cuisine that you'll find that packs any heat is Basque – a bit surprising for people living in a rainy and generally cool climate, but by now you should realize that Basques are exceptions to the rule. In fact, perhaps the ultimate test of one's Basquehood is not the ability to play *pelota*, run with boulders, or speak Euskera, but the capacity for eating a mess of *piments d'Espelette* without flinching.

sausages. The famous **Bayonne ham** is hung for over a year; it has a strict set of rules and an *appellation d'origine contrôlée* (AOC) status like fine wines. In the north, you'll also find the archetypal delights of southwest France: duck and goose *confits*, *magrets* and *foie gras*. Other meaty staples include *txistorra*, a long, thin, spicy red sausage which is normally eaten fried in small chunks, and *morcilla*, a pungent black pudding. For a special treat, tuck into a *chuletón*, a great slab of T-bone steak grilled over charcoal, at a local *asador*.

Red **peppers**, notably the *piments d'Espelette* that pack a bit of heat (*see* above), are another icon of the Basque kitchen; Basque housewives still hang strings of them on the walls of their houses for drying (and for decoration). The season for fresh ones is short, from September to November. They go into spicy sausages, or into *piperade*, a kind of ratatouille made from roast red peppers, green peppers, tomatoes, garlic and whipped eggs, lightly fried and served with *jambon de Bayonne*. Milder peppers turn up everywhere: in omelettes, or in *poulet basquaise*, a free-range corn-fed chicken stewed in a pot with peppers, onions and tomatoes. In Álava, chard leaves are stuffed with ham and cheese and fried in batter, and the wide variety of vegetables from the plains gets mixed up into *menestra*. Everywhere in winter you'll find *purrusalda*, a hearty leek and potato soup. In Bilbao they make a sweetish spinach pie, and the bunches of sweet, plump asparagus piled up at the markets throughout the Basque country are famous throughout Spain.

The Basques, like their Spanish and Gascon neighbours, are also partial to **beans**, which were a mainstay at the table for centuries. A winter favourite, *cocido*, is a thick bean stew flavoured with a ham bone and miscellaneous pork parts; in Labourd, where it's called *eltzekari*, the beans are flavoured with duck fat, making it a bit like cassoulet. One classic is *habas a la vitoriana*, the broad beans of Vitoria, although the Basques swear the best by test is a hearty mess of *alubias de Tolosa* served with cabbage and chunks of cured sausage like chorizo or *morcilla*, and sometimes pickled green *guindilla* peppers.

And *après* beans? The Basque cure for indigestion is curdled milk (*mamia* or *cuajada*). Other treats made the old-fashioned way include pure **sheep's milk cheese**. On the Spanish side it's called *Idiazabal*, DO (*denominación de origen*) since 1988, a strong cheese with bite made only from the milk of *latxa* ewes, a special Basque race of sheep; it's delicious with grapes or slices of quince or a handful of plump walnuts. To the north, the best-known Basque cheeses are Etorki and Kerkou, sold everywhere in France. There's also the AOC (*appellation d'origine contrôlée*) Ossau-Iraty. Some of the real mountain cheeses pack a wallop.

The Basques in the south often end things fairly simply with cheese or maybe an apple, but you may be able to finish a meal in grand **dessert** style with a *pantxineta*, an almondy *gâteau basque* filled with cream or cherry jam (made with special Basque cherries from Itxassou). In Bilbao, try the *canutillos*, rolls of flaky pastry stuffed with custard, or the sweeter version in the south of Álava, *hojaldres a la crema*. Around Pamplona, the sweet-toothed shouldn't miss the *crema frita de almendras*, a quickly fried ball of almond dough. Otherwise, desserts, even in the smartest restaurants, are often quite restrained in the Spanish Basque lands: tarts piled with fresh fruits are a summer favourite, and bittersweet lemon tarts do the rounds in spring. Bayonne is a different story, with chocolate gâteaux, mousses, ice-creams and the ultimate treat, the *pavé de chocolat*, a dense, rich truffle cake.

New Basque Cuisine

Franco's régime has been compared to stale white bread, and in 1976 it had scarcely come to an end when two Basque chefs, Juan Mari Arzak and Pedro Subijana, attended a course run by *nouvelle cuisine* pied piper Paul Bocuse. At the time Basque cooking was suffering from a certain malaise and boredom, and, while the old recipes still held sway, they had begun to seem lacklustre; restaurants kept their clients with quantity rather than quality. A dose of Bocuse was enough to send the chefs off on their own path of *cocina nueva vasca* to transform the age-old Basque ingredients into new and exciting dishes such as *ensalada de angulas* (baby eel salad), *lubina a la pimienta verde* (sea bass with green pepper), *crepes de txangurro* (spider crab crêpes), and (on the French side) *petits piments rouges farcis à la morue sauce brune* (baby red peppers stuffed with cod in a brown wine sauce), and *brochette de langoustines au sésame*. New Basque cuisine also makes good use of wild mushrooms. Álava province is the best place to go for these, particularly for the exquisite and very delicate spring mushroom, *perretxiku* (*Lyophylum georgii*), served lightly cooked with eggs. Truffles are found in Álava, too, around Campezo, and modern Basque chefs are not having too much trouble inventing new dishes to put them in.

Nowadays, chefs like Arzak, Irizar, Subijana and Pildain, leading figures of the revolution in Basque cuisine, are household names throughout Spain, and the mere mention of their celebrated restaurants can bring a longing gasp to the lips of admirers. A new generation – Martín Berasategui, Hilario Arbelaitz, Ramón Roteta and José Juan Castillo, as well as bright new stars like Koldo Lasa and Alberto Elorza – has sprung up under their tutelage, and Karlos Arguiñano even has his own hugely popular TV show. Today, the old recipes in the hands of the new Basque maestros are no longer stuck-in-the-mud reruns, but personalized culinary variations on a theme, prepared with centuries of savvy, and always *el punto*.

Washing it Down: Wine, *Sidra* and Other Nice Things

Biba Rioja, Biba Nafarroa Haren famaren izarra
Hemen guziak aneiak gira Hustu dezagun Pitxarra
Glugluglu glu glugluglu glu glugluglu glugluglu glugluglu
Glu glugluglu glu glugluglu gluglu glu glugluglu gluglugluglulglu glu.

popular Basque drinking song

With its gentle climate, the Basque region has been making wine at least since Roman times. On the French side, the best known are the soft AOC reds and rosés of Irouléguy from the Pyrenean foothills (*see* p.276), good with chicken dishes and grilled or roast lamb. The most distinctive Basque vintage is a tangy young 'green' wine called **txakoli** (in 1994 made a DO, the Spanish equivalent of AOC), which is poured into the glass with bravura from a height. There are red and rosé versions, but the *gree* (white) is by far the most common. *Txakoli* was made according to old family recipes which were passed down from generation to generation, but the tradition had almost died out by the mid-19th century. Technological improvements have meant that it is once again everyone's favourite tipple, an emblematic, entirely Basque accompaniment to *pintxos* (*see* p.63). It is made along the coast with just a modicum of sunlight around Getaria and Zarautz, as well as in small areas in Vizcaya and Álava provinces, and is especially good with seafood.

Navarra grows its own DO Navarra, mostly reds, using traditional grapes such as tempranillo and grenache, although other varieties – merlot and cabernet sauvignon – are becoming increasingly popular. The rosés are renowned for their quality, and the rosé of Olite is especially good. An extraordinary percentage of it never gets beyond Pamplona, in the week of *Los Sanfermines*. The Navarrese also have a grand tradition of mellow muscatel dessert wines.

Then there's **Rioja**, the best-known wine region in Spain, famous for its soft, warm, mellow, full-bodied reds, with a distinct vanilla bouquet. The Carthaginians, it seems, introduced the first vines, which, after the various invasions, were replanted by the Church; the first law concerning wine was decreed by Bishop Abilio in the 9th century. The arrival of masses of thirsty pilgrims in the Middle Ages proved a boon to business, much as mass tourism would do in the 1960s and '70s.

Despite a long pedigree, the Rioja we drink today dates from the 1860s, when growers from Bordeaux, their own vineyards wiped out by phylloxera, brought their techniques south of the border and wrought immense improvements on the native varieties. By the time the plague reached La Rioja in 1899, the owners were prepared for it with disease-resistant stock. During the First World War, when the vineyards of the Champagne region were badly damaged, the French returned to buy up *bodegas*, sticking French labels on the bottles and trucking them over the

Pyrenees. Rioja finally received the respect it deserved after Franco. On the bad side, prices have skyrocketed as the *bodegas* have attracted investors from around the world.

La Rioja's growing area covers 64,000 hectares, comprising three zones: **Rioja Alta**, home of the best red and white wines, followed by **Rioja Alavesa** (on the left bank of the Ebro in the Basque province of Álava) known for its lighter, perfumed wines, and the decidedly more arid **Rioja Baja**, where the wines are coarse and mostly used for blending – a common practice in La Rioja. The varieties used for the reds are mostly spicy, fruity tempranillo (covering some 30,000 hectares alone), followed by garnacha tinta (a third of the red production, a good alcohol booster) with smaller portions of graciano (for the bouquet) and high-tannin mazuelo (for acidity and tone). Traditional Rioja whites are relatively unknown but are excellent, golden and vanilla-scented like the reds: viura grapes are the dominant grape, with smaller doses of malvasía and garnacha blanca.

Unlike French wines, Riojas are never sold until they're ready to drink (although of course you can keep the better wines even longer). DOC rules specify that La Rioja's Gran Reserva, which accounts for only three per cent of the production, spends a minimum of two years maturing in American oak barrels (six months for whites and rosés) then four more in the *bodega* before it's sold. *Reservas* (six per cent of the production) spend at least one year in oak and three in the *bodega*. *Crianzas* (30 per cent of the production) spend at least a year in the barrel and another in the bottle. The other 61 per cent of La Rioja is *sin crianza* and labelled CVC (*conjunto de varias cosechas*, 'combination of various vintages'); this includes the new young white wines and light reds (*claretes*) fermented at cool temperatures in stainless steel vats, skipping the oak barrels altogether and losing most of the vanilla tones.

Besides wine, Basques make good hard **cider** (*sidra* or *sagardo*) in an enclave in Guipúzcoa. The story goes that paradise was located in the Basque country (it's now gone underground) and that when the first Basques, Adam and Eve, were given their marching orders Adam was so furious that he hurled the rest of the apples he had picked into a hole, and for good measure ground them up with stones so he would never have to see them again. A few days later, Eve was thirsty and found a fermented juice that resembled liquid gold. The Basques then (they say) passed the secret knowledge on to the Vikings, who went on to become the more famous cider makers of Normandy. Back in the 16th century, Basque fishermen used to trade the stuff to the American Indians for furs. *Sidra*, like *txakoli*, has to be poured from a great height, and is best drunk in February.

Anís (*anisette*, sweet or dry) is also quite popular; mixed with cognac it becomes a *sol y sombra* (which, however, isn't as vile as a *kalimotxo*, red wine mixed with Coke, the crazy-juice favoured by the bull-runners in Pamplona). Look for Bayonne's famous **Izarra**, a potent mix of Pyrenean herbs with spices, based on armagnac, which comes in either green or the less potent yellow. For something more unusual, you can top off your meal with a **carajillo** (coffee with cognac or rum flambé), **manzana** (a liqueur made from apples), or a tipple of Basque hooch, **patxaran** or **pacharán**, made from sloes grown around Pamplona and soaked in *anís*.

Practicalities

Learning to Eat Like a Basque

Jan-edanaren gozoa! Kontu-emanaren gaiztoa!
('How sweet it is to eat and drink! How terrible to have to pay the bill!')
old Basque saying

The essential fact is that Basques like to eat all day long – this scheme spreads the gratification evenly throughout the waking hours. Give it some consideration (only the quantities will probably kill you). Go into a village restaurant at nine in the morning on a market day, and just watch the boys tuck into their three-course breakfasts – soup, tons of meat, fish and potatoes, with a gallon or so of wine for each. If you're planning to spend an afternoon running around with boulders or doing some other Basque sport, join them. Otherwise, start out with a big coffee and a pastry, or find a progressive-looking bar (usually called a **taberna**, but you may also see **ardangedi**, 'wine place'), where you might find a more fitting breakfast – a glass of wine or brandy, and a salami sandwich or a glazed doughnut. These will be around all day, the piles of treats under the glass cases growing by the hour. They peak mid-morning, when Basques stop off for their *hamaiketako* ('elevenses', literally). Lunch at 2pm or so is fairly substantial, followed at around 5pm by a late-afternoon snack, or *merienda*. Then come *apéritifs* on the run (*see* 'Bar Life and the *Txikiteo*', pp.64–5), which help work up an appetite for dinner at 10pm; this is usually the main meal of the day, taking an hour or two to eat with all its courses, wine and coffee (at the end of the meal, ask for a *completo* – coffee, cognac and a cigar). And more drinks (*kopas*).

At the upmarket end of the scale you'll find plenty of new restaurants serving New Basque cuisine, but there are still plenty of old-fashioned restaurants around – along with many of the sort that travellers have been complaining about for centuries. The worst offenders are often the **cafeterías**, those flag-bedecked places that feature faded photographs of their *platos combinados* ('combination plates') to eliminate any language problem in the most touristy areas, and in general you'd do better to buy some bread, cheese and a bottle of Rioja red, and have a picnic.

In any coastal town or village, the best seafood restaurants sit around the harbour. The fancier ones will post set menus, while at the rest a chalkboard lists the prices for grilled fish or prawns or whatever else came in that day; just choose a dish, or negotiate a full dinner with the waiter. Don't expect seafood to be a bargain, though; a plate of prawns in garlic all by itself usually goes for about €8.50. Places called **marisquerías** serve only fish and shellfish. Don't neglect the rapidly disappearing shacks on the beach – they often serve up barbecued sardines that are completely out of this world.

Away from the sea, you'll find **asadores** that specialize in roast or grilled meat, and **sidrerías** (or *sagardotegiak*) that specialize in cider and serve simple dishes such as cod omelettes, T-bone steaks, pork chops and fried potatoes, all accompanied by as much *sidra* as you can drink. The season is between 21 January and Easter, when the *sidra* is in wooden barrels (once it's bottled it's not as good). Expect to be splashed:

rather than the *sidra* being poured from a jug, the big wooden barrel is unbunged, the cider gushes out in a stream and everyone queues up to fill their glass. Don't bother dressing up, and do wear sturdy shoes. Both *asadores* and *sidrerías* are often packed out with families at weekends, when it's a good idea to book.

If you dine where the locals do, you'll be assured of a good deal, if not necessarily a good meal. Almost every restaurant offers a *menú del día / menu du jour* or a *menú turístico / menu touristique* featuring a starter, a main course, dessert, bread and drink at a set price, always lower than if you had ordered the items *à la carte*. These menus are always posted outside the restaurant, in the window or on the plywood chef by the door; memorise what you want before going in, because these bargains are hardly ever listed on the menu the waiter gives you at the table. In Spain, unless it's explicitly written on the bill (*la cuenta*), service is not included in the total, so tip accordingly (between five and ten per cent). In France, service is generally included on the *addition*; if not, it will say s.n.c. or *service non compris*.

The Basque country is celebrated for its **pintxos** (Basque tapas), little morsels served on a slice of bread or with a toothpick, which have evolved into one of the world's great snack cultures. Bars that specialize in them offer platter after platter of delectable titbits, from shellfish to slices of omelette, mushrooms baked in garlic, vegetables in vinaigrette and stews. All you have to do is pick out what looks good and order a *porción* (two or three bites), or a *ración* (a big helping). It's hard to generalize about prices, but on average €10 of tapas and wine or beer can fill you up. You can always save money in bars by standing up; sit at a charming table on the terrace and prices jump considerably. The hard part comes when trying to remember what you've had (if you ever knew the name in the first place) when the time comes to settle up, as drinks and *pintxos* are on the honour system and you pay as you leave.

Another advantage of *pintxos* is that they're available at what most Americans or Britons consider normal dining hours. If you stay for a few months, late dining makes perfect sense, but it's exasperating to the average visitor whose stomach growls at a much earlier hour. On the coasts, restaurants tend to open earlier to accommodate foreigners, but you may as well do as the Basques do – if you can find a restaurant at all. In non-touristy areas they will be inconspicuous. If you ask around, however, you should find a nice **comedor** (dining room), with home-cooked meals for around €8–12, tucked behind a bar – if you hadn't asked you never would have found it. You'll find as many good ones as real stinkers, where the food and décor are equally drab.

Vegetarians are catered for in the cities, which always manage to come up with one or two veggie restaurants, usually rather good ones too. In the countryside and away from the main resorts, proper vegetarians and vegans will find it hard going, though tapas make it easier to get your nutrition than in some other southern European countries.

In France you can also find *pintxos*, although the cult isn't as ingrained as it is farther west, perhaps because people tend to dine earlier, getting in the door by 8.30pm. Along the Côte Basque you'll find as many, if not more, French restaurants as Basque. Don't overlook hotel restaurants, some of which are absolutely top notch, even if a certain red book refuses on some obscure principle to give them their full quota of stars. To avoid disappointment, call ahead in the morning to reserve a table, especially in the summer. In French restaurants, if you order a *rouge*, *blanc* or *rosé*, you'll usually get a decent *vin de pays*, by the glass (*un verre*), the quarter-litre (*un pichet*) or the bottle (*une bouteille*). Don't neglect the wines with less-exalted labels, especially those labelled VDQS (*vin de qualité supérieure*). *Vin ordinaire* (or *vin de table*), at the bottom end, may not send you to seventh heaven, but is usually drinkable and cheap. Think twice before you order champagne (or *cava* in Spain) if you have any opinion whatsoever of age-old Basque wisdom, which warns *Ez ardo bizidunik, ez andre bizardunik* ('Beware of sparkling wine and bearded women').

Bar Life and the *Txikiteo*

It has been suggested that, just as geneticists study Basque DNA and linguists bruise their brains trying to find a cousin to the Basque language, anthropologists should study the basic form of Basque socializing. This is the *txikiteo*, where bands of friends (a *koadrila*) gather before dinner and lurch from bar to bar, staying just as long in each as it takes to drink a glass of wine or a *zurito* (a tiny glass of beer, or a bigger *caña* for quick chug-a-luggers) and devour a *pintxo* or two. Speed and noise are of the essence: one should never linger more than 15 minutes in a single spot; everyone should talk as loudly as possible, mostly about the fortunes of the Bilbao or Donostia-San Sebastián football teams, usually while smoking as furiously as an old Bilbao chimney; and it's anathema to address the opposite sex, even among members of one's *koadrila*. After a hard day at work, this is what the Basques do to relax.

At least the drink is cheap. No matter how much other costs have risen in Spain, wine has remained refreshingly inexpensive by northern European or American standards. A restaurant's *vino del lugar* or *vino de la casa* is always your cheapest option when dining out; it usually comes out of a barrel or glass jug and may be a surprise either way. In bars, the one question is *tinto* (red) or *blanco* (white)?

Many Basques prefer **beer**, which is generally nondescript. The most popular brand is San Miguel, but try Mahou Five Star if you see it. Imported **whisky** and other spirits are pretty inexpensive, although even cheaper are the versions Spain bottles itself, which may come close to your home favourites. **Coffee**, **tea**, all the international **soft drink** brands and the locally made **Kas** round off the average café fare. Spanish coffee is good and strong; if you want a lot of it order a *doble* in a *vaso*.

On the French side, you can get all the old standbys in a café or bar. Prices are listed on the *tarif des consommations*: note that they go up depending whether you're served at the bar (*le comptoir*), at a table (*la salle*) or outside (*la terrasse*). If you order *un café* you'll get a small black espresso; if you want milk, order *un crème*. If you want more than a few drops of caffeine, ask them to make it *grand*. For decaffeinated, the word is *déca*. The French only order *café au lait* (a small coffee topped off with lots of hot milk) when they stop in for breakfast, and, if what your hotel offers is expensive or boring, consider joining the bar crowd. *Chocolat chaud* (hot chocolate) is usually good; Bayonne is famous for it. If you order *thé* (tea), you'll get an ordinary bag. An *infusion* is a herbal tea – *camomille*, *menthe* (mint), *tilleul* (lime or linden blossom), or *verveine* (verbena). These are kind to the all-precious *foie*, or liver.

Mineral water (*eau minérale*) can be addictive, and comes either sparkling (*gazeuse* or *pétillante*) or still (*non-gazeuse* or *plate*). If you feel run down, Badoit has lots of peppy magnesium in it. Some bars also do fresh lemon and orange juices (*citron pressé* or *orange pressée*). Then there are the fruit syrups – red grenadine and ghastly green *menthe* (mint), which becomes positively demonic with the addition of lemonade (*diabolo menthe*).

Beer (*bière*) in most bars and cafés is run-of-the-mill big brands from Alsace, Germany and Belgium. Draft (*à la pression*) is cheaper than bottled beer. Red and white wine round out the usual fare. Nearly all resorts have bars or pubs offering wider selections of draughts, lagers and bottles; some even do cocktails, although the prices can be a kick in the pants.

Spanish Menu Reader

Entremeses (Hors d'œuvres)
aceitunas olives
alcachofas con mahonesa artichokes with mayonnaise
ancas de rana frogs' legs
caldo broth
entremeses variados assorted hors d'œuvres
huevos de flamenco baked eggs in tomato sauce
gambas pil pil prawns in hot garlic sauce
gazpacho cold soup
huevos al plato fried eggs
huevos revueltos scrambled eggs
sopa de ajo garlic soup
sopa de arroz rice soup
sopa de espárragos asparagus soup
sopa de fideos noodle soup
sopa de garbanzos chickpea soup
sopa de lentejas lentil soup
sopa de verduras vegetable soup
tortilla Spanish omelette, with potatoes
tortilla a la francesa French omelette

Pescados (Fish)
acedías small plaice
adobo fish marinated in white wine
almejas clams
anchoas anchovies
anguilas eels
angulas baby eels (elvers)
ástaco crayfish
atún tuna fish
bacalao codfish (usually dried and salted)
besugo sea bream
bogavante lobster
bonito tunny

boquerones anchovies
caballa mackerel
calamares squid
cangrejo crab
centollo spider crab
chanquetes whitebait
chipirones baby squid
...en su tinta ...in its own ink
chirlas baby clams
cocochas hake cheeks
dorado sea bass
escabeche pickled or marinated fish
gambas prawns (US: shrimps)
langosta lobster
langostinos giant prawns
lenguado sole
lubina sea bass
mariscos shellfish
mejillones mussels
merluza hake
mero grouper
navajas razor-shell clams
ostras oysters
pejesapo monkfish
percebes barnacles
pescadilla whiting
pez espada swordfish
platija plaice
pulpo octopus
rape monkfish
raya skate
rodaballo turbot
salmón salmon
salmonete red mullet
sardinas sardines
trucha trout
ttoro Basque fish stew
veneras scallops
zarzuela fish stew

Carnes y Aves (Meat and Fowl)

Note: *cazuelas, cocidos, estofados, guisados, fabadas* and *potajes* are all kinds of stew.

albóndigas meatballs
asado roast
bistec beefsteak
buey ox
callos tripe
cerdo pork
chorizo spiced sausage
chuletas chops
cochinillo suckling pig
cola de toro see under 'rabo'
conejo rabbit
corazón heart
cordero lamb
faisán pheasant
fiambres cold meats
filete fillet
hígado liver
jabalí wild boar
jamón de Bayonne cured ham
jamón Iberico cured ham
jamón serrano raw cured ham
lengua tongue
liebre hare
lomo pork loin
morcilla blood sausage
paloma pigeon
pato duck
pavo turkey
perdiz partridge
pinchitos spicy mini-kebabs
pollo chicken
rabo/cola de toro bull's tail with onions and tomatoes
riñones kidneys
salchicha sausage
salchichón salami
sesos brains
solomillo sirloin steak
ternera veal

Verduras y Legumbres (Vegetables)

ajo garlic
alcachofa artichoke
apio celery
arroz rice
arroz a la marinera rice, saffron and seafood
berenjena aubergine (US: eggplant)
cebolla onion
champiñones mushrooms
col, repollo cabbage
coliflor cauliflower
endibia endive (US: chicory)
ensalada salad
espárragos asparagus
espinacas spinach
garbanzos chickpeas (US: garbanzo beans)
judías (verdes) French beans
lechuga lettuce
lentejas lentils
patatas potatoes
   ...*fritas/salteadas* ...fried/sautéed
   ...*al horno* ...baked
pepino cucumber
pimiento pepper
puerro leek
remolacha beetroot (US: beet)
setas Spanish mushrooms
zanahoria carrot

Frutas y Nuecas (Fruit and Nuts)

albaricoque apricot
almendras almonds
avelanas hazelnuts
cacahuetes peanuts
castañas chestnuts
cerezas cherries
ciruela plum
ciruela pasa prune
dátiles dates
durazno nectarine
frambuesas raspberries
fresas strawberries
   ...*con nata* ...with cream
fruta de la pasión passion fruit
granada pomegranate
grosellas redcurrants
grosellas o casis blackcurrants
higos figs
lima lime
limón lemon
mandarina mandarin
mango mango
manzana apple
melocotón peach
melón melon
membrillo quince
moras blackberries
naranja orange
nueces walnuts
pera pear
picotas black cherries
piña pineapple
plátano banana
pomelo grapefruit
sandía watermelon
uvas grapes

Postres (Desserts)

arroz con leche rice pudding
bizcocho/pastel/torta cake
blanco y negro ice cream and coffee float
canutillos rolls of flaky pastry filled with custard
flan crème caramel

galletas biscuits (US: cookies)
helado ice cream
pajama flan (see p.66) with ice cream
pantxineta almondy gâteau basque filled with cream or cherry jam
pasteles pastries
queso cheese
requesón cottage cheese
tarta de frutas fruit pie
turrón nougat

Miscellaneous
aceite oil
arroz rice
azúcar sugar
ensalada salad
huevos eggs
mantequilla butter
pan bread
pimienta pepper
tortilla omelette
sal salt
vinagre vinegar

Bebidas (Drinks)
agua con hielo water with ice
agua mineral mineral water
   ...sin/con gas ...without/with fizz
agua potable drinking water
batido de leche milkshake
botella (media) bottle (half)
brandy brandy
café (con leche) coffee (with milk)
caña draught (beer)
cava Spanish champagne
cerveza beer
chocolate caliente/hecho hot chocolate
dulce sweet (wine)
granizado slush, iced squash
hielo ice
leche milk
seco dry
semi-seco semi-dry
spumoso sparkling (wine)
té (con limón) tea (with lemon)
vaso glass
vino (tinto, rosado, blanco) wine (red, rosé, white)
zumo de manzana/naranja apple/orange juice

Useful Phrases
menu carta
fixed price lunch menu, set meal menú del día
change cambio
waiter/waitress camarero/a
Do you have a table? ¿Tiene una mesa?
   ...for one/two? ¿... para uno/dos?
The menu, please Déme el menú, por favor

Do you have a wine list? ¿Hay una lista de vinos?
The bill (US: check), please La cuenta, por favor
Can I pay by credit card? ¿Puedo pagar con tarjeta de crédito?

French Menu Reader

Hors-d'œuvre et Soupes (Starters and Soups)
amuse-gueule appetizers
assiette assortie mixed cold hors-d'œuvre
bisque shellfish soup
bouchées mini vol-au-vents
bouillabaisse famous fish soup of Marseille
bouillon broth
charcuterie mixed cold meats, salami, ham, etc.
consommé clear soup
coulis thick sieved sauce
crudités raw vegetable platter
potage thick vegetable soup
tourrain garlic and bread soup
velouté thick smooth soup, often fish or chicken
vol-au-vent puff-pastry case with savoury filling

Poissons et Coquillages (Crustacés) (Fish and Shellfish)
aiglefin little haddock
alose shad
anchois anchovies
anguille eel
bar sea bass
barbue brill
baudroie angler fish
belons flat oysters
bigorneau winkle
blanchailles whitebait
brème bream
brochet pike
bulot whelk
cabillaud cod
calmar squid
carrelet plaice
colin hake
congre conger eel
coques cockles
coquillages shellfish
coquilles St-Jacques scallops
crabe crab
crevettes grises shrimps
crevettes roses prawns
cuisses de grenouilles frogs' legs
darne slice or steak of fish
daurade sea bream
écrevisse freshwater crayfish
éperlan smelt
escabèche fish fried, marinated and served cold

escargots snails
espadon swordfish
esturgeon sturgeon
flétan halibut
friture deep-fried fish
fruits de mer seafood
gambas giant prawns
gigot de mer a large fish cooked whole
grondin red gurnard
hareng herring
homard Atlantic (US: Norway) lobster
huîtres oysters
lamproie lamprey
langouste spiny Mediterranean lobster
langoustines Norway lobster (often called
   Dublin Bay prawns)
limande lemon sole
lotte monkfish
loup (de mer) sea bass
louvine sea bass (in Aquitaine)
maquereau mackerel
merlan whiting
morue salt cod
moules mussels
oursin sea urchin
pagel sea bream
palourdes clams
poulpe octopus
praires small clams
raie skate
rascasse scorpion fish
rouget red mullet
St-Pierre John Dory
saumon salmon
sole (meunière) sole (with butter, lemon and
   parsley)
stockfisch stockfish (wind-dried cod)
telline tiny clam
thon tuna
truite trout
truite saumonée salmon trout

Viandes et Volailles
(Meat and Poultry)

agneau (de pré-salé) lamb (grazed in fields
   by the sea)
ailerons chicken wings
aloyau sirloin
andouillette chitterling (tripe) sausage
autruche ostrich
biftek beefsteak
blanc breast or white meat
blanquette stew of white meat, thickened
   with egg yolk
bœuf beef
boudin blanc sausage of white meat
boudin noir black pudding
brochette meat (or fish) on a skewer

caille quail
canard, caneton duck, duckling
carré crown roast
cassoulet haricot bean stew with sausage,
   duck, goose, etc.
cervelle brains
chair flesh, meat
chapon capon
châteaubriand porterhouse steak
cheval horsemeat
chevreau kid
chorizo spicy Spanish sausage
civet meat (usually game) stew, in wine and
   blood sauce
cœur heart
confit meat cooked and preserved in its
   own fat
côte, côtelette chop, cutlet
cou d'oie farci goose neck stuffed with pork,
   foie gras and truffles
crépinette small sausage
cuisse thigh or leg
dinde, dindon turkey
entrecôte ribsteak
épaule shoulder
estouffade a meat stew marinated, fried
   and then braised
faisan pheasant
faux-filet sirloin
foie liver
frais de veau veal testicles
fricadelle meatball
gésier gizzard
gibier game
gigot leg of lamb
graisse, gras fat
grillade grilled meat, often a mixed grill
grive thrush
jambon ham
jarret knuckle
langue tongue
lapereau young rabbit
lapin rabbit
lard, lardons bacon, diced bacon
lièvre hare
maigret, magret de canard breast of duck
manchons duck or goose wings
marcassin young wild boar
merguez spicy red sausage
moelle bone marrow
mouton mutton
museau muzzle
navarin lamb stew with root vegetables
noix de veau topside of veal
oie goose
os bone
perdreau, perdrix partridge
petit salé salt pork

pieds trotters
pintade guinea fowl
plat-de-côtes short ribs or rib chops
porc pork
pot au feu meat and vegetables cooked in stock
poulet chicken
poussin baby chicken
quenelle poached dumplings made of fish, fowl or meat
queue de bœuf oxtail
ris (de veau) sweetbreads (veal)
rognons kidneys
rosbif roast beef
rôti roast
sanglier wild boar
saucisses sausages
saucisson dry sausage, like salami
selle (d'agneau) saddle (of lamb)
steak tartare raw minced beef, often topped with a raw egg yolk
suprême de volaille fillet of chicken breast and wing
taureau bull meat
tête (de veau) calf's head, fatty and usually served with a mustardy vinaigrette
tortue turtle
tournedos thick round slices of beef fillet
travers de porc spare ribs
tripes tripe
veau veal
venaison venison

Légumes, Herbes, etc.
(Vegetables, Herbs, etc.)

ail garlic
aïoli garlic mayonnaise
algue seaweed
aneth dill
anis anis
artichaut artichoke
asperges asparagus
aubergine aubergine (US: eggplant)
avocat avocado
basilic basil
betterave beetroot (US: red beet)
blette Swiss chard
bouquet garni mixed herbs in a little bag
cannelle cinnamon
céleri celery
céleri-rave celeriac
cèpes ceps, wild boletus mushrooms
champignons mushrooms
chanterelles wild yellow mushrooms
chicorée curly endive (US: chicory)
chou cabbage
choucroute sauerkraut
chou-fleur cauliflower
choux de bruxelles Brussels sprouts
ciboulette chives

citrouille pumpkin
clou de girofle clove
cœur de palmier heart of palm
concombre cucumber
cornichons gherkins
courgettes courgettes (US: zucchini)
cresson watercress
échalote shallot
endive chicory (US: endive)
épinards spinach
épis de maïs sweetcorn (on the cob)
estragon tarragon
fenouil fennel
fèves broad (US: fava) beans
flageolets white beans
fleurs de courgette courgette (US: zucchini) blossoms
frites chips (US: French fries)
genièvre juniper
gingembre ginger
haricots blancs white beans
haricots rouges kidney beans
haricots verts green (French) beans
jardinière with diced garden vegetables
laitue lettuce
laurier bay leaf
lavande lavender
lentilles lentils
maïs (épis de) sweetcorn (on the cob)
marjolaine marjoram
menthe mint
mesclun salad of various leaves
morilles morel mushrooms
moutarde mustard
navet turnip
oignons onions
oseille sorrel
panais parsnip
persil parsley
petits pois peas
piment pimento
pissenlits dandelion greens
poireaux leeks
pois chiches chickpeas (US: garbanzo beans)
pois mange-tout sugar peas or mangetout
poivron sweet pepper (US: capsicum)
pomme de terre potato
potiron pumpkin
primeurs young vegetables
radis radishes
raifort horseradish
riz rice
romarin rosemary
roquette rocket
safran saffron
salade verte green salad
salsifis salsify
sarrasin buckwheat

sarriette savory
sauge sage
seigle rye
serpolet wild thyme
thym thyme
truffes truffles

Fruits et Noix (Fruit and Nuts)

abricot apricot
amandes almonds
ananas pineapple
banane banana
bigarreaux black cherries
brugnon nectarine
cacahouètes peanuts
cassis blackcurrant
cerise cherry
citron lemon
citron vert lime
coing quince
dattes dates
figues (de Barbarie) figs (prickly pear)
fraises (des bois) strawberries (wild)
framboises raspberries
fruit de la passion passion fruit
grenade pomegranate
groseilles redcurrants
mandarine tangerine
mangue mango
marrons chestnuts
mirabelles mirabelle plums
mûre (sauvage) mulberry, blackberry
myrtilles bilberries
noisette hazelnut
noix walnuts
noix de cajou cashews
noix de coco coconut
pamplemousse grapefruit
pastèque watermelon
pêche, pêche blanche peach, white peach
pignons pine nuts
pistache pistachio
poire pear
pomme apple
prune plum
pruneau prune
raisins, raisins secs grapes, raisins
reine-claude greengage plums

Desserts

Bavarois mousse or custard in a mould
biscuit biscuit, cracker, cake
bombe ice-cream dessert in a round mould
bonbons sweets (US: candy)
brioche light sweet yeast bread
charlotte sponge fingers and custard
  cream dessert
chausson turnover
clafoutis baked batter pudding with fruit

compote stewed fruit
corbeille de fruits basket of fruit
coulis thick fruit sauce
coupe ice cream: a scoop or in cup
crème anglaise egg custard
crème caramel vanilla custard with
  caramel sauce
crème Chantilly sweet whipped cream
crème fraîche slightly sour cream
crème pâtissière thick pastry cream filling made
  with eggs
gâteau cake
gaufre waffle
génoise rich sponge cake
glace ice cream
macarons macaroons
madeleine small sponge cake
miel honey
mignardise same as *petits fours*
mousse 'foam': frothy dessert
œufs à la neige floating islands/meringues
  on a bed of custard
pain d'épice gingerbread
parfait frozen mousse
petits fours sweetmeats; tiny cakes and
  pastries
profiteroles choux pastry balls, often filled with
  chocolate or ice cream
sablé shortbread
savarin a filled cake, shaped like a ring
tarte, tartelette tart, little tart
tarte tropézienne sponge cake filled with
  custard and topped with nuts
truffes chocolate truffles
yaourt yoghurt

Fromage (Cheese)

cabécou sharp local goat's cheese
chèvre goat's cheese
doux/fort mild/strong
fromage blanc yoghurty cream cheese
fromage de brebis sheep's cheese
fromage frais a light, high-water white cheese
fromage sec general name for solid cheeses
plateau de fromage cheese (board)

Cooking Terms and Sauces

bien cuit well-done steak
à point medium steak
saignant rare steak
bleu very rare steak
aigre-doux sweet and sour
aiguillette thin slice
à l'anglaise boiled
à la bordelaise cooked in wine and
  diced vegetables
à la broche roasted on a spit
à la châtelaine with chestnut purée and
  artichoke hearts

à la diable in spicy mustard sauce
à la grecque cooked in olive oil and lemon
à la jardinière with garden vegetables
à la périgourdine in a truffle and foie gras sauce
à la provençale cooked with tomatoes, garlic
  and olive oil
allumettes strips of puff pastry
au feu de bois cooked over a wood fire
au four baked
auvergnat with sausage, bacon and cabbage
barquette pastry boat
béarnaise sauce of egg yolks, shallots and
  white wine
beignets fritters
broche roasted on a spit
chasseur mushrooms and shallots in
  white wine
chaud hot
cru raw
diable spicy mustard or green pepper
  sauce
émincé thinly sliced
en croûte cooked in a pastry crust
en papillote baked in buttered paper
épices spices
farci stuffed
feuilleté flaky pastry
flambé set aflame with alcohol
forestière with bacon and mushrooms
fourré stuffed
frais, fraîche fresh
frappé with crushed ice
frit fried
froid cold
fumé smoked
galantine cooked food served in cold jelly
galette puff pastry case or pancake
garni with vegetables
(au) gratin topped with cheese and
  breadcrumbs and browned
grillé grilled
haché minced (US: ground)
hollandaise a sauce of egg yolks, butter
  and vinegar
marmite casserole
médaillon round piece
mijoté simmered
Mornay cheese sauce
pané breaded
Parmentier with potatoes
pâte pastry, pasta
pâte brisée shortcrust pastry
pâte à chou choux pastry
pâte feuilletée puff pastry
paupiette thin slices of fish or meat, filled
  and rolled
pavé slab
piquant spicy hot

poché poached
pommes allumettes thin chips (US: fries)
raclette melted cheese with potatoes, onions
  and pickles
salé salted, spicy
sucré sweet
timbale pie cooked in a dome-shaped mould
tranche slice
vapeur steamed
Véronique grape, wine and cream sauce
vinaigrette oil and vinegar dressing

Miscellaneous
addition bill (US: check)
baguette long loaf of bread
beurre butter
carte non-set menu
confiture jam
couteau knife
crème cream
cuillère spoon
formule set menu
fourchette fork
fromage cheese
huile (d'olive) (olive) oil
menu set menu
nouilles noodles
pain bread
œufs eggs
poivre pepper
sel salt
service compris/non compris service
  included/not included
sucre sugar
vinaigre vinegar

Snacks
chips crisps (US: potato chips)
crêpe thin pancake
croque-madame toasted ham and cheese
  sandwich with fried egg
croque-monsieur toasted ham and
  cheese sandwich
croustade small savoury pastry
frites chips (US: French fries)
gaufre waffle
sandwich canapé open sandwich

Boissons (Drinks)
bière (pression) (draught) beer
bouteille (demi) half-bottle
brut very dry
café coffee
café au lait white coffee
café express espresso coffee
café filtre filter coffee
café turc Turkish coffee
chocolat chaud hot chocolate
citron pressé fresh lemon juice

demi a third of a litre

doux sweet (wine)

eau (minérale, non-gazeuse ou gazeuse) water (mineral, still or sparkling)

eau-de-vie brandy

eau potable drinking water

gazeuse sparkling

glaçons ice cubes

infusion or *tisane (camomille, verveine, tilleul, menthe)* herbal tea (camomile, verbena, lime flower, mint)

jus juice

lait milk

menthe à l'eau peppermint cordial

moelleux semi-dry

mousseux sparkling (wine)

orange pressée fresh orange juice

pastis anis liqueur

pichet carafe

pression draught

ratafia home-made liqueur made by steeping fruit or green walnuts in alcohol or wine

sec dry

sirop d'orange/de citron orange/lemon squash

thé tea

verre glass

vin blanc/rosé/rouge white/rosé/red wine

Planning
Your Trip

05

When to Go

Climate

You have just one guess to figure out what makes the Basque country so luxuriantly green. The Cordillera Cantábrica and the western Pyrenees meet all the weather fronts coming over the Atlantic and squeeze out all the precipitation. It rains on average over 200 days a year all along the Spanish–French border, which includes some 50 or so days of snow. The coast gets 3–4 inches (7.5–10mm) of rain in August – and the real rainy season doesn't start until September. It all adds up to 7 or 8ft (2–2.5m) of the stuff a year, as much as Wales or the west of Ireland; no wonder the ancient Basques worshipped the sun.

Southern Euskadi, especially in La Rioja Alavesa, enjoys a more reasonable, drier climate, which is very good for the vines. On the bright side, the pocket around the Basque coast enjoys something of a microclimate, with winter temperatures often as warm as the Mediterranean coast. Winds can make it nippy, though.

The weather from March into May is wonderfully inconsistent: it can be hot enough for a dip in the pool or so cold that you need a coat, and it can vary from week to week. May and June are often good months to come: usually summer has set well in, and the sights are open while hotel rates are still low. The high season is intense, squeezed in between June and September, when the ocean is warm enough for water sports, the festival calendar is in full swing and everything is open; July is by far the driest month (with only an inch or two of rain). Of course, July and August also coincide with school holidays, when everything is packed, prices are high, and the Pyrenees are apt to be pummelled by violent thunderstorms.

The region often looks its best in October, when most of the tourists have gone (although late August to October are fine months for surfing). November and December can be dismal and overcast when not spewing down buckets, but wild mushrooms, game dishes and masses of holiday oysters offer some consolation.

Festivals

One of the most spiritually deadening aspects of Francoism was the banning of many local and regional *fiestas* in Spain. These are now celebrated with gusto, while the pronounced Spanish influence in the French Basque lands, added to the inhabitants' natural panache, tends to make its *fêtes* among the liveliest in France. Besides those listed in the Calendar of Events, every single village or town in this book puts on a party at least once a year, usually in honour of its patron saint, and if you can arrange your itinerary to include one or two you'll be guaranteed an unforgettable holiday.

Music, dancing, food, wine and fireworks are all necessary ingredients of a proper *fiesta* or *fête*, while the bigger ones often include bullfights, funfairs, circuses, Basque sports and sometimes poetry competitions. In Euskadi and Navarra, summer *fiestas* often feature a loose bull or two stampeding through the streets – an *encierro*. The music is often provided by local *bandas* (brass bands of 20–40 local musicians in dashing costumes), who play Basque tunes.

Tourist Information

A little preparation will help you to get much more out of your holiday. Check the list of events (*see* box, right) to help you decide where you want to be and when, and book your accommodation early: if you plan to base yourself in one area, contact the local tourist offices listed in the text for complete lists of accommodation in their areas. For

Average Maximum Temperatures in °C (°F)					
	Jan	Feb	Mar	April	May	June
Bayonne	13/55	14/57	16/61	18/64	21/70	25/77
Bilbao	9/48	10/50	11/52	13/55	16/61	19/66
	July	Aug	Sept	Oct	Nov	Dec
Bayonne	28/82	27/81	26/79	24/75	19/66	13/55
Bilbao	21/70	21/70	20/67	16/61	12/53	9/48

Calendar of Events

Note that many of these dates are subject to change (to fit weekends, etc.); a call ahead to the tourist office is always a good idea, or check local websites.

January

19–20 St Sebastian's Day, *Tamborrada*, when scores of drum corps bang their way through the streets, followed by feasting, in Donostia-San Sebastián (Guipúzcoa).

Third Sun *San Vicente*, bachelors' party, Los Arcos (Navarra).

Last Tues and Wed *Foire aux Pottoks*, Basque horse fair, Espelette (Pays Basque).

Last Mon and Tues *Zanpantzar*, pre-Christian dances of the *joaldunaks*, with pointed hats, sheepskins and big bells, Ituren and Zubieta (Navarra).

31 St Agatha, traditional Basque singing in the streets in many places.

February

Carnival A big affair everywhere in Spain. Some of the biggest celebrations are in Bilbao, Donostia-San Sebastián, Vitoria-Gasteiz, Tolosa (with a *pelota* championship) and Lantz, where a huge dummy representing Miel Otxin, a famous bandit, is paraded. There are cavalcades on Carnival Sunday in Valcarlos, Uhart-Cize and Lasse. On Carnival Tuesday in Altsasu there's a parade of *momotxorroaks*, monsters dressed in sheep pelts stained with blood.

Every Sun Horse-racing in Donostia-San Sebastián.

March

Two Sundays after 4th *Javierada*, two important pilgrimages for St Francis Xavier, Javier (Navarra).

Mid-month International organ competitions, Biarritz (Pays Basque).

Late March/early April *Semana Santa* (Holy Week):

Good Friday *Los Picaos*, medieval-style self-flagellants, San Vicente de la Sonsierra (La Rioja); mystery play, Balmaseda (Vizcaya); processions in Fuenterrabia and Segura (Guipúzcoa).

Thurs, Fri, Sat Ham fair, Bayonne (Pays Basque).

Easter Sat *Volatin* – Judas Iscariot gets his come-uppance in Tudela (Navarra).

Easter Sun *Aberri Eguna*, Basque National Day, celebrated everywhere, beginning with a mass in Euskera, followed by dancing, singing and Basque sports. 'Descent of the Angel' in Tudela (Navarra).

April

First Sun after Easter Easter Fair, Tardets (Pays Basque); festivities for San Telmo, including bull-running on the beach, Zumaia (Guipúzcoa).

May

First weekend *Día de las Almadías*: rafts are built and floated downriver to commemorate the ancient method of log transport, followed by picnics in the Irati and Salazar valleys (Navarra).

Mid-month Sheepdog trials at Mt Jaïzkibel (Guipúzcoa).

End of May/early June Corpus Christi (Thursday after Trinity Sunday), four days of general festivities in Spain.

Last three days *Arrain Azoka*, sea fair, Bermeo (Vizcaya).

June

First week *Fêtes locales*, Boucau and Urcuit (Pays Basque).

Second Sun Cherry festival, Itxassou (Pays Basque).

Second week *Fêtes locales*, Arcangues (Pays Basque).

Second Sun after Pentecost *Processions de la Fête-Dieu*, Bidarray and Iholdy (Pays Basque).

21 Midsummer's Day, 'bonfires of San Juan' in many Basque villages. On the nearest Saturday, Sorcerers' Festival at Zugarramurdi (Navarra).

21–24 *La Magdalena*, with Basque sports, Bermeo (Vizcaya), followed by a nautical *romería* to the isle of Izaro.

24 *Fiesta de San Juan*, Laguardia (Álava).

26 *Fiesta de San Pelayo*, Zarautz (Guipúzcoa).

24–27 St John's Day festival, St-Jean-de-Luz (Pays Basque).

Last week *Fêtes locales*, St Pierre-d'Irube, Hasparren (Pays Basque).

29 *Fiesta de San Pedro*, Orio and Zumaia (Guipúzcoa).

30 *Fiesta de San Marcial*, Irún (Guipúzcoa).

End of June *San Felices de Bilibio*, a pilgrimage and drunken 'wine battles', Haro (La Rioja); *La Semana Gastronomica*, Donostia-San Sebastián.

July

Month-long International Jazz Festival, Donostia-San Sebastián.

Early July *Fêtes locales*, St-Pée-sur-Nivelle, St-Jean-Pied-de-Port and Lahonce (Pays Basque).

5–9 Getxo Jazz Festival, both international and national bands, Getxo (Vizcaya).

7–14 Famous running of the bulls and mad party for *San Fermín*, Pamplona (Navarra).

Second Sun Tuna Festival, St-Jean-de-Luz (Pays Basque).

Second fortnight International horse-racing competition, Donostia-San Sebastián.

Mid-month Jazz festival and medieval market, Bayonne; international piano recitals, St-Jean-de-Luz (Pays Basque).

13 *Fête du Chipiron*, Hendaye (Pays Basque); *Tributo de las Tres Vacas*, Piedra de San Martín, French mayors from the Baretous valley give Spanish mayors from the Roncal valley a tribute of three cows, renew their peace vows and name the keepers who will watch the common grazing land.

14 Re-enactment of a Basque wedding, St-Etienne-de-Baïgorry; medieval fair featuring bullfights in Bayonne (both Pays Basque).

Third week Surfing championships and Basque folklore, Biarritz (Pays Basque); jazz festival, Vitoria-Gasteiz (Álava).

22 Boat races, Basque sports and dancing, Bermeo (Vizcaya); *Fiesta de Santa María Magdalena*, Rentería (Guipúzcoa).

24–30 *Santa Ana*, music and dancing for a week, Tudela (Navarra).

25 Vitoria and Bilbao's saint's day, Santiago, known in Vitoria as the 'Day of the Blouse'; *fêtes locales*, Gotein-Libarrenx (Pays Basque).

29 *Fiesta de San Pedro*, Mundaka (Vizcaya).

31 *Fiesta de San Ignacio*, Getxo (Vizcaya) and Azpeitia (Guipúzcoa).

End of month International festival of humorous drawing, Anglet (Pays Basque); *Fête de la Madeleine*, with a 'competition of the unusual', St-Palais (Pays Basque); *fêtes locales*, La Bastide-Clairence and Arbonne (Pays Basque).

August

1 Sheepdog competitions, St-Jean-Pied-de-Port (Pays Basque); *Foire de Garris*, cattle fair, St-Palais (Pays Basque).

First Wed Beginning of huge five-day *Fêtes de Bayonne*, Bayonne (Pays Basque).

First Sat Irrintzi (Basque yodelling, *see* p.48) contest, Urcuray (Pays Basque).

3–9 Ancient fiesta, with giants and a rowdy *encierro* where everyone runs with the bulls,

Estella (Navarra); Basque sport finals, Biarritz (Pays Basque).

4–10 Giants, music, bonfires and more, for the *Virgen Blanca* – Vitoria-Gasteiz (Álava).

6 *Fiesta de San Salvador*, Getaria (Guipúzcoa).

First weekend *Fêtes Basques*, Hendaye (Pays Basque); crafts fair, Mauléon, Soule (Pays Basque); *Pastorale*, shepherds' festival (first Sun), Gotein Libarrenx (Pays Basque).

8–15 Basque Sports Week, with *pelota* and *force basque* competitions everywhere in the Basque lands.

10 *San Juan Dantzak*, procession and traditional dancing at Berástegui (Guipúzcoa).

Second week *Fêtes locales*, St-Etienne-de-Baïgorry, Cambo-les-Bains (Pays Basque).

13 Basque shepherd hollering contest, Hasparren (Pays Basque); sardine festival, Ustaritz (Pays Basque).

13–25 Assumption Day fêtes, Bayonne and Ainhoa (Pays Basque).

14 Festival of Basque song, Garindein (Pays Basque).

15 *Nuit Féerique* and fireworks, Biarritz (Pays Basque); espadrille festival, Mauléon, Soule (Pays Basque); regional products fair, St-Pée-sur-Nivelle (Pays Basque); also fêtes in Bidart and Bardos (Pays Basque); *Zikiro-Jatea* festival in Zugarramurdi (Navarra) with a popular picnic held in the caves on the 17th.

15–16 *Fiesta de San Rocco*, Gernika (Vizcaya); on the Saturday after the 15th, Bilbao starts its *Aste Nagustia* or *Semana Grande* ('Great Week'), with Basque sports and races; a week-long international fireworks festival starts in Donostia-San Sebastián (Guipúzcoa).

19 Cheese fair, Tardets (Pays Basque).

19–21 Gastronomic and crafts fair, St-Jean-Pied-de-Port (Pays Basque).

20 International professional *Cesta Punta* finals, St-Jean-de-Luz (Pays Basque).

Third Sun Fair and smugglers' cross-country race, Sare (Pays Basque); *force Basque* festival, St-Palais (Pays Basque).

Last Sun *Encierro del Pilón*, bull-running in a small village.

Last week *Fêtes locales*, Bassussarry (Pays Basque).

31 St Ignacio de Loyola Day, Loyola (Guipúzcoa).

September

First half Quiksilver Surf master championships and *Musique en Côte Basque*, big-name recitals, Biarritz (Pays Basque); *corridas*,

Bayonne (Pays Basque); *fêtes patronales*, Urrugne (Pays Basque).

First week Basque food festival, Donostia-San Sebastián (Guipúzcoa).

1–8 Festival with Basque 'goose games', a contest between boatmen to pull the head off a goose with a greased neck, Lekeitio (Vizcaya).

First Sat *Fêtes du ttoro*, Basque fish soup competition, St-Jean-de-Luz (Pays Basque).

First two Sundays Traditional regattas at Donostia-San Sebastián.

8 *Fiesta de la Virgen de Guadalupe*, Fuenterrabía (Guipúzcoa); Virgin's birthday, celebrations in many places.

8–10 *Fiesta de Santa Eufemia*, Bermeo (Vizcaya).

12 International Film Festival, Donostia-San Sebastián.

2nd week Basque fun and games, Zarautz (Guipúzcoa).

Second fortnight *Quincena Musicale*, classical music fortnight in Donostia-San Sebastián.

14 Festival, Altsasu (Navarra).

Second Sun *Fêtes de Sare*, Sare (Pays Basque).

19 *Fête des Corsaires*, St-Jean-de-Luz (Pays Basque).

Mid-month World *Cesta Punta* championship, Biarritz (Pays Basque).

Third week Festival of stories and storytellers from around the world, Hasparren (Pays Basque).

29 *Fiesta de San Miguel*, Oñati (Guipúzcoa); traditional Basque dancing, Markina (Vizcaya).

End of month International festival of Latin American cinema and culture, Biarritz (Pays Basque); world championship fishing from boats competition, Anglet (Pays Basque).

October

13 *Fiesta de San Fausto*, Durango (Vizcaya).

Mid-month Important international theatre festival, Bayonne (Pays Basque).

Last Sun *Fête du Piment*, Espelette (Pays Basque).

November

7–11 *Fêtes du St-Martin*, Biarritz (Pays Basque).

19 *Fiesta de San Andrés*, Estella (Navarra).

24–25 *Pottok* fair, Helette (Pays Basque).

December

Throughout month *Marchés de gras* – foie gras, fattened duck and goose markets – are held in most towns in the Pays Basque.

4–5 *Fêtes patronales*, Guéthary (Pays Basque).

6 *San Nicolás Obispillo*, Segura (Guipúzcoa).

13 *Santa Lucía* fair, Zumárraga (Guipúzcoa).

21 *Santo Tomás* fair, with processions, San Sebastián, Bilbao and Azpeitia.

Last weekend before Christmas *Olentzero* processions in many villages, honouring the Basques' jovial pre-Christian 'Santa Claus'.

more general information, get in touch with the French or Spanish national tourist offices.

Spanish National Tourist Offices

UK: 6th floor, 64 North Row, London W1K 7DE, t 00 800 10 10 50 50, *www.spain.info/en_GB*.

USA: Water Tower Place, Suite 915 East, 845 North Michigan Avenue, Chicago, Illinois 60611, t (312) 642 1992, *www.okspain.org*; 8383 Wilshire Blvd, Suite 960, Beverly Hills, California 90211, t (323) 658 7188; 666 Fifth Avenue, New York, NY 10103, t (212) 265 8822; 1395 Brickell Avenue, Miami, Florida 33131, t (305) 358 1992.

Canada: 2 Bloor St West, Suite 3402, Toronto, Ontario M4W 3E2, t (416) 961 3131, *www.spain.info/ca*.

Japan: Daini Toranomon Denki Building, 6F, 3-1-10 Toranomon, Minato Ku, Tokyo 105-0001, t + 81 (3) 3432 6141, *www.spain.info/jp*.

Also provides information for Australian and New Zealand nationals.

French Government Tourist Offices

UK: French Tourist Board, 300 High Holborn, London W1V 7JH, t 09068 244 123, *www.uk.franceguide.com*.

USA: 16th Floor, 444 Madison Av, New York, NY 10020, t (212) 838 7800; Suite 715, 9454 Wilshire Bd, Beverly Hills, Los Angeles, CA 90212, t (310) 271 6665, *www.us.franceguide.com*.

Canada: 1800 Av McGill College, Suite 101, No.490, Montreal, Quebec H3A 2W9, t (514) 288 2026, *www.ca-en.franeguide.com*.

France: 79–81 Rue de Clichy, 75009 Paris, t 01 42 96 70 00, *www.fr.franceguide.com*.

Useful Websites

There are several good websites offering information on the region:

www.bilbao.net
www.euskadi.net
www.navarra.es
www.basquecountry-tourism.com
www.tourisme64.com
www.franceguide.com
www.buber.net/Basque – this is the most extensive Basque site on the web.

Embassies and Consulates

Embassies are based in Madrid and Paris. Ireland, France and the UK have consulates in Bilbao. Otherwise, the nearest consulates in Spain are in Madrid (there are also consulates in Barcelona). In France, there are British and American consulates in the southwest.

Generally, consulates are only open for visa enquiries on weekday mornings.

Foreign Embassies, etc. in Spain

UK: Alameda Urquijo 2, Bilbao, **t** 94 415 76 00, *www.ukinspain.com*.

Ireland: C/Elcano 5, Bilbao, **t** 94 423 04 14.

USA: C/Serrano 75, Madrid, **t** 91 587 22 00. Consulate: Paseo de la Castellana 52, *www. embusa.es*.

Canada: C/Núñez de Balboa 35, Madrid, **t** 91 423 32 50, *www.canadainternational.gc.ca*.

France: C/Iparraguirre 26, Bilbao, **t** 94 425 51 80, *www.ambafrance-es.org*, *www.consulfrance-bilbao.or*g.

Spanish Embassies, etc. Abroad

UK: 20 Draycott Place, London SW3 2RZ, **t** (020) 7589 8989; 1a Brook House, 70 Spring Gardens, Manchester M2 2BQ, **t** (0161) 236 1262; 63 North Castle Street, Edinburgh EH2 3LJ, **t** (0131) 220 1843.

Ireland: 17a Merlyn Park, Ballsbridge, Dublin 4, **t** (01) 269 1640.

USA: 31 St James Ave, Suite 905, Boston, MA 02116, **t** (617) 536 2506; 180 North Michigan Avenue, Chicago, IL 60601, **t** (312) 782 4588; 2655 Le Jeune Road, 203 Coral Gables, Miami, FL, **t** (305) 446 5511; 5055 Wilshire Blvd, Suite 960 Los Angeles, CA 90036, **t** (323) 938 0158; 150 East 58th Street, New York, NY 10155,

t (212) 355 4080; 2375 Pennyslvania Avenue NW, Washington, DC 20009, **t** (202) 728 2330.

Canada: 1 West Mount Square, Montreal H3Z 2P9, **t** (514) 935 5235; 200 Front Street, Toronto, Ontario, **t** (416) 977 1661.

Foreign Embassies, etc. in France

The only consulates in the region are:

UK: 353 Bd de Président Wilson, Bordeaux, **t** 05 57 22 21 10.

USA: 25 Allée Jean-Jaurès, 31000 Toulouse, **t** 05 34 41 36 50.

Embassies and consulates in Paris include:

Ireland: 4 Rue Rude, 16th, **t** 01 44 17 67 00, Ⓜ Charles de Gaulle/ Etoile.

Canada: 35 Av Montaigne, 8th, **t** 01 44 43 29 00, Ⓜ Franklin D. Roosevelt.

French Embassies, etc. Abroad

UK: 58 Knightsbridge, London SW1X 7JT, **t** (020) 7073 1000, *www.ambafrance-uk.org*; 21 Cromwell Rd, London SW7 2EN, **t** (020) 7073 1200, *www.consulfrance-londres.org* (for visas); 11 Randolph Crescent, Edinburgh EH3 7TT, **t** (0131) 225 7954 – recorded visa information only, *www.consulfrance-edimbourg.org*.

Ireland: 36 Ailesbury Rd, Ballsbridge, Dublin 4, **t** (01) 277 5000, *www.ambafrance.ie*.

USA: 4101 Reservoir Rd NW, Washington, DC 20007-2185, **t** (202) 944 6000, *www. ambafrance-us.org*; 205 North Michigan Avenue, Suite 3700, Chicago, IL 60601, **t** (312) 327 5200, *www.consulfrance-chicago.org*; 10390 Santa Monica Bd, Suite 410, Los Angeles, CA 90025, **t** (310) 235 3200, *www.consulfrance-losangeles.org*; 934 Fifth Av, New York, NY 10021, **t** (212) 606 3600, *www.consulfrance-newyork.org*. There are also French consulates in Atlanta, Boston, Houston, Miami, New Orleans and San Francisco.

Entry Formalities

Passports and Visas

Holders of EU, US, Canadian, Australian and New Zealand passports do not need a visa to enter Spain or France for stays of up to three months; most other nationals do.

If you intend staying longer in Spain, you should report to the Foreign Nationals Office (*oficina de extranjeros*). Non-EU citizens should apply for a resident's card (*tarjeta de residente comunitario*). EU citizens will be issued with a printed Residence Certificate stating name, address, nationality, NIE number (*Número de Identificación Extranjeros*) and date of registration. Non-EU citizens had best apply for an extended visa at home, a complicated procedure requiring proof of income, etc. You cannot get a *tarjeta* without this visa.

Non-EU citizens had best apply for an extended visa at home, a complicated procedure requiring proof of income, etc. You can't get a *carte de séjour* or *tarjeta* without this visa. A lawyer is the best bet if you need to pick your way through European bureacracy.

Customs

Duty-free allowances have been abolished within the EU. **EU nationals** over the age of 17 can now import a limitless amount of goods for their personal use. For travellers coming from **outside the EU**, the duty-free limits are one litre of spirits or two litres of liquors (port, sherry or champagne), plus two litres of wine and 200 cigarettes. Much larger quantities – up to 10 litres of spirits, 90 litres of wine, 110 litres of beer and 3,200 cigarettes – bought locally and provided you are travelling between EU countries, can be taken through customs if you can prove that they are for private consumption only and taxes have been paid in the country of purchase.

If you are travelling from the UK or the USA, don't bother taking any alcohol – it's cheaper to buy it from supermarkets locally.

Residents of the USA may each take home US$400-worth of foreign goods without attracting duty, including the tobacco and alcohol allowance. Canadians can bring home $300 worth of goods in a year, plus their tobacco and alcohol allowances.

Disabled Travellers

Eurotunnel is a good way to travel to the Basque country by car from the UK, since passengers are allowed to stay in their vehicles. By train, Eurostar gives wheelchair passengers first-class travel for second-class fares. Most **ferry** companies will offer special facilities if contacted beforehand. Vehicles fitted to accommodate disabilities pay reduced tolls on *autoroutes* through France. **SNCF (French railways)** publish a booklet for disabled travellers (in French); either pick one up at major rail stations, or apply in writing to the Délégation à l'Accessibilité et aux Voyageurs Handicapés, 2 Rue Traversière, 75571 Paris Cedex 12.

Disability Organizations

France

Association des Paralysés de France, 22 Rue du Père-Guérin, 75013 Paris, **t** 01 44 16 83 83, *www.apf.asso.fr*. A national organization with an office in each *département*, providing in-depth local information. It also organizes holidays (*see* website).

Association Handiplage, 39 Rue des Faures, Bayonne 64100, **t** 05 59 93 12 42. All kinds of useful information, from accommodation to sporting activities for wheelchair-users in the Pays Basque.

CNRH (Comité National Français de Liaison pour la Réadaptation des Handicapés), 236 bis Rue de Tolbiac, Paris 75013, **t** 01 53 80 66 66. Provides information on access and useful guides to various regions in France.

Spain

Coordinadora Estatal de Minusvalidos Fisicos, Luis Cabrera 63, Madrid, **t** 91 744 36 00, *www.cocemfe.es*. Provides general services and advice for people with disabilities.

ECOM, Gran Vía 562, Barcelona, **t** 93 451 55 50, *www.ecom.es*. A federation of private Spanish organizations that offer services for people with disabilities.

ONCE (Organización Nacional de Ciegos de España), C/José Ortega y Gasset 18, **t** 91 577 37 56, *www.once.es*. Association for the blind, offering a number of services for the traveller (e.g. maps in Braille).

UK

Access Travel, 6 The Hillock, Astley, Lancashire M29 7GW, **t** (01942) 88 88 44, *www.access-travel.co.uk*. Travel agent for people with disabilities: air fares, car hire and accommodation.

Holiday Care Information Unit, Tourism for All, Hawkins Suite, Enham Place, Enham Alamein, Andover, Hants SP11 6JS, t 0845 124 9971, *www.holidaycare.org.uk.* Information on accessible hotels and attractions.

RADAR (Royal Association for Disability and Rehabilitation), Unit 12, City Forum, 250 City Road, London EC1V 8AF, t (020) 7250 3222, *www.radar.org.uk. Open Mon–Fri 10–4.*

RNIB (Royal National Institute for the Blind), 105 Judd Street, London WC1H 9NE, t 0845 766 9999, *www.rnib.org.uk.* Information for the blind or visually impaired.

USA

Alternative Leisure Co., 165 Middlesex Turnpike, Suite 206, Bedford, MA 01730, USA t (718) 275 0023, *www.alctrips.com.* Organizes vacations abroad for people with disabilities.

American Foundation for the Blind, 2 Penn Plaza, Suite 112, New York, NY 10121, t (212) 502 7600, or t 800 232 5463, *www.afb.org.* The best source of information in the USA for visually impaired travellers.

Mobility International USA, 132 Broadway, Suite 343, Eugene, OR 97440, t (541) 343 1284, *www.miusa.org.* Provides information on international educational exchange programmes and volunteer service overseas for people with disabilities.

SATH (Society for Accessible Travel and Hospitality), 347 5th Ave, Suite 610, New York, NY 10016, t (212) 447 7284, *www.sath.org.* Travel and access information; also details other access resources on the web.

Other Useful Contacts

Emerging Horizons, *http://emerginghorizons. com.* International on-line travel newsletter for people with disabilities.

Global Access, *www.globalaccessnews.com.* Online network for travellers with disabilities.

Once you arrive, facilities for travellers with disabilities are limited. Within Spain, public transport is not particularly wheelchair-friendly, though the rail operator **RENFE** usually provides wheelchairs at main city stations (they often require 24 hours' notice), and many trains are slowly being upgraded to provide services for travellers with disabilities (lift acess to platforms, etc.).

The Spanish tourist office has compiled a fact sheet and can give general information on accessible accommodation; more useful is the official Spanish hotel guide (*Guía Oficial de Hoteles*), published annually, which covers hotels throughout the country (available in most bookshops, €14), and uses a symbol for wheelchair-accessible hotels.

France's official tourism websites now have a dedicated section for travellers with disabilities (click on the 'Special Needs Tourism' button, or use this link: *http://uk.franceguide. com/travellers/special-needs-travellers*). This provides lists of accommodation, sights and monuments which are equipped for disabled travellers.

Unfortunately, the otherwise excellent Spanish tourism site offers no specific advice for travellers with disabilities. For wheelchair-accessible beaches on the Spanish side of the border, see *www.esplaya.com.*

Insurance and EHIC Cards

No inoculations are required to enter Spain or France, though it never hurts to check that your tetanus jab is up to date.

Citizens of the EU are entitled to a certain amount of free medical care in EU countries if they have a free **European Health Insurance Card** or **EHIC** (available online at *www.dh. gov.uk/travellers,* or *www.ehic.org.uk,* or by calling t 0845 605 0707, or by post using the forms available from post offices). You will need a card for every family member.

If you need urgent medical treatment while in **Spain,** ensure that you are taken to a public hospital or clinic and show your EHIC card on arrival. Private healthcare is not covered by the EHIC card. Note that dentistry, even emergency dentistry, is not covered by the reciprocal agreements.

In **France** you pay up front for medical care and prescriptions, and 75–80 per cent of the costs will be reimbursed later. Canadians are usually covered in France by their provincial health coverage. US citizens and those of other nations should check their individual policies.

As an alternative, consider a **travel insurance** policy covering theft and losses and offering 100 per cent medical refund plus repatriation costs if necessary; check to see if it covers extra expenses if you get bogged down in airport or train strikes. Beware that accidents resulting from sports are rarely covered by ordinary insurance. Make sure you save all doctor's and pharmacy receipts, plus police reports for thefts.

Maps

Rural Spain is not well mapped or sign-posted; rural France does a bit better, but you can still get lost. For general touring, a Michelin map or the equivalent is fine; for walking or finding dolmens and so on, the best maps are the IGN maps (Instituto Geográfico Nacional in Spain, Institut Géographique National in France), comparable to the Ordnance Survey or US Geodetic Survey map. They come in several different scales, from the highly detailed 1:25000 on up. The maps distributed by local tourist offices are often the best for pinpointing places of interest, beaches and so on.

You can buy maps and travel books online from the Spanish travel bookshop **Altaïr**, *www.altair.es*. If in the UK, visit **Stanfords** at 12 Long Acre, WC2, for the biggest selection, or you can buy online at *www.stanfords.co.uk*.

Money and Banks

The currency of both Spain and France is the **euro**. Coins are issued in denominations of 1, 2, 5, 10, 20 and 50 cents, and 1 and 2 euros. Notes are issued in denominations of 5, 10, 20, 50, 100, 200 and 500 euros. For the latest exchange rates, check out *www.xe.com/ucc*.

Traveller's cheques are the safest way to carry money. Pre-paid holiday cards have become popular, but shop around before you purchase as fees and charges vary considerably.

Major international **credit cards** are widely used in France and Spain, although American Express is often not accepted and Diners' Club cards are almost never accepted.

Cash withdrawals in euros can be made from bank and post office automatic cash machines (**ATMs**) using your PIN; the specific cards accepted are marked on each machine, and all give instructions in English. Credit card companies charge a fee for cash advances, but exchange rates are often better than in banks.

Most banks will change traveller's cheques and cash. For opening hours, *see* p.98. Exchange rates vary, and nearly all take a commission of varying proportions. Places that do nothing but exchange money (and hotels and train stations) usually have the worst rates or take the heftiest commissions, so be careful.

Getting There

By Air

There is an astounding variety of flight options to Spain and France these days, especially from the **UK**. A high-season **scheduled** return costs from around £80 on a no-frills carrier, up to £200 on a national airline. However, even Air France and Iberia offer special deals. Discounts are also available for domestic flights and for under-12s. No matter how you go, you can always save by travelling off-season and booking in advance.

There are international **airports** in Bilbao and Biarritz, and smaller airports in Donostia-San Sebastián, Pamplona and Hondarribia.

Air France flies to Biarritz from Paris Orly.

British Airways has a daily flight to Bilbao from London Heathrow (code-sharing with Iberia).

easyJet operates daily flights to Bilbao from London Stansted (twice daily in summer); Manchester to Bilbao (three days a week); daily flights from London Gatwick to Biarritz (summer only).

Iberia flies direct to Bilbao from London Heathrow daily, and to Bilbao via Barcelona or Madrid from Manchester. There are connections with major UK cities via London Heathrow. There are also direct flights to Santiago de Compostela, and flights to Pamplona and Donostia-San Sebastián via Madrid or Barcelona.

Ryanair has daily no-frills cheap flights to Biarritz (France) from London Stansted; flights four times a week to Manchester and to Dublin.

Vueling fly from London Heathrow to Bilbao.

There are no direct flights to Bilbao or other airports in the Basque region from the **USA and Canada**, but numerous carriers fly direct to Madrid, Barcelona and Paris. A high-season

Airline Carriers

UK

British Airways, t 0844 493 0787, *www.ba.com*.
easyJet, t 0843 104 5000, *www.easyjet.com*.
Iberia, t 08706 090 500, *www.iberia.com*.
Ryanair, t 0871 246 0000, *www.ryanair.com*.
Vueling, t 0906 754 7541, *www.vueling.com*.

USA and Canada

Air Canada, t 1-888 247 2262, *www.aircanada.ca*.
American Airlines, t 1-800 433 7300, *www.aa.com*.
British Airways, t 1-800 247 9297, *www.ba.com*.
Continental Airlines, t 1-800 231 0856, *www.continental.com*.
Delta, t 1-800 221 1212, *www.delta.com*.
Iberia, t 1-800 772 4642, *www.iberia.com*.
United Airlines, t 1-800 864 8331, *www.ual.com*.

Discounts and Special Deals

UK and Ireland

Flightbookers, UK **t** 0821 223 5000, *www.ebookers.com*.
Trailfinders, UK **t** 08450 58 58 58, *www.trailfinders.com*.
CIE Tours International, Ireland **t** (01) 703 1888, *www.cietours.ie*.
Joe Walsh Tours, Ireland **t** (01) 241 0800, *www.joewalshtours.ie*.
www.cheapflights.co.uk.
www.expedia.com.
www.lastminute.com.
www.skyscanner.net.

USA and Canada

Air Brokers International, USA **t** 800 883 3273, *www.airbrokers.com*.

Last Minute Travel Club, USA **t** 1-888 868 7722, Canada **t** 877 970 3500, *www.lastminuteclub.com*. Payment of an annual membership fee gets you cheap standby deals; there are also special rates for the major car rental companies in Europe, and train tickets.
Club ABC Tours, 200 Broadacres Drive, Bloomfield, NJ 07003, **t** 1-888 868 7722, *www.clubabc.com*.
www.traveldiscounts.com. Members get special discount rates on flights, hotels and tours.
www.orbitz.com. Cheap flights, hotels and car rental companies.

Student Discounts

Students and under 26s are eligible for considerable reductions on flights, train fares, admission fees to museums, concerts and more. Agencies specializing in youth travel can help you apply for the correct ID cards, as well as filling you in on the best deals.

Europe Student Travel, 6 Campden Street, London W8, **t** (020) 7727 7647.

STA Travel, *www.sta-travel.com/www.statravel.co.uk*. Has over 450 branches in countries all over the world, including more than 50 in the UK. Check the website, or call intersales: UK **t** 0871 230 0040; USA **t** 1 800 781 4040.

Student Universe, UK: **t** 0808 234 41 07, USA and Canada: **t** 1 800 272 9676, *www.studentuniverse.com* Online travel agency specializing in youth/student fares, cheap accommodation, tours and activities, etc.

Travel Cuts, 187 College St, Toronto, Ontario M5T 1P7, **t** 1-866 246 9762, *www.travelcuts.com*. Canada's largest student travel specialist.

USIT, Aston Quay, Dublin 2, **t** (01) 602 1906, *www.usit.ie*. Also: Belfast, **t** (028) 903 27111; Cork, **t** (021) 427 0900; Galway, **t** (091) 565177; Limerick, **t** (061) 415 069; Waterford, **t** (051) 351 762.

return will cost around US$1,000–2,000. Alternatively, it may be cheaper to fly to London and then on to Spain from there, especially off-season.

By Train

Travelling by high-speed train makes an attractive alternative to flying from the UK. **Eurostar** (**t** 08705 186 186, *www.eurostar.com*) departs from London St Pancras with direct connections to Paris (Gare du Nord; 2hrs 15mins) and Lille (1hr 40mins). Fares are

cheaper if booked in advance and/or include a Saturday night away. You must check in at least 30mins before departure or you will not be allowed on to the train. Prices range from around £55 (if booked more than 21 days in advance) to £300 for a standard return. Once you reach Paris or Lille, France's high-speed **TGVs** (*trains à grande vitesse*) shoot along at an average of 180mph, when they're not breaking world records. TGVs from Paris go to Bayonne (4½hrs) and Biarritz (5hrs) in the Pays Basque. Fares are only minimally higher than on slower trains; some weekday departures require a supplement and all require seat reservations, which you can make when you buy your ticket or at the station before departure. People aged under 26 are eligible for a 30 per cent discount on fares (see the student travel agencies) and there are other discounts if you're over 65, available from major travel agents.

From London to Bilbao or San Sebastián it's a full day's trip, changing trains in Paris and usually at Bordeaux or Hendaye in the small hours of the morning. For Bilbao you will have to change at San Sebastián for the slow but scenic **EuskoTren** service, which takes 2½ hours. The TGV service from Paris to Bordeaux can cut some hours off the trip if the schedule works for you. Another option is to take a direct train from Paris to Vitoria, and take a bus or local train from there. Spain is currently expanding its **high-speed AVE network**, which will cut travel times considerably (the completion date is currently 2020, although some sections will open from 2013).

If you plan to take some long train journeys, it may be worth investing in a rail pass. The good-value **Inter-Rail Global Pass**, *www.interrail.net* (for European residents of at least six months) offers 15 days', 22 days' or one month's unlimited travel in Europe, plus discounts on trains to cross-Channel ferry terminals, and returns on Eurostar from £59. Inter-Rail cards are not valid on UK trains. You can also get an **Inter-Rail One Country Pass** for three days (£169, under-26s £114) or eight days (£229, under 26s £173).

Visitors from North America have a wide choice of passes, including **Eurailpass**, **Europass** and **France 'n' Spain Pass**, which can all be purchased in the USA. A one-month Eurailpass costs $995/1,110 for those aged under/over 26 years. There are also **Senior Passes** for the over-60s.

For long-distance train travel, **bicycles** need to be transported separately and must be registered and insured. They can be delivered to your destination, though this may take several days. On Eurostar you need to check in your bike at least 24 hours before you travel, or wait 24 hours at the other end. For more details, call **t** 08705 186 186.

Rail Europe handles bookings for all services, including Eurostar and French Motorail (trains that can carry your car), and sells rail passes:

Rail Europe (UK), 1 Lower Regent St, London SW1Y 4XT, **t** 08448 484 064, *www.raileurope.co.uk*.

Rail Europe (USA), **t** 1-800 622 8600; Canada **t** 1-800 361 7245, *www.raileurope.com*.

By Coach

Eurolines runs services (all require a change, usually in Paris or Tours) from London to Bilbao (22hrs 45mins; £100–159 return), Donostia-San Sebastián (21hrs; £99–149 return), Vitoria-Gasteiz (23hrs; £85–120 return) and Bayonne (23hrs; £86–120 return); there are usually two or three services a week. There are discounts for those aged under 26, for senior citizens and for children under 12. In summer, the coach is the best bargain for anyone over 26; off season you'll probably find a cheaper flight.

Eurolines, **t** 08717 818181, *www.eurolines.com*.

By Sea

To Spain

Brittany Ferries, **t** 0871 244 0744, *www. brittany-ferries.co.uk*. Ferries from Portsmouth to Bilbao; fares vary throughout the year. A high-season return for two adults, two children and a car in an outside 4-berth cabin currently costs £748. They also operate services to Santander from Portsmouth and from Plymouth.

Note that Bilbao's ferry port is at Santurzi, 13km from the centre.

To France

If you prefer to cross the Channel to France, it is cheapest by ferry from Dover, but quickest via the Channel Tunnel (*see* p.84). For ferries, check out *www. directferries.co.uk*, and try price-comparison websites such as *www. ferrysmart.co.uk* and *www.ferrybooker.com*.

Brittany Ferries, **t** 0871 244 0744, *www. brittany-ferries.co.uk*. As well as the ferries to Bilbao and Santander (*see* above), Brittany Ferries operate services to Caen, Cherbourg, Roscoff and St-Malo from Portsmouth; and to St-Malo from Plymouth.

DFDS Ferries, t (020) 8127 8303, *www.dfdsseaways.com*. Dover to Dunkirk.

P&O Ferries, t 08716 642 121, *www.poferries.com*. Dover to Calais; Hull to Rotterdam or Zeebrugge.

Seafrance, t 0871 423 7119, *www.seafrance.co.uk*. Dover to Calais.

By Car

From the UK via France you have a choice of routes. If you get a ferry (*see* above) or the Eurotunnel (*see* below) to Calais, you may face going through or around Paris on the abominable *périphérique*, a task best tackled either side of rush hour. To avoid this, you can get a ferry from Portsmouth to Cherbourg, Caen, Roscoff or St-Malo. From any of these ports, the most direct route takes you to Bordeaux down the western coast of France, past Biarritz to the border at Irún and on to Donostia-San Sebastián and Bilbao.

For something different, opt for one of the routes the pilgrims to Santiago followed over the Pyrenees, through Somport-Canfranc (down the N134/E7/N330 south of Pau) or the classic route through Roncesvalles (on the D933 from St-Jean-Pied-de-Port).

Eurotunnel trains carry cars and their passengers through the Channel Tunnel from Folkestone to Calais on a simple drive-on, drive-off system (journey time 35mins). Payment is made at toll booths (which accept cash, cheques or credit cards). Prepaid tickets and booked spaces are available, but at off-peak times you can just turn up and take the next available service. Eurotunnel runs 24 hours a day, all year round, with a service at least once an hour through the night. Return fares range from around £84 (5-day return fare) to £398 (fully flexible return fare).

Drivers must carry **registration** and **insurance** papers. If you're coming from the UK or Ireland, the dip of the **headlights** must be adjusted to the right (you can buy patches to stick on the headlights). Carrying a **warning triangle** is mandatory, and it should be placed 50m (55 yards) behind the car if you have a breakdown. **Seat belts** are mandatory; in addition, all cars in France and Spain are required to have rear seat belts and these must be worn by rear seat passengers. Drivers with a valid licence from an EU

Drivers' Clubs

For more information on driving abroad, contact the AA, RAC or, in the USA, the AAA:

AA, t 0870 600 0371, *www.theaa.com*.

RAC, t 0870 572 2722, *www.rac.co.uk*.

AAA (USA), **t** 800 222 4357, *www.aaa.com*.

country, Canada, the USA or Australia don't need an international licence for Spain or France.

Eurotunnel trains, info and bookings t 08443 35 35 35, *www.eurotunnel.com*.

Getting Around

By Train

If you're using public transport in Spain for short distances, it is almost always better to take a bus than a train – they are faster, cheaper and more direct. In the French Basque Lands, however, the opposite is often true. Trains often take a more scenic route around rural villages, which can be worth the extra time and cost.

For long distances, trains in Spain are usually faster. High-speed services throughout Spain are being substantially improved, and the government aims to bring all provincial cities within three hours' train journey of the capital by 2020. Faster train links between the three main Basque cities (Bilbao, Donostia-San Sebastián and Vitoria-Gasteiz) are under construction.

Trains in Spain

RENFE, t 902 320 320, *www.renfe.com* (website has timetables, types of ticket available and fares, also in English). For international trains, visit *www.elipsos.com*.

Democracy in Spain has made the trains run on time, but western Europe's most eccentric railway, RENFE, still has a way to go. The problem isn't the trains themselves – they're almost always clean and comfortable, and do their best to keep to the schedules – but that the RENFE network remains phenomenally complex.

There are basically four kinds of train service: the high-speed inter-city AVE trains (Alto Velocidad Española, which means Spanish High Speed); fast inter-city services with a bewildering variety of names including Talgo, Alvia, Estrella and Diurno; the slower and less expensive *regionales*, which link major towns and cities; and *cercanías*, which are local services connected to a major hub like Bilbao.

Every variety of train has different services and a different price – yet the system is efficient, albeit confusing for the visitor. There are **discounts** for children, large families, senior citizens and regular travellers. If you buy a single ticket, hang on to it, because if you decide to return you are still elegible for a discount. The under-26s in possession of a *tarjeta joven* (youth card) issued in Spain or abroad are elegible for discounts.

Every city has a RENFE travel office in the centre, and you can make good use of these for information and tickets. Always buy tickets in advance if you can, particularly at small stations; one of RENFE's little tricks is to close station ticket-windows 10 minutes before your train arrives, and if you show up at the last minute you could be out of luck. You can also book tickets online, or by telephone and pick them up at automatic ticket terminals in the main stations.

To add to the confusion, northern Spain has two private narrow-gauge railway lines: in Euskadi, the **EuskoTren** (Basque Railways) connects Bilbao and Donostia-San Sebastián by way of Zarautz and Zumaia; and **FEVE** has tracks along the north coast of Spain connecting Bilbao to Oviedo via Santander. Both these lines show off rural Spanish life and scenery at their best and both are fun to ride, though again, they are slower and often more expensive than the bus. The EuskoTren line maintains an electric train from the 1920s with wooden carriages, and runs it in summer for excursions around Donostia-San Sebastián; ask at the train station there for details. Passes are not valid on these.

After disappearing for many years because of terrorism, **left luggage** facilities have reappeared in Spanish stations; the word in Spanish is *consigna*.

Trains in France

SNCF general information, **t** 36 35 (within France only), *www.sncf.com*.

The southwest of France has a decent network of trains, although many of the smaller lines have only two or three daily connections. In some places SNCF buses have taken over former train routes. Most visitors to the French Pays Basque will probably make most use of the TER regional network; for timetable information, *see www.ter-sncf.com* and click on Aquitaine.

Prices, if not a bargain, are still reasonable and discounts are available if you travel at off-peak times, or purchase one of the several travel cards available. (Note that travel cards are valid for one year and are usually only worth the expense if you are travelling long distances within France, or intend to make heavy use of the high-speed services.) These include: the *Carte Sénior*, for those aged over 60, which offers discounts of between 25–50 per cent; the *Carte 12–25* for children and young people up to the age of 25, with discounts of between 25–60 per cent; the *Carte Escapades*, valid for weekend travel of distances over 200km and offering 25–50 per cent discounts; and the *Carte Enfant +*, which provides discounts for a child between 4 and 12 plus an adult.

Anyone can also save money by buying a second-class ticket in advance, the only condition being that you must use it at the designated time on the designated train.

Tickets must be stamped in the little orange machines by the door to the tracks that say *Compostez votre billet* (this puts the date on the ticket, to stop you from using the same one over and over again). Any time you interrupt a journey until another day, you have to re-*compost* your ticket.

Nearly every station has banks of mechanical **left luggage** lockers (*consignes automatiques*) that spit out a slip with the lock combination when you use them.

By Bus

Buses in Spain

Like the trains, buses in Spain are cheap by northern European standards. Usually, whether you go by train or bus will depend on simple convenience – in some places the train station is a long way from the centre; in others the bus station is out of town.

Small towns and villages can normally be reached by bus only through their provincial capitals.

Buses are usually clean and dependable, and there's plenty of room for baggage in the compartment underneath. On the more luxurious buses you even get air-conditioning and a movie. Tourist information offices are the best sources of information; they almost always know every route and schedule.

Buses in France

Do not count on seeing the rural Pays Basque by public transport. The bus network is barely adequate between major cities and towns (places often already well served by rail) and rotten in rural areas, where the one daily bus fits the school schedule, leaving at the crack of dawn and returning in the afternoon. More remote villages are linked to civilization only once a week or not at all.

Buses are run either by the SNCF (replacing discontinued rail routes) or private firms. Rail passes are valid on SNCF buses. Private bus firms, especially when they have a monopoly, tend to be a bit more expensive than trains.

Some towns have a *gare routière* (coach station), usually near the train station, while in others the buses stop at bars or any other place that catches their fancy. Stops are hardly ever marked, though in some areas there are conspicuous bus stops everywhere while in fact no service exists.

The posted schedules are not always to be trusted. The tourist office or shopkeepers near the bus stop may have a more accurate instinct for when a bus is likely to appear.

By City Bus and Taxi

City Buses and Taxis in Spain

In Spain, every city in Euskadi and Navarra has a perfectly adequate system of public transport. You won't need to make much use of it, though, for even in the big cities nearly all attractions are within walking distance.

City buses usually cost around €1, and if you intend using them often there are books of tickets called *abonamientos* or *bono-Bús*, or *tarjeta* cards to punch on entry, available at reduced rates from tobacconists (*estancos*). Bus drivers will give change if you don't have the correct amount (although most will only accept notes up to the value of €20). In many cities, the entire route will be displayed on the signs at each bus stop (*parada*).

Taxis are cheap enough for the Spaniards to use them regularly on their shopping trips. The average fare for a ride within a city will be €8–12. Taxis are metered and the drivers are usually quite honest; they are entitled to certain surcharges (for luggage, night or holiday trips, to the train or airport, etc.), and if you cross the city limits they can usually charge double the fare shown. It's rarely hard to hail a cab from the street, and there will always be a few around the stations. If you get stuck where there is none, or in a small village, call information (t 11811 is just one of the numbers in Spain for directory enquiries) for the number of a radio taxi.

City Buses and Taxis in France

On the French side, the only **city buses** you'll find are in Biarritz and Bayonne.

Nearly every town, however, has at least one **taxi** service; the numbers are usually posted in the phone booths or bars.

By Car

Driving in Spain

Petrol is less expensive in Spain than most places in Europe, but not by much. In cities, parking is often difficult; another problem is that only a few hotels – the more expensive ones – have garages or any sort of parking. Spaniards may still have a reputation as hotheads behind the wheel, but you will find that the Basques potter about rather serenely, and on the whole they are as careful and courteous as you could wish. Basque nationalists, however, are keen that you learn the Basque names for towns and tend to black out the Spanish ones on the bilingual road signs; you may want to check the Basque place names in this text before setting out.

Spain's **highway network** is good, and many major cities are now linked by motorways (called *autovías* or, if a toll is charged, *autopistas*) or dual carriageways. The government has invested a considerable sum on a full-scale motorway system, including one following the entire length of the northern coast. However, the Bilbao area is a motorist's nightmare – even if you're just passing through, you'll probably get good and lost among the bizarre topography and endless roadworks. Be warned that tolls on the motorways are sheer highway robbery.

The **speed limit** is 120kph (75mph) on the *autopistas*, and 100kph (62mph) on all other national highways unless otherwise marked.

Driving in France

A car is, regrettably, the only way to get around the rural Pays Basque. This, too, has its drawbacks: high car-rental rates and Europe's priciest petrol, and an accident rate double that of the UK (and much higher than the USA). Go slowly and be careful; never expect any French driver to be aware of the possibility of a collision. Generally, roads are excellently maintained, but anything of lower status than a departmental route (D road) may be uncomfortably narrow.

Petrol stations are rare in rural areas and they are closed on Sunday afternoons, so consider your fuel supply while planning any forays into the back country. The scoundrels will expect a tip for oil, wind-screen-cleaning or air. The price of petrol (*essence*) varies considerably, with motorways always more expensive.

France used to have a rule of giving priority to the right at every intersection. This has largely disappeared, although there may still be intersections, usually in towns, where it applies – these will be marked. Watch out for the *Cédez le passage* (Give way) signs and be careful. Generally, as you'd expect, give priority to the main road, and to the left on roundabouts. If you are new to France, think of every intersection as a new and perilous experience. Watch out for byzantine street parking rules (which would take pages to explain: do as the natives do, and be careful about village centres on market days).

Speed limits are 130km/80mph on the *autoroutes* (toll motorways); 110km/69mph on dual carriageways (divided highways); 90km/55mph on other roads; 50km/30mph in an 'urbanized area': as soon as you pass a white sign with a town's name on it and until you pass another sign with the town's name barred. Fines for speeding, payable on the spot, can be astronomical if you flunk the breathalyser. The French have one admirably civilized custom of the road: if oncoming drivers unaccountably flash their headlights at you, it means the *gendarmes*

Car Hire Companies

Auto Europe, UK t 0800 223 5555; USA t 1-800 223 5555; Spain t 900 801 879, *www.autoeurope.com*.

Avis, UK t 0844 581 0147; Spain t 94 427 57 60, *www.avis.com*.

Atesa, Spain t 902 100 101, *www.atesa.es*.

Budget, UK t 08701 56 56 56; USA t 800 527 0700; Spain t 902 112 585, *www.budget.com*.

Europcar, UK t 08706 075 000; USA t 877 940 6900; Spain t 902 105 055; France t 08 25 35 83 58, *www.europcar.com*.

Hertz, in UK t 08708 44 88 44; Spain t 91 749 77 78; France t 01 39 41 91 95 25, *www.hertz.com*.

Holiday Autos, UK t 0870 400 4461; Spain t 902 887 210, *www.holidayautos.com*.

are lurking just up the way. If you wind up in an **accident**, the procedure is to fill out and sign an official report called a *constat amiable*. If your French isn't sufficient to deal with this, hold off until you find someone to translate for you so you don't accidentally incriminate yourself.

If you have a **breakdown** and are a member of a motoring club affiliated to the Touring Club de France, ring the latter; if not, ring the police, t 112 (across Europe).

Car Hire

This is slightly cheaper in **Spain** than elsewhere in Europe. Most of the big international companies are expensive, but budget firms like Auto Europe, Holiday Autos and ATESA offer cheaper rates. Prices for the smallest cars begin at about €300 (£260) per week with unlimited mileage, but full insurance can add considerably to the costs. Small local firms can sometimes offer a better deal, but should be treated with some caution.

Car rental can also be booked through most of the airlines, including British Airways, Iberia and easyJet.

Check out rental prices on price comparison websites such as *www.compare carhire.co.uk*, but carefully check hidden charges (such as limited mileage).

By Bicycle

The Basques, who produced Tour de France winners Miguel Indurain and Carlos Sastre, are keen cyclists, and if you haven't brought your own bike the main towns and holiday centres always seem to have at least one shop that hires out mountain bikes (BTT in Spanish, VTT in French) or touring/racing bikes; local tourist offices have lists. Be prepared to pay a fairly hefty deposit on a good bike, and you may want to enquire about theft insurance. Do take into account how fit you are: Basqueland is a seriously steep and hilly place, although one advantage in the summer is that the (relatively) cool temperatures should keep sunstroke at bay. Roads, however, are often distressingly narrow. Wear a helmet.

Maps and information are available from the following federations and clubs:

Real Federación Española de Ciclismo, C/ Ferraz 16, 28008 Madrid, Spain, **t** 91 540 08 41, *www.rfec.com.*

Fédération Française de Cyclotourisme, 12 Rue Louis Bertrand, 94207 Ivry-sur-Seine, **t** 01 56 20 88 88, *www.ffct.org.*

Cyclists' Touring Club, Parklands, Railton Rd, Guildford, Surrey, **t** 0844 736 8450, *www.ctc.org.uk.*

On Foot

A network of long-distance paths, the *Grandes Randonnées*, or GRs for short (marked by distinctive red and white signs), take in some of the most beautiful scenery in France, and the Pyrenees make up some of the most gorgeous walking territory in Europe. The most popular trails are: the **GR10**, which goes straight across the Pyrenees on the French side, passing through many villages, and is accessible to any fit walker; and the more demanding **GR11**, higher up and more or less following the French–Spanish frontier, and passing through fewer villages.

Each French GR is described in a *Topoguide*, with maps and details about campsites, refuges, *gîtes d'étape* and so on, available in area bookshops or from the **Fédération Française de la Randonnée Pédestre**, 64 Rue du Dessous des Berges, 75013 Paris, **t** 01 44 89 93 93, *www.ffrp.asso.fr.*

In the French Pyrenees, the best maps and trail guides and much of the mountain accommodation is administered by the Randonnées Pyrénéennes. For details, contact the **Centre d'Information sur la Montagne et les Sentiers (CIMES)**, 4 Rue Maye Lane, 65420 Ibos, **t** 05 62 90 09 92.

Spain's GR trails are usually poorly marked on the ground; the guides which cover them are usually out-of-date or in Basque; and the paths are not marked on most maps. Contact the **Euskadi Mendizale Federazioa** (Basque Mountain Federation), Anoeta Pasealekua 24. Donostia-San Sebastián, **t** 94 347 42 79 , *wwww.emf-fvm.com* (in Basque and Spanish only) for the most up-to-date information.

Where to Stay

Spain

The Spanish government regulates hotels more intelligently, and more closely, than any other Mediterranean country. Room prices must be posted in hotel lobbies and in rooms, and if there's a problem you can ask for the complaints book, or *Libro de Reclamaciones*. No one ever writes anything in these – written complaints must be passed to the authorities immediately, and hotel keepers would always rather correct the problem.

The prices given in this guide do not include **VAT** (IVA), charged at 8 per cent. Prices for single rooms will average about 60 per cent of a double, while triples or an extra bed are around 35 per cent more.

Within the price ranges shown, the most expensive are likely to be in the big cities, while the cheapest places are always in provincial towns. On the whole, prices are surprisingly consistent. Look for the little blue plaques next to the doors of all *hoteles*, *hostales*, etc., which identify the classification and number of stars. Local tourist offices have complete accommodation lists for their province, and some can be very helpful with finding a room when things are tight.

Accommodation Price Ranges

Note that prices listed here and elsewhere in this book are for a double room in high season.

luxury	€€€€€	over €200
very expensive	€€€€	€160–200
expensive	€€€	€120–160
moderate	€€	€80–120
inexpensive	€	under €80

Paradores

The government, in its plan to develop tourism in the 1950s, started this nationwide chain of classy hotels to draw attention to little-visited areas. They restored old palaces, castles and monasteries for the purpose, furnished them with antiques and installed fine restaurants featuring local specialities.

Paradores for many people are one of the best reasons for visiting Spain. Not all are historic landmarks; in resort areas, they are as likely to be cleanly designed modern buildings, usually in a good location with a pool and some sports facilities. As their popularity has increased, so have their prices; in most cases both the rooms and the restaurant will be the most expensive in town, though most offer substantial off-season discounts.

There are also discounts for the over-55s and the under-35s (but these must be booked in advance, see under 'Offers and Promotions' at *www.parador.es*). There is also a good-value pass called the Five-night Card, offering five nights in any *parador* for a discounted price. Note that you will have to book months in advance for the most popular *paradores*.

Hoteles

Hoteles (H) are rated from one to five stars, according to the services they offer. These are the most expensive places, and even a one-star hotel will be a comfortable middle-range establishment. Many of the more expensive hotels have some rooms available at prices lower than those listed; you'll have to ask. You can often get discounts in the off season but will be charged higher rates during big festivals (in Pamplona, for example, prices usually quintuple during the Sanfermines festival). If you want to attend any of these big events, be sure to book as far in advance as possible.

Spanish hotel breakfasts are usually served buffet style and are very rarely good, although often expensive. You'll do much better at a local café.

Hostales, Pensiones and Fondas

Hostales (Hs) are rated with from one to three stars. *Pensiones* and *fondas* no longer have an official category, but many establishments still bear the name. Like *hostales*, these are usually more modest places, often a floor in an apartment block; a two-star *hostal* is roughly equivalent to a one-star hotel, but not always. A few may require full- or half-board in high season. *Hostales* and *pensiones* with one or two stars will often have cheaper rooms without private baths.

You can also ask in bars or at the tourist office for unidentified **casas particulares**, private houses with a room or two. In fact, in most towns and resorts you will not have to look at all. Someone will probably find you in the bus or train station, and ask if you need a room. Almost all of these will be pleasant enough. Prices are usually negotiable (before you are taken to the place). Always make sure the location suits you – 'five minutes away' can mean five minutes on foot or in a car. In many villages these rooms will be the only accommodation on offer, but they're usually clean. In cities, the best places to look are right in the centre, not around the stations. Some may ask you to pay a day in advance.

Alternative Accommodation

Youth hostels exist in Spain, but they're rarely worth the trouble. Most are open only in summer, there are the usual inconveniences and silly rules, often they're in out-of-the-way locations – and they can be block-booked by schools. You're better off with the inexpensive *hostales*.

Ask at the local tourist office for rooms that might be available in **university halls**.

If you fancy some tranquillity, several **monasteries and convents** welcome guests. Accommodation and meals are simple and guests can usually take part in the religious ceremonies. We have listed some of these in the text; for others, ask for details at local tourist offices.

Camping

Campsites are rated from one to three stars, depending on their facilities. As well as the ones listed in the official government handbook, there are always others, rather primitive, that are unlisted. Facilities in most first-class sites include shops, restaurants, bars, laundries, hot showers, first aid, swimming pools, phones and, occasionally, a tennis court. Caravans (trailers) converge on all the more developed sites, but if you just want to pitch your little tent or sleep out in some quiet field, ask around in the bars or at likely farms. Camping is forbidden in many forested areas because of the danger of fire, as well as on the beaches. If you're doing some hiking, bring a sleeping bag and stay in the *refugios* along the major trails.

The government handbook *Guía Oficial de Campings*, published by Turespaña, can be found in most bookstores and at tourist offices. See also *www.spain.info*.

The excellent Spanish tourist information website *www.spain.info* has a search engine for locating campsites.

Private Accommodation, Self-Catering and *Casas Rurales*

With the rise in hotel prices, staying in private homes has become an increasingly popular way of holidaying in Spain. *Casas rurales*, rural accommodation in farms or country houses, has become extremely popular and is a wonderful way to enjoy the spectacular countryside of northern Spain. Some are rented whole, while others offer B&B accommodation. Some even offer special activities such as cheese-making. Some provincial tourist offices have full lists of *casas rurales* and other self-catering properties. This type of accommodation is also called *Agriturismo*, or *Turismo Rural*, or in Basque (wait for it) *Nekazalturismoa*. Kitchen facilities may or may not be available, and prices generally fall in the range of €40–80 per day for a double room. A very useful website is *www.toprural.com*, which lists all kinds of rural accommodation throughout Spain and is also in English. You can also contact the following:

Asociacion Nekazalturismoa, Edificio Kursaal, Av. de Zurriola 1, Donostia-San Sebastián t 902 130 031, *www.nekatur.net*.

Agroturismo de Navarra, C/ José Manuel Martínez de Irujo San Pedro 4, 31173 Izane (Cendea de Olzo), t 94 817 67 74, *www. agroturismosnavarra.com*.

There are numerous private firms offering all sorts of different types of self-catering accommodation. *See* also 'Self-catering and Special-interest Operators', p.92.

France

Hotels

As in Spain, French tourist authorities grade hotels by their facilities (not by charm or location) with a star system. Some places with good facilities have no stars at all, though, simply because the hotel owners have not applied to be graded.

Almost every establishment has a wide range of rooms and prices: a large room with a view and a bathroom can cost much more than a poky back room with the WC down the hall. Most two-star hotel rooms have their own showers and WCs. Most one-stars offer rooms with or without.

Single rooms are relatively rare and usually cost two-thirds the price of a double. Rarely will a hotelier give you a discount if only doubles are available (because each room has its own price). Prices are posted at the reception desk and in the rooms. Flowered wallpaper, usually beige, comes in all rooms at no extra charge. Breakfast (coffee, a croissant, bread and jam for €5–12) is nearly always optional: you'll do as well for less in a bar. As usual, rates rise in the busy season, when many hotels with restaurants will require that you take **half-board** (*demi-pension* – breakfast and set lunch or dinner). Many hotel restaurants are superb, and non-guests are welcome.

Book ahead, especially from May to October. July and August are the only really impossible months. Many tourist offices will call around and book a room for you on the spot for free or a nominal fee.

There are various umbrella organizations like Logis et Auberges de France, Relais de Silence, and the prestigious Relais et Châteaux, which promote and guarantee the quality of independently owned hotels and their restaurants. Many are recommended in this guide. Larger tourist offices usually stock their booklets.

Bed and Breakfast

In rural areas there is plenty of opportunity to stay in a private home or farm. *Chambres d'hôtes*, in the tourist office brochures, are listed separately from hotels with the various *gîtes* (*see* below). Some are connected to ferme-auberge restaurants, others to wine estates or a château; prices tend to be moderate to inexpensive. Local tourist offices will usually provide you with a list if you ask.

Youth Hostels, Gîtes d'Etape and Refuges

Most cities have youth hostels (auberges de jeunesse) which offer dormitory accommodation and breakfast to people of any age for around €15–20 a night. Most also offer kitchen facilities or inexpensive meals. They are the best deal for people travelling alone. For people travelling together, a one-star hotel can be just as cheap. A downside is that most are either in the suburbs, where the last bus goes by at 7pm, or miles from any transport at all in the country. In summer, the only way to be sure of a room is to arrive early. To stay in some hostels you need to be a member of Hostelling International.

Fédération Unie des Auberges de Jeunesse (FUAJ), 27 Rue Pajol, 75018 Paris, t (01) 44 89 87 27, www.fuaj.org.

Youth Hostels Association (YHA), Trevelyan House, Dimple Rd, Matlock, Derbyshire, DE4 3YH, t (01629) 592600, www.yha.org.uk.

American Youth Hostelling International, 8401 Colesville Road, Suite 600, Silver Spring, MD 20910, t (301) 495-1240, www.hiayh.org.

A gîte d'étape (www.gite-etape.com) is a shelter with bunk beds (no bedding) and a rudimentary self-catering kitchen set up by a village along GR footpaths or scenic bike routes. In the mountains, similar rough shelters along the GR paths are called refuges; most of them are open in summer only. Both charge around €15–18 a night.

Camping

Camping is a very popular way to travel, especially among the French themselves, and there's at least one campsite in every town – often an inexpensive, no-frills municipal site (Camping Municipal). Other campsites are graded with stars like hotels from four to one: at the top of the line you can expect lots of trees and grass, hot showers, a pool or beach, sports facilities, and a grocer's, bar and/or restaurant, for prices rather similar to one-star hotels. Camping on a farm is especially big in the southwest, and is usually less expensive than organized sites. If you want to camp wild, ask permission from the landowner first, or you risk a furious farmer, his dog and perhaps even the police.

Tourist offices have complete lists of campsites in their regions. If you plan to move around a lot, the Guide Officiel Camping/ Caravanning is available in most French bookshops. Also see www.campingfrance. com. A number of UK holiday firms book camping holidays and offer discounts on Channel ferries: **Canvas Holidays**, t 0845 268 0827, www.canvasholidays.co.uk; **Eurocamp**, t 0844 406 0402, www.eurocamp.co.uk; **Keycamp Holidays**, t 0844 7406 0200, www. keycamp.co.uk. The French National Tourist Office has complete lists. The Michelin Green Guide Camping/Caravanning France is very informative and also lists sites with facilities suitable for disabled visitors. In the UK, a couple of useful organizations are **Camping and Caravanning Club**, Greenfields House, Westwood Way, Coventry CV4 8JH, t 0845 130 7631, www.campingandcaravanning club.co.uk; and **Caravan Club**, East Grinstead House, East Grinstead, Sussex RH19 1UA, www.caravanclub.co.uk.

Gîtes de France and Other Self-catering Accommodation

The Pays Basque offers a vast range of self-catering accommodation, from inexpensive farm cottages to fancy villas. The **Fédération Nationale des Gîtes de France** is a French government service offering inexpensive accommodation by the week in rural areas. Lists with photos for the Pays Basque are available from the French National Tourist Office, from most local tourist offices, or online at www.gites-de-france.com (also in English). Prices range from €350–1,200 a week, depending very much on the time of year as well as facilities; nearly always you'll be expected to begin your stay on a Saturday.

The Sunday papers are full of options, or contact one of the firms listed below. The accommodation they offer will nearly always be more comfortable and costly than a gîte, but the discounts holiday firms offer on ferries, plane tickets or car rentals can make up for the price difference.

Self-catering and Special-interest Operators

Companies are springing up offering infor‐ mation and online booking only. Try *www. francedirect.co.uk*, which has a large selection of cottages and villas. The Spanish tourist information site *www.spain.info* has accommo‐ dation listings for the Basque region.

To stay in a rural farmhouse, log on to *www.gites-de-france.fr*, for the French Pays Basque; or **t** 90 213 00 31, *www.nekatur.net*, for the Spanish Basque Lands.

In Spain

Euro Adventures, C/ Velázquez Moreno 9, Vigo, Pontevedra, Galicia, **t** 98 622 13 99, *www. euroadventures.net*. Gastronomic tours, walk‐ ing tours, and tailor-made holidays in the Basque country.

Tandem, C/Pasajes 4, 20013 Donostia-San Sebastián, **t** 94 332 6705, *www.tandem sansebastian.com*. Spanish courses and cultural exchanges, based at a building in the old part of San Sebastián.

Tenedor, PO Box 5070, San Sebastián, **t** 94 331 39 29, *www.tenedortours.com*. A superb range of cultural (art, food, wine and architecture) tours of the Basque country and northern Spain, lasting from one to 13 days in length.

Totally Spain, Barrio Zoña, 39193 Castillo, Cantabria, Spain **t** 94 263 73 58, UK **t** 0871 666 0214, USA **t** (561) 828 0238, *www.totallyspain. com*. Tailor-made and themed holidays in Bilbao and the Spanish Basque lands, as well as tours and city breaks.

In the UK

ATG Oxford, 274 Banbury Road, Oxford OX2 7GH, **t** (01865) 315 678, *www.atg-oxford.co.uk*.

Offers a delightful eight-day walking trip in the western Pyrenees, from Biarritz along the French–Spanish frontier to Hendaye, staying in Basque farmhouses along the way.

Exsus Travel, 118–119 Tenchurch St, London EC3 M5BA, **t** (020) 7337 9010, *www.exsus.com*. Luxury, tailor-made tours in the Basque region.

Martin Randall, Voysey House, Barley Mow Passage, London W4 4GF, **t** (020) 8742 3355, *www.martinrandall.com*. Lecturer-accompanied cultural tours.

Pico Verde, 792 Wilmslow Road, Didsbury, Manchester, M20 6UG, **t** (0161) 773 5335, *www.picoverde.com*. Walking holidays in north‐ ern Spain, including the Atlantic Pyrenees.

Pyrenean Experience, UK **t** (0121) 711 3428, *www.pyreneanexperience.com*. Beginners' Spanish and walking holidays, painting and tailor-made holidays in the Spanish Pyrenees.

Pyrenees Adventures, UK **t** 08701 904 125, *www.pyreneesadventures.com*. Arranges tailor‐ made guided walks in the Pyrenees, based at a farmhouse in southeast France.

VFB Holidays, **t** (01242) 240 340, *www.vfb holidays.co.uk*. Accommodation in France, from rustic *gîtes* to luxurious farmhouses.

In the US

Classic Journeys, 7855 Ivanhoe Avenue, Suite 220, La Jolla, CA 92037, **t** 800 200 3887, *www.classicjourneys.com*. Offers a 'cultural walking adventure' from St-Jean-de-Luz to Bilbao and Biarritz, over seven days.

NRCSA, PO Box 1393, Milwaukee, W153201, **t** (414) 278 0631, *www.nrcsa.com*. Language and cultural courses in San Sebastián.

Wilderness Travel, 1102 9th Street, Berkeley, CA 94710, **t** 800 368 2794, *www.wilderness travel.com*. Hiking in the Basque country.

Practical A–Z

06

Imperial–Metric Conversions

Length (multiply by)
Inches to centimetres: 2.54
Centimetres to inches: 0.39
Feet to metres: 0.3
Metres to feet: 3.28
Yards to metres: 0.91
Metres to yards: 1.1
Miles to kilometres: 1.61
Kilometres to miles: 0.62

Area (multiply by)
Inches square to centimetres square: 6.45
Centimetres square to inches square: 0.15
Feet square to metres square: 0.09
Metres square to feet square: 10.76
Miles square to kilometres square: 2.59
Kilometres square to miles square: 0.39
Acres to hectares: 0.40
Hectares to acres: 2.47

Weight (multiply by)
Ounces to grams: 28.35
Grammes to ounces: 0.035
Pounds to kilograms: 0.45
Kilograms to pounds: 2.2
Stones to kilograms: 6.35
Kilograms to stones: 0.16
Tons (UK) to kilograms: 1,016
Kilograms to tons (UK): 0.0009
1 UK ton (2,240lbs) = 1.12 US tonnes (2,000lbs)

Volume (multiply by)
Pints (UK) to litres: 0.57
Litres to pints (UK): 1.76
Quarts (UK) to litres: 1.13
Litres to quarts (UK): 0.88
Gallons (UK) to litres: 4.55
Litres to gallons (UK): 0.22
1 UK pint/quart/gallon = 1.2 US pints/quarts/gallons

Temperature
Celsius to Fahrenheit: multiply by 1.8 then add 32

Fahrenheit to Celsius: subtract 32 then multiply by 0.55

°C	°F
40	104
35	95
30	86
25	77
20	68
15	59
10	50
5	41
-0	32
-5	23
-10	14
-15	5

Spain and France Information

Time Differences
Spain/France: + 1hr GMT; + 6hrs EST
Daylight saving from last weekend in March to end of October

Dialling Codes
Note: to dial within Spain and within a province, include the area code (9X). For France, omit the first zero of the area code.

Spain country code 34; **France country code** 33

To Spain or France from: UK, Ireland, New Zealand 00 / USA, Canada 011 / Australia 0011 then dial 33 or 34 and the number

From Spain or France to: UK 00 44; Ireland 00 353; USA, Canada 001; Australia 00 61; New Zealand 00 64 then the number without the initial zero

Directory enquiries: Spain 11811, **France** 118 000
International directory enquiries: Spain 176; **France** 00 33 12

Emergency Numbers
General EU emergency number: 112
Police: Spain 091, **France** 17
Ambulance: France 15
Emergencias Osakidetza (Basque Emergency Health Service), **Spain,** 94 410 00 00
Fire: Spain 080, **France** 18

Embassy Numbers in Spain
UK: 94 415 76 00 (Bilbao); **Ireland** 94 423 04 14 (Bilbao); **USA:** 91 587 22 00 (Madrid); **Canada** 91 423 32 50 (Madrid); **Australia** 91 441 93 00 (Madrid); **New Zealand** 91 523 02 26 (Madrid)

Embassy Numbers in France
UK: 05 57 22 21 10; **Ireland** 01 44 17 67 00; **USA:** 05 34 41 36 50; **Canada** 01 44 43 29 00; **Australia** 01 40 59 33 00; **NZ** 01 45 01 43 43

Women's Clothing

Europe	UK	USA
34	6	2
36	8	4
38	10	6
40	12	8
42	14	10
44	16	12

Basque Names and Places

Names are a bugbear for anyone writing about the Basque country. Many places have at least two, with a few spelling variations thrown in for fun. We've tried to list all, Spanish or French and Basque, in the text, but in general we have used the Basque for towns and villages in Spain, or the official combined names such as Donostia-San Sebastián or Vitoria-Gasteiz. In France you are far more likely to see the French name, and this is what we have used.

There are seven Basque provinces: Vizcaya (Bizkaia in Basque), Álava (Araba), Guipúzcoa (Gipuzkoa), Navarra (Nafarroa), Labourd, Basse-Navarre (Behe Nafarroa) and Soule (Zuberoa). The first four are in Spain, and yet even in the New Spain of autonomous communities they are divided in two. Vizcaya, Álava and Guipúzcoa make up what were known for centuries as the Bascongadas or Vascongadas, but are now called **Euskadi**, or officially the Euskal Autonomia Erkidegoa in Basque and the Comunidad Autonoma Vasca in Spanish. **Navarra**, which has a higher percentage of Spaniards than Basques in the south, is its own autonomous community, the Comunidad Foral de Navarra. Labourd, Basse-Navarre and Soule form the French **Pays Basque**, comprising half of the *département* of the Pyrénées Atlantiques.

The Basques have traditionally called their country Euskal Herria, 'the Country of Basque-speakers'. What most people call the 'Spanish' or 'French' Basque country, the Basques prefer to call the South and North Basque country – Hego Euskal Herria (Hegoalde) for the south, and Ipar Euskal Herria (Iparralde) for the north.

Crime and the Police

General emergency number t 112 (EU)

Police t 091 (Spain), **t** 17 (France)

The Basque country on both sides of the border – because of the terrorist activities of ETA (which very rarely involve tourists) – is the most densely policed corner of Europe, and the presence of several different kinds of police does keep the everyday crime rate relatively low. Pickpocketing and robbing parked cars are the specialities; and, except for some quarters of the largest cities, walking around at night is no problem. Crime is increasing in the tourist areas; even there, though, you're generally safer than you would be at home: the national crime rate of Spain is roughly a quarter that of Britain.

There are several species of police in the Spanish Basque country, and their authority varies according to the area. The Spanish Basque country has its own police force, the **Ertzaintza**. You'll see them looking dapper in their red berets, waiting by the roadsides for motorists in a barely legal hurry. The Ertzaintza has an important anti-terrorist unit, and also has a history of being notably unsympathetic to the Basques, partly in an attempt to prove their trustworthiness to the national government.

Franco's old goon squad, the Policía Armada, was reformed and relatively demilitarized into the **Policía Nacional**, known as 'chocolate drops' for their brown uniforms. Nowadays they wear blue and white, and their duties seem to consist largely of driving around and drinking coffee. The **Policía Municipal** (**Udaltzaingoa** in Basque) in some towns do control crime, while in others they are limited to directing traffic.

Mostly in rural areas, you will also see the **Guardia Civil**, with green uniforms. They, too, are resented by the Basques for historical reasons (*see* pp.31–8), and because today they often break up demonstrations and torture the Basques they arrest. Basques are nearly unanimous in wanting them to go away. For visitors, they are probably most conspicuous as a highway patrol, assisting motorists and handing out tickets (ignoring 'no passing' zones is the easiest way to get one). Most traffic violations are payable on the spot, but the traffic cops have a reputation for honesty.

The French Pays Basque isn't a high crime area either. Isolated holiday homes get burgled, as anywhere else; cars are occasionally broken into or stolen. By law, *gendarmes* can stop anyone anywhere and demand ID; in practice, they tend only to do it to harass minorities, the homeless and scruffy hippy types.

On either side of the border, report thefts to the nearest police station – not a pleasant task, but the reward is the bit of paper you need for an insurance claim. You can also call t 902 102 112, make the report over the phone, and then go into the police station to sign it. If your passport is stolen, contact the police and your nearest consulate for emergency travel documents.

The drug situation is the same in **France** as anywhere in Europe: soft and hard drugs are widely available, and the police only make an issue of victimless crime when it suits them (your being a foreigner may just rouse them to action). Smuggling any amount of marijuana into France can mean a prison term, and there's not much your consulate can or will do about it. Note that in **Spain**, possession of any quantity of recreational drugs is illegal; even a small amount may earn you the traditional 'six years and a day'.

Eating Out

Basques in Euskadi and Navarra share the **Spanish** habit of dining late. In the morning it's a coffee and a roll grabbed at the bar, followed by a huge meal at around 2 or 3pm, then after work at 8pm a few tapas at the bar to hold them over until supper at 10pm.

In non-touristy Spanish areas restaurants are inconspicuous and few. Just ask someone, and you will find a nice *comedor* with home cooking tucked in a back room behind a bar. If you dine where the locals do, you'll be assured of a good deal if not necessarily a good meal. Almost every restaurant offers a *menú del día* (usually only available on weekdays, as they are designed to cater for local workers) or a *menú turístico*, featuring an appetizer, a main course, dessert, bread and drink at a set price, always a certain percentage lower than if you had ordered the items *à la carte*.

French restaurants generally serve between 12 and 2pm and in the evening from 7 to 9pm, with later summer hours. In the southwest people tend to arrive early, to have a better choice of dishes and to get a crack at the specials or *plats du jour* – turn up at 1 for lunch or 8 for dinner and your choice may be very limited. All restaurants post menus outside the door so you'll know what to

Restaurant Price Categories

Price categories in the 'Eating Out' sections throughout this book indicate the cost of a three-course meal with wine for one person. The set menus can drop prices considerably.

expensive	€€€	over €45
moderate	€€	€25–45
inexpensive	€	under €25

expect; if prices aren't listed, you can bet it's not because they're a bargain. If you have the appetite to eat the biggest meal of the day at noon, you'll spend a lot less money.

In France, there's often a choice of dishes on the set price menu. Some restaurants offer a gourmet *menu dégustation* – a selection of chef's specialities, which can be a great treat. At the other end of the scale, in the bars and brasseries, is the no-choice *formule*, which is more often than not steak and *frites*. If you're vegetarian you may have a hard time, especially if you don't eat eggs or fish. But most establishments will try to accommodate you.

In **Spain**, unless it's explicitly written on the bill (*la cuenta*), service is not included in the total, so **tip** accordingly. In **France**, if service is included it will say *service compris* or s.c., if not *service non compris* or s.n.c.

For further information about eating and drinking in the Basque lands, including local specialities and wines and a menu decoder, *see* the **Food and Drink** chapter, pp.55–72.

Electricity

The current is 225 AC/220V, the same as most of Europe.

North Americans will need converters, and Brits will need the usual two-pin adapters for the different plugs.

Health and Emergencies

Ambulance t 112 (all of EU), t 15 (France)

Fire Brigade t 080 (Spain), t 18 (France)

Police t 091 (Spain), t 17 (France)

Emergencias Osakidetza (**Basque Emergency Health Service**), Spain, t 94 410 00 00

The tap water in both Spain and France is safe to drink, but at the slightest twinge of queasiness, switch to the bottled stuff.

Citizens of the EU are entitled to a certain amount of free medical care in EU countries if they have a European Health Insurance Card (EHIC). *See* **Planning Your Trip**, p.80.

In an emergency ask to be taken to the nearest *hospital de la seguridad social/urgences*. Tourist offices can supply lists of local English-speaking doctors, but, if it's not an emergency, consider consulting a **pharmacist** first. They are trained to administer first aid and dispense free advice for minor problems.

Make sure you save all doctor's receipts, pharmacy receipts and police documents (if you're reporting a theft).

Internet

Getting online is easy in **Spain**. WiFi is widely available in most hotels and some cafés (curiously, smaller establishments rarely charge for use, while the big hotels can charge up to €25 for 24 hours). Some cities, including Bilbao, have introduced free WiFi hotspots (check the website *www.bilbao.net*, which lists the locations in English).

Outside of big towns in the **French** Pays Basque, however, you'll be lucky to find any internet cafés, particularly inland; tourist offices should be able to guide you to the closest possibilities. However, most hotels usually offer WiFi – even the smallest and humblest establishments.

Natural Parks

The Basque country has several areas of outstanding natural beauty which have been designated Natural Parks or Biosphere Reservations. The **Uridaibai Reservation**, near Bermeo, covers the Gernika-Mundaka estuary and is an important migrating ground for barnacle geese, eider ducks and sawbills, among other species, which flock here on their way to the warmer African climates.

The **Pagoeta Natural Park**, inland from Orio and Zarautz, offers dense forests, river valleys and the impressive Hernio-Gaztume massif. Mountain birds such as the mountain greenfinch, pipits and peregrine falcons, and animals such as the cat-like genet, martens, badgers and foxes live here, and in autumn the leaves change colour dramatically. To the northeast, the monumental granite **Aia Rocks** (Aiako Harrio) are the oldest piece of land in the Basque country, with three main summits called the Three Crowns, the Battles or the Face of Napoleon – you may spot booted eagles, polecats and roe deer among the oak forests. There is a stunning 330ft waterfall in the Aitzondo gulley.

In the heart of Euskadi lies **Urkiola**, one of the least populated of the natural parks, which has inspired dozens of legends – Mari (*see* pp.45–6) was said to inhabit one of the spectacular caves scooped out of the limestone. All kinds of wildlife have made this area their home: vultures, peregrine falcons and Egyptian vultures circle lazily overhead and reptiles like the Seoane viper and the green lizard sun themselves on the rocks.

The **Aralar Sierra**, part of which is in Navarra, has the greatest density of dolmens in the region; the emblematic silhouette of Txindoki (also known as Larrunari) can be seen from afar and is a much-loved symbol of Guipúzcoa. The sierra has provided grazing grounds for millennia, and tiny shepherds' huts dot the landscape. There is wonderful walking among the beech woods, and lots of waterfalls along the Amundarain river.

The **Gorbea Massif** is the highest point in Vizcaya and was once one of the five Basque 'signal' mountains, when messages were sent by horn or fire to the surrounding villages. There are several pretty hermitages lost in the forests and valleys and the park is home to birds of prey as well as kingfishers, the aquatic blackbird and otters. **Aizkorri**, spreading into Navarra, has dolmens, cave remains and other megalithic monuments as well as the lovely Sanctuary of the Virgin of Arantzazu. Beech groves, oak forests, peat bogs and limestone crags are home to a wide variety of birds and beasts: wild boar, martens and snow rats, as well as the Egyptian vulture, chough and mountain greenfinch.

The **Entzia Sierra**, which spreads across the Navarrese border, is a very popular spot for walking and mountaineering, partly because it is easily accessed (from the delightful village of Salvatierra, for example). There are stunning beech groves, some curious megalithic monuments and several species of fauna: jays, royal redstars, birds of prey, peat-bog lizards, polecats and wild boar. The **Izki mountains**, in the southeastern corner of Álava, are covered with magnificent white oak forests and dotted with peat bogs and small springs. Abrupt limestone crags offer spectacular views across the surrounding Álavan mountains. You might spot a golden eagle, eagle owl, goshawk or spotted woodpecker, or catch a glimpse of an otter, or the flash of a kingfisher upriver.

Over in Navarra, the **Parque Natural del Señorío de Bértiz** in the Bidasoa valley has a dense oak, beech and chestnut forest attached to a park of exotic trees. And up in the Salazar valley, in the Pyrenees of Navarra, the **Forest of Irati** is not only the largest primeval beech and yew forest in Spain, but has more animal species than most places in the mountains, including the extremely rare white-backed woodpecker and the Pyrenean aquatic shrew.

To the south, near Lumbier, the **Foz de Arbayún** is one of Spain's most spectacular gorges, with soaring, sheer-sided limestone walls. This is the home of Spain's largest colonies of mighty griffon vultures and eagles. In southern Navarra, near Tudela, you'll find the most exotic natural park of them all, the **Bardenas Reales**, a slice of Arizona's Monument Valley.

Although the Pays Basque doesn't have any natural parks, it does have places that are beautiful, quiet and unspoiled. The holy mountain of **La Rhune**, reached by a tramway and covered with megalithic monuments, is one; the so-called '*Route des Contrebandiers*' (smugglers) over the Pyrenees between Sare and Zugarramurdi, and the valleys around St-Jean-Pied-de-Port are others, especially if you aim for the primeval beech **Forêt d'Orion**.

Opening Hours, Museums and National Holidays

Shops

Spain: Shops usually open at 9.30am, boutiques an hour or so later. Spaniards take their main meal at 2pm and, except in the larger cities, most shops close for 2–3 hours in the afternoon, usually from 1pm or 2pm. In the evening, most establishments stay open until 7 or 8pm.

France: Most shops close on Sunday afternoons and some on Mondays, though some grocers and *supermarchés* open on Monday afternoons. In many towns, Sunday morning is a big shopping period. Markets (daily in cities, weekly in villages) are usually mornings only, although clothes, flea and antiques markets run into the afternoon.

Banks

Spain: Mon–Fri 8.30–2. A few open until 4pm on Thursdays.

France: 8.30–12.30 and 1.30–4. They close on Sunday, and most close either on Saturday or Monday as well.

Post Offices

Spain: Main **post office** opening hours are Mon–Fri 8.30–8.30, Sat 9.30–1, but smaller branches may open only in the morning.

National Holidays

On national holidays, banks, shops and businesses close. In France, some museums and most restaurants stay open, while in Spain you are likely to find many establishments shut.

1 January New Year's Day
6 January Epiphany (Spain)
Holy Thursday (Spain)
Good Friday (Spain)
Easter Sunday
Easter Monday (France)
1 May Labour Day
8 May Victory Day (France)
Ascension Day (France)
Pentecost (Whitsun) and Monday (France)
Corpus Christi May/June (Spain)
14 July Bastille Day (France)
25 July St James' Day (Spain)
15 August Assumption
12 October Columbus Day (Spain)
1 November All Saints' Day
11 November First World War Armistice (France)
6 December Constitution Day (Spain)
8 December Immaculate Conception (Spain)
25 December Christmas Day

Many post offices close early in summer, particularly in August.

France: In the cities, opening hours are Mon–Fri 8–7, Sat 8–12. In villages, offices may not open until 9am and close at 4.30 or 5pm; they also close for lunch.

Museums

We've done our best to include opening hours in the text, but don't be surprised if they're not exactly right, as they are liable to change. Most close on national holidays and give discounts if you have a student ID card, or are an EU citizen under 18 or over 65 years old; most charge admission.

Spain: Museums and historical sites tend to follow shop hours, though they are shorter in winter. Nearly all close on Mondays. Seldom-visited sites have a raffish disregard for their official hours, or open only when the mood strikes them. Don't be discouraged: bang on doors and ask around.

France: With a few exceptions, museums close on Mondays or Tuesdays, and for lunch, and sometimes for all of November or the entire winter. Hours change with the season: longer summer hours begin in May or June and last until September – usually. Some places change their hours every month.

Churches

Spain: Most of the less important churches are always closed. If you're determined to see one, it will never be hard to find the *sacristán*, or caretaker. Usually they live close by and will be glad to show you around for a tip. Don't be surprised when cathedrals and famous churches charge for admission – just consider the cost of upkeep.

France: Churches are usually either open all day, or closed all day and only open for mass. Sometimes notes on the door direct you to the *mairie* or *presbytère* (priest's house), where you can pick up the key. If not, ask at the nearest house – they may well have it. There are often admission fees for cloisters, crypts and special chapels.

Post Offices

Every city in **Spain**, regardless of size, seems to have one post office (*correos*) and no more.

Send everything by airmail (*por avión*) and don't send postcards unless you don't care when they arrive. **Postboxes** (marked *correos*) are bright yellow.

You can receive mail *poste restante* (in Spanish, *lista de correos*) at any main post office; the postal codes in this book should help your mail get there in a timely fashion. To collect it, bring some ID.

In **France**, post offices are known as PTT or *bureaux de poste* and are marked by a blue bird on a yellow background. For opening hours, *see left*.

Post offices will often be crowded, but unless you have packages to send you may never need visit one: most tobacconists sell stamps and they'll usually know the correct postage for whatever you're sending.

Shopping

In most villages and towns, market day is the event of the week, and rightfully so. Celebrated for their fresh farm produce, markets are fun to visit, and become even more interesting if you're cooking for yourself or are just gathering the ingredients for a picnic. In the larger cities they take place every day, while smaller towns and villages have markets but once a week; they double as social occasions for the locals. Most finish at around noon.

With a striking inclination for combining beauty and utility, Basque artisans excel at the simple things of everyday life: furniture and woodcarving, and especially linens. *Linge basque*, whether factory-made or woven on an old wooden loom, may be your best bet for a beautiful and practical souvenir. Other archetypal Basque buys are hand-sewn espadrilles, berets, sheep's cheese, ham, red peppers (dried whole, powdered or in a paste), bottles of wine or *patxaran* (Basque firewater), figurines (Christmas crib or characters from Basque folklore) and recordings of traditional music.

For the ultimate Basque souvenir, a *makila* (walking stick), the best place is the 200-year-old family firm of Ainciart-Bergara (*www.makhila.com*), in the village of Larressore, or else the Fabrique de Makilas on Rue de la Vieille Boucherie in old Bayonne – but they don't come cheap.

Sports and Activities

The Basque country's rare combination of ocean, rivers and mountains offers plenty of opportunities to play in the great outdoors. The Basques themselves are crazy about sport, from football to running in front of bulls, and have even invented a few games of their own (see pp.51–4) that you can attempt – or at least lose some money on.

Individual tourist offices in the regions have literally reams of information on local activities. If you speak some Spanish, a wide range of adventure sports from paragliding to white-water rafting in the Basque country are offered by dozens of 'active tourism' companies, including **Troka Abentura**, *www.troka.com*. Several other companies are listed at *www.bideak-navarraactiva.com*.

The Basque government publishes several helpful leaflets, with comprehensive lists of local tour operators, and guides to which sports are on offer where, including *Everything Worth Seeing, Visiting and Knowing in Euskadi, The Active Basque Country* and, for Spanish-speakers, *Espacios Naturales y Tursimo Activo*. These are worth ordering in advance if you are interested in adventure sports.

Bullfighting

The *corrida* is still big in parts of Northern Spain, although its popularity has waned considerably in the last decades. A recent poll showed that less than 10 per cent of Spaniards were in favour of bullfighting, and in Catalunya it has now been completely banned on the grounds of cruelty.

In Spanish newspapers, you will not find accounts of the bullfights (*corridas*) on the sports pages: you should look in the 'arts and culture' section, for that is how Spain has always thought of this singular spectacle. Bullfighting combines elements of ballet with the primal finality of Greek tragedy. To Spaniards, it is a ritual sacrifice without a religion, and it divides the nation irreconcilably between those who find it brutal and demeaning and those who couldn't live without it.

The origins of bullfighting are obscure and a continuing source of debate. Some claim it

Bullfight Calendar

Corridas tend to coincide with the big holidays; see box.

6–14 July Pamplona (Los Sanfermines)
14 July Bayonne, which also has fights most weekends, and on 14–15 Aug
25 July and 4–9 Aug Vitoria-Gasteiz
8–15 Aug Donostia-San Sebastián
3rd week in Aug Bilbao

derives from Roman circus games, others that it started with the Moors, or in the Middle Ages, when the bull faced a mounted knight with a lance. The present form of bullfighting had its beginnings around the year 1800 in Ronda in Andalucía, when Francisco Romero developed the basic pattern of the modern *corrida*; some of his moves and passes are still in use today. Fernando VII, the reactionary post-Napoleonic Spanish monarch who also brought back the Inquisition, founded the Royal School of Bullfighting in Seville, and promoted the spectacle across the land.

In keeping with its ritualistic aura, the *corrida* is one of the few things in Spain that begins strictly on time. The show commences with the colourful entry of the *cuadrillas* (teams of bullfighters or *toreros*) and the *alguaciles*, officials dressed in 17th-century costume, who salute the 'president' of the fight. Usually three teams fight two bulls each, the whole performance taking only about two hours.

Each of the six fights, however, is a self-contained drama performed in four acts. First, upon the entry of the bull, the members of the *cuadrilla* tease him a bit, and the *matador*, the team leader, plays him with the cape to test his qualities.

Next come the *picadores*, riding on padded horses, whose task is to slightly wound the bull in the neck with a short lance or *pica*. They are accompanied by the *banderilleros*, who deftly plant sharp darts in the bull's back while avoiding the sweep of its dangerous horns. The effect of these wounds is to weaken the bull physically without diminishing any of its fighting spirit, and to force it to keep its head lower for the third and most artistic stage of the fight, when the lone *matador* conducts his *pas de deux* with the deadly, if doomed, animal.

Ideally, this is the transcendent moment, the *matador* leading the bull in deft passes and finally crushing its spirit with a tiny cape called a *muleta*. Now the defeated bull is ready for 'the moment of truth'. The kill must be clean and quick, a sword thrust right to the heart. The corpse is then dragged out by horses to the waiting butchers behind the scenes.

More often than not the job is botched. Most bullfights, in fact, are a disappointment, especially if the *matadores* are beginners, or *novios*, but to the aficionado the chance to see one or all of the stages performed to perfection makes it all worthwhile. When a *matador* is good, the band plays and the hats and handkerchiefs fly; a truly excellent performance earns as a reward from the president one of the bull's ears, or both; or rarely, for an exceptionally brilliant performance, both ears and the tail.

You'll be lucky to see a bullfight at all; there are only about 500 each year in Spain, mostly coinciding with holidays or a town's fiesta. Tickets can be astronomically expensive and hard to come by, especially for a well-known *matador*; sometimes ticket touts buy the whole lot. Buy in advance, if you can, and directly from the *plaza de toros* to avoid the hefty commission charges. Prices vary according to the sun – the most expensive seats are entirely in the shade.

Bull-running

The biggest and most famous bull-running festival is **Los Sanfermines** in Pamplona (*see* pp.211–12), but bull-running (called *encierros* in Spanish) is also a highlight of plenty of local festivals in the smaller villages of central Navarra. The custom dates back to the times when herds of cattle were chased down from their summer pastures in the mountains, a hair-raising journey which now takes place in the village streets.

The most popular *encierros* outside Pamplona take place in Tudela (last week of July), Pilón (last week of August), Tafalla (20 January) and Sangüesa (mid-September) during their local festivals.

Caves

Speleology, potholing, spelunking – whatever you want to call it, it's very popular.

Euskadi

Several adventure tourism companies in Euskadi offer potholing trips, including:

Uraik Aventura, Huertas de la Villa 5, 4th floor, 48007 Bilbao, t 94 445 19 73.

Naturlan, Avda Aguirre 11, 48014 Bilbao, t 94 947 78 11, www.naturlan.es.

Lurraska Centro Medioambiental, B. Kanpantxu, Ajangiz, t 94 625 72 45, www.lurraska.com.

Pays Basque

Cocktail Aventure, Herran, Haute-Garonne, t 05 61 97 52 74.

Fédération Française de Spéléologie, 28 rue Delandine, Lyon, t 04 72 56 09 63, http://ffspeleo.fr.

Comité de Spéléologie Régionale Midi-Pyrénées, 7 Rue André-Citroën, 31130 Balma, t 08 73 18 03 28, www.comite-speleo-midipy.com.

Cycling

See 'Getting Around', pp.87–8.

Deep-sea Diving

The Côte Basque has a number of schools that also hire out equipment.

Union Sportive de Biarritz, Allée des Passereaux, Biarritz, t 05 59 03 29 29, http://union.sportive.free.fr.

Fédération Française d'Etudes et de Sports Sous-Marins, 24 Quai de Rive-Neuve, 13284 Marseille, t 04 91 33 99 31, www.ffessm.fr.

Fishing

This is a popular pastime in the Basque region. You can fish in the sea without a permit as long as your catch is for local consumption. Freshwater fishing (extremely popular in this region of rivers and lakes) requires an easily obtained permit from a local club; tourist offices can tell you where to find them. Often the only outdoor vending machine in a town sells worms and other bait. Ocean-fishing excursions (for tuna and other denizens of the deep) are organized by the day and half-day, arranged in advance.

Contact local tourist offices for details of the necessary licences.

Football (Soccer)

In Bilbao, football is a passion (*see* p.137); in Donostia-San Sebastián it ranks not far behind food.

Goitibehera

In Basque this means 'from up to down', and it is just that: an unmotorized soapbox derby for home-made three-wheeled vehicles, many of which bear more than a passing resemblance to a wheelbarrow. Naturally, only the steepest, most winding mountain roads are chosen for the course, although in an attempt to spare life and limb the most dangerous sections are lined with tyres and hay bales. It's a popular summer sport throughout the Basque lands; in the north, the *Goitibehera* championship takes place over a month in three stages, at Ustaritz, Ascain and Hasparren.

Golf

In the 19th century, the English introduced golf to Biarritz (which now has some of France's oldest courses), while employees built Spain's first golf course at the Rio Tinto mines.

Most golf courses hire out clubs. Green fees have taken a leap in recent years, however, and even the humblest clubs charge €18. On the French side, you'll find some of the oldest and most beautiful fairways. Summer green fees for 18 holes are €45–53.

Euskadi and Navarra

Bilbao: Real Sociedad Golf Neguri, t 94 491 02 00.

Hondarribia: Golf de Hondarribia (Real Club de Golf de San Sebastián), t 94 361 68 45.

Pamplona: Golf Gorraiz, Valle de Egües, t 94 833 70 73, *www.golfgorraiz.es*; Valle de la Ulzama, Ctra Ostiz-Lizaso Km.6.8, t 94 830 51 62, *www.ulzama.com*.

Donostia-San Sebastián: Golf de Basozabal, Camino de Goyaz-Txiki 41, t 94 346 76 42.

Urturi: Hotel Borja y Yon Golf (designed by Severiano Ballesteros), t 94 537 82 32.

Vitoria: Complejo Izki Golf, t 94 537 82 62, *www.izkigolf.com*.

Zarautz: Real Club de Golf, t 94 383 01 45.

Pays Basque

Anglet: Golf de Chiberta, t 05 59 63 83 20.

Arcangues: t 05 59 43 10 56.

Bassussarry: Makila Golf, t 05 59 58 42 42.

Biarritz: Le Phare, t 05 59 03 71 80.

Ciboure: Golf de la Nivelle, t 05 59 47 18 99.

St-Jean-de-Luz: Chantaco, t 05 59 26 14 22.

Souraïde: Golf Epherra, t 05 59 93 84 06.

Fédération Française de Golfe, 68 Rue Anatole France, 92300 Levallois-Perret, t 01 41 49 77 00, *www.ffgolf.org*.

Harri Alzatzea (Force Basque)

Don't pass up a chance to watch the Basques flex their mighty muscles (*see* p.51). *Force basque* competitions are usually held in July and August. Many villages put something on for Basque Sports Week, the second week in August; the biggest festivals are at St-Palais (in August) and St-Etienne-de-Baïgorry (mid-July and early August).

Horse-riding

Tourist offices have lists of riding centres that hire out horses. Most offer group excursions, although if you prove yourself an experienced rider you can usually head off down the trails on your own.

The Basque government publications listed on p.100 include a comprehensive list of horse-riding centres. You'll also find online lists at *www.fvh.org* (Basque Horse-riding Federation), *www.fnhipica.com* (Navarrese Horse-riding Federation); and at *www.fref-france.com*, the French Horse-riding Federation.

Microlites

For microlite clubs (ULM in French) in the Pays Basque, try **Planet'Air**, Chemin de Brané, Navarrenx, t 05 59 66 23 37.

Pelota/Jaï-Alaï/Pelote

The Basques invented the fastest game in the world (*see* pp.51–2) and show no sign of slowing down. In summer, matches take place at least once a week and there are games indoors year-round in the *trinquetes*, which are let out by the hour if you feel like playing. Serious summer training courses can be arranged on either side of the border through the federations.

International Pelota Federation, C/Bernardino Tirapu 67, Pamplona, **t** 94 816 40 80, *www.fipv.net*.

Fédération Française de Pelote Basque, Trinquet Moderne, 60 Avenue Dubrocq, 64100 Bayonne, **t** 05 59 59 22 34, *www.ffpb.net*.

Most of the championships are held in the summer. One of the biggest events is the August International *Cesta Punta au Jaï-Alaï* tournament in St-Jean-de-Luz.

Rowing Regattas

The Basques have been fishing in small boats (*traineras*) in the open sea for over a thousand years, and some say they may have even invented the regatta. The biggest events are in July, at St-Jean-de-Luz, and in September, in Bilbao and San Sebastián.

Rugby

The sturdy Basque physique makes for natural rugby players, and there are usually one or two Basques on the French national team (Imanol Harinordoquy is from Biarritz and former French rugby captain Raphaël Ibañez is also a Basque). Bayonne always fields a good team, and in the summer rugby tournaments (*le rugbeach*) are organized on the sands.

The Côte Basque rugby committee, **t** 05 59 63 36 57, *www.comitecbl.com*, has schedules.

Skiing

The Pyrenees don't get as much of the white stuff as the Alps and anyway, snow has been fiendishly unpredictable of late. The Basque region is at the westernmost end of the French Pyrenees, where rains and mists

can be troublesome. Resorts include **Iraty**, **t** 05 59 28 51 29 (cross-country, 3,940–4,920ft/1,313–1,640m), and **St-Jean-Pied-de-Port**, **t** 05 59 28 51 29 (cross-country and snowshoes, 3,280–4,760ft/1,093–1,386m).

Fédération Française de Ski, 50 Rue des Marquisats, 74011 Annecy, **t** 04 50 51 40 34, *www.ffs.fr*.

Surfing

Surf bums from all across Europe flock in late summer to ride the big rollers that hit the Bay of Biscay. Hendaye, St-Jean-de-Luz, Anglet, Guéthary and Biarritz are the major spots on the French side (for wave conditions, contact **Ocean Surf Report**, **t** 08 92 68 13 60, *www.surf-report.com*).

In Euskadi, San Sebastián, Zarautz, Mundaka, Bakio, and Punta Galea and Sopelana near Bilbao, are the main centres. There are schools to learn and world championships to watch, but you'll also find plenty of small clubs that hire out both surfboards and body boards.

Walking

See 'Special-interest Operators', p.92.

Practical companions if you are walking the road to Santiago include: *Walking the Camino de Santiago* by Davies and Cole (Pili Pala Press, 2003); *A Pilgrim's Guide to the Camino Frances* by John Brierley (Findhorn Press, 2003), *The Pilgrimage Road to Santiago* by Gitlitz and Davidson (St Martin's Press, 2000).

Telephones

Calls within **Spain** are expensive (25–80 cents for a short local call), and overseas calls from Spain are among the most expensive in Europe: calls to the UK cost about €2 a minute, to the USA substantially more. Most tobacconists sell PIN-**phonecards** that make international phone calls much cheaper.

Public **phone booths** have instructions in English and accept phonecards, from news stands, tobacconists and post offices. In some Spanish phone booths, there will also be a little slide on top that holds coins.

In every big city (and many smaller ones) in Spain, there are **calling centres** (*locutorios*) where you telephone from a metered booth. These offer cheap international calls, but national calls or calls to mobiles are expensive. They open and close with alarming frequency but can usually be found around bus and train stations. Expect to pay a big surcharge if you make any phone calls from your hotel. For directory enquiries, dial **t** 11811.

Calling internationally from **France** is a bit cheaper. Nearly all **public telephones** have switched over from using coins to *télécartes*, which you can purchase at any post office or newsstand at €7.41 for 50 *unités* or €14.74 for 120 *unités*. The easiest way to **reverse charges** is to spend a few euros ringing the number and giving your number in France (always posted by public phones). For **directory enquiries**, dial **t** 118 000, or see *www.pagesjaunes.com* (the French *Yellow Pages* online) or try your luck and patience on the free, slow, inefficient Minitel electronic directory in post offices.

In both countries, telephone codes have now been incorporated into the telephone numbers. All numbers in this guide are listed as they must be dialled. If you're ringing from abroad, the code for Spain is 34 followed by the number; for France the code is 33, but drop the first zero of the 10 digit number.

For international calls from Spain, dial **t** 00, wait for the higher tone and then dial the country code and the rest of the number (omitting the zero in any area code). To make an international call from France, dial **t** 00, then the country code and the number. Country codes are: Australia 61, New Zealand 64, Canada 1, Republic of Ireland 353, UK 44, and USA 1.

Time

France and Spain are one hour ahead of UK time and six hours ahead of North American EST. Summer time runs from the last Sunday in March to the last Sunday in October; clocks change on those days.

Toilets

Apart from bus and train stations, public facilities are rare on both sides of the border. On the other hand, every bar on every corner has a toilet. Just ask for *los servicios* in Spain, *les toilettes* in France, and take your own toilet paper to be on the safe side.

Bilbao

Not so long ago, if you were to say that Bilbao was destined to become an international art Mecca, the select few who had ever visited the place would have laughed in your face. Bilbao meant rusty old steel mills and shipping. Travellers who weren't there on business didn't linger, unless they got lost in the maddening traffic system. Getting lost, however, would have allowed more people to better appreciate Bilbao's uncommon setting, tucked in the lush green folds of Euskadi's coastal mountains, the city filling up every possible pocket for miles along the Nervión.

07

Don't miss

⭐ Frank Gehry's titanium masterpiece
Guggenheim Museum **p.122**

⭐ Walking around medieval Bilbao
The Siete Calles **p.112**

⭐ A fine art collection
Museo de Bellas Artes **p.118**

⭐ Contemporary art – with a pool
Alhóndiga **p.117**

⭐ A ritual bar crawl with *pintxos*
An evening *txikiteo* **p.146**

See map overleaf

MADARIAGA

PLAZA
SAN PÍO
X

HERMANOS AGUIRRE

FRANCISCO MACÍA

PUENTE DE DEUSTO

AVENIDA DE LAS UNIVERSIDADES

Universidad
de Deusto

HELIODORO DE LA TORRE

LUIS POWER

AS DE OTERO

RIBERA DE BOTICA

RIBERA DE DEUSTO

Ría de Bilbao

MUELLE DE EVARISTO CHURRUCA

ABANDOIBARRA

*Museo
Guggenheim*

AVENIDA DE LERCHUNDI

ABANDOIBARRA

PUENTE DE LA SALVE

PUENTE EUSKALDUNA

*Palacio Euskalduna de Congresos y
de la Música*

ALAMEDA DE MAZARREDO

*Museo Marítimo
Ría de Bilbao*

PLAZA
DEL SAGRADO
CORAZÓN

PASEO JOSÉ ANSELMO CLAVÉ

*Parque de Doña
Casilda de Iturrizar*

PLAZA
EUSKADI

*Museo de
Bellas Artes*

ALAMEDA DE RECALDE

LERSUNDI

LOS HEROS

ALAMEDA DE

CECHEBARRIETA

*Campo de
San Mamés*

AVENIDA DE SABINO ARANA

GRAN VÍA DE DON DIEGO LÓPEZ DE HARO

PLAZA
TEÓFILO
GUIARD

COLÓN

PLAZA
SAN JOSÉ

HENAO

ELCANO

IPARRAGUIRRE

HENAO

ERCILLA

LUIS BRIÑAS

RODRÍGUEZ ARIAS

MARÍA DÍAZ DE HARO

ALAMEDA DOCTOR AREILZA

PLAZA DE
CAMPUZANO

RODRÍGUEZ ARIAS

PLAZA
SAN JOSÉ DE LARREATEGUI

ABANDO

PLAZA
ENSANCHE

COLÓN DE LARR

PLAZA
VÍCTOR
CHÁVARRI

ALAMEDA DE URQUIJO

LICENCIADO
POZA

INDAUTXU

PLAZA
DE FEDERICO
MOYÚA

M

GRAN VÍA DE DON DIEGO L

DIPUTACIÓN

ASTARLOA

LEDES

SIMÓN

JOSÉ MARÍA ESCUZA

MARÍA DÍAZ DE HARO

ALAMEDA DOCTOR AREILZA

GREGORIO DE LA REVILLA

M

PLAZA DE
INDAUTXU

PLAZA
PÁRROCO
GARAIZAR

ESPAÑA

IPARRAGUIRRE

ALAMEDA DE RECALDE

Rodríguez
Arias

PLAZA PEDRO
EGUILLOR

*Palacio
Foral*

GENERAL CONCHA

LICENCIADO POZA

ELCANO

ALAMEDA DE URQUIJO

AVENIDA DEL FERROCARRIL

BOLÍVAR

MANUEL ALLENDE

GORDÓNIZ

ALAMEDA DE SAN MAMÉS

PLAZA DE
ARRIQUIBAR

Alhóndiga

FERNÁNDEZ DE CAMPO

EUSKALDUNA

PLAZA DEL
BOMBERO
ETXANIZ

IPARRAGUIRRE

EGAÑA

AUTONOMÍA

ALAMEDA DE RECALDE

GENERAL CONCHA

HURTADO DE AMÉZAGA

JUAN DE GARCÍA SALAZAR

SAN FR

AUTONOMÍA

ZUGASTINOVIA

PLAZA
GUARDIA
CIVIL

AMETZOLA

LABAYRU

PLAZA DE
ZABÁLBURU

PM ARTOLA

LAS CORTES

PLAZA
GENERAL
LATORRE

AVENIDA DEL FERROCARRIL

ALZOLA

GORDÓNIZ

GENERAL SALAZAR

PLAZA MACHÍN
AMETZOLA

PABLO PICASSO

*Museo
Taurino*

M

SAN

*ento de
uchinos*

VICTOR DÍAZ EMPARANZA

*Park
Ametzola*

*Plaza
de Toros
Vista Alegre*

IRALA

AVENIDA KIRKIÑO

JUAN DE GARCÍA SALAZAR

CAMILO VILLABASO

TA SOLUCIÓN SUR

DOCTOR DÍAZ EMPARANZA

ANDRÉS ISASÍ

IRALA

AVENIDA KIRKIÑO

JUAN DE GARCÍA SALAZAR

ZABALA

N

Don't miss

☆ Guggenheim Museum p.122

☆ The Siete Calles p.112

☆ Museo de Bellas Artes p.118

☆ Alhóndiga p.117

☆ An evening *txikiteo* p.146

VÍA VIEJA DE LEZAMA

VÍA VIEJA DE

AVENIDA DE MAURICE RAVEL

URIBARRI

PLAZA SALVE

CASTAÑOS

TÍBOLI

CASTAÑOS

Funicular de Artxanda

HUERTAS DE LA VILLA

PLAZA DE MORAZA

PASEO CAMPO DE VOLANTÍN

PLAZA DE LA VILLA

ANSELMA DE SALCES

TÍBOLI

MATIKO

URIBARRI

TRAVESÍA DE URIBARRI

MONTE

AVENIDA DE ZUMALAKARREGI

PUENTE ZUBIZURI

URIBITARTE

MAZARREDO

Parque de Etxebarria

AVENIDA DE ZUMALAKARREGI

MUELLE DE URIBITARTE

URIBITARTE PÍO BAROJA

PLAZA

Ayuntamiento

PLAZA ERNESTO ERKOREKA

QUITANA

ALAMEDA DE MAZARREDO

PLAZA SAN VICENTE

San Vicente Mártir

Jardines de Albia

PRÉATEGUI DE MAZARREDO

BERÁSTEGUI

PUENTE DEL AYUNTAMIENTO

SENDEJA

VILLARÍAS

RIPA

VIUDA DE EPALZA

ESPERANZA

LÓPEZ DE HARO

PLAZA CIRCULAR

Ⓜ Estación de Abando

Estación de Santander

NAVARRA PUENTE DEL ARENAL

Paseo del Arenal

San Nicolás

PLAZA DE LOS FUEROS

BEGOÑA

VIRGEN DE BEGOÑA

HURTADO DE AMÉZAGA

BAILÉN

LA RIBERA

SANTA MARÍA

JARDINES

VÍCTOR

PERRO

PLAZA DE ARRIAGA

i 🏛 Teatro Arriaga

CORREO

SOMBRERERÍA

PLAZA NUEVA

PLAZA DE MIGUEL DE UNAMUNO Ⓜ

PRIM

ITURRIBIDE

To Basilica Nuestra Señora de Begoña

AMADEO DEPRIT

BIDEBARRIETA

CASCO VIEJO

LOTERÍA BANCO DE ESPAÑA

Museo Vasco

PRIM

ITURRIBIDE

DOS DE MAYO

HERNANI

PUENTE DE LA MERCED

PLAZA SANTIAGO

✝ Catedral

ARTEKALE

SOMERA

PLAZA ZUMÁRRAGA

SOLOKOETXE

FRANCISCO

PLAZA CORAZÓN DE MARÍA

Museo de Reproducciones Artísticas

PUENTE DE LA RIBERA

JULIÁN ECHEVARRÍA CAMARÓN

LA LONDA

PELOTA

RONDA

ZUMÁRRAGA

FIKA

ZABALBIDE

ITURRIBIDE

CONCEPCIÓN

LA RIBERA

MUELLE DE MARZANA

PLAZA SANTOS JUANES

SAN ANTÓN

ZABALBIDE

SANTUTXU

FRANCISCO

Mercado

Río de Nervión

SAN FRANCISCO

LA CONCEPCIÓN

ATXURI

FIKA

Monte de Miribilla

Estación de Atxuri

PLAZA DE LA ENCARNACIÓN

Diocesan Museum of Sacred Art

ATXURI

FIKA

PLAZA DEL CARMEN

250 metres
250 yards

The city's name is Bilbo in Basque, just like the hobbit, but its inhabitants lovingly call it the *Botxo*, the Basque word for hole, or orifice. The orifice was originally a scattering of fishing hamlets huddled on the left bank of a deep *ría*, where the hills offered some protection from the Normans and other pirates. In 1300, when the coast was clear of such dangers, the lord of Vizcaya, Diego López de Haro, founded a new town on the right bank of the Ría de Bilbao. It quickly developed into the Basques' leading port and Spain's main link to northern Europe, exporting Castile's wool to Flanders and the swords Shakespeare called 'bilbos'. In 1511 the merchants formed a council to govern their affairs, the Consulado de Bilbao, an institution that survived and thrived until 1829.

The 19th century had various tricks in store: the indignity of a French sacking in 1808, and sieges by the Carlists in both of their wars; Bilbao was the 'martyr city' of the Liberal cause. But the 19th century also made Bilbao into a great industrial dynamo. Blessed with its fabled iron mountain, nearby forests, cheap hydraulic power and excellent port, Bilbao got a double dose of the Industrial Revolution. Steel mills, shipbuilding and other industries sprang up, quickly followed by banks and insurance companies and all the other accoutrements of capitalism. Workers from across the country poured into gritty tenements, and smoke clogged the air. It became the fifth city of Spain, and still is; it was Spain's Pittsburgh, and still looks like it, and back at the turn of the last century it was just as full of worker misery and exploitation. Social activism combined with Basque nationalism made a sturdy anti-fascist cocktail; during the Civil War, Bilbao was besieged again and Franco punished it crushingly. Then, in the late 1950s, Bilbao was whipped forward to become once more the industrial powerhouse of Spain, but on an artificial life-support system that was unplugged in the new Spain of the EU. The iron mines gave out. In the 1980s, unemployment soared from 6 per cent to 20 per cent.

Something had to be done to save the *Botxo* from becoming a real hole, and the Basques found the political will to do it. Thanks to banking, insurance and such less obviously dirty business, the economy was doing pretty well in spite of all the lay-offs, and this allowed the city to embark on an ambitious redevelopment programme, reclaiming vast areas of the centre formerly devoted to heavy industry. The rusting machinery has been removed and the once-seedy dock area gentrified. The hugely popular Guggenheim Museum, which opened in 1997, has by itself significantly boosted the city's prestige, attracting around 100,000 visitors annually. Other new projects include César Pelli's soaring Torre Iberdrola, one of the tallest skyscrapers in Spain, completed in 2011, and Philippe Starck's conversion of an old wine warehouse, the Alhóndiga, into a superb arts and leisure centre (2010). These

Getting to Bilbao

By Air

Bilbao's **airport** lies 10km north of the city centre in Loui and is the busiest in northern Spain, with regular flights from London, Manchester, Dublin, Paris, Brussels, Frankfurt, Munich and Milan, and from most airports in Spain (for information, t 91 321 10 00, *www.aena.es*).

There is also an **airport bus** service (no. A-3247, **t** 902 222 265), which runs roughly every 20mins from 6.20am to midnight to the Plaza Moyúa (with a metro connection) with stops at Gran Vía 79, and Alameda Recalde 11 (note that the bus back to the airport runs roughly every 20mins from 5.20am to 10pm). A **train line** is under construction. The bus fare is included in the Creditrans ticket (*see* 'Getting around Bilbao', p.110).

Note: If you arrive early for your departing flight, don't go through the departure gates until you have to, as there are very few facilities.

Airline Numbers in Bilbao

Air Europa: t 902 310 510, *www.air-europa.com*.
Aer Lingus: t 902 502 737, *www.aerlingus.com*.
Air Berlin: t 901 320 737, *www.airberlin.com*.
Air France: t 94 486 97 50, or **t** 902 207 090, *www.airfrance.com*.
Alitalia: t 94 486 97 85, or **t** 90 210 03 23, *www.alitalia.com*.
easyJet: t 90 229 99 92, *www.easyjet.com*.
Iberia: t 902 400 500, *www.iberia.com*.
Lufthansa: t 902 883 882, *www.lufthansa.com*.
Spanair: t 902 131 415, *www.spanair.es*.
Vueling: t 902 333 933, *www.vueling.com*.

By Train

Bilbao has several train lines and about a dozen stations, although as a non-suburban commuter you have to be aware of only three of them.

The main **RENFE** station, **Estación de Abando** (**t** 902 320 320, *www.renfe.es* for information), on Plaza Circular, has connections to France, Madrid, Barcelona and Galicia. Next to Abando, at C/Bailén 2, facing the river with a colourful tiled front, is the **Estación de Santander** (**t** 94 423 22 66, *www.feve.es*), also known as **La Concordia**, where scenic narrow-gauge **FEVE** trains set off for Santander and Oviedo.

The pretty little **Estación de Atxuri**, at C/Atxuri 6 in the Casco Viejo, is used by the Basque regional line, **EuskoTren, t** 902 543 210, *www.euskotren.es*, running slow but equally scenic services to Donostia-San Sebastián by way of Durango, Zarautz and Zumaia. A separate line serves Gernika, Mundaka and Bermeo.

By Bus

All inter-city bus lines arrive and depart from **Termibús** (**t** 94 439 5077, *www.termibus.es*) near San Mamés stadium. There are hourly services to Donostia-San Sebastián, Vitoria and Santander, and several buses a day to Pamplona, Madrid, Barcelona, Galicia and Castilla-León.

BizkaiBus (**t** 902 222 265, *www.bizkaia.net*) serves destinations within Vizcaya, including Durango, Gernika and the coastal villages, from Termibús and from stops around the city (these are listed, along with timetables, on its useful website).

By Car

Bilbao is well connected to France and other major Spanish cities – the only problem is that each motorway has several different numbers, reflecting the slow standardization of motorway identification numbers throughout Europe. Motorway tolls in Spain are expensive.

For Madrid take the *autovía* (A68/E-80) to Burgos and then the A1/E-5 motorway from there.

For Barcelona, take the AP-68 motorway to Zaragoza, then the AP-2/E-90.

Closer at hand, the A-8/E-70 motorway runs between Bilbao and Donostia-San Sebastián, from where it soon becomes the A63 (also known as the E-5, E-70, and E-80) and crosses into France.

By Ferry

Brittany Ferries operate a twice-weekly service from Portsmouth to Bilbao, which arrives in the suburb of Santurtzi, 13km from the centre of town. There is an information and booking office at Muelle Vizkaya, Espigón 3, **t** 94 236 0611.

Getting around Bilbao

Nearly all of Bilbao's attractions are within walking distance of each other in the centre; the city bus line (**Bilbobus**), the metro and the shiny modern tram will take you there if you're elsewhere. There is a card available, the **Creditrans**, which offers reduced fares on the bus, tram and metro services (it is also valid for the airport bus). Creditrans fares can be bought at machines in metro stations, bus and tram stops, or at some tobacconists. Cards cost €5, €10 or €15, and can be topped up with any amount once purchased.

The **BilbaoCard** provides low fares on city transport as well as discounts to museums, shops, restaurants, leisure facilities and shows. Cards cost €6 (1 day), €10 (2 days) and €12 (3 days). Buy online at *www2.bilbao.net/bilbaoturismo/ingles*, at Bilbao tourist offices (*see* p.135) or the airport.

By Metro

The metro consists of two lines: a main line (L1) from Etxebarri to Plentzia, and a branch line (L2), which splits off at Sarriko to head up the left bank of the river to Portulaguete. The metro offers the easiest way to the beaches at Getxo and Plentzia; there are stations at the Casco Viejo, Abando (for long-distance trains), Plaza Moyúa (closest to the Guggenheim), Indautxu and San Mamés (for Termibús). A single ride costs €1.45–1.70 depending on the distance travelled, or 72–96 cents with Creditrans (see above). There is also a €4.50 ticket which offers unlimited metro travel for one day, or you can buy a Creditrans card (see above). Metro services run about every 2 minutes within the centre, and every 30 minutes to Plentzia.

For information call t 94 425 40 25, or visit the website *www.metrobilbao.net*.

By Tram

The modern tram system, the **EuskoTran**, t 902 543 210, *www.euskotren.es*, fills the last gap in inner Bilbao's public transport network. The line runs alongside the Nervión, connecting Estación Atxuri with San Mamés via Abando, the Guggenheim and Abandoibarra. Single tickets cost €1.35 (67 cents per journey if you're using Creditrans), and there's also a one-day card offering unlimited use of the tram network for €3.85. Trams run every 10 minutes and you can buy tickets from easy-to-use machines at tram stops, or use the Creditrans card (*see* above). Date-stamp your ticket before boarding.

By Bus and Taxi

It is unlikely you will need the local **bus** service in this pocket-sized city with such an efficient metro and tram service. The local buses, run by **Bilbobus**, have red and white stripes and each stop has a route map. To continue around the coast from Plentzia without your own transport, take a taxi to Mungia (€15–20) from where buses go to Bermeo. **Taxis** in Bilbao are white with a red stripe. A green light on the roof indicates they are free. For a **radio taxi**, call t 94 444 88 88 or t 94 410 21 21.

By Boat

Bilboats, *www.bilboats.com*, t 644 442 055 (mobile), offer one- and two-hour sightseeing trips with multilingual audioguides along the River Nervión; the longer trip goes out to sea. Boats depart from next to the city hall bridge (Puente del Ayuntamiento), one bridge south of the Zubizuri bridge. Prices are €10 for adults for the one-hour trip, €16 for the two-hour trip, with discounts for seniors and children.

By Car

Bilbao's excruciatingly complex topography of hills and valleys makes it a beast to negotiate by car; miss one turn and you may have to circle 40km (no exaggeration) back and around. If you ever make it to the centre, parking will prove equally frustrating; you'll find municipal garages at Plaza Nueva, Plaza del Ensanche, Plaza de Indautxu and near the Termibús. If the car you parked in the street vanishes, call the Grúa Municipal (towing authorities), t 94 420 50 98.

Car Hire Companies
Aquilbilbo: t 94 441 20 12.
A-Rental: t 94 427 07 81.
Avis: t 94 427 57 60.
Hertz: t 94 415 36 77.
National-Atesa: t 94 442 32 90.

There are several car hire booths (Avis, Budget, Hertz, National-Atesa) at the airport in the arrivals hall next to the luggage carousels. As with the airport tourist information office, you can't get back to them once you have passed through customs.

Funicular Railway

The Funicular de Artxanda departs every 15 minutes from Plaza Funicular, off C/Castaños, and heads up to the summit of Artxanda (Mon–Sat 7.15am–10pm, Sun 8.15am–10pm, until 11pm in summer on Sat, Sun and hols).

Tours

The tourist office offers two **walking tours**, one around the Casco Viejo (departures from the tourist information office at the Teatro Arriaga) and the other around the Ensanche (departures from the tourist office in front of the Guggenheim). Both last around 1½ hours and cost €4.50.

The **Bus Turistikoa, t** 696 429 848, *www.busturistikoa.com*, is a hop-on, hop-off tourist bus which has 13 stops around the city, including the Casco Viejo and the Guggenheim. Tickets are valid 24 hours and cost €12 for adults, with concessions for seniors, students and children (under-6s are free).

Bilbao Paso a Paso, t 94 415 38 92, *www.bilbaopasoapaso.com*, organizes walking tours around the city, guided visits of the Guggenheim, tastings, and special trips into the surrounding hills.

are just the latest of a long string of celebrity architects associated with the city: the metro, with sleek modern stations, was designed by Sir Norman Foster and completed in 1995, and the airport got an elegant new terminal designed by Santiago Calatrava in 2000. The port has been given a boost as part of a vast harbour expansion project which includes a striking conference centre and auditorium, the Palacio Euskalduna (1999), and an excellent Maritime Museum (2004). Further upriver, Zaha Hadid has come up with an ambitious plan for the regeneration of the Zorrozaurre neighbourhood. Bilbao is shaping up to become one of the cities of Europe's future; come back in a few years and see.

The Casco Viejo

The Casco Viejo, the centre of the city from the 15th to the 19th centuries, is a snug little quarter on the east bank of the Nervión. Tucked out of the way, across the Puente del Arenal from the bustling centre, it remains the city's heart. The bridge takes you to **Plaza de Arriaga**, known familiarly as El Arenal from the sand flats that stood here long ago.

Fittingly for a Basque city, El Arenal's monuments are both musical: a small Art Nouveau **pavilion** in steel and glass (with concerts every Sunday afternoon) and the opera house, the **Teatro Arriaga**, with its frilly neo-Baroque façade. This is really the third opera house to stand on the site; the first was demolished after only a decade, and the second was built in 1890 when business was booming and the newly rich entrepreneurs decided to bring a little culture to city life. It opened to much fanfare and was equipped, as befitted the new industrial age, with all the latest gadgets, including electric lighting. The townspeople were invited to connect with the theatre and hear the opening opera, *La Gioconda*, down their telephone lines. In 1915 fire broke out and rapidly gutted the building. It took four years to restore it and the present theatre, in its third incarnation, opened in 1919. It is named after Crisóstomo de Arriaga, a child prodigy known as the 'Spanish Mozart', who went to Paris and passed away poetically of consumption just before his 20th birthday. After half a century of neglect, the Teatro Arriaga was bought by the city council and has been thoroughly primped up. Opera, dance, *zarzuela* (a kind of Spanish popular opera) and concerts take place in the refurbished auditorium, now equipped with all the latest technological developments. Nearby is the **Café Boulevard**, with its winking neon light, which was built to accommodate the smart audiences attending the opera; refurbished in glorious Art Deco style in the early 20th century, it has recently been expensively restored and is once again one of the city's most popular haunts.

Across the *plaza* stands the imposing, if now rather bleary, church of **San Nicolás de Bari**, built on the ruins of a chapel of the same name and inaugurated in 1756. It is dedicated to the patron saint of sailors, who couldn't save it from the French, or the Carlists, who ransacked it and used it as a barracks for most of the 19th century. Inside, shiver in the Baroque gloom or admire the handful of sculptures by Basque artist Juan Pascal de Mena. Behind the church, the Casco Viejo metro station and EuskoTren station for local services is burrowed into the rock. Head down Calle Esperanza, pausing at the *pelota* court if the players are practising, and you'll find the entrance to the *ascensor* (lift) which will lift you up to the heights of Begoña. It may look like the watchtower of a Soviet labour camp, but your reward will be wonderful views across the old quarter.

From here it's a short but steep walk to the Vizcayans' holy shrine, the **Basílica de Begoña**, with its unusual spire stuck on an early 16th-century church. Inside, a venerated statue of the Virgin holds court with some huge paintings by the slapdash Neapolitan Luca Giordano, probably the most popular painter of his day. This church lies closest to the hearts of Bilbaínos, and it's where the much-loved football team, Atlético de Bilbao, come to celebrate their victories. There are more fine views of the old town below.

The Siete Calles

Steep, worn steps lead all the way down the hill to **Plaza Unamuno**, named after the influential philosopher and writer Miguel de Unamuno (*see* box, p.114), who was born on nearby Calle La Ronda, not far from the little *plaza* which bears his name.

🛡 Siete Calles

Calle La Ronda is as good as its name and, together with Calle La Ribera, encircles the **Siete Calles**, the seven original streets of medieval Bilbao. Once contained by a girdle of stone walls, the prosperous little city was bulging in all directions by 1843 when, directly after the first Carlist War, the walls were demolished by royal decree. New homes and shops immediately sprang up, and the centrepiece of all this urban development was the arcaded, enclosed **Plaza Nueva**, symbol of Bilbao's growth and prosperity, and still the heart of the old town. Edged with cafés, bars and shops stuffed with souvenirs and religious ornaments, it gets especially lively on Sunday afternoons, when families come to eat out on the terraces and stroll around the weekly market, a tradition which has earned the *plaza* the nickname of 'the living room'.

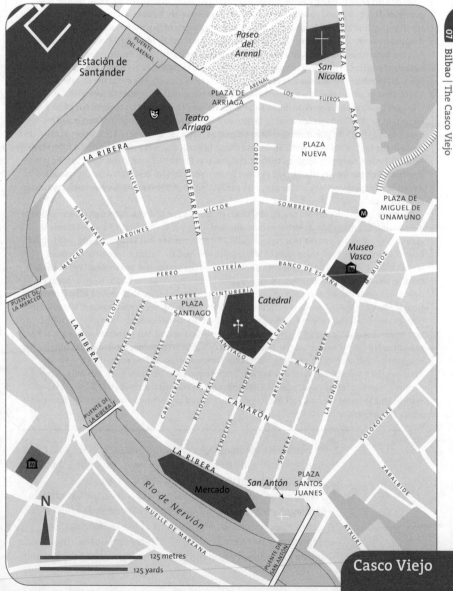

Casco Viejo

The Basque Philosopher

Although he cared deeply for Spain, Miguel de Unamuno (1864–1937) was always very proud of being Basque. More clear-sighted than some of his contemporaries, he ridiculed nationalist attempts (notably those of Sabino Arana) to romanticize and mythologize the race in one of his first works, *Critique on the Issue of the Origin and Prehistory of the Basque Race*. After gaining his doctorate, he wanted to stay in Bilbao and applied for a professorship in Euskera at the Instituto Viscazíano. He came in second place (Arana, who also applied, came in last), which may have been unfortunate for the history of Basque letters, but Unamuno, who had 15 other languages under his belt, didn't stay unemployed for long, and soon found a post as a professor of Ancient Greek at the University of Salamanca.

Despite his pride in being Basque, Unamuno always wrote in Spanish. Yet a certain Basque angst permeated his essays and novels. One of the early existentialists, he believed that individual integrity was the only true and reliable thing in an ever-changing world of lies and fanaticism (just as the Basques have often seen themselves, as they try to hold on to their identity). Also, being Basque gave him the detachment to see Spain as it really was. In *On Casticismo* (1895) he dissected Spain's singularly backward position in the modern world, and three years later, after Spain's traumatic defeat in the Spanish-American War and the loss of its last colonies, he became the leader of the so-called 'Generation of 98', analyzing what went wrong with Spain and seeking ways to revitalize it.

In 1901, Unamuno was made rector of Salamanca University and went on to write one of his most important works, *The Tragic Sense of Life in Men and Peoples* (1913). In spite of the fame it and his novels brought him, he was dismissed from his post as rector for speaking out in support of the Allied cause in the First World War (when Spain, and Bilbao in particular, was making a fortune from staying neutral). He was so openly opposed to the dictatorship of Primo de Rivera in the 1920s that he was imprisoned on the Canary Islands, and became Spain's most famous dissident. A daring rescue led by a Paris newspaper freed him, and in 1931, with the setting up of the Republic, he was re-elected rector at Salamanca.

Unamuno's own integrity led to a most famous incident in the Civil War. Although his opposition to dictatorship had made him a celebrity, Unamuno had come out at first for the Francoist rebels. It wasn't long before he realized that he had made a terrible mistake, but Salamanca was well behind Franco's lines, and in 1936, three months after Franco revolted, the Falange decided to celebrate National Day (Columbus Day) there with a special ceremony. Franco was unable to attend at the last minute, and the unwilling Unamuno had to replace him on the stage. He had to listen as speakers called the Catalans and Basques (both on the Republican side) 'cancers' that needed to be removed from the body of Spain. Then General Millán Astray, the one-eyed, one-armed leader of the Spanish Foreign Legion, set the audience on fire shouting his motto: '¡Viva la muerte!' (Long live death!). Unamuno's concluding remarks were struck from the official record, but witnesses recalled that he proudly defended his Basque origins, that he called Astray to account for mutilating the nation in the image of himself, and that his parting shot, as the frenzied Astray and his supporters screamed, 'Death to the intellectuals!', was: 'You will win, because you have the brute force. But you will not convince.' Surrounded by rabid Falangists, Franco's wife performed the service of a bodyguard and escorted the philosopher safely off the stage; he was placed under house arrest and died of a heart attack two months later.

Known for its antique books, coins and postcards, the market doesn't stop there and has everything from clamouring songbirds (unhappily penned in tiny cages) to dog food and mops.

A couple of blocks to the south of Plaza Nueva, the **Catedral de Santiago** sends its graceful spire up over the centre of the Casco Viejo. Begun in the 13th century, most of this understated but elegant grey stone church is 14th–15th-century Gothic (though the façade was added only in the 1880s). The highlight of the building is the magnificent Renaissance portico, constructed in 1581, where town councils were once held under the pale, cool arches.

Museo Vasco
Plaza Miguel de Unamuno 4, www. euskal-museoa.org; open Tues–Sat 11–5, Sun 11–2; closed Mon; adm

Around the corner from the cathedral is the delightful **Museo Vasco**, set around a peaceful cloister which once formed part of the city's first Jesuit church and college, established in 1604. In the centre stands the ancient Idolo de Mikeldi, the museum's treasure, which probably dates back to the Iron Age and looks like the prototype of the cow that jumped over the moon. Gravestones, other funerary pieces and strange stone statues discovered in caves and dating back millennia are also on display. On the first floor, a series of tableaux recreates the old Basque occupations of shepherd, fisherman and whaler, their domestic lives and pastimes and their religious devotions, all set to a murmuring soundtrack of seagulls, creaking sails and wood being whittled. Photographs document pilgrimages to local churches, and with them are displayed an eclectic range of *ex votos*, including a huge and wonderfully detailed sailing ship found at the Hermitage de Santa María de Olabeaga. Upstairs again, you'll find a scale model of Vizcaya and a reconstruction of the rooms of the Consulate (the old merchants' organization), as well as tools and model ships.

Wander down to the river through the Siete Calles, all but deserted during the afternoon siesta, yet crammed in the evenings with shoppers and strollers taking in the busy bars, cafés and shops, some of which have remained unchanged for generations. The street names often reveal their history: **Carnicería** was the butchers' street, **Tendería** was packed with shops, and **Barrenkale** is named after the Barrondo family in recognition of their staunch support for Pedro of Castile, who lived on this street in a tower which has long since disappeared. The 'Seven Streets' run down to the river, where they join the arcaded **Porte de la Ribera**, all that remains of the old Plaza Mayor, where stallholders once came to sell their wares. By the beginning of the 20th century they had become such a fixture that it was decided to build them a home, the fabulous Art Deco **Mercado de la Ribera** on the riverfront, the largest covered market in Spain. Next door stands the sturdy church of **San Antón**, showing off its pretty, garlanded portico and bell tower. It overlooks a bridge of the same name, where tolls used to be levied for entrance to the city.

Diocesan Museum of Sacred Art
9 Plaza de la Encarnación, www. eleizmuseoa.com; open Tues–Sat 10.30–1.30 and 4–7, Sun 10.30–1.30; closed Mon; adm

Farther upriver again, past the ornamental Atxuri train station, is tiny **Plaza de la Encarnación**. Here, at No.9, is the **Diocesan Museum of Sacred Art**, which occupies the former Convento de la Encarnación and is set around a peaceful Renaissance cloister. It displays over eight centuries' worth of religious art and finery: vestments of gold brocade and embroidery, sculptures and paintings by Basque artists, and a vast silver collection, one of the country's finest, with pieces from across Spain and the Americas.

07

Bilbao | The Casco Viejo

The Ensanche

Nobody in the 19th century had a sharper sense of urban design than the Spaniards, and, wherever a town had money to do something big, the results were impressive. Like Barcelona, Bilbao in its industrial boom years had to face exponential population growth, and its mayors chose to plan instead of just letting things happen. The area across the river from Bilbao, the Anteiglesia de Abando, was mostly farmland in the 1870s when the city annexed it. A trio of planners, Severino de Achúcarro, Pablo de Alzola and Ernest Hoffmeyer, got the job of laying out the streets of what came to be known as the Ensanche, or 'extension', and they came up with a simple-looking but rather ingenious plan, with diagonal boulevards dividing up the loop of the river like orange sections.

The Ensanche begins across from El Arenal; just over the bridge from the old town, a statue of Bilbao's founder, Diego López de Haro, looks benignly over the massive banks and circling traffic in the Plaza de España, more commonly known as **Plaza Circular**. This has become the business centre of the city, with the big grey skyscraper of the Banco Bilbao Vizcaya, built in the 1960s, to remind us who is the leading force in the city's destiny today. The RENFE station occupies one corner of the square; you'll have to walk around behind it to the riverfront to see one of the city's industrial-age landmarks: the tiny Bilbao–Santander train station, a charming Art Nouveau work with a wrought-iron and tile façade designed by Severino de Achúcarro.

Southwest of the Plaza Circular

Plaza Zabálburu marks the beginning of Bilbao's less salubrious quarters, which are gradually becoming gentrified. The artists and funky bars have moved in, but the prostitutes, especially those on Calle de las Cortes, are still a going concern. Southwest of Plaza Zabálburu lies the **Vista Alegre bullring**, carpeted with weird black sand brought from the mines around the city. It is packed during the *Semana Grande*, the week following 15 August every year, when bullfighters quake at the thought of facing the notoriously tough Bilbaíno audience. The **Museo Taurino de Bilbao** holds mementos from over 250 years of bullfighting history, from posters, costumes and photographs to the heads of famous bulls – or, in the case of Ofendido, who stands massively at the entrance, the whole beast. Poor Ofendido ('offended') was a magnificent bull deprived of his chance for glory because he'd chipped his horns. At least he got a second chance posthumously. The highlight of these exhibits is a magnificent embroidered cape decorated with figures by Goya, which was created for the Enlightenment-era matador Joaquín Rodríguez. The museum also outlines Basque contributions to

Museo Taurino de Bilbao
www.plazatoros bilbao.com; open April–Oct Mon–Thurs 10.30–1 and 4–6, Fri 10.30–1; Nov–Mar Mon–Fri 10–2; adm

bullfighting, traditionally regarded as an Andalucían sport, and defiantly points out that the first *toreros* to face a bull on foot were in fact from northern Navarra and Aragón (they probably had a lot of practice during the *Festa de San Fermín*; *see* pp.211–12). The most famous Basque bullfighter was Castor Jaureguibeitia, nicknamed Cocherito de Bilbao, who made his debut as a matador here at the Vista Alegre bullring in 1905. Fifteen years later it was also the scene of his final performance, given in front of King Alfonso XIII, who awarded him the prized bull's ear as the crowds gave him a roaring standing ovation.

The Gran Vía and the Plaza Moyúa

From Plaza Circular, the main boulevard of the Ensanche extends westwards: the **Gran Vía de Don Diego López de Haro**. Designed to be the city's 'backbone', it was the obvious place in the new city for prominent families and businesses to vie for the most modern and progressive houses. A later addition to the street, but still exhibiting the same pride and optimism, is **El Corte Inglés** department store at Nos.7–9, its façade one vast, high-relief mural evoking the industry and history of Bilbao. Further along is the **Palacio Foral** (the seat of the provincial council), another product of the city's boom times. Completed in 1900, this building was conceived as a means of flaunting the new prosperity, and the façade is a dizzying reminder that less is usually more: swirls, curlicues, garlands and ornamentation of every kind jostle together. The contemporary reaction was horror, particularly from those who had to work in the labyrinthine, impractical interior, but attitudes have mellowed over the years and now its eccentricity earns it an affectionate regard.

The centre of the Ensanche scheme is **Plaza de Federico Moyúa**, better known as La Elíptica. The **Hotel Carlton**, at No.2, still one of the city's posh establishments, served as the seat of the Basque government under the Republic and during the Civil War. At No.5 is the spiky, stripy **Chavarri Palace**, inspired by a celebrated Brussels hotel; it's famous for the fact that each window is different.

✪ **Alhóndiga**
Plaza Arriquibar 4,
t 94 401 40 14;
information on events
at www.alhondiga
bilbao.com

Three blocks south, along Alameda Recalde, is the city's biggest new landmark, the **Alhóndiga**, a huge wine warehouse from 1909 which occupies an entire block of the Ensanche. After languishing empty for decades, it has been spectacularly transformed into an arts and leisure complex by Philippe Starck. The central atrium is supported by a forest of columns, each different – one is Chinese laqueur red, with gold dragons, while another is a fat Baroque swirl of white marble – and lit by a huge virtual 'sun'. There's an exhibition space, a cinema, library, gym, a clutch of restaurants and cafés, a great gift shop with designer goodies, and a wonderful glass-bottomed **swimming pool** with a sun terrace.

A block up from the Alhóndiga, on the corner of Alameda Recalde and Licenciado Poza, check out the award-winning new building housing the **Basque health service (Sede de Osakidetza)**, with a multi-faceted mirrored façade reflecting an ever-changing mosaic of images from the street.

Museo de Bellas Artes

⭐ **Museo de Bellas Artes**
open Tues–Sat 10–8, Sun 10–2; adm; for guided tours (in English also) call **t** *94 439 61 37*

From La Elíptica, Calle Elcano takes you to the Plaza del Museo and the Museum of Fine Arts on the edge of the large and beautiful Parque de Doña Casilda de Iturrizar. Although this museum contains one of the finest art collections in Spain, until fairly recently few visitors made it to this quiet corner. However, this changed when the overflow from the Guggenheim brought more visitors, and the museum has been enlarged to accommodate them. Tours of culture-hungry visitors from around the world now throng the revamped galleries, and a glassy lobby has been added, with an excellent gift shop and an airy cafe overlooking the park, along with gleaming white galleries.

The collection begins in the 13th century with a pair of Catalan Romanesque panels; a simple *Noah and the Ark* surmounted by a monstrous, awkward dove, and a spindly *Descent from the Cross*, in which Christ bears up with an expression of mild bemusement. The early collection is rich in Catalan art, partly because the Catalans themselves were doing very nicely and could afford to grant plenty of commissions. There is a clutch of late-Gothic, Italian-influenced Mannerist paintings by another Catalan, Pere Serra (d. 1405), and a remarkable gilded altarpiece by Pere Nicolau. By the mid-15th century, Flemish realism had stamped its imprint across Spanish painting; Bartolomé Bermejo's cold, cruel *Flagellation of St Grace* is unnervingly realistic. There are several Flemish works here, too, including Metsys' *The Money Changers*, some gentle pastoral scenes by Jan Brueghel, and a later, unnerving *Lamentation* by Van Dyck, with desperate red-eyed women holding Christ's limp, dead body.

The luminous 16th-century *Piedad* is by Luis de Morales who, despite being dismissed from court by Philip II for being 'too old-fashioned', remained extremely popular and was nicknamed 'El Divino' for his ecstatic saints. They look pallid and contrived next to the intensely emotional canvases of El Greco; the blazing colours of his rapturous *Annunciation* (c. 1596–1600) seem to stun even Mary, while in *St Francis and the Cross* the gaunt saint's face gleams palely from the shadows as he contemplates death and resurrection. Another bold colourist was José Ribera, whose *St Sebastian Treated by the Holy Women* depicts the saint tethered by his arm as arrows are drawn from his body in the rather dim heavenly light provided by a couple of angels.

For something a bit fluffier and less intense, there are a few Murillos, including a pudgy-faced *St Lesmes* and a couple of portraits. Untouched by the histrionics of lesser mortals, Zurbarán's sublimely simple still-life paintings reveal a serene, orderly world. *The Virgin with the Infant Jesus*, one of Velázquez's last paintings, is restrained, contemplative and utterly moving.

Goya, who started out making designs, or cartoons, for the local carpet factory in Madrid, was appointed Principal Painter to the king in 1799, shortly after being struck with deafness (probably thanks to syphilis). Plunged into silence, he ended by painting vast, apocalyptic visions of a world 'where reason sleeps'. Before these visions became all-consuming, his portraits, such as those here of Martín Zapater and the poet Moratín, provided much of his income and are strikingly frank, acute and utterly unconcerned with rank. But by the 19th century Spanish art had lost its fire, as the smug portraits and bland landscapes attest. There are a few pieces by French artists, among them Gauguin's *Washerwomen at Arles* and Cézanne's *Great Bathers*, and some soft portraits by the American Impressionist Mary Cassatt. Later Spanish works include a bleak portrait of grim-faced prostitutes by Solana, and a touching study of an ineffably *Sad Child* by Moroccan-born Carlos Sárez de Tejada.

The collection of Basque works is very strong and includes wonderful portraits by Echevarría and Zuloaga, particularly his

Jorge de Oteiza

Oteiza, the fiery 5ft-tall *enfant terrible* of the Spanish art world, was born in 1908 in the seaside resort of Orio. He was sent to Madrid to study medicine, but it wasn't long before he abandoned his studies in favour of sculpture and mounted his first exhibition in Donostia-San Sebastián in 1931. From about 1935, he began his career as a plastic artist with a series of pieces based on found objects, but, disgusted with Francoism and the apathetic dreariness of Spain, he set off for South America, where he spent several years teaching ceramics to students in Buenos Aires and Bogotá. In the 1950s he began to make the pieces for which he is most famous, the 'Metaphysical Boxes', a series of massive forms based on cubes with hollow centres, which reflected his increasing preoccupation with what he described as 'spatial de-occupation'. These works brought him widespread acclaim and recognition, but, when he set out the theoretical ideas behind their conception in the *Propósito Experimental* (written 1956–7), the art world reacted with consternation at his radical new ideas.

Oteiza was enormously influential on a new generation of sculptors who became known as Equipo 57; this group saw art as a form of behaviour within society and rejected its commercial exploitation. Having riled the critics in the 1950s, Oteiza had another go at goading them in 1963, when he published *Quousque Tandem*, which became the unofficial manifesto of the Escuela Vasca (the Basque School), of which Chillida (*see* p.187) was a long-standing member. He exhorted Basque artists to define their art in terms of the Basque character and bound together his principal theories by stating: 'Rejecting the occupation of space, Basque art is natural, irregular. I reject whatever is not essential, whatever fails to respond to constructive truth'. This Basque character is already apparent in the cromlechs, the rings of sacred stones that lead us into the realm of magic, the basis of our tradition.' Still sculpting and still mischievous until his death at the age of 94, Oteiza never passed up an opportunity to throw out a few fireworks. The very suggestion that art should be sold drove him to distraction, which is why the main body of his work lies stacked in his studio in Zarautz, and why he was, for a long time, famously contemptuous of 'the other sculptor' (Chillida) who was famously prolific – and rich.

sultry, sloe-eyed *La Condesa Mathieu de Noailles* (1913). The dreamy *Bridge of Burceña* is by Bilbao-born painter Aurelio Areta Errasti, and depicts a silent figure slumped, musing, over the railings. The highlights are, of course, the sculptural pieces, such as *Portrait of a Soldier called Odyssey* by Jorge de Oteiza (*see* p.119) and *Around a Void I* by Eduardo Chillida (*see* p.187); both artists were interested in the concept of what Oteiza called 'spatial de-occupation'.

The leafy park itself is an agreeable place to spend an hour or two, with exotic trees carefully labelled, a lagoon with ducks, and a light-and-colour bauble called the 'Cybernetic Fountain'.

Along the Nervión

When Bilbao's urban planners embarked on post-industrial regeneration in the late 1980s, it was inevitable that the riverbank would be identified as the project's linchpin. The significance of the Nervión (which becomes the Ría de Bilbao) to Bilbao is as much symbolic as practical; for years it has been synonymous in Spain with massive industrial pollution, but clean-up efforts since 1981 have succeeded in making the river habitable to fish for the first time in over a century.

Major developments have taken place above water, too, as several kilometres of old rusting jetties and dock installations have been torn out to make room for a riverside park, stretching downstream from the Arenal bridge past the Guggenheim Museum and down to the Palacio Euskalduna. Bilbaínos have taken to the development with gusto – thousands of them pour on to the riverbanks every evening to walk their dogs and eat ice-cream. New gardens have been laid out, with kiosk cafés and play areas for kids, making for a very pleasant space.

Overlooking the river at the Arenal end is the city's **Ayuntamiento** (town hall), which hasn't followed the big banks and wealthy businesses across the river. It used to sit next to the long-demolished Plaza Mayor on the other side of the Casco Viejo, part of a formidable and powerful trinity along with the church of San Antón and the Trade Court. It was shifted to this spot (where it can keep an eye on everyone) a century or so ago and housed in a brand new building with an 'Arab Hall' decorated with Mudéjar-style tiles. The grand houses continue along this side of the river, and the old warehouse district on the opposite bank is transforming itself with loft-style apartments and artists' galleries.

Halfway along, the glass-floored **Puente Zubizuri** ('white bridge' in Basque) was one of the first additions to the riverfront landscape; its nautical theme – the bridge billows out like a great sail – has become a widespread motif in the architecture of New

Bilbao. The bridge was controversially modified by Isozaki Atea in 2008 (Calatrava didn't approve), and now connects to a pair of glassy towers containing fancy apartments and a posh gym and spa. The architect-engineer Santiago Calatrava of Valencia has become a favourite here and was also responsible for the bridge at Ondárroa and the airport terminal.

Heading off Campo de Volantín into the little *barrio* of Castaños, a **funicular** (every 15mins; *see* 'Getting around Bilbao', p.111) glides up from Plaza Funicular to the hilltop park on **Monte Artxanda**, where there are a couple of restaurants and extensive views of the Casco Viejo, the Guggenheim and, on really clear days, the sea, 10 miles to the north. For an authentic cultural experience go up on a weekend, when half of Bilbao squeezes into the rattling cars and hangs out on the mountain, picnicking, chattering and enjoying the view. It's a great place to watch the greening of the city, as lines of turf unfurl along the riverbanks.

Back at the bottom of the hill, cross the river on the Zubizuri, and follow the riverside walkway to the **Alamedo Mazarredo**, where there are several restaurants and the graceful **Palacio Ibaigane**, which once belonged to the powerful Sota family and is now the seat of Atlético de Bilbao football club.

Head back down the riverbank, past the Guggenheim, to the sleek **Puente Euskalduna**, which arches in a broad sideways curve across the river. The bridge is named, like the concert hall and conference centre, after the old shipyard which once stood here, commemorated by an old shipyard crane, 'La Carola', supposedly named after a pretty girl who crossed the Deusto bridge every day and brought all the workers out to watch and whistle. The great hunk of rusting steel and glass is the high-tech **Palacio de Congresos y de la Música Euskalduna** (1998), designed by the architects Federíco Soriano and Dolores Palacíos. An incoherent jumble of metal and concrete, it is supposed to represent the last ship made in the Euskalduna shipyards, churning up the Nervión.

More tangible reminders of the old trade are housed in a spectacular museum devoted to Bilbao's maritime history, the **Museo Marítimo Ría de Bilbao**, downriver towards Olabeaga in the old Euskalduna dry docks. Here a permanent collection, displayed both in immense indoor galleries and out in the docks, traces the city's maritime history, with restored fishing boats, sailing ships, historic nautical instruments and maps on show, accompanied by film clips and all kinds of high-tech exhibits. The old lock system which once operated on the river is still kept in working order. Temporary exhibitions are always huge crowd-pullers, and the museum is in general a family-pleaser, with plenty of child-friendly activities going on.

Museo Marítimo Ría de Bilbao
Muelle Ramón de la Sota 1, t 902 131 000, www.museomaritimo bilbao.org; open summer Tues–Sun 10–8; winter Tues–Fri 10–6, Sat–Sun 10–8; closed Mon; adm

07 Bilbao | Along the Nervión

San Mamés
museum open Tues–Sat 10–2 and 4–6.30, Sun 10–2; adm; guided tours of stadium at 10.30, 11.30, 12.30, 1.15, 4.30, 5.30 and 6

It's difficult to miss Bilbao's San Mamés stadium, also known as 'the Cathedral', which has a small museum and runs guided tours. Ground was broken in 2010 for the new stadium, yet to be named, which will seat 55,000 when completed.

The Guggenheim Museum

① Guggenheim Museum

The greatest building of our time.
Philip Johnson

Downstream from the Zubizuri, a 6oft tower of steel and golden limestone heralds the presence of Bilbao's art Mecca and the centrepiece of the city's river-front redevelopment, Frank O. Gehry's stunning Museo Guggenheim. Gehry's softly glowing titanium clipper ship occupies the Abandoibarra flats, until 1987 home to Bilbao's biggest shipyard and now a worldwide symbol of successful urban renewal. The museum fits into the landscape perfectly, looking utterly futuristic and yet in keeping with the city's industrial past. Its massive popularity and high public visibility have helped to spawn an economic boom, the so-called 'Guggenheim Effect', which has been felt throughout the Basque lands and shows no sign as yet of slowing down. How it all came into being is as intriguing as the building itself.

The Guggenheims

It really looks a good deal like they'd gobble all in sight

On top of earth or under it, so fearful is their might.

They'll gobble all there is to get and turn you inside out.

The Guggenheims will get you if you don't watch out.
Washington Times, 1910

By the 1970s, even most Americans only remembered the Guggenheims for the extraordinary museum in New York that bears their name, forgetting how, only a few decades before, their names were splashed regularly across the front pages as one of the dozen richest families in the United States. The one link they have with Bilbao is metals: iron made Bilbao, copper made the Guggenheims. And the fruit of their unlikely marriage, fittingly, is a titanium miracle child.

The Guggenheims were one of the great American sagas of rags to riches. Anti-Semitism in a Swiss ghetto is what pushed Simon Guggenheim the tailor to emigrate to Philadelphia in 1847, where he and his 20-year-old son, Meyer, first worked as itinerant pedlars. Meyer had no formal education, but he realized that his best-selling item was stove polish, and soon began making a better polish at home with the help of a second-hand sausage-stuffer. From stove polish Meyer went on to coffee extract, then to food and clothing during the Civil War, spices, lye, Swiss lace and embroideries. The turning point came in 1881, with a haphazard purchase of two waterlogged lead and silver mines in Colorado. Meyer had them drained, and they proved far richer than anyone had imagined. Meyer soon built his first smelter and, like the other robber barons of the era, he did his share to found the American labour movement; starvation wages for miners were the rule, and strikers were clobbered into submission.

Unlike the other robber barons, though, Meyer had seven sons who took over the mining business as a formidable unit. Operations soon expanded to Mexico. In 1900 they battled a Rockefeller-controlled trust for control of America's mines and smelters, and ended up owning 51 per cent of the trust. With J. P. Morgan they bought Kennecott, a mountain of solid copper in Alaska, and built a $25 million railroad over a moving glacier to exploit it, scooping up much of the rest of Alaska's mineral wealth while they were at it with such assiduousness that they also helped to spark the American conservationist movement. They joined with financier Thomas Ryan to exploit the Congo's gold mines and diamonds for its owner-slavemaster, King Leopold II of Belgium. They expanded into diamond mines in Angola. They acquired a huge copper mine in Bingham canyon in Utah, and then topped that by buying the Chuquicamata mine in Chile, the world's richest copper mine. They owned tin mines in Malaysia. By the First World War, the Guggenheims controlled 75 per cent of the earth's silver, copper and lead.

The family, however, was beginning to fray. One brother went down on the *Titanic*. The youngest brother sued the older brothers. No one had seven sons; in fact, male heirs interested in the business were exceedingly rare. In 1923 the five remaining brothers sold Chuquicamata to Anaconda Copper, sat back on their multi-millions, and decided it was time to give them away.

The Guggenheims were remarkable for the speed with which they made their fortune, but perhaps are even more so for how quickly and farsightedly they dispersed it. One brother financed the first aeronautics studies in America, the rocket experiments of Robert H. Goddard, the ancestors of the jet propulsion labs at Princeton and Caltech, and the masterminds of the US space programme. Another set up a free dental clinic for the children of New York, and left millions to Mount Sinai Hospital and the Mayo Clinic. Another set up a foundation to dispense grants to promising scholars, artists and scientists to do with as they pleased, enabling hundreds of people to start their careers or work on their masterpieces: Linus Pauling, Aaron Copland, Katherine Anne Porter, Vladimir Nabokov, Gian Carlo Menotti, Henry Kissinger, W. H. Auden, Samuel Barber, Thomas Wolfe and Marianne Moore were all Guggenheim fellows.

Then there was brother Solomon, the charmer, who acquired a sudden interest in nonobjective art at the age of 65, after meeting a 36-year-old German baroness named Hilla Rebay. Solomon was captivated, and took it to heart when she told him it was his duty to stop collecting Old Masters and patronize the new. Under her guidance he acquired the Kandinskys, Delaunays, Légers, Feiningers and Moholy-Nagys that became the basis of the Solomon R. Guggenheim Foundation. Rebay was the first director. The collection went on tours around America, and with its success Rebay pressed Solomon into building a temple for his collection in New York, and getting America's greatest architect, Frank Lloyd Wright, to design it. Finished in 1959, the Guggenheim Museum was the most controversial and the most organic, sculpturally beautiful building erected in America in the 20th century.

But even before its completion the Guggenheims were expanding. In the early 1940s, keen collector Peggy Guggenheim (whose father had gone down with the *Titanic*) wowed the New York art world with her 'Art of the Century' exhibition, displaying her collection of works by Duchamp, Ernst, Mondrian, Tanguy, Arp, Brancusi, Giacometti and Klee, many of whom were scarcely known in America. 'Art of the Century' was a major force behind Abstract Expressionism, led by Peggy's protégé Jackson Pollock (who started off as a carpenter in Solomon's museum) and Robert Motherwell. After the war, Peggy bought a *palazzo* in Venice to exhibit her collection, and since her death in 1979 it, too, has been owned by the Guggenheim Foundation.

Expanding into Bilbao

The Guggenheims always knew that mines eventually give out, but the fact that countries like Chile and Angola would nationalize theirs in the 1970s caught them unawares. Share prices collapsed and the Solomon R. Guggenheim Foundation's original endowment, which depended on the dividends, could no longer meet operating costs. Money-spinners like a museum restaurant and shop were opened, but the Foundation, concluding that its biggest assets were its fabulous permanent collection and its prestigious name, decided that a satellite was in order.

In his quest to find a site for another Guggenheim, Thomas Krens, the head of the Foundation, went around the world, to Salzburg, Tokyo, Moscow, Vienna, London and elsewhere, ready to wheel and deal. None of the proposed marriages worked out for one reason or another – until Krens met the Basques, who were ready to come up with the dowry.

At the time, Bilbao's movers and shakers were already well along in their grand scheme for converting the dirty old rust bucket along the Nervión into a magnet for service and high-tech industries. Although a dramatic string of dazzling architectural projects (including Sir Norman Foster's metro, the Calatrava airport terminal and the new congress and performance centre) were under way, they were still casting about for a prestigious state-of-the-art project to anchor their redevelopment schemes, something that would encourage outside investment, something truly bodacious which would give the Basque country headlines that didn't mention the word terrorism. After the huge success of an exhibition of the Guggenheim's permanent works at the Reina Sofía museum in Madrid, the Basques realized that a Guggenheim museum was just what they were looking for, and boldly suggested Bilbao to Krens.

It just so happened that this was a time when Bilbao city, Vizcaya province and the autonomous regional government were all in the hands of the Basque Nationalist Party (PNV), which enabled them to head off the considerable political opposition to the idea. Nor was Krens immediately convinced – although impressed by the PNV's determination to give Bilbao a new direction, he and the other Guggenheim administrators were appalled by the site earmarked for the new museum, a run-down warehouse district punctuated by a brutally ugly bridge, the busiest in Bilbao. Undeterred, the PNV came up with the convincing $100 million (in spite of indignant squawks from the opposition) to ensure that the new museum would be housed in a building of spectacular character, one that would come to identify the city in the same way as the Opera House in Sydney. To this end, Krens provided three names for an architectural competition: Arata Isozaki, the Viennese Coop Himmelblau and Frank Gehry. They were each given $10,000, one site visit, and three weeks.

When the design of the museum was put out to competition, both Krens and Bilbao had their own demands. Krens wanted the museum to be thoroughly new, both in form and function. The building itself was to have the same dramatic effect as a cathedral of the Middle Ages; the gallery space should be large enough to accommodate the massive works of modern art that had outgrown traditional museums; and the building should interact with the collection rather than simply provide a blank space for its presentation. The local administration wanted the museum to be a fully integrated part of the city, and Gehry's design was chosen because it fulfilled this condition most completely.

Gehry fell in love with Bilbao, the industrial setting (so very different from the Fifth Avenue Guggenheim) and the city's gritty determination. He wanted the museum to be a link between their 19th and 21st centuries, a building that would be 'a good neighbour'. Surrounded by pools, the museum seems to float by the riverside, echoing the great ships which once made the city's fortune. The materials used – limestone and titanium – evoke the industrial past and the creamy stone of the Deusto university on the opposite bank. The Puente de la Salve bridge, a major access road to the city centre, is embraced by the limestone tower which has no exhibition purpose but exists simply to knit together the city and the museum. A walkway sweeps across the river, around the museum and up a flight of movie-star steps, and gives pedestrian access to the bridge. Instead of an imposing elevated main entrance, visitors descend a grand stairway into the main lobby. Even the walls themselves melt into the interior atrium through the glass façade, blurring the sense of inside and outside. From within the museum, glass angles frame the university, the new music and conference centre and the old opera house, deliberately embracing the city's landmarks.

Frank Gehry's Titanium Sculpture

He is an architect of immense gifts who dances on the line separating architecture from art but who manages never to let himself fall.
Paul Goldberger,
New York Times
architecture critic

Gehry, born in Toronto in 1929 but long-time resident of Los Angeles, has often been accused of kookiness, along with an impressive assortment of other labels: Postmodernist, Cubist, Deconstructionist, Expressionist, 'punky', 'funky', Nouveau Californian or simply 'that chain-link guy', referring back to his first works that caused a stir: his own house in Santa Monica (1978) and the Temporary Contemporary Museum (1983) in a former LA bus garage, made of concrete, plywood, chain-link and corrugated metal. His buildings, made of low-cost 'found' materials, resembled 3-D collages – unfinished, spontaneous, even explosive at times.

The leap from 'that chain-link guy' to master of the voluptuous, organic, high-tech Guggenheim Bilbao may seem huge but, according to Gehry's own vision of his work, nothing could be more natural. He believes that architecture itself is art, or sculpture to be precise, because it has three dimensions, and he has made the often-complicated synthesis between the two his territory, trying to match the form and materials to the context of each project. Not bound by any other criteria, his buildings are shot through with an engaging delight and freedom. Architecture as art can serve both life and art, Gehry would argue; it can be poetic, dynamic, sensual, restless, spiritual, lyrical or even irreverent. Unlike many trendy architects who sink into frivolity and kitsch to avoid the cardinal postmodern sin of boring the audience, there's always a method behind Gehry's madness, an inner order to his buildings, an often complex meshing of form and function. His favourite building is Le Corbusier's church at Ronchamp in the Vosges (1955), a sculptural masterpiece by the otherwise supreme rationalist, celebrated for its deeply spiritual spaces. 'I approach each building as a sculptural object, a spatial container, a space with light and air, a response to context and appropriateness of feeling and spirit,' Gehry wrote in 1980, in *Contemporary Architects*. 'To this container, this sculpture, the user brings his baggage, his program, and interacts with it to accommodate his needs. If he can't do that, I've failed.'

More recently, for his big projects – such as the provocative, swirling Vitra Museum (1988) in Weil-am-Rhein, in Germany, the Experience Music Project in Seattle (2000), or the rippling skyscraper at 8 Spruce Street in New York City (2011) – Gehry the sculptor of buildings has used the latest technology to help him make buildings bend to his will. His preliminary drawing for the Guggenheim was a wildly Expressionist sketch, full of verve and energy. He then built a series of models and scanned the final one on CATIA, a computer program developed in France for designing Mirage jet fighters, which can digitize a sculptural form into a 3-D electronic model. The data translated the undulating curves into numbered sections, making it possible to have each piece of steel, stone and glass cut to measure and fitted on to a swirling skeleton of steel. Gehry has opened the doors of a new architecture without limits, as Richard Serra has said, but it would never have been possible without computers.

Gehry's original idea for the Guggenheim Bilbao was to sheath it in lead and copper, but he realized that lead would slowly leach into the river. He then considered stainless steel, but realized that in the often rainy and cloudy climate of Bilbao it would look dull. As he experimented with ways to make stainless steel somehow warmer, he came across a small piece of titanium in his office. Titanium is a malleable white metal resembling aluminium, a material guaranteed not to rust and used mostly in medical instruments and aircraft design. Intrigued, Gehry stuck it on the wall, and by chance the next day in Los Angeles was rainy and overcast. Yet the titanium still gave off a golden glow. At sunset it had a purple sheen. Gehry was convinced. And thanks to the collapse of the titanium market after the fall of the Soviet Union, prices were low. Also a little goes a long way: on the roof, the titanium panels are only a third of a millimetre thick, but guaranteed, Gehry was told, to last a hundred years.

Most visitors spend as much time wandering around Gehry's enormous sculpture as they do inside it. Like the three blind men and the elephant, your interpretation will depend on which part of the building you are looking at; ships' hulls, truncated fish bodies and palm trees all protrude from the bulging mass in a wonderful juxtaposition of natural forms and 21st-century technology. The curves and titanium give the building a remarkable sense of movement. Some of the best views are to be had from the Puente de la Salve, a classic lump of 1960s concrete that Bilbao would rather have forgotten but which Gehry's design embraces. In 2007, to celebrate the Guggenheim's 10th anniversary, French artist Daniel Buren crowned the bridge with his sculpture *Arcos Rojos* (Red Arches). One of Gehry's skylights looms up towards the bridge, looking for all the world like a giant open-mawed basking shark.

Puppy, or Life Imitates Art, Again

Before you even get a chance to step through the doors of the museum, you'll be mugged by the Guggenheim's first (and biggest) exhibit, a 40ft mountain of flowers and love created by kitsch guru Jeff Koons and answering to the name of 'Puppy' (pronounced 'poopy'). Puppy, presumably a West Highland terrier, is a familiar sight at galleries worldwide – he's made appearances in New York and Sydney, amongst other cities – a kind of vegetarian version of the Littlest Hobo, who wanders from city to city lending his support wherever art exhibitions need him, before turning tail and trotting off into the sunset. But, like the Littlest Hobo, eventually the time came to settle down, and Puppy has put down his roots firmly in Bilbao, to the delight of almost everyone. He's been adopted as the city's *de facto* mascot, his image decorating everything from T-shirts to Vizcaya government literature.

Puppy's meteoric rise to mass adulation no doubt amuses his creator. When Koons came across the dog, it was no more than a tacky porcelain souvenir, a mass-produced piece of commercial crassness. Having based a career on taking just this kind of tat and elevating it to the status of High Art, Koons saw potential in Puppy; a couple of months, one CAD program and a few thousand begonias later and *voilà!* – a star was born. Yet just as junk can be made into art, art can be made into junk and before long the poor pooch was back where he came from; cuddly Puppys are the hot souvenir in Bilbao.

The vantage point also looks on to an area of the roof where unsightly brown stains once spread across some of the titanium scales, to the consternation of the world's press. Apparently, one of the contractors spilled a fireproofing sealant on them during the construction, and the oxide film which coats titanium as soon as it's exposed to oxygen thickened and dulled, like cataracts on an eye. Fortunately, a new oxide scrubbing foam has been developed to clean up the surface, and all is now shining again.

A Day at the Guggenheim

Don't underestimate the Guggenheim's popularity. Attendance rates have vastly exceeded projections, and queues of up to an hour to get in have become frequent, especially at weekends. Once you're through the door it's easy enough to wander round the galleries on your own; alternatively, audioguides can be hired (free), with recorded information on the key works. Free guided tours cover each installation daily, in English, but there's a definite skill to getting on one – spaces are limited to 20 people and there's no possibility of signing up more than 30 minutes in advance.

The interior spaces are as remarkable as the exterior. The building's heart is a sublime 150ft-high atrium of swooping curves, in every sense the museum's centre – galleries radiate from it on all sides, and you'll inevitably pass through time and again at different levels – but also a sculptural work of art in itself. Light floods in through glass curtain walls and cascades down from skylights in the roof, dancing and jumping yet never finding an absorbent surface to stop its flow. Watch out for Gehry's cheeky nod of the head to Frank Lloyd Wright's famous spiral design; Gehry claims that Thomas Krens egged him on to 'take on the Guggenheim in New York'. It is a worthy successor, but radically different, unrestrained by anything but the imagination, 'a metaphoric visionary city, *à la* Fritz Lang', as Gehry sees it.

Outside the atrium, the Nervión is incorporated into the design by way of an ingenious raised walkway, rising and curving and creating a union between river and water garden.

Although not a few people end up just wandering about the building, enchanted like Alice in Wonderland, Gehry's intention was to provide a perfect and warm setting for contemporary art. Frank Lloyd Wright's spiral ramp, captivating as it is, has always made viewing awkward for many people. Gehry hoped his own non-rational forms would sharpen the visitor's senses and open the mind to the give and take of contemporary art, but also provide ample space to view it. Even in the more conventional galleries,

Guggenheim Practicalities

Address: Avenida Abandoibarra 2, 48001 Bilbao, **t** 94 435 90 80. The website, *www.guggenheim-bilbao.es*, is a good place to see what temporary exhibitions are on and what's coming up. You can also pre-book admission tickets (although not guided visits).

Opening hours: Tues–Sun 10–8, daily in July and August. Ticket sales stop 30mins prior to closing.

Information centre: There's a visitor information desk in the main entrance hall. Multilingual staff provide leaflets and information on guided tours, and answer general queries.

Cloakroom: In the main lobby; there is no charge for leaving your coats.

Toilets and telephones: In the basement.

Bank machines: There are two ATMs which accept credit cards by the ground floor entrance closest to the river.

Guided tours: Free guided tours in English, Spanish and Basque take place four times per day, with a special family tour Sun at 12pm. Call **t** 94 435 90 90 for schedule information. It is not possible to pre-book guided tours; you can register for a tour up to 30mins before it starts (register at the Information desk in the main lobby). Otherwise, audioguides, included in the admission price, have recorded information about the exhibits. There is a special audioguide for children.

Group admissions: For groups holding reservations, there is a special entrance on the side of the building that faces the river. Groups of more than 20 people must request authorisation by calling **t** 94 435 90 23.

Shop: The shop is arranged on three levels: on the ground floor you'll find stationery and souvenirs (such as mugs, posters, puzzles, keyrings, postcards, tapestry kits to embroider your own 'Puppy', T-shirts, calendars, umbrellas, etc.). On the mezzanine level there is a wide selection of handmade jewellery and glassware, hand-painted silk scarves, ceramics, candles, designer sunglasses, handmade paper products and other gift items. On the 1st floor you'll find the bookshop, where there are museum guides, monographs on several of the artists featured, art history, design and architectural books, as well as a small selection of local history books.

Library: The library (**t** 94 435 90 83) specializes in 20th-century and contemporary art and is open to investigators, students, and the general public. *Closed Aug.*

Cafés: There's a café-bar with dining room on the first floor by the entrance, with a large outdoor terrace. The pale wood panelling, frosted glass screens and wooden furniture in undulating forms are all Gehry-designed. The bar serves simple breakfasts, drinks and snacks, with more elaborate fare in the dining area: see *www.bistroguggenheimbilbao.com*. There's also a summer café-kiosk outside by the river, overlooking a huge play area for kids.

Restaurant: Try superb New Basque cuisine under the innovative direction of chef Josean Martínez Alija at Nerua (*menú degustación* is €75). Book in advance: **t** 94 423 93 33, *www.nerua.com*.

Guggenheim Floor Plan

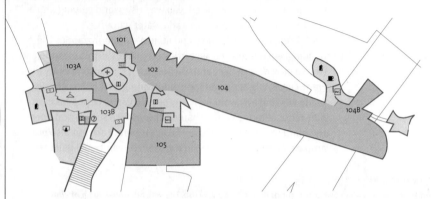

▣	lift	⑦	information	▦	exhibition space
ᴡᴄ	toilets	⚲	cloakroom		
🎫	ticket office	🔊	auditorium		
■	café	📖	bookshop		
⑈	restaurant	♿	wheelchair access		

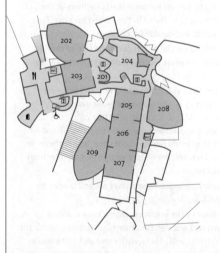

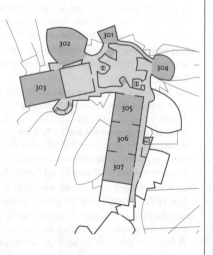

ceilings are extremely high. The architect has also created some revolutionary gallery spaces, especially the cavernous Fish Gallery (gallery 104), which is 420ft long by 100ft wide with whalebone-like ribs supporting the ceiling, and designed to hold the biggest and heaviest works of modern art without any structural columns getting in the way. *Snake*, a heavy iron sculpture designed especially for the gallery by Gehry's close friend Richard Serra, throws down the gauntlet to future artists; too heavy to move and too big to fit anywhere else, it's one of the few exhibits that's guaranteed to be on show. This isn't art you *look* at – you have to participate in it by entering the narrow corridors formed by the six massive undulating steel plates. Serra said that he was trying to reproduce the sensation of a walk through the narrow streets of a medieval city, a feeling underlined by the great iron sides leaning in and swaying out. *Snake* was later augmented with Serra's seven-part sculpture *A Matter of Time* (2005), seven enormous (they even dwarf the *Snake* itself) swirls of steel that were also created specifically for this space. A meditation on time, both physical and experiential, a journey to the centre of these swaying steel ellipses and spheres is curiously dislocating – walls appear and fall away when you least expect them to.

The Collection

After Gehry's architectural fireworks and Koons' giant dog, the collection itself has a hard act to follow; whether or not it succeeds will depend on when you go. Thanks to its family connections with New York, Venice and Berlin, the Guggenheim has access to more masterworks of 20th-century art than a museum of its tender age has any right to. Yet the shifting nature of the exhibits means there's no guarantee that the piece you're desperate to see will be on show. However, the site-specific works by Koons and Serra will be there, as will Jenny Holzer's *Installation for Bilbao* (1997), in gallery 101, just off the atrium, a characteristically spiky LED monologue scrolling upwards into a reflective ceiling via nine vertical columns. Very private feelings – expressions of desire, obsession, betrayal, even violence – are emblazoned in public neon signs: shooting, searing red words in English and Spanish. All the effects that neon signs provide are made use of: flashing lights, different typography and eye-catching symbols. Step between the vertical posts and the same messages unravel in Basque on the other side in an unearthly blue, dimly reflected in the grey walls.

If the permanent collection is up, look out for a good selection of European avant-garde art: there's a pivotal work by Miró, *The Tilled Field* (1923–4), a bold and relatively accessible prelude to his later, more figurative style; a selection of Kandinskys; some elongated heads by Modigliani; and scattered works by Picasso and Klee,

07 Bilbao | The Guggenheim Museum

mostly on permanent loan from the Guggenheim in New York. Underpinning these is Bilbao's own distinguished collection of abstract expressionists, including pieces by some of the movement's leading figures, among them Robert Motherwell's stark assessment of the Civil War, *Elegy to the Spanish Republic IV* (1955–60), a swirling late-period Pollock (*Ocean Greyness*, 1953) and De Kooning's forceful *Composition* (1955), a gestural riot of primary colours. The polychromatic chaos is balanced by a tranquil Rothko (*Untitled*, 1956) and Yves Klein's *Large Blue Anthropometry* (1960), which the artist created by smearing naked women in paint (the famously patented *International Klein Blue*) and dragging them across the canvas while a 20-piece orchestra played his own *Symphonie Monotone*, a single note sustained for 10 minutes alternating with 10 minutes' silence.

There's a fairly patchy collection of pop art, perhaps best represented by Lichtenstein's unusually subdued *Interior With Mirrored Wall* (1991); some fine pieces by Schnabel, Dubuffet and Basquiat; and a moving monographic exhibition devoted to Anselm Kiefer, one of the artists that the museum has chosen to focus on in its acquisition policy. This juxtaposes the historically laden works of his early period – the notorious faces of Nazi Germany glare down from a chaotic monochrome swirl in *The Paths to Worldly Wisdom: Hermann's Battle* (1982–3) – with the unburdened, redemptive inner landscapes that characterize Kiefer's work in the 1990s. In *Sun Ship* (1994–5), a dried sunflower glides over devastated landscapes of ash and fallen trees, heading off to a brighter future, a future perhaps realized in the cracked desert colours of *Alone With Wind, Time and Sound* (1997).

Elsewhere, there's a small collection of works by Basque and Spanish artists: sculptures by Eduardo Chillida (*see* p.187) and Cristina Iglesias, such as her *Untitled (Jealousy II)* (1997), a strange, seemingly impenetrable 'room' made of Arab-style carved panels; a few textural paintings by Tapiés; and some startling mixed-media still lifes and landscapes from Miguel Barceló – which the museum's directors have pledged to augment with future purchases. They tried hard to get the one work that the Basques feel really belongs here – Picasso's *Guernica* – but Madrid refused to send it even on loan for the opening in 1997, out of fears, they say, that the Basques wouldn't give it back.

Temporary Exhibitions

Nothing draws the crowds to Bilbao like a big new **temporary exhibition** – until the collection matures, they're the best guarantee of seeing a really strong body of work – and the Guggenheim has achieved a few stunning successes. Features in the past have included a major exhibition of photographs by

German cult cinematographer Wim Wenders, wide-ranging retrospectives of Chillida and Iglesias, an assemblage of sculpture and photography by Picasso, Degas and Rodin, and a hugely successful retrospective of fashion house Emporio Armani. Nothing so far has been able to compete with the runaway success of 2000's 'The Art of the Motorcycle' exhibition; all of a sudden, half the Basque country was in gallery 104 dribbling over the lusty iron horse.

Postscript: The Guggenheim Effect

No new building has been more praised in recent years, and no one disputes that Gehry's massive sculpture marks a significant break with traditional museum models. But there have been some detractors, among them the architectural historian Juan Antonio Ramírez, who describes it as 'a cultural franchise, a sign of the McDonaldization of the universe', and perceives a 'California jokiness at the expense of the tribal tragedy of the Basques'. ETA, seeing it as a symbol of globalization, killed a guard there just before it was opened in 1997 by King Juan Carlos. Security, understandably, remains tight. Others, while marvelling at the building, worry that Guggenheim Bilbao is in the vanguard of the trend of art museums as entertainment centres, with their restaurants, cafés and shops, and that the meaning of the art itself (the serious works at any rate – sorry, Puppy!) is co-opted by the very sort of consumer culture that the avant-garde sought to challenge. The popular appeal of a motorcycle show is used in evidence of this, and the issue has been raised again with an exhibition devoted to fashion designer Giorgio Armani which, for all the negative press, was a sellout in both New York and Bilbao.

'Cultural tourism' may elicit sneers from architects and art historians, but many other cities gaze enviously at the enormous financial and regenerative benefits that Bilbao has reaped from the Guggenheim. Since opening in 1997, the museum has already recouped every penny invested in it. The city agreed to pay an annual subsidy of around 20 per cent of its budget, but the museum has become entirely self-financing long before anyone ever dreamed it would be possible.

The Guggenheim's success has spawned an ambitious series of restoration projects throughout Bilbao, including Philippe Starck's conversion of a former wine warehouse into the glossy Alhóndiga cultural centre (*see* p.117). Perhaps most extraordinary is the transformation taking place on the **Abandoibarra flats**. Acres of railway sidings have disappeared, making way for a new development crowned by a huge skyscraper, the Torre Iberdrola, designed by César Pelli and completed in 2010. More office blocks,

Rafael Moneo's boxy university library building, and various shops are sprouting up alongside the Guggenheim, and an extensive park area is unfolding, completing the 'green corridor' between Parque de Doña Casilda Iturrizar and Paseo del Arenal. The thick-set **Palacio Euskaldena** completes the project, its massive hulk evoking the days when rusty freighters laboured up the Nervión.

Around Bilbao

Only a third of Bilbao's million-odd souls live within the city itself. Bilbao is the heart of a sprawling conurbation which lines the Nervión for 20 miles, with factories and tower blocks squeezing in wherever the terrain permits.

Industrial archaeologists may want to head for **Sestao**, site of the impressive ruins of the Altos Hornos de Vizcaya, once one of the biggest steel mills in Europe; all the bars in the area have evocative photos. Neighbouring **Ansio** now contains the massive Bilbao Exhibition Centre (BEC), used for trade fairs, concerts and sports events. As for the fancier suburbs, these are found near the coast, where there are dramatic cliffs and a number of beaches.

The most distinguished suburb is **Getxo** (Neguri, Algorta and Bidezabal metro stations), a combination suburb, marina and beach resort whose waterfront is lined with lovely villas. Getxo claims one of the youngest populations in Vizcaya, and the closest beaches to downtown Bilbao, yet retains a distinctly refined atmosphere; signs politely request that swimming costumes should not be worn on the beachfront promenade. A few traces of the town's more earthbound past continue to linger, particularly in the graceful old fishing port of **Algorta**, which cascades down the cliffs from a defiantly modern *urbanización*. Look out for 19th-century **San Nicolás de Bari**, built in late neoclassical style, where stoups made of giant clam shells prop up the walls by the main door.

Almost everything else in Getxo was built in the 20th century, including the grandiose villas that line the waterfront between Arriaga and Las Arenas beaches. New money from iron and the shipyards paid for these mansions; it couldn't guarantee good taste, but at least in the 1920s it bought a nice view. Nowadays, however, the crumbling old castles look across to the proletarian suburbs of Bilbao's superport, sprawling along the left bank of the estuary from Santurtzi to Portugalete.

Puente Colgante
www.puente-colgante. com; t 94 480 10 12, Areeta or Portulaguete metro; open daily 10–9; adm

The *ría*, and a social chasm, are bridged at the Nervión's mouth by one of Vizcaya's great industrial-age landmarks, the **Puente Colgante**, or 'hanging bridge'; the name refers to a system (unique in its day) of transporting people and goods across the river by way of a suspended gondola, allowing free passage to tall ships without the palaver of swinging or raising the bridge. This is Bilbao's proudest monument from the 19th century – locals like to call it 'the Eiffel Tower of Vizcaya' – and was as much a symbol of a vigorous economy in its day as the Guggenheim is now. Modern-day visitors can take a lift to the uppermost span for a commanding view of the port and estuary.

The beaches continue eastwards along the coast. Though they're jam-packed with Bilbaínos at weekends, they can be fun; both the beaches and the water are surprisingly clean. Two of the most popular are at **Sopelana** and **Plentzia**; the latter is an agreeably sleepy town on weekdays, with a handsome medieval quarter. Plentzia lacks any real sights, but it's a good place to wander around when the beach scene gets too frantic; the main monuments are the Gothic church of Santa María Magdalena and the 16th-century town hall, now home to a small Museo Municipal, which has exhibits on Plentzia's fishing history.

Tourist Information in Bilbao

ⓘ **Bilbao >**
Plaza Ensanche 1,
t 94 479 57 60,
www.bilbao.net

Airport, t 94 471 03 01

The main **tourist offices** are in Plaza Ensanche, in front of the Guggenheim at Abandoibarra 2, and in the Teatro Arriaga, Plaza Arriaga, on the edge of the Casco Viejo. There is also an **airport office**, near the luggage carousel; visit it before you leave the luggage hall as it isn't accessible once you have passed through customs.

Post offices: The main post office is at Alameda de Urquijo 19, **t** 94 422 05 48, *www.correos.es*. There is another branch at Alameda de Mazarredo 12. You can also buy stamps (*sellos*) at *estancos* (tobacconists), recognizable by their maroon and yellow sign marked *tabacos*.

Telephones: There are public telephones on many street corners, in stations and in most museums (in the basement of the Guggenheim, for example), which usually take cards (*tarjeta telefónica*, bought at news-agents and tobacconists for €5 or €10) and coins. For international calls, buy a phonecard with a scratch-off PIN from *estancos* – these are cheaper than Telefónica's exorbitant international rates.

Banks: The section of the Gran Vía between Plaza Moyúa and Plaza Circular has dozens of banks where you can change money.

Internet and email: Note that many hotels and *hostales* throughout the Pais Vasco have WiFi access: ask when you book your accommodation. The city operates a **free WiFi** network, with hotspots throughout the city, including at the outdoor café next to the Guggenheim, and the café of the Museo de Bellas Artes. For *ciber cafés*, ask at the tourist office, or try the Laser Internet Center, C/Sendeja 5, **t** 94 445 35 09.

Magazines and newspapers: There are local versions of Spain's two major publications, *El País* and *El Mundo*, but everyone reads *El Correo*, Bilbao's local newspaper. It contains listings for music, exhibitions, cultural events and cinemas in Spanish. The *Bilbao Guide*, available from tourist information offices and some hotels, has plenty of listings, in English and Spanish.

Useful websites: As well as the official city site, *www.guggenheim-bilbao.es* (the official Guggenheim site) and *www.spain.info* (the official Spanish tourist office site) are useful. Best of all is *www.euskadi.net*, a Basque government website with a wide range of useful information.

Tours: *see* p.111.

Festivals in Bilbao

2 February: the *Romería San Blas* ends at San Nicholas, just off El Arenal.

16 July: a marine procession navigates the Río de Nervión in honour of the Virgin Mary.

Semana Grande/Aste Nagustia: begins on the Saturday after 15 August, a city-wide party with balls, parades of papier-mâché giants, fireworks and bullfights. The tourist office has information on the different events.

Shopping in Bilbao

There's no shortage of opportunities to spend your money in Bilbao. The Siete Calles of the Casco Viejo are a good place to start, particularly C/Bidebarrieta and C/Correo, with plenty of upmarket clothing and shoe shops, and tacky souvenir places knocking out ceramic Puppys (à la Guggenheim). For something slightly funkier, try C/Somera, where youthful fashions dominate and subversive 'grow shops' line the street. The trendiest boutiques are concentrated in the Ensanche, mostly south of the Gran Vía around Plaza Indautxu; C/Ercilla is a good place to start. Best buys are leather goods, food and wine.

Department Store

El Corte Inglés, Gran Vía Pastelería 7–9. Everything you would expect from Spain's largest department store chain – fashion, leather goods, books, music, cosmetics and more. There is also a bureau de change. Another branch across the street has a wide selection of books and music.

Fashion and Leather Goods

Calzados Ayestaran, Gran Vía 27. High quality shoes and leather garments designed by established local chain. You can preview the goods at www.ayestaran.es.

The Closet, C/Ledesma 18. Gorgeous women's clothing and accessories in a loft-style space from a range of hip international labels.

Javier de Juana, Gran Vía 18. Long-established, prestigious tailor and fashion shop with beautiful evening clothes and classic outfits.

Loewe, Gran Vía 39 (next door to Bolsos Ferrara). Expensive, elegant leather clothes, bags, shoes and other goods.

Mica, C/Lotería 2. A showcase of Spanish designers from Barcelona and Madrid, plus some young Bilbao designers such as Carlos Diez Diez.

Persuade, C/Villarias 8. A wonderful selection of antiques and exquisite fashions at this stylish shop.

Zara, Gran Vía 16. Very popular Spanish chain with well-priced fashion for men, women and children.

Books

La Casa del Libro, Colón de Larreategui 41. Part of a Spanish chain, this has a wide range of maps and books, including a good selection in English (several branches).

Urretxindorra, C/Iparraguirre 26. More of the same (including Basque cookbooks in English), plus one of the best selections of Basque music.

Food and Wine

Almacen Coloniales y Bacalao Gregorio Martín, C/Artekale 22. A wonderful old shop in the Casco Viejo, still with its old fittings, almost overtaken by the sheets of bacalao (salted cod) hanging from the ceiling. All kinds of regional fishy specialities are sold, some easily transportable in jars or tins.

Arrese, Gran Vía 24. An old and very famous confectioners which is renowned for its chocolate truffles and the best pastries in Bilbao.

Chocolates de Mendaro, C/Licenciado Poza 16. This chocolate-maker has been concocting luxury chocolates since 1850. Sample from more than a hundred varieties.

Mercado de la Ribera (see p.115). One of the biggest covered markets in the world, with a wealth of fresh produce.

El Rincón de Vino, Euskalduna 5. Excellent range of Spanish and Basque wines. They also offer tastings and run courses for those who want to learn more about Spanish wines. More information from www.pasionporelvino.com.

Gifts and Souvenirs

Basandere, C/Iparraguirre 4. Just a skip away from the Guggenheim, this attractive Basque boutique has ceramics, glassware, hand-crafted jewellery, tasteful household linens and other goods. There are also Basque music CDs, T-shirts and mugs.

Kukuxumusu, C/Rodríguez Arias 27. Souvenirs, from T-shirts, postcards and mugs, to posters and hand-made ceramics. Several branches.

Regalos Rui-Wamba, Plaza Nueva 10. All kinds of kitsch, from religious ornaments to souvenirs.

Shopa, Alhóndiga. The Alhóndiga's gift shop is crammed with designer goodies, from art and design books, to T-shirts and tableware.

Sports and Activities in Bilbao

Football

Football is a highly charged national passion and something of a war without bullets throughout Spain, but in Bilbao it becomes almost a religion. Even the stadium (at San Mamés, near the Plaza del Sagrado Corazón) is known as 'the Cathedral'.

Atlético was founded in 1898 by Englishmen working in the city, and unlike most European teams staunchly fields only Basque players, yet manages to remain in the top ranks of the Spanish leagues. One of its first great stars in the 1920s was José Antonio Aguirre, who became the president of Euskadi during the Republic. If you want to see a game, buy tickets at branches of the BBK bank, or at the San Mamés stadium (see also *www.athletic-club.es*).

Pelota

The biggest *frontón* in the Basque Lands opened in 2011, and can seat up to 3000 spectators. It's in the rapidly growing new district of Mirabilia, on the hill south of the Casco Viejo (take bus nos. 30, 71 or 75 from the old town). It plays host to a huge *frontón* festival held in March or April; ask at the tourist office for details.

One of the most atmospheric places to watch a *frontón* match is at Deportivo Bilbao, Alameda Rekalde, **t** 94 423 11 08, *www.club-deportivo. com*. This century-old club organises important *pelota* matches throughout the year and has a capacity for 1,500 spectators.

Bullfighting

The bullfighting season runs from April to October, although the highlight is the *Semana Grande* (*see* 'Calendar of Events', p.76) in August. Tickets can be purchased through the website: *www.plazatorosbilbao.com*.

Where to Stay in Bilbao

Bilbao ✉ 48000

The 'Guggenheim Effect' has filled Bilbao's hotels to the brim with the kind of educated, culture-seeking tourist other cities dream of, so book in advance. Most of the inexpensive rooms are in the Casco Viejo.

Luxury–Very Expensive

Bilbao has quite a few luxury hotels catering for the business people who pass through; some offer up to 50 per cent discount at weekends.

15 *****Gran Hotel Domine Bilbao**, Alameda de Mazarredo 61, **t** 94 425 33 00, *www.granhoteldominebilbao. com*. This has a fabulous location right opposite the Guggenheim; the bold, playful interior design is by Javier Mariscal. The sleekly luxurious rooms offer every imaginable comfort. The excellent restaurant, **Beltz the Black**, and hip bar are open to non-residents.

11 *****Carlton**, Plaza de Federico Moyúa 2, **t** 94 416 22 00, *www. aranzazu-hoteles.com*. Once the headquarters of the Republican Basque government, this plush 19th-century hotel has lodged famous bullfighters, along with Hemingway, Ava Gardner and Lauren Bacall, and is perfectly placed for shopping and the Guggenheim.

Expensive

12 *****Lopez de Haro**, C/Obispo Orueta 2, **t** 94 423 55 00, *www. hotellopezdeharo.com*. This classically elegant hotel has one of the city's finest restaurants, **Club Náutico** (*see* p.142). Not much to look at from the outside, but the interior is opulent. Close to the pretty Jardines de Albia, it's 5mins from the Guggenheim.

10 ****Hotel Miro**, Alameda Mazarredo, 77, **t** 94 661 18 80, *www. mirohotelbilbao.com*. Very close to the Guggenheim, this intimate boutique

⭐ Hotel Miro **>>**

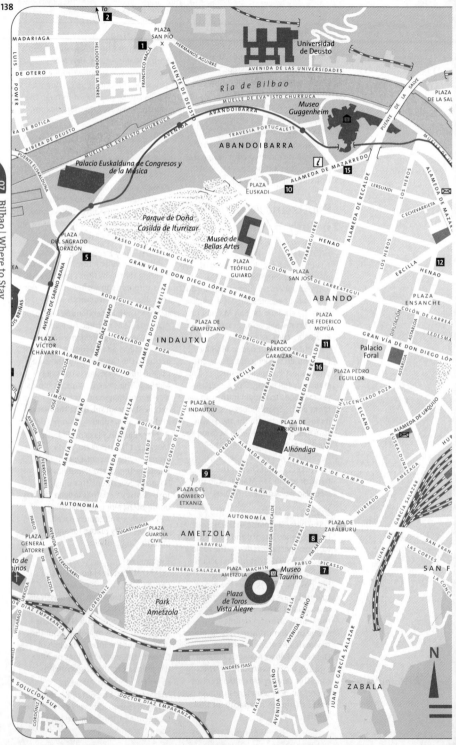

AVENIDA DE MAURICE RAVEL

VÍA VIEJA DE LEZAMA

URIBARRI

VÍA VIEJA DE LEZAMA

CASTAÑOS

CASTAÑOS

HUERTAS DE LA VILLA

PLAZA DE LA VILLA

Funicular de Artxanda

PLAZA DE MORAZA

CASCO VIEJO

PASEO CAMPO DE VOLANTÍN

TÍBOLI

TÍBOLI

PUENTE ZUBIZURI

URIBITARTE

18

26

14

LA RIBERA

SANTA MARÍA

PLAZA DE LOS FUEROS

PLAZA DE ARRIAGA

CORREO

PLAZA NUEVA

19 20

BIDEBARRIETA

13

VÍCTOR

SOMBRERERÍA

21 JARDINES

23 22

PERRO

LOTERÍA BANCO DE ESPAÑA

24

PLAZA SANTIAGO

† Catedral

ARTEKALE

SOMERA

LA RONDA

SOLOKOETXE

ZABALBIDE

MUELLE DE URIBITARTE

PLAZA PÍO BAROJA

PLAZA SAN VICENTE

† San Vicente Mártir

Jardines de Albia

ALAMEDA DE MAZARREDO

PLAZA DE MAZARREDO

BERASTEGUI

EZ DE HARO

RDO

PUENTE DE LA RIBERA

JULIÁN ECHEVARRÍA CAMARÓN

LA RIBERA

Río de Nervión

SAN FRANCISCO

Mercado

PLAZA SANTOS JUANES

ATXURI

PLAZA CIRCULAR

4

17

VILLARIAS

RIPA

Paseo del Arenal

VDA. DE ESPERANZA

ESPERANZA

San Nicolás

BEGOÑA

VIRGEN DE BEGOÑA

To Basílica Nuestra Señora de Begoña

Estación de Abando

Estación de Santander

BAILÉN

DOS DE MAYO

HERNANI

Teatro Arriaga

PLAZA DE LOS FUEROS

PLAZA DE ARRIAGA

CORREO

PLAZA NUEVA

LA RIBERA

BIDEBARRIETA

VÍCTOR

SANTA MARÍA

JARDINES

SOMBRERERÍA

PLAZA DE MIGUEL DE UNAMUNO

PRIM

ITURRIBIDE

CASCO VIEJO

PERRO

LOTERÍA BANCO DE ESPAÑA

Museo Vasco

PLAZA SANTIAGO

† Catedral

ARTEKALE

SOMERA

LA RONDA

SOLOKOETXE

PLAZA ZUMÁRRAGA

ZUMÁRRAGA

FIKA

AMADEO DEPRIT

PRIM

ITURRIBIDE

SOLOKOETXE

JULIÁN ECHEVARRÍA CAMARÓN

PLAZA CORAZÓN DE MARÍA

FRANCISCO

Museo de Reproducciones Artísticas

LA RIBERA

PELOTA

PUENTE DE LA MERCED

LA RIBERA

Río de Nervión

MUELLE DE MARZANA

SAN FRANCISCO

Mercado

PLAZA SANTOS JUANES

PUENTE SAN ANTÓN

ZABALBIDE

ZABALBIDE

ATXURI

FIKA

SANTUTXU

LA CONCEPCIÓN

Monte de Miribilla

Estación de Atxuri

PLAZA DE LA ENCARNACIÓN

25 Diocesan Museum of Sacred Art

ATXURI

PLAZA DEL CARMEN

250 metres
250 yards

hotel has sleekly designed rooms, a small spa (which can be booked for private use), and delightful staff. A lounge area with free coffee and soft drinks is provided for guests.

18 ****Hesperia Bilbao, Campo Volantín 28, t 94 405 11 00; www. hesperia-bilbao.es. It's difficult to miss the multicoloured window panes of this designer hotel, which is located next to Santiago Calatrava's footbridge over the Nervión River. Like the Miro, the hotel is superbly located near the Guggenheim but has lower rates.

9 ****Hotel Indautxu, Plaza del Bombero Etxaniz, t 94 444 00 04, www.hotelindautxu.com. This giant glass cube has all the necessary comforts in a good, quiet location. Like its sister hotel, the Gran Domine, it attracts a glossy cosmopolitan clientele, and the house restaurant, Etxaniz (see p.142), is very good.

Moderate

26 ****Best Western Hotel Conde Duque, Paseo Campo de Volantin 22, t 94 44560 00, www.bestwestern hotelcondeduque.com. Modern chain hotel, with good-value spacious rooms in a central location.

5 ****NH Villa de Bilbao, Gran Vía 87, t 94 441 60 00, www.nh-hotels.com. On the city's grandest street, near Plaza del Sagrado Corazón, this sleek modern hotel with its striking marble and iron façade offers all the amenities. Particularly geared towards business people, but that means its weekend prices offer excellent value.

14 ***Barceló Hotel Nervión, Paseo del Campo de Volantín 11, t 94 445 47 00, www.bchoteles.com. A modern hotel, this presents a sleek glass façade overlooking the river not far from the town hall.

1 ***NH Deusto, C/Francisco Maciá 9, t 94 476 00 06, www.nh-hotels.com. A business hotel, well located near the University of Deusto and the Guggenheim. Check out the weekend deals.

19 ***Petit Palace Arana, C/Bidebarrieta 2, t 94 415 64 11, www. petitpalacearana.com. A tastefully refurbished hotel in a 19th-century building very near the Teatro Arriaga,

(★) Hostal Begoña >>

with smallish but comfortable rooms. Good Internet deals.

8 **Hotel Zabálburu, C/Pedro Martínez Artola 8, t 94 443 71 00, www.hotelzabalburu.com. Pleasant rooms in a modern setting, with parking facilities. It is family-run, friendly and in a quiet neighbourhood just down from the Plaza de Zabálburu. It's also handy for the bus and train stations. Prices drop a bracket outside high season.

25 **Sirimiri, Pza de la Encarnación 3, t 94 433 07 59, www.hotelsirimiri.com. A peachy little hotel that offers a comfortable, reasonably priced option, situated on a pretty square near the old church of San Anton and Atxuri train station. Extras include a small gym and sauna.

7 **Vista Alegre, C/Pablo Picasso 13, t 94 443 14 50. Good facilities at a reasonable price, although it is a bit more of a trot to the main sights.

21 **Hostal Iturrienea Ostatua, C/Santa María 14, t 94 416 15 00. María 14, t 94 416 15 00. A nice choice in the Casco Viejo; simple rooms are furnished with a mix of antique and new pieces, while flowering plants trail from the balconies. You can't miss its brightly painted façade.

3 **HR Rio de Bilbao, C/Ribera de Deusto 32, t 94 476 50 60, www. riobilbao.es. This quiet riverside hostal is mainly used as a student residence and has a garden and cooking facilities. Several rooms are reserved for visitors; useful if you don't mind being away from the centre.

4 **Hostal Begoña, C/Amistad, 2, t 94 423 0134, www.hostalbegona.com. This charming option in the Casco Viejo has six spacious, brightly decorated suites, with small fridges and microwaves. One of the historic centre's best deals.

16 **Pension Central, Alameda Recalde, 35a, 1°, t 94 410 63 39, www.hostalcentral.com. It may lack the flair of Begoña but the price is fair for the modern, clean rooms with internet access. The location, just off Moyua square, is also convenient.

17 *Hotel Ripa, C/Ripa 3, t 94 423 96 77, www.hotel-ripa.com. On the riverfront opposite the Casco Viejo;

nice, renovated rooms with balconies overlooking the old opera house and town hall.

20 **Arriaga Suites,** Bidebarrieta 3, t 635 707 247, *www.arriagasuites.com*. This charming option in the Casco Viejo has six spacious, brightly decorated suites, each with small fridge and microwave.

Inexpensive

13 ****Bilbao Jardines,** Jardines 94, t 94 479 42 10, *www.hotelbilbaojardines. com*. A clean, light and modern hotel in the Casco Viejo, conveniently located close to the *pintxos* circuit. One of the historical centre's best deals.

6 ****Estadio,** Avda J. Antonio Zunzunegui 10, t 94 442 42 41. On the other side of town, handy for the Termibús (see p.109). A little pricy for what it offers.

2 ****Hotel Artetxe,** Carretera Enékuri-Artxanda Km.7, t 94 474 77 80, *www.hotelartetxe.com*. A delightful option, this is a traditional Basque house on a hill above the city with charming rooms and fabulous views. Best if you have your own transport. Good restaurant and they also rent apartments in an annexe.

22 ****Hostal Gurea,** C/Bidebarrieta 14, t 94 416 32 99. From the outside this looks pretty shabby and tumbledown, but inside you'll find clean rooms (with bath) and friendly owners.

24 ***Hostal Estrella,** C/María Muñoz 6, t 94 416 40 66. Refurbished, clean and bright *hostal* near the cathedral. Better for night owls, as it can be a bit noisy.

23 **Pension Mendez I and II,** Santa Maria 13, fourth floor (Pension I) and first floor (Pension II), t 94 416 03 64, *www.pensionmendez.com*. The rooms are rather small but clean and painted an elegant turquoise blue. You pay more for the Pension II because it's on the first floor and rooms have baths and TV. The higher options (fourth floor) come with shared baths.

Around the City ✉ 48990

****Ercilla Embarcadero, Avda Zugazarte 51, Getxo, t 94 480 31 00, *www.hotelembarcadero.com* (€€€€). A sumptuous hotel in a traditional Basque villa set amid landscaped gardens on the riverfront, with striking 1920s-style interior design.

***Gran Hotel, C/María Díaz de Haro 2, Portugalete, t 94 401 48 00, *www. granhotelpuentecolgante.com* (€€€). Across from the lively Getxo neighbourhood, this is a plush hotel situated in an historical building at the foot of the Vizcaya Bridge.

**Artaza, Avda Los Chopos 12, Neguri, t 94 491 28 52, *www.hotelartaza.com* (€€€). Elegant comfort in a refined mansion surrounded by tranquil parkland, near Neguri metro station.

Pensión Areeta, C/Mayor 13, Getxo, t 94 463 81 36 (€). Comfy rooms with bath.

Plentzia ✉ 48630

*Hotel Kaian, C/Areatza 38, t 94 677 54 70, *www.kaianplentzia.com* (€€–€). Charming, peach-painted villa in its own little garden on the seafront, with just a handful of spacious rooms.

*Hotel Casa de Marinos Uribe, C/Erribea 13, t 94 677 44 78, *www. hoteluribe.com* (€€–€). Restored mansion overlooking the *ría*. Some rooms boast luxurious glassed-in balconies.

Eating Out in Bilbao

Donostia-San Sebastián might get all the fanfare, but you can eat just as well in Bilbao. For the purest Basque cuisine, look for the strangest names. If you want to do as the locals do, go for a *txikiteo*, the local, civilized version of a pub-crawl, stopping for *pintxos* and tapas accompanied by a glass of Rioja or a beer at lots of different bars (see 'Tapas/*Pintxos*', pp.146–8).

Note that many restaurants close during the week before, or the week after, *Semana Grande* (the week before the 15th August).

Expensive

6 **Zortziko,** Alameda de Mazarredo 17, t 94 423 97 43, *www.zortiko.es*. Splurge at this spectacular restaurant, in a historic building. The lunch menu is a relative bargain. *Closed Sun, Mon eve.*

15 **Bermeo,** C/Ercilla 37 (Hotel Ercilla), t 94 470 57 00. This offers a delicate

blend of new and old Basque cuisine in sumptuous surroundings. *Closed Sat lunch, Sun eve.*

7 **Guría**, Gran Vía 66, **t** 94 441 57 80, *www.restauranteguria.com*. Old favourite serving traditional Basque fare since 1920. *Closed Sun eve.*

8 **Mina**, Muelle Marzana, **t** 94 479 59 38, *http://restaurantemina.es*. This serves spectacular New Basque cooking including fabulous desserts, served in a set menu which changes daily. There are very few tables, so reserve in advance. *Closed Sun eve, Mon, Tues.*

17 **Gorrotxa**, Alameda de Urquijo 30, **t** 94 422 05 35. In spite of its shopping mall setting, this restaurant offers spectacular New Basque cooking by Carmelo Gorrotzategui, served in a sophisticated ambience. Try the *lubina al horno con gambas* (oven-baked sea bass with prawns) or the *rodaballo encebellado* (turbot with onion sauce). *Reservations essential. Closed Sun, first 2 weeks Sept, and Holy Week.*

25 **Víctor**, Plaza Nueva 2, **t** 94 415 16 78, *www.restaurantevictor.com*. Víctor has overcome the disadvantage of having a pronounceable name and has, over the last 60 years, built up an enviable reputation as one of the Casco Viejo's best restaurants.They also have an excellent tapas bar. *Closed Sun (exc May), Easter, last 2 weeks Jan and first 2 weeks Sept.*

22 **El Perro Chico (Perrotxico)**, C/Arechaga 2, **t** 94 415 05 19. Close to Ribera market, this has deep blue walls, tiles, lots of paintings and a boho-chic atmosphere. Dine on traditional Basque favourites like *bacalao con berenjanas* (cod with aubergine) or *lomo de merluza con kokotxas* (fillet and cheeks of hake). *Book in advance. Closed Sun–Mon.*

 Nerua >

2 **Nerua**, Guggenheim Museum, **t** 94 423 93 33, *www.nerua.com*. Book weeks in advance for a table at this light-filled restaurant. Superb, incredibly technical yet flavoursome cuisine by award-winning young chef Josean Martínez Alija. Go for the *menú de degustación* (€75). *Closed Sun eve, Mon, and Tues eve.*

5 **Club Náutico**, C/Obispo Orueta 2 (Hotel López de Haro), **t** 94 423 55 00.

Innovative New Basque cuisine in elegant surroundings. Grilled monkfish, steamed hake with baby squid and delicious desserts are among the specialities on offer. *Closed Sat lunch and Sun, 15 June–Aug.*

18 **Etxaniz**, C/Gordóniz 15 (Hotel Indautxu), **t** 94 421 11 98. This renowned establishment serves excellent New Basque cuisine. Crisply elegant surroundings complement the beautifully presented dishes: fillet of hake with mushroom and clam sauce, or a wonderful lobster salad are recommended. *Closed Sun, first 2 weeks Aug, and Easter.*

11 **Matxinbenta**, C/Ledesma 26, **t** 94 424 84 95. In a street full of old-fashioned bars and eating places, this is one of Bilbao's most established restaurants. Formal and popular with businessmen, it offers robust, traditional Basque dishes using seasonal specialities, including plenty of seafood, game and mushrooms. *Closed Sun eve.*

4 **Yandiola**, Alhóndiga, **t** 94 413 36 36, *www.yandiola.com*. The most upmarket of the three restaurants in the Alhóndiga; refined dishes from dynamic chef Ricardo Perez in a plush dining room designed by Philippe Starck. Follow up with drinks on the roof terrace. *Closed Sun, Mon eve, Tues eve, Easter Week and first 2 weeks Sept.*

14/16/29 **Serantes**, C/Licenciado Poza 16, **t** 94 421 21 29; **Serantes II**, Alameda de Urquijo 51, **t** 94 410 26 99; **Serantes III**, Alameda Mazarredo 75, **t** 94 424 80 04, *www.marisqueriaserantes.com*. Famous local favourites, these classic restaurants are always busy. Specializing in fish, but with a good selection of options for carnivores too, the secret of their success is very fresh, simply prepared dishes. The *menú del día* is attractively priced at €22, but be warned that *à la carte* can be three times the price. *Closed Sun, three weeks in July.*

(off maps) **Azurmendi**, Barrio Leguina, Larrabetzu (10km east of Bilbao), **t** 94 455 88 66, *www.azurmendi.es*. Extraordinarily inventive cuisine by top chef Eneko Atxa, who has two Michelin stars, in a theatrical restaurant which combines rusticity with contemporary design. Don't miss his signature 'reverse egg', in which the yolk is replaced with black truffle. *Closed Sun, Mon eve.*

Moderate

21 **Bola-Viga**, C/Enrique Eguren 4, t 94 443 50 26. This friendly little place, famous across the city, specializes in the three things the Basques do best: *merluza* (hake), *bacalao* and *rabo de toro* (oxtail). *Closed Sun, and Sept.*

12 **Nicolás**, C/Ledesma 10, t 94 424 07 37. Another of the old-fashioned gems on Calle Ledesma, this restaurant is particularly, although not exclusively, acclaimed for its fish dishes. Definitely a good place to try local *bacalao* (salted cod) and *merluza* (hake) in traditional sauces. Come just for the *pintxos* at the bar if you don't want to sit down to a full meal. *Restaurant closed Sun eve, all day Sun mid-June–mid-Sept.*

28 **Arriaga-Sidrería Asador**, C/Santa María 13, t 94 416 56 70. A grill and *sidrería* house specializing in roasted meats and fish, this long, brick-walled restaurant is packed with tables and can get very busy. *Closed Sun eve.*

10 **Metro-Moyúa**, C/Gran Vía 40, t 94 424 92 73. Set on the corner of the Plaza Moyúa, this family-run restaurant serves good Basque cooking with flair. There's a cafetería offering a very reasonable *menú del día* (€11) and a huge terrace where you can watch the world go by as you tuck into *mero al txakoli* (halibut with tart white wine) followed by a piquant *tarta de limón.* *Closed Sun, 25 Dec and 1 Jan.*

★ **Bascook** >

13 **Bascook**, Barroeta Aldamar 8, t 94 400 99 77, *www.bascook.com.* Hidden away in a cleverly renovated old salt warehouse, Bascook serves imaginative Basque dishes designed to share, with the emphasis on the freshest local produce. A gem.

1 **Casa Vasca**, C/Avda Lehendakari 13–15, t 94 475 47 78. Over in Deusto, this offers innovative interpretations of regional dishes in elegant surroundings, plus a well-priced set lunch menu. Smart bar offering upmarket *pintxos. Closed Sun eve.*

23 **Atea**, Paseo Uribitarte 4, t 94 400 58 69, *www.atearestaurante.com.* Chic designer bistro, with a pale wood and stone interior and a small summer terrace near the Guggenheim. It serves well-priced but highly imaginative tapas and *raciones*, which are perfect for sharing.

27 **Amboto**, C/Jardínes 2, t 94 415 61 48. A bustling seafood place off Plaza de Arriaga that specializes in *merluza* (hake) in a sauce made from crabs. As well as the *à la carte* options, they also offer a pair of good set menus (at €14 and €23). *Closed Tues eve, Wed eve and September.*

3 **La Pizarra**, Juan de Ajuriaguerra 16, 4, t 94 424 60 82. On a charming street behind the Gran Vía, with a lively, modern tapas bar at the front, and a beautiful (if minuscule) salon-style dining room at the back lined with bottles and lit with a crystal chandelier. *Closed Mon eve.*

30 **La Gallina Ciega**, C/Máximo Aguirre 2 (near the Museo de Bellas Artes), t 94 442 39 43. A tiny, eclectically decorated bar with utterly charming hosts, this serves superb lunches at the single wooden table. There's no menu – you'll be served whatever looked good at the market that day, although the emphasis is usually on fish – but it's always excellent. Book well in advance.

31 **Kikara**, C/Iparraguire 20, t 94 423 68 40, *www.kikara.com.* Fashionable, retro-chic restaurant-bar near the Guggenheim which offers elaborate contemporary cuisine (including a good set menu for about €30 which comprises seven tasting-size dishes). It usually offers a couple of vegetarian choices. DJ sessions at the weekend.

33 **Río Oja**, C/Perro 4. Another old-fashioned establishment with plenty of charm. It's a great place to try regional specialities like *bacalao al pil pil* or *a la vizkaína*, or *rabo de toro* (oxtail). At the bar, top tapas include the *txipirones* (baby squid) and anchovies. *Closed Mon.*

32 **Víctor Montes**, Plaza Nueva 8, t 94 415 70 67. One of the city's most celebrated eating places, a *belle époque* classic with a florid ebony and gilt façade. A vast array of *pintxos* wait inside, such as crisp *croquetas de bacalao.* Sunday lunchtime is the best time to come – local families turn up to eat and chat with their neighbours,

★ **La Gallina Ciega** >>

MADARIAGA

To **1**

LUIS

S DE OTERO

POWER

D

PLAZA
SAN PÍO
X

HERMANOS AGUIRRE

FRANCISCO MACÍA

HELIODORO DE LA TORRE

PUENTE DE DEUSTO

Universidad
de Deusto

AVENIDA DE LAS UNIVERSIDADES

Ría de Bilbao

MUELLE DE EVARISTO CHURRUCA

PLAZA
DE LA SA

PUENTE DE LA SALVE

RIBERA DE BOTICA

RIBERA DE DEUSTO

PUENTE EUSKALDUNA

MUELLE DE EVARISTO CHURRUCA

AVENIDA DE DEUSTO

ABANDOIBARRA

TRAVESÍA PORTUGALETE

2

Museo
Guggenheim

ABANDOIBARRA

MUELLE M

Palacio Euskalduna de Congresos y
de la Música

ALAMEDA DE MAZARREDO

PLAZA
EUSKADI

LERSUNDI

LOS HEROS

ALAMEDA DE RECALDE

C ECHEVARRIETA

ALAMEDA DE MAZA

PLAZA
DEL SAGRADO
CORAZÓN

Parque de Doña
Casilda de Iturrizar

Museo de
Bellas Artes

PASEO JOSÉ ANSELMO CLAVÉ

7

GRAN VÍA DE DON DIEGO LÓPEZ DE HARO

PLAZA
TEÓFILO
GUIARD

COLÓN

PLAZA
SAN JOSÉ DE LARREATEGUI

ELCANO

IPARRAGUIRRE

HENAO

LOS HEROS

ERCILLA

HENAO

3

5

ABANDO

AVENIDA DE SABINO ARANA

LUIS BRIÑAS

PLAZA
VÍCTOR
CHÁVARRI

RODRÍGUEZ ARIAS

MARÍA DÍAZ DE HARO

ALAMEDA DOCTOR AREILZA

LICENCIADO

POZA

J

K

INDAUTXU

Q

N

PLAZA DE
CAMPUZANO

RODRÍGUEZ ARIAS

PLAZA
PÁRROCO
GARAIZAR

ARIAS

PLAZA
DE FEDERICO
MOYÚA

10

DIPUTACIÓN

COLÓN DE LARREA

PLAZA
ENSANCHE

I

C **H**

11

ASTARLOA

LEDESMA

L

ALAMEDA DE URQUIJO

SIMÓN

MARÍA ESCUZA

JOSÉ MARÍA ESCUZA

ALAMEDA DE URQUIJO

M

ERCILLA

14

IPARRAGUIRRE

ALAMEDA DE RECALDE

GRAN VÍA DE DON DIEGO LÓP

Palacio
Foral

PLAZA PEDRO
EGUILLOR

LICENCIADO POZA

P

AVENIDA DEL FERROCARRIL

MARÍA DÍAZ DE HARO

BOLÍVAR

GREGORIO DE LA REVILLA

MANUEL ALLENDE

O **15**

16

PLAZA DE
INDAUTXU

GORDÓNIZ

ALAMEDA DE SAN MAMÉS

PLAZA DE
ARRIQUIBAR

4

Alhóndiga

17

19

GENERAL CONCHA

ELCANO

EUSKALDUNA

ALAMEDA DE URQUIJO

HURT

AUTONOMÍA

18

PLAZA DEL
BOMBERO
ETXANIZ

IPARRAGUIRRE

EGAÑA

FERNÁNDEZ DE CAMPO

20

HURTADO DE AMÉZAGA

AUTONOMÍA

PABLO

PLAZA
GENERAL
LATORRE

AVENIDA DEL FERROCARRIL

ALZOLA

nto de
chinos

ZUGASTINOVIA

PLAZA
GUARDIA
CIVIL

LABAYRU

AMETZOLA

AUTONOMÍA

ENRIQUE EGUREN

ALAMEDA DE RECALDE

GENERAL CONCHA

PM ARTOLA

PLAZA DE
ZABÁLBURU

JUAN DE GARCÍA SALAZAR

SAN FRAN

LAS CORTES

SAN F

LA CONCE

DÍAZ EMPARANZA

VILLABASO

CHURRUCA

CAMILO

GORDÓNIZ

21

GENERAL SALAZAR

PLAZA
AMETZOLA

MACHÍN

Museo
Taurino

Plaza
de Toros
Vista Alegre

PABLO PICASSO

IRALA

KIRKIÑO

Park
Ametzola

ANDRÉS ISASI

DOCTOR DÍAZ EMPARANZA

IRALA

AVENIDA KIRKIÑO

JUAN DE GARCÍA SALAZAR

ZABALA

N

TA SOLUCIÓN SUR

GORDÓNIZ

Tap

AVENIDA DE MAURICE

PLAZA
LA SALVE

CASTAÑOS

Funicular de
Artxanda

PLAZA DE
MORAZA

PUENTE DEL ARENAL

PLAZA DE
ARRIAGA

LOS FUEROS

HUERTAS DE LA VILLA

CASTAÑOS

PASEO CAMPO DE VOLANTÍN

LA RIBERA

24

CORREO

25

PLAZA
NUEVA

32

TIBOLI

PUENTE DE URIBITARTE

SANTA MARÍA

28

E

26 V

JARDINES

27

VÍCTOR

BIDEBARRIETA

SOMBRERERÍA

PLAZA DE MAZARREDO

23

URIBITARTE PÍO BAROJA

T

PERRO

X Y

33

LOTERÍA BANCO DE ESPAÑA

5

6

A

PLAZA
SAN
VICENTE

San Vicente Mártir

13

9

PLAZA
SANTIAGO

Catedral

JULIÁN ECHEVARRÍA CAMARÓN

ARTEKALE

LA RONDA

SOLOKOETXE

SOMERA

ZABALBIDE

LA RIBERA

LA RIBERA

PUENTE DE
LA RIBERA

Río de Nervión

PLAZA
SANTOS
JUANES

L

B

34

Jardines
de Albia

G F

12

U

SAN FRANCISCO

Mercado

LÓPEZ DE HARO

R

PLAZA
CIRCULAR

VILLARÍAS

RIBA

VIUDA DE EPALZA

ESPERANZA

Estación de
Abando

Estación de
Santander

Paseo
del
Arenal

San
Nicolás

BEGOÑA

HURTADO DE AMEZAGA

NAVARRA PUENTE DEL ARENAL

PLAZA DE
ARRIAGA

LOS FUEROS

VIRGEN DE BEGOÑA

BAILÉN

Teatro
Arriaga

CORREO

PLAZA
NUEVA

To Basílica Nuestra
Señora de Begoña

LA RIBERA

SANTA MARÍA

JARDINES

BIDEBARRIETA

VÍCTOR

SOMBRERERÍA

CASCO VIEJO

PLAZA DE
MIGUEL DE
UNAMUNO

PRIM

ITURRIBIDE

AMADEO DEPRIT

PRIM

DOS DE MAYO

HERNANI

PERRO

LOTERÍA BANCO DE ESPAÑA

Museo
Vasco

PLAZA
SANTIAGO

Catedral

JULIÁN ECHEVARRÍA CAMARÓN

ARTEKALE

SOMERA

LA RONDA

PLAZA
ZUMÁRRAGA

SOLOKOETXE

SOLOKOETXE

ITURRIBIDE

N FRANCISCO

PLAZA
CORAZÓN
DE MARÍA

Museo de
Reproducciones
Artísticas

22

8

LA RIBERA

Mercado

Río de Nervión

MUELLE DE MARZANA

PLAZA
SANTOS
JUANES

ZUMÁRRAGA

FIKA

ZABALBIDE

ZABALBIDE

CONCEPCIÓN

LA CONCEPCIÓN

SAN FRANCISCO

ATXURI

SANTUTXU

FIKA

Estación de
Atxuri

PLAZA DE LA
ENCARNACIÓN

ATXURI

Diocesan
Museum of
Sacred Art

250 metres
250 yards

Tapas Bars   Restaurants

followed by a stroll around the Sunday market. *Closed Sun eve.*

Inexpensive

26 La Deliciosa, C/Jardines 7. A pretty, stylish, white-painted café-restaurant which attracts a hip young crowd and offers an excellent lunch menu for around €10 (prices go up a category if you go *à la carte*). The chef has won awards for the fresh, innovative modern cuisine.

34 Iruña, C/Berastegi 5, t 94 423 70 21. A stunning tribute to the Alhambra, this legendary, beautiful Mudéjar-style café comes alive with the evening crowd.

⭐ *Txikiteo* >>

9 Saibigain, Barrencalle Barrena, 16, t 94 415 01 23. Well established since the 1950s; with a cheap *menú del día* and a bar full of *pintxos. Closed Sun.*

⭐ **Café Boulevard** >

24 Café Boulevard, C/Arenal 3, t 94 415 31 28. First opened in 1871, giving opera-goers a meeting place, and revamped 50 years later, the café retains its elegant Art Deco interior - which has recently been beautifully restored. Pop in for an afternoon iced coffee, an early evening *copa*, or a cocktail in its fashionable new basement bar.

Vegetarian

19 Vegetariano, Alameda de Urquijo 33, t 94 444 55 98 (€). Great-value menus full of simple vegetable-based dishes, with the emphasis on salads. *Closed Sun.*

20 Garibolo, C/Fernández del Campo 7, t 94 422 32 55 (€). Another pleasant little place with a daily *menú* for around than €10.

By the Sea (Getxo and Plentzia)

Jolastoki, Avda Los Chopos 24, Neguri, t 94 491 20 31 (€€€). Has an enviable reputation for its elaborate fish and fowl dishes. They also have a cheaper tavern, still elegant, with a well-priced set lunch menu. *Closed Sun eve, Mon, Easter week, and first 2 weeks Aug.*

El Puerto-Zabala, C/Aretxandra 20, Getxo, t 94 491 21 66 (€€€–€)€. This old-time portside restaurant in Algorta keeps things simple and unadorned, serving mighty portions of fresh fish out on a breezy terrace.

Basalbo Braseria, Estrada de Martiturri 18, Getxo, t 94 491 34 91, *http://basalbobaserria.com* (€€). A stylishly converted stone *caserio* set in the hills behind Getxo, this serves an excellent *menú del día* for €20 (with wine). *Closed Sun eve and Mon.*

Bar Urizarra, C/Artekale 14, Plentzia, t 94 677 28 70 (€). Looks a bit dingy but comes up with the goods for cheap Basque soul food; all the beans, fish and wine you could want for around €10.

Tapas/*Pintxos* in Bilbao

One of the city's greatest pleasures is the *txikiteo*, the ritual bar crawl, selecting titbits from the groaning bar tops (*see* pp.62–5). There are three main areas to enjoy this: in the Casco Viejo, in the streets around C/Ledesma in the Ensanche, and the central area around C/Licenciado Poza and the Plaza Indautxu. Among the local specialities are *tigres de Yurre*, mussels served in a piquant tomato and anchovy sauce; endless varieties of *bacalao* (salted cod) with different sauces, such as the mild, green *pil-pil* sauce; *champis*, mushrooms cooked in a garlic, parsley and lemon sauce; *pimientos*, slivers of fried or roasted pepper; fresh squid cooked in its own ink; and the ubiquitous little slices of bread with a breathtaking variety of toppings. Wash it all down with a glass of Rioja or *txakoli*.

Many of the city's finest restaurants also serve *pintxos* at the bar, and it's a great way to taste some of the best cuisine in the city if you can't quite manage a big blowout.

The annual *pintxos* competition takes place in March or April: for a list contending bars, or to see who won, see: *www.depintxos.net*.

Casco Viejo

The pretty arcaded Plaza Nueva is a good place to start.

S Los Fueros, C/Los Fueros 6. This tiled bar has a huge range of tapas, but the *gambas a la plancha* – fresh, simply cooked prawns – are the highlight. Try them with a glass of chilled amontillado sherry.

V **Berton**, C/Jardines 11, **t** 94 416 70 35. Filled with locals at weekends; this bar is brimming with a zillion varieties of hefty pieces of heaven. *Closed Sun pm and Mon.*

Y **Egiluz**, C/El Perro 4. One of the excellent, almost unchanged little bars in this busy street full of drinking and eating places. The house speciality is the *cazuelitas*, stews cooked in a small earthenware pot.

X **Xukela**, C/Perro 2, **t** 94 415 97 72. Another good bar on this narrow street, though this one has only been going for 30 years – a mere child compared to its venerable neighbours. There is an enormous variety of *pintxos*, including one with *queso de Cabrales* (a strong blue cheese from Asturias) topped with anchovies that is especially delicious.

T **Txiriboga**, C/Santa María 13. A minute bar hidden under piled-up platters of tiny slices of bread with dozens of different toppings. The *croquetas* are good too.

D **Oriotarra**, C/Blas de Otero 30. Across the river in Deusto, this atmospheric bar offers more than 150 varieties of *pintxos* – including an award-winning millefeuille pastry filled with pig's ear.

⭐ **Gatz >**

E Gatz, C/Sant María 10, *www. bargatz.com*. A tiny little bar in the heart of the Casco Viejo with fabulous and unusual tapas, including cherries stuffed with blue cheese.

W **Gure Toki**, Plaza Nueva 12, **t** 94 415 80 37. Winner of the 2011 Bilbao tapas championship, this modern bar serves superb, creative *pintxos* such as baby squid stuffed with black sausage.

The Ensanche

Across in the Ensanche, the streets around Calle Ledesma keep going until a bit later than other areas of the city.

⭐ **Bitoque de Albia >**

U Bitoque de Albia, C/Alameda Mazarredo 6, **t** 94 423 65 45. The creator of some of the best *pintxos* in the Basque Lands is Englishman Darran Williamson, whose exquisite miniature creations include baby squid ravioli in its own ink. The downstairs restaurant serves superb, creative cuisine and a good set lunch; but book early for a table. (There's another, smaller, branch at C/Rodríguez Arias 43, **t** 94 441 88 30, not far from the Museo de Bellas Artes.)

B **Jardines**, Avda de Mazarredo 8. Across the Jardines de Albia from the Iruña, this is an elegant little spot with a popular terrace in summer. You'll find all the usual *pintxos* here, from good tortilla to very tasty fried anchovies. *Closed Sun.*

C **Lasa**, C/Diputación 3, **t** 94 424 01 03. Elegant, classic bar with excellent *pintxos*; try the *brocheta* with monkfish and prawns. Also has a dining room for sit-down meals.

A **María Mani**, C/Henao 3. Up the road from the Jardines de Albia, this bar serves an imaginative range of *pintxos*: *morros* (pig's cheeks) *a la vinagreta*, *salpicón*.

R **La Granja**, Plaza Circular 3, **t** 94 423 08 13. Another of the city's stalwarts, a lively, lovely Art Nouveau-style bar with wooden tables, little alcoves and a good selection of traditional *pintxos* on one of the city's main *plazas*. *Menú del día* €13. *Closed Sun.*

L **Antomar**, C/Ledesma 14, **t** 94 424 85 70. Fine hams and *embutidos* (cured meats and sausages) are the speciality of this popular bar. *Closed Sat and Sun, plus first 2 weeks Aug.*

G **Artajo**, C/Ledesma 7. There's never any room in this large bar, despite its size. Everyone is here for the *tigres*, mussels in a spicy tomato and anchovy sauce – the best in Bilbao.

F **La Taberna Taurina**, C/Ledesma 5, **t** 94 424 13 81. One of the oldest, most traditional bars around, this gets packed during the summer bull-fighting season. The tortillas, with dozens of different fillings, are the highlight here. *Closed Sun.*

I **El Globo**, C/Diputación 8, **t** 94 415 42 21. A genial, modern bar which has won awards for its elaborate *pintxos*; it's also a good place to find imaginative vegetarian toppings, but the star is their *gratinado de bacalao*. *Closed Sun.*

H **Lekeitio**, C/Diputación 1, **t** 94 423 92 40. This attractive bar has a reputation for serving some of the best *pintxos* in Bilbao. Try the famous three-tiered tortilla, stuffed with tuna and ham, or the stuffed artichokes in season. *Closed Sat, Sun, first 2 weeks Aug, first 2 weeks Sept.*

Around Plaza Indautxu

There are dozens of bars lining the Calle Licenciado Poza, and plenty of good ones just off the main *plaza*.

N **Okela**, C/Maestro García Rivero 8. Bright, modern bar, that specializes in an endless variety of seafood tapas, and attracts a young hip crowd.

O **Urdazpi**, Alameda de Urquijo 48. This bar has a good restaurant serving Basque favourites. The *jamón de pata negra*, served as a *ración* at the bar, is excellent, and the wine list includes a good range of *txakoli* wines.

Q **El Huevo Frito**, Calle Garcia Rivero Maestro, t 94 441 22 49. This bar's name, 'Fried Egg', belies the sophistication of its elaborately prepared *pintxos* (some of which include fried eggs).

P **Tabernilla de Poza**, C/Licenciado Poza 3. A delightful throwback, this old-fashioned tavern still serves its wines in a *porrón*, a ceramic jug with a long spout. Accompany the wine with *anchoas con pimientos rojos* (anchovies with red peppers).

M **New Or Konpon**, C/Licenciado Poza 33. A young place serving gourmet sandwiches (try the grilled chicken and apple) and creative tapas.

J **Ziripot**, C/Licenciado Poza 40. All manner of beers on tap and sturdy *pintxos* to mop them up. There's a young, lively crowd enjoying the *croquetas de jamón* (ham croquettes) and tortilla served with a hunk of fresh bread.

K **Busterri**, C/Licenciado Poza 43. This café-bar also has a very decent restaurant if you are not in the mood to face the crowds at the bar. The *pintxos* and *raciones* are good and the wine list is excellent.

Entertainment and Nightlife in Bilbao

For listings, check the back pages of the local newspaper, *El Correo*, or pick up the bi-monthly *Bilbao Guide*, available at tourist information offices.

Music and Theatre

Teatro Arriaga, Plaza de Arriaga, t 94 479 20 36. Regular performances of opera, theatre and comedy.

Palacio Euskalduna de Congresos y de la Música, Avda Abandoibarra 4, t 94 403 50 00. Also puts on plays and musicals, and sometimes big-name foreign acts.

Cinemas

Undubbed films are listed as v.o. (*versión originale*), though showings are few and far between in Bilbao. **Multicines**, José María Escuza 13, is the only cinema that regularly shows undubbed films.

Live Music and Bars

C/Barrenkale is a busy place with a number of music bars and clubs, while C/Somera has friendly and funky bars that are very popular with the Basque nationalist community. In the Ensanche there are more on C/Pérez Galdós and C/Licenciado Poza.

Burton Bar, C/Dos de Mayo 16. A retro-chic bar decorated with fleamarket finds that plays lounge music and mellow electro-pop.

La Antigua Cigarrería, C/Astarloa 5. Stylish bar with a glossy crowd, serving oysters and champagne as well as cocktails. Occasionally hosts live music.

The Cotton Club, C/Gregorio de la Revilla 25, *www.cottonclubbilbao.es*. Offers live music (everything from funk to jazz).

Palladium, C/Iparraguire 11, t 94 424 61 65. Live jazz and blues.

Kafé Antzokia, C/San Vicente (by the Jardines de Albia), *www.kafeantzokia. com*. Set in a former cinema: a Basque-speaking café by day, and a bar and club by night.

Discotecas

Congreso, C/Uribitarte 8, t 94 424 73 82, *www.congresoclub.com*. Hugely popular club for house and techno.

Conjunto Vacío, C/Muelle de la Merced 4, *www.conjuntovacio.net*. Another good club; check the website to see what's on.

Public Lounge, C/Henao 54. A spectacularly over-the-top restaurant-bar-cum-club.

Euskadi

Vizcaya (Bizkaia), Álava (Araba) and Guipúzcoa (Gipuzkoa), the three provinces of the autonomous region of Euskadi, are rural and vertical for the most part, lush and green, crisscrossed by a network of rushing mountain streams that travel every which way through steep, narrow valleys in their search for the sea. Pretty Basque houses with long, sloping roofs and floppy-eared sheep decorate the emerald slopes, while below to the north the surf pounds against the wild coast, which relents here and there to admit a busy fishing port or sheltered beach. Signs on restaurants, tabernas, and shops are packed full of 'x's 'k's and 'z's, all written in a special Basque fairytale font, and add to the otherworldly air.

08

Don't miss

⭐ The *Fiesta de la Virgen Blanca*
Vitoria-Gasteiz **p.153**

⭐ Country church hiding glorious Gothic frescoes
Gazeo (Gaceo) **p.159**

⭐ Glorious birch forests
Parque Natural Urkiola **p.166**

⭐ Fishing villages
Getaria and Mundaka **pp.176 and 170**

⭐ *Belle époque* elegance and New Basque cuisine
Donostia-San Sebastián **p.179**

See map overleaf

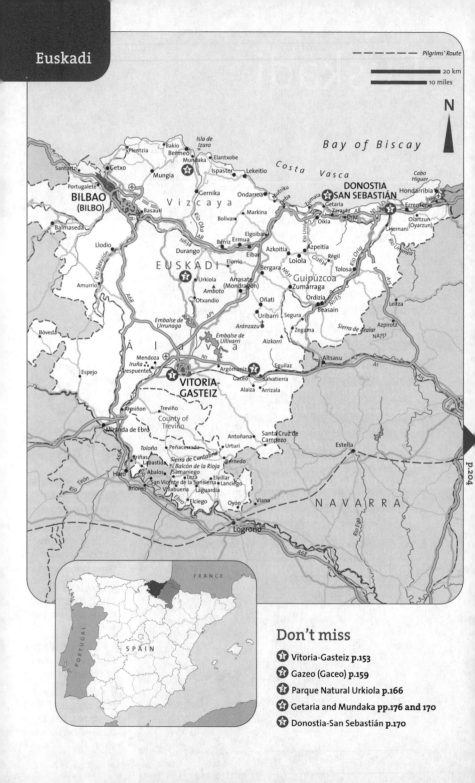

Pilgrims' Route

20 km
10 miles

N

Bay of Biscay

Costa Vasca

Plentzia
Bakio
Isla de Izaro
Bermeo
Getxo
Mundaka
Elantxobe
Santurtzi
Ispaster
Lekeitio
Portugalete
Mungia
Ondarroa
Mutriku
Cabo Higuer
BILBAO (BILBO)
Gernika
Deba
Zumaia
Getaria
Zarautz
DONOSTIA SAN SEBASTIÁN
Hondarribia
Irun
Errenteria
Basauri
Oikia
Orio
Oiartzun (Oyarzun)
Balmaseda
Bolivar
Markina
Vizcaya
Hernani
Llodio
Elgoibar
Azkoitia
Azpeitia
Régil
Tolosa
Leitza
Berriz
Ermua
Eibar
Durango
Loiola
EUSKADI
Elorrio
Bergara
Amurrio
Urkiola
Arrasate (Mondragón)
Zumarraga
Guipúzcoa
Ordizia
Beasain
Otxandio
Oñati
Uribarri
Segura
Embalse de Urrunaga
Aránzazu
Zegama
Sierra de Aralar
Azpiroz
Amboto
Embalse de Ullivarri
Aizkorri
Altsasu
Á L A V A
Mendoza
Iruña
Trespuentes
Espejo
VITORIA-GASTEIZ
Argómaniz
Gaceo
Eguilaz
Salvaterra
Alaiza
Arrizala
Bóveda
Armiñón
Treviño
County of Treviño
Antoñana
Santa Cruz de Campezo
Urturi
Estella
p.204
Miranda de Ebro
Toloño
Peñacerrada
Bernedo
Briñas
Labastida
Sierra de Cantabria
Balcón de la Rioja
Haro
Samaniego
Elvillar
Ábalos
Leza
Lanciego
San Vicente de la Sonsierra
Villabuena
Laguardia
Briones
Elciego
Oyón
Viana
N A V A R R A
Logroño
FRANCE
PORTUGAL
SPAIN

In most places in Euskadi, the industry of Bilbao seems remote. Basque nationalism, on the other hand, is ever present: every bridge, underpass and *frontón* has been painted with the Basque flag and slogans of ETA and Herri Batasuna. Everywhere, big white flags showing Euskadi in silhouette with big red arrows pointing at it demand that Basque prisoners be held in prisons in the Basque country rather than spread throughout Spain and in the Canary Islands, where they are often rotated without notice to their families.

With the notable exception of the big cities of Donostia-San Sebastián and Vitoria-Gasteiz, Euskadi is not chock-a-block with 'sights' *per se*; go there rather for the atmosphere, to pootle about, to take in a *pelota* match, or to be on hand as the fishing fleet brings in the catch. Wander down country lanes in search of dolmens, watch a furious game of *mus* in a bar, or try to keep up with Basque trenchermen at the table. But if you like to have destinations to aim for, try the Gothic frescoes at Gazeo and the cartoonish murals at Alaiza; Laguardia and the Rioja vineyards basking in the sun; San Miguel de Arretxinaga with its bizarre Neolithic altar, in Markina; the pagan Basque cemetery of Argiñeta, near Elorrio; the extraordinary Castillo de Butrón; the hermitage-topped islet of San Juan de Gaztelugatxa, near Bakio; the Palaeolithic Cueva de Santimamiñe, near Gernika; the bijou fishing port of Elantxobe and dramatic coast around Deba; picturesque Getaria and its lopsided church; palace-filled Oñati and Bergara; the Jesuit extravaganza at Loyola; and colourful seaside Hondarribia, on the French border.

Vitoria-Gasteiz

Vitoria has style. It also has the air of a little Ruritanian capital – because it is one. The seat of the inland province of Álava and, since 1980, the capital of Euskadi, Vitoria has grown to be one of Spain's modern industrial centres, a phenomenon that has so far done little harm to one of the most surprisingly urbane cities in the nation. Founded as Victoriacum by the Visigothic King Leovigild after he smashed the Basques in 581, the name stuck along with the Basque name, Gasteiz, because it recalls the height (*Beturia* in Basque) on which the city was built. In the Middle Ages this was a hot border region between the kingdoms of Navarra and Castile. King Sancho VI founded a fortress and town here, 'Nueva Victoria', in 1181 and gave it a charter of *fueros* (*see* p.24), but the Castilians managed to snatch it away from the Navarrese soon after. Like everything else in medieval Castile, Vitoria boomed and extended

Getting to and around Vitoria-Gasteiz

By Air

The **airport**, 9km northwest of Vitoria in Foronda, is mainly a freight airport, but has summer charter connections with holiday destinations in the Mediterranean (**t** 91 321 10 10, *www.aena.es*).

By Train and Bus

Vitoria's stylish **train station** (call RENFE **t** 902 320 320 for information) is at the head of C/Eduardo Dato, six blocks from the old town. Trains between Donostia-San Sebastián and Madrid pass through Vitoria, with at least five daily services heading for the capital (approx. 5hrs 30mins, high-speed service 3hrs 40mins), and Salvatierra is a stop along RENFE's Vitoria–Pamplona run. Otherwise you'll have to take the bus. The **bus station** (**t** 94 525 84 00) is at C/Los Herran 50, a short walk east of the old town. There are regular services to San Donostia-Sebastián, Bilbao and Logroño, as well as to the provincial villages, and, because of the city's position on the main route north from Madrid, you can get a bus to nearly anywhere.

By Car

Though small, Vitoria can be a puzzle if you are driving. Most of the centre is a closed-off pedestrian zone, and parking is hard to find.

---

itself logically in concentric rings of streets – oddly enough, a plan exactly like Amsterdam's, without the canals.

Hard hit by the wars and plagues of the 14th century, Vitoria stagnated for centuries, although one bright spot was the reflected glory of its greatest son, Francisco de Vitoria (1486–1549), an eloquent theologian who lectured at the University of Salamanca. Often called the 'father of international law', he strongly challenged the morality of Europeans colonizing the New World (even the plea of needing to convert the pagans didn't wash with friar Francisco); he defended the human rights of Native Americans and set forth reasoned discussions on the limitations of war, which under his terms was hardly ever justified. His opinions were highly influential in Renaissance university circles – even Charles V asked his advice, although history says neither he nor his successors bothered to follow it.

Vitoria next made the headlines when it saw the decisive battle in the Peninsular War on 21 June 1813, when Wellington, after retreating from his failed siege of Burgos, caught up with the French here and routed them, although his troops, whom Wellington himself called 'the scum of the earth', let the French escape over the Pyrenees as they pillaged their baggage in a drunken orgy. News of the victory, however, did rally the Europeans to unite against Napoleon, and the next year the war came to an end with Napoleon's abdication. Vitoria's own recovery as a city came only with the industrial boom of the 1890s. It has preserved itself beautifully throughout, probably an important factor in getting Vitoria – now officially Vitoria-Gasteiz – named the Basque capital in the autonomy agreement of 1981. It is also the home of the Euskal Herriko Unibertsitatea (EHU), the University of the Basque Country, established by the government shortly after it took power, and now the world's leading centre for the study of the Basque language and its history.

Fiesta de la Virgen Blanca

The important thing to know about Vitoria is the *Fiesta de la Virgen Blanca*, from 4 August. It's a typically berserk six-day Basque blowout, with sparkling *cava* everywhere, lots of high-powered fireworks and parties until dawn, but the image of it that sticks in the mind is Celedón, a dummy in a beret and workman's clothes. Celedón holds an umbrella aloft, which is attached to a wire from the top of the cathedral tower; from this he descends as gracefully

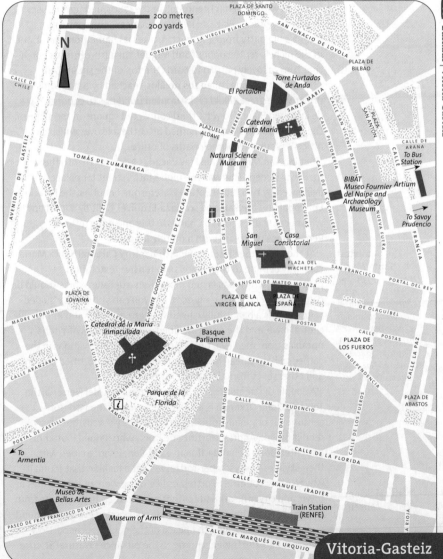

Vitoria-Gasteiz

as Mary Poppins, gliding across the *plaza* to start the festival. On the morning of 10 August, he glides up the wire and pops magically back into the belltower, and it's all over for another year.

The Casco Viejo

The old city, with its core of neat, concentric streets, begins with **Plaza de la Virgen Blanca**, a delightful example of asymmetrical medieval town design. Adjacent to it, the enclosed and studiously symmetrical **Plaza de España** provides a perfect contrast; this grand neoclassical confection was built at the height of Spain's flirtation with the Enlightenment, in the 1780s, and now houses mostly city offices. Plaza de la Virgen Blanca is the centre of Vitoria's big party from 4 August; it takes its name from the statue in the niche over the door of **San Miguel**, the 14th-century church that turns a lovely portico towards the top of the square. An 18th-century arcade called **Los Arcillos**, reached by a stair, runs under some graceful old glass-fronted buildings to connect Plaza de la Virgen Blanca to yet a third connected square on the slope of the hill, **Plaza del Machete**, named after the axe over which city officials would swear their oaths of office.

Behind San Miguel, Calle Fray Zacarías leads north into the medieval streets. This was the high-status street for palaces, as evidenced by two 16th-century Plateresque beauties, the **Palacio Episcopal** and the **Palacio Escoriaza-Esquivel**, built by a local boy who became physician to Charles V; this one has a refined Renaissance courtyard with a marble loggia.

Catedral Santa María
t 94 525 51 35, www. catedralvitoria.com; for tours, email visitas@ catedralvitoria.com or book through the adjacent visitor centre (Centro de Acogida al Visitante) at Plaza de la Burullería, s/n; adm

At the top of the street is the 14th-century **Catedral Santa María**, currently coming to the end of an extensive restoration programme which has lasted more than a decade. Works should be complete by end 2012–early 2013, but you can still visit by guided tour. There is a beautifully carved western doorway and impressive central nave, and the aisles are lined with the tombs of Vitoria's notables from medieval times. Archaeological excavations in the cathedral have unearthed remains of an ancient fortified church and other relics from the 13th century.

A couple of streets west of the cathedral, on C/del Herrería, the **Torre de Doña Otxanda** is a defensive tower of the 15th–16th centuries. It originally formed part of the city's walls, but was rebuilt by Don Andrés Martínez de Iruña who named it after his daughter, Doña Ochanda. Italian early-Renaissance cities, with their skylines of skyscraper-fortresses, set a fashion that found its way to other countries. Fortresses like these were private castles in town, and city officials had to fight hard to keep their owners from acting like rustic barons on their manors, bossing everyone around and generally disturbing the peace of the neighbourhood. Now fully restored, the tower is home to the province's **Natural Science**

Natural Science Museum
open Tues–Fri 11–2 and 4–6.30, Sat 10–2, Sun 11–2; closed Mon

Museum. Another conspicuous tower nearby, the **Torre Hurtados de Anda**, lurks just to the north of the cathedral on C/Correría: this is a blank-walled fort with a half-timbered house planted on top – a proper urban castle. Also on C/Correría, a rambling brick and timber structure called **El Portalón**, built in the early 16th century, is one of the oldest buildings in town, and it gives an idea of what most of Vitoria must have looked like at the time.

Palaces are fewer in the eastern quarter of old Vitoria, across C/Las Escuelas; the houses here are generally plainer, though older, especially those in the former **Judería**, the medieval Jewish ghetto that covered much of this area. On C/Cuchillería, a pair of museums dedicated to playing cards (a local speciality) and archaeology have re-opened under the umbrella name of **BIBAT**. The **Museo Fournier de Naipes**, in the Plateresque Palacio Bendaña, has the oldest surviving card (14th-century), as well as card-making machinery and paintings. The collection includes Tarot decks too; originally there was no difference between the cards for fortune-telling and those for playing games. Slotted in beside it, in a sleek glass and metal cube (2009) designed by Patxi Mangado, is the **Archaeology Museum** containing Roman finds and Basque discoidal tombstones, as well as some fascinating medieval art, such as the exceedingly strange *Relief of Marquinez*.

BIBAT
(Archaeology
Museum and
Museo Fournier
de Naipes)
*C/Cuchilleria 53,
t 94 520 37 07; open
Tues–Fri 10–2 and
4–6.30, Sat 10–2, Sun
11–2; closed Mon*

Just east of here, at C/Francia 24, is Vitoria's exciting **Artium** (Basque Museum of Contemporary Art), with a permanent collection of more than 1,600 contemporary paintings, sculptures, drawings and photos by Basque and Spanish artists.

Artium
*www.artium.org;
open Tues–Fri 11–8, Sat
and Sun 10.30–8;
closed Mon; adm;
'you decide' on Wed*

The New Cathedral and Museum of Fine Arts

The tourist information office shares the pretty **Parque de la Florida**, Vitoria's monumental centre, with the stern, no-nonsense **Basque Parliament** building and the remarkable 'new cathedral', the **Catedral de la María Inmaculada**. Here, the Basques, who don't like anything frumpy but do like the Middle Ages, got together to build a completely 'medieval' building, by medieval methods, beginning in 1907. Most of it is already finished, although there is enough decorative work to do inside to last them another century or two. The style seems to be part English Gothic, part Viollet-le-Duc, and the most endearing feature is the rows of comical modillions around the cornices – lots of satirical and monster faces, including caricatures of the architects and masons. It contains the **Museo Diocesano de Arte Sacro**, with an appealing collection of medieval Madonnas, over-the-top Baroque religious paintings, and lavish church plate and ornaments.

**Museo Diocesano
de Arte Sacro**
*t 94 515 06 31; open
Tues–Fri 10–2 and
4–6.30, Sat 10–2, Sun
11–2; closed Mon*

Vitoria is a city of unexpected delights; one example, completing the park's monumental ensemble, is one of the most resplendent Art Deco petrol stations in Europe, just behind the cathedral.

Another, a few blocks southeast on Calle Eduardo Dato, is the fantastical **RENFE station**, done in a kind of Hollywood-Moorish style with brightly coloured tiles. The spare, modern **Plaza de los Fueros**, a square just southeast of Plaza de la Virgen Blanca, designed and decorated by Eduardo Chillida. It's a strange space – part Roman amphitheatre, part basketball court. At one end, an untitled Chillida sculpture is enclosed within angular walls.

The wonderful **Parque de la Florida**, laid out in 1855, retains much of the Romantic spirit of its times, with grand promenades, hidden bowers and viewpoints. It was the centre of the city's fashionable district, and a shady walkway from the southern end of the park, the Paseo de la Senda, takes you to the elegant **Paseo de Fray Francisco de Vitoria**, lined with the Hispano-Victorian mansions of the old industrialists. One of these houses, now the **Museo de Bellas Artes**, features a well-displayed collection ranging from early paintings to Picasso and Miró, with a handful of great Spanish masters in between; all in a beautifully restored space, with original features such as a Tiffany-style stained-glass skylight.

Museo de Bellas Artes
open Tues–Fri 10–2 and 4–6.30, Sat 10–2 and 5–8, Sun 11–2; closed Mon

Some of the finest works are of the type that museums here call *Escuela Hispanoflamenca*, paintings from the early 16th century, at a time when the influence from the Low Countries was strong; most are anonymous, and it is impossible to tell which country the artist was from. One of the finest works, a triptych of the *Passion* by the 'Master of the Legend of Santa Godelina', shows the same sort of conscious stylization as an Uccello; the longer you look at it, the stranger it seems. Medieval painted carved-wood figures are well represented, and there are no fewer than three paintings by Ribera, including a *Crucifixion*. As in all Basque museums, Basque painters are more than well represented. Here you'll find some surprises, such as a great early 20th-century landscapist named Fernando de Anarica, or his contemporary Ramon Zubiaurre, whose *Autoridades de mi Aldea* shares the not-quite-naïve sensibility of Rousseau or Grant Wood. The façade of a 13th-century hermitage has been reconstructed in the museum's garden. Back along the Paseo at No.3, the **Museum of Arms** houses suits of armour, medieval weapons, and dioramas and displays on Wellington's victory at the Battle of Vitoria.

Museum of Arms
open Tues–Fri 10–2 and 4–6.30, Sat 10–2, Sun 11–2; closed Mon

Seeing the last of Vitoria's little secrets means a pleasant 20-minute walk to the southwest (from the Paseo de Fray Francisco, take Paseo de Cervantes and Avenida de San Prudencio), to the **Basílica of San Prudencio**, in Armentia, a village swallowed up by the city's suburbs. The church was built at the end of the 12th century, remodelled in the 18th century, but preserving its original Romanesque doorway and curious reliefs and carved capitals inside. It is dedicated to Santo Prudencio, a 6th-century bishop from Armentia, who is now the patron saint of Álava.

West of Vitoria you can visit Roman ruins, including a long, 13-arched bridge at **Trespuentes**, near the remains of a pre-Roman town, the *oppidum* of Iruña. In 2006, it was declared that some of the oldest examples of Basque writing had been found here, but, scandalously, the texts were subsequently declared forgeries. Two kilometres away at Mendoza, near the airport on the A3302, a 13th-century defensive tower with great views over the countryside has been restored to house the **Museo de Heráldica**, one of Spain's only museums dedicated to the origins and graphic styles of heraldic escutcheons. The exhibits give special attention to the histories of the great families of the Basque country.

Oppidum of Iruña
open Tues–Sat 11–3;
Sun 11–2; closed
Mon; adm

Museo de
Heráldica
open Tues–Sat 11–3;
Sun 10–12; closed
Mon; adm

Market Days in Vitoria-Gasteiz

Thursdays, in Plaza de Abastos; flea market on Sundays in Plaza de España; clothes market on Thursdays and Saturdays in C/Simón Bolívar.

Where to Stay in Vitoria-Gasteiz

(i) Vitoria >
Plaza General Loma 1,
t 94 516 15 98,
www.vitoria-gasteiz.
org/turismo

(★) La Casa de
Los Arquillos >>

Vitoria-Gasteiz ✉ 01000

*****Gran Hotel Lakua, C/Tarragona 8, t 94 518 10 00, *www.granhotelakua.com* (€€€). The fanciest option, in a huge modern building 4km from the centre, with suites and apartments, plus a small spa, and restaurant. Online packages offer great bargains.

****NH Canciller Ayala, C/Ramón y Cajal 5, t 94 513 00 00, *www.nh-hotels.com* (€€€). Modern tower hotel next to the Florida Park, with elegant rooms, a restaurant, and a short walk across the park to the old quarter.

***Hotel Palacio de Elorriaga, C/Elorriaga 15, t 94 526 36 16, *www.hotelpalacioelorriaga.com* (€€€). Pretty hotel on the outskirts of the city, in an elegant 17th-century mansion surrounded by gardens. Rooms are stylishly decorated and there's a restaurant for guests.

****Hotel Silken Ciudad de Vitoria, Portal de Castilla 8, t 94 514 11 00, *www.hotelciudaddevitoria.com* (€€€–€€). More character than most, central, with smart rooms, friendly staff and an indoor garden. Bargain packages, especially at weekends. The restaurant serves some of the best *pintxos* in town.

***AC General Álava, Avda de Gasteiz 79, t 94 521 50 00, *www.ac-hotels.com* (€€€–€€). A large hotel in the new part of town, with modern rooms geared towards business travellers.

***Almoneda, C/de la Florida 7, t 94 515 40 84, *www.hotelalmoneda.com* (€€). Welcoming, central hotel with simple rooms and a pleasant lounge with an eclectic collection of antiques.

La Casa de Los Arquillos, C/Los Arquillos 1–2º, t 94 515 12 59, *www.lacasadelosarquillos.com* (€€). A delightful, intimate bed-and-breakfast on the second floor of a medieval building which used to be a tailor's workshop. The décor blends exposed stone walls and solid wooden floors with pristine white linen and comfortable bathrooms. Book early, as there are only eight rooms. Only avoid if you dislike the ringing of church bells.

**Hotel Desiderio, C/San Prudencio 2, t 94 525 17 00, *www.hoteldesiderio.es* (€). Functional rooms, but close to the old town and friendly.

**Dato 28, C/Eduardo Dato 28 (near the train station), t 94 514 72 30, *www.hoteldato.com* (€€). Conveniently located, with imaginative Art Deco furnishings, if a tad overpriced.

**Guesthouse Casa 400, C/Florida 46, 3ºD, t 94 523 38 87, (€). A decent bet if you are on a budget. Close to the cathedral and medieval town.

**Pension Araba, C/Florida 25, 1st floor, t 94 523 25 88, *www.pensionaraba.com* (€). Simple but spotless *hostal* in the centre of town; also has triples and quadruples.

Eating Out in Vitoria-Gasteiz

Most of the most atmospheric bars and restaurants in Vitoria are in the old town. Look out for the 'Semana Del Pintxo' ('Pintxo Week'), an annual gastronomic competition to find the best tapas (late Mar/early April).

Ikea, C/Portal de Castilla 27, **t** 94 514 47 47, www.restauranteikea.com (€€€). One of the most renowned restaurants in Euskadi; original cuisine prepared with the finest seasonal ingredients. Push the boat out with the menú de degustación (€75), which includes wine pairings. Closed Sun eve and Mon, plus last 3 weeks Aug.

Zaldiarán, Avda de Gasteiz 21, **t** 94 513 48 22, www.restaurantezaldiaran.com (€€€). Superb restaurant serving award-winning modern cuisine, famous for its spectacular desserts. Closed Tues eve and Sun.

El Portalón, C/Correria 151, **t** 94 514 27 55, www.restauranteelportalon.com (€€€). Especially good, with tables on three floors of a 15th-century building and traditional Basque food. Set lunch for €35 Mon–Fri: other menus €39–€69. Closed Sun eve.

Dos Hermanas, C/Madre Vedruna 10, **t** 94 513 29 34 (€€). A local institution for over a century. Closed Sun eve.

⭐ **La Cocina de Plágaro** ❯ La Cocina de Plágaro, C/Florida 37, **t** 94 527 96 54 (€€). This deceptively humble spot serves some of the best cuisine in town. The talented young chef is equally at home with traditional and modern interpretations of local cuisine, prepared, where possible, with ingredients sourced from within a 100km-radius of the city. Closed Sun eve, all day Mon, Tues eve, Wed eve.

Mesa, C/de Chile 1, **t** 94 522 84 94 (€€). Flavoursome, down-to-earth local dishes including game and mushrooms in season. Closed Wed, and mid-Aug to 1st week Sept.

Olárizu, C/Tomás de Zumárraga 54, **t** 94 521 75 00, www.olarizu.com (€€). Creative fusion cuisine in colourful surroundings. Great value lunch menu served Mon–Fri.

Saburdi, C/Eduardo Dato 32, **t** 94 514 70 16 (€). Lively little bar, lined with bottles, serving fresh, inventive tapas and good wines.

Oleaga, C/Adriano VI 15, **t** 94 524 68 53 (€). Counters heaving with pintxos and a dining room with home cooking at bargain prices. Closed Sun eve and Mon, and 2nd half Aug.

Toloño, La Cuesta de San Francisco 5, **t** 94 523 33 36 (€). A local institution, which regularly wins the top awards at the annual pintxo competition.

La Malquerida, C/Correría 10, **t** 94 525 70 68 (€). Stylish little café-bar with a lovely terrace near the Plaza del Virgen Blanca, serving delicious, contemporary pintxos which change according to what's in season. Make your choice from the menu scrawled up on the two huge blackboards, and tuck into such delights as scallops with caramelised onions.

Cuatro Azules, C/Postas 28 (€). This is a friendly, stylish tapas bar serving delicious gourmet pintxos.

Nightlife in Vitoria-Gasteiz

Vitoria has its share of nightlife, mostly in the Casco Viejo, though C/Dato, near the station, can also be buzzy. Don't miss the annual **Jazz Festival**, held in July: see www.jazzvitoria.com.

Café Dublín, Plaza de la Virgen Blanca (corner of C/Herrería), **t** 94 528 67 62. Live music, running the gamut from jazz to pop, as well as DJ sessions.

Jimmy Jazz, C/Coronación de la Virgen Blanca s/n, http://jimmyjazz gasteiz.com. Probably the city's most popular jazz club, although it regularly hosts pop, rock and indie bands too, as well as theatre and comedy events. There's a club upstairs, with DJs performing nightly.

Datura, C/La Paz 5, **t** 637 132 386, www.saladatura.com. One of the liveliest and biggest clubs in the city; check the website for club nights.

Hell Dorado, C/Venta De La Estrella 6, www.helldorado.net. A warehouse venue run by an artists' co-operative on the edge of town, with regular live gigs and other events.

Álava Province

Just because the Basque capital is located here, you might think that Álava (Araba in Basque) is the Euskadi heartland. In fact, speakers of Basque make up precisely four per cent of the population, by far the lowest in the seven Basque provinces. One senses that, having lost ground to the Spaniards for centuries during their long economic decline, the Basques purposely planted their parliament here as part of a careful plan to reclaim the soil. Álava is home to the historical oddity of the County (*Condado*) of Treviño, an enclave of Castilian Spaniards smack in the middle of the province. They are quite happy being part of Castile, just as they were in the Middle Ages, making Álava the only province in Spain, maybe in the world, that is shaped like a doughnut.

Gazeo (Gaceo) and Alaiza

There aren't a lot of sights here, but for anyone interested in things medieval the province offers something truly outstanding – and almost totally unknown outside the area. The minuscule village of **Gazeo** (Gaceo), on the N1 east of Vitoria, offers nothing less than one of the finest ensembles of Gothic fresco painting anywhere in Europe. The frescoes are in the simple church of **San Martín de Tours**; covered in plaster, they were not rediscovered until 1966.

San Martín de Tours
guided tours available through Tour Agurain; for details call t 94 531 25 35 or t 608 901 670

Research places these works some time between about 1325 and 1450. The style, a bit archaic with its Romanesque attention to flowing draperies, is distinctive enough for scholars to speculate about an obscure 'Basque-Navarrese' school of artists, perhaps centred in Vitoria. A Byzantine influence is also strongly present, though details like the gnarled, rugged cross are uniquely Spanish (such a cross was the symbol of the 19th-century Carlist rebels). Thanks to the plaster, most of the paintings are well preserved, though oddly enough many of the faces have vanished, as in the *Trinity*, with a grand figure of God enthroned, supporting Jesus on the cross, painted on the apse over the altar. True fresco work requires that the plaster underneath the paintings, applied fresh each morning for an artist's day's work, be absolutely right in composition and application. The secrets were just being rediscovered in the 14th century in Italy; artists elsewhere hadn't got it quite right. The figures around the *Trinity* on the apse seem to be arranged to represent the commemoration of All Saints' Day: various scenes of *Los Bienaventurados*, the Blessed – apostles, martyrs, confessors, virgins and more – all arranged neatly by category. On the right, note the conspicuous figures of St Michael, weighing souls on Judgement Day, and Abraham, gathering the fortunate to his bosom. The choir vault too is entirely covered in frescoes, stock images from the life of Christ divided by charming borders of *trompe l'œil* designs and fantasy architecture. At the bottom right is something no medieval mural picture book could be without: the souls of the damned getting variously swallowed up in the mouth of hell or cooked in a big pot.

Gazeo is not such an illogical spot for art as it seems. The modern N1 that connects Vitoria to Burgos and Pamplona roughly follows the course of the main Roman road into the north. Enough of this survived in medieval times to keep it an important route, heavily used by pilgrims on their way to Santiago de Compostela. Perhaps no one ever imagined Gazeo would grow into a metropolis, but it may well have been that the village was a popular pilgrim stop, and some pious gentleman or lady paid for the paintings to edify the sojourners' spirits and give them something to think about as they made their way westwards.

While you're out in Gazeo, you might as well carry on a little further and see some quite different paintings at another tiny hamlet, **Alaiza** (from the A1/E5/E80 motorway, take the A3100 south from Salvatierra). The Iglesia de la Asunción here is a barn-like 13th-century building; it too has a painted apse and choir, but the contrast with Gazeo's is like day with night. Instead of flowing Gothic draperies, Alaiza has one-colour cartoons so weird and primitive they might have been done by a Palaeolithic cave artist on a bad day. The central work, on the apse, shows soldiers besieging a castle, while on the choir vault and walls bizarre hooded figures joust, murder or indulge in bodily functions not often seen on church walls. There is a contrastingly precise inscription underneath in Gothic letters, but no one has ever managed to decipher it. The best guess the Spaniards can come up with for this singular work is that these scenes were done *c.* 1367, while Alaiza was under the control of some rough English mercenary soldiers; one of them might have done it.

The closest village of any size in this region, **Salvatierra**, is a pleasant old village of warm stone within striking distance of two of Euskadi's best dolmens – **Aizkomendi** at Eguilaz, visible in a little roadside park off the N1, and Sorginetxe in Arrizala.

North of Vitoria, the biggest features on the landscape are the dams and lakes of **Urrunaga** and **Ullívarri**. The lakes are popular spots for water sports; Ullívarri even has a nudist beach. Farther north, on the road to Durango, **Otxandio** was the original Basque iron town, a fact commemorated by a statue of the god Vulcan in the main square.

South of Vitoria: The Ebro Valley and La Rioja Alavesa

South of Vitoria, the Castilian fief of the County of Treviño looks strangely compelling on the map, but in reality there are plenty of oak woods and good farmland, and that's it. There is one village, Treviño, and, just to the east of the county, in the pretty, hilly region near Bernedo, is a public 18-hole golf course at **Urturi**, designed by Severiano Ballesteros.

Some of the best Rioja wines come from **La Rioja Alavesa**, a 40km growing area along the Ebro, facing the autonomous region of La Rioja and extending to Oyón, just north of Logroño. Sheltered from gusts and clouds by the Cantabrian mountains, the climate is midway between Atlantic and Mediterranean and by far the sunniest in Euskadi. The first vines here were introduced by the monastic orders, and the first rules governing the quality go back to 1650; today some 25 per cent of Riojas originate in Euskadi.

Perched high over the river, the key wine town of La Rioja Alavesa is walled **Laguardia** (**Biasteri** in Basque), founded in the 10th century. You can learn all about local wines and their production at **La Casa del Vino**, and visit the *bodegas*; one, **Bodegas Palacio**, offers classes on wine appreciation. The *bodega* is modern, but the original buildings have been converted into a pretty hotel and restaurant. Another, the Bodegas Ysios, just outside the village, was designed by Santiago Calatrava, the distinguished Spanish architect. This is not the only example of world-class *bodega* design in the area (*see* 'Elciego', below). Don't miss the 14th-century portal of Laguardia's Gothic **Santa María de los Reyes**, with the most spectacular sculpted tympanum in Euskadi, still in mint condition and bearing its original bright colours.

Bodegas Palacio
San Lázaro 1, t 94 560 00 51 or t 94 560 00 57, www.bodegaspalacio.es

In 1935 archaeologists discovered Laguardia's prehistoric ancestor just to the north; the **Poblado de la Hoya** was occupied from the end of Bronze Age until the late Iron Age (about 1500–250 BC). You can stroll around part of the site and visit the adjacent small **museum**, with a model of what La Hoya may have looked like and finds from the site; the explanations are entirely in Castilian and Basque. Some believe it was founded by peoples from the north who mixed with the indigenous proto-Basques. Further evidence of the importance of this area in prehistoric times is the quantity and quality of its **dolmens**, so numerous that a dolmen route has been laid out: the most important are the Dolmen de la Hechicera, east on the A3228, just beyond Elvillar, while west of Laguardia the A124 leads past two others.

Poblado de la Hoya Museum
t 94 518 19 18/t 94 562 11 22; open May–Oct Tues–Fri 11–2 and 4–8, Sat 11–3, Sun 10–2; Nov–April Tues–Sat 11–3, Sun 10–2; closed Mon

If, like the old song says, you like 'wine, wine, wine, all the time, time, time', La Rioja Alavesa will not disappoint. In **Elciego**, south of Laguardia, you'll find the *bodega* of the **Marqués de Riscal**, a famous producer who helped establish the reputation of Riojas in the 19th century. The vineyard has a reputation for knowing just how to age wines, and some 30,000 barrels patiently sit in the cellars here, some for as long as 50 years. An added attraction is the administrative wing, designed by Frank Gehry, architect of the

Marqués de Riscal
C/Torrea 1, Elciego, t 94 160 60 00, www. marquesderiscal.com

Guggenheim Museum in Bilbao. Gehry has once again used titanium for the undulating roof of the building, which houses a shop, museum and Basque restaurant.

To the north, in **Leza**, little *bodegas* specialize in *vino de cosechero* (harvester wine) made through 'carbolic maceration' of the whole grape; it ferments in a few days, after which men stomp the grapes to produce a fresh, perfumed, slightly acidic wine, the best of which is 'heart's wine', or *vino de corazón*. Further west, **Samaniego**, another wine town, is bunched up around the parish church of the *Asunción*, converted from a 15th-century fortress. Perhaps the most famous *bodega* here belongs to **Fernando Remírez de Ganuza**, whose exquisite, highly personalized wine is a true *vino de autor*.

Fernando Remírez de Ganuza
www.remirezde ganuza.com

For the best overview of La Rioja Alavesa, head north of here to the Balcón de la Rioja, at the top of the Herrera mountain pass; if you carry on north, you'll come to **Peñacerrada** (**Urizaharra**), still embraced by perfectly preserved walls.

Granja de Nuestra Señora de Remelluri
t 94 133 18 01, www.remelluri.com; closed Aug

West of Samaniego, towards Haro and the green Montes del Toloño, **Labastida** has the Romanesque hermitage of Santo Cristo at its highest point, which once belonged to the Monasterio del Toloño. The monks' farm, the 16th-century **Granja de Nuestra Señora de Remelluri**, is now a prestigious family-run bodega open for visits. Others are just west in Briñas (*see* opposite).

Haro

Bodegas Bilbaínas
Barrio de la Estación 3, t 94 131 01 47, www. bodegasbilbainas.com

While here, you might as well slip over the river and visit Haro, the capital of Rioja Alta wines, in the autonomous region of La Rioja. At the confluence of the Ebro and the Tirón, Haro is built around a large arcaded square. Its chief monuments are a handful of noble houses, the attractive **Casa Consistorial** (1775) and the 16th-century church of **Santo Tomás** up in Plaza Iglesia, bearing a Plateresque façade with sculpture and reliefs in several registers, paid for by the *condestables* of Castile.

Bodegas Roda
t 94 130 30 01; www.roda.es

CVNE
t 94 130 48 00, www.cvne.com

López de Heredia
t 94 131 02 44, www. lopezdeheredia.com

Rioja Alta
Avda Vizcaya, t 94 131 03 46, www.riojalta.com

Federico Paternina
Avda de Santo Domingo 1, t 94 131 05 50, www.paternina.com

The *bodegas* are clustered around the train station. While most *bodegas* welcome visitors, they usually require advance notice (the tourist office has a useful booklet listing them all). An exception is **Bodegas Bilbaínas**, with a pretty façade in *azulejos*, usually open mornings and late afternoons. Nearby, you'll find one of the newer – and among the most praised – wine-producers: **Bodegas Roda**. Along Costa del Vino, you'll find the celebrated cellars of the CUNE, or **CVNE**, home of a fine bubbly; Chilean-owned **López de Heredia**, makers of one of the best Riojas, Viña Tondonia and with a tasting pavilion designed by award-winning architect Zaha Hadid; and the vast, French-founded **Rioja Alta**, with 25,000 barrels. The even larger **Federico Paternina**, founded in 1896 by the Plaza de Toros,

**Martínez
Lacuesta Hnos**
*C/Ventilla 71,
t 94 131 00 50, www.
martinezlacuesta.com*

**Selección Vinos
de Rioja**
*Plaza Paz 5,
t 94 130 30 17*

Wine Museum
*Avda Bretón de los
Herreros 4, t 94 131 05
47; open Tues–Fri 10–2
and 4–8, Sat and Sun
10–8; adm, free on Wed*

houses four million bottles, and welcomes visitors. Another, **Martínez Lacuesta Hnos**, is in the old gas company that became obsolete back in 1891, when Haro became the first city in Spain to have public electric street lighting. Among the shops, **Selección Vinos de Rioja** offers tastings and a wide variety of different Riojas.

Since 1892, Haro's **Estación Enológica** (just behind the bus station) has tested new wine-making techniques and varieties; its excellent **Wine Museum** offers detailed explanations of the latest high-tech processes used in La Rioja. For a far less serious initiation, or rather baptism, in Rioja, come on 29 July when San Felices is celebrated with a Batalla del Vino. Everyone dresses in white and, after the Mass, fortified with *zurracapote* (Rioja sangría, made with red wine, citrus fruit and cinnamon) and armed with every conceivable squirter, splasher and sprayer, opposing groups douse one another with 100,000 litres of wine. This Dionysian free-for-all takes place 3km from Haro at the **Peña de Bilibio**, below the striking rock formation and pass of the **Conchas de Haro**, 'the Shells of Haro', where Felices, a hermit-follower of San Millán, lived in a cave. A 10th-century church and the ruins of a Roman town, Castrum Bilibium, or Haro la Vieja, were discovered under the rocks.

Around Haro: The Sonsierra

There aren't many landmarks around Haro, but a handful of villages are worth a look if you're trawling about looking for that perfect bottle. A good place to start is the Sonsierra, a pocket of La Rioja on the left bank of the Ebro. **Briñas**, just north of Haro, has a number of noble escutcheoned manors left over from the days when it was the playground of the Haro nobility. These days, wine is the be-all and end-all; there's even a *bodega* under the church.

Don't confuse Briñas with **Briones** to the southeast, where there is a nubbly church tower and a bridge to **San Vicente de la Sonsierra**, a village best known in La Rioja since 1499 for its Guild of Flagellants, Los Picaos, headquartered at Ermita de Vera Cruz. During Holy Week, clad in anonymous hoods, the Picaos whip themselves across the shoulders, then pique the bruises with wax balls full of crystal splinters until the blood runs. Just outside San Vicente, the curious 12th-century Romanesque church of **Santa María de la Piscina** was founded by Ramiro Sanchez, son-in-law of the Cid, who allegedly brought back a piece of the True Cross from the Crusades. Over the door there's a shield carved with mysterious symbols. Paintings inside represent the *piscina probática* ('waters of the flock') of Jerusalem and the Holy Grail. Just east, **Abalos** has

**Bodegón de la
Real Divisa**
t 94 133 41 18

one of the oldest cellars in Spain, the **Bodegón de la Real Divisa**, owned by descendants of the Cid, and a 16th-century church, **San Esteban Protomártir**, decorated with dragons.

⭐ Hotel Castillo
El Collado >

ⓘ Antoñana
Cuesta de Lavadero 1,
t 94 541 02 26
(summer only)

ⓘ Laguardia >
Palacio Samaniego,
Plaza de San Juan,
t 94 560 08 45, www.
laguardia-alava.com

⭐ Hotel Marqués
de Riscal >>

Market Days in Álava Province

Laguardia: Sunday.
Arco de Santa Bárbara: Tuesday and Saturday.

Where to Stay and Eat in Álava Province

Argómaniz ✉ 01192

***Parador de Argómaniz**, Ctra N1 Km. 363, **t** 94 529 32 00, *www.parador.es* (€€€). Small and simple, but still very charming, with some rooms in the original building, a 17th-century mansion with iron balconies. Tiny Argómaniz is 10km east of Vitoria, near the paintings of Gazeo. Great restaurant.

Urturi ✉ 01119

**Hotel Urturi Golf, t 94 537 82 32, *www.hotelurturigolf.com* (€€). Small hotel overlooking the golf course, with a comfortable lounge and open fire for *après*-golf. It's on the fringes of a beautiful nature reserve, which can be explored on foot, by bike, or on horseback (these can be arranged through the hotel).

Laguardia and Around ✉ 01300

Laguardia is definitely the place to stop over if you are passing through La Rioja Alavesa. Be warned, it is crowded with locals on Sundays.

Posada Mayor de Migueloa, C/Mayor de Migueloa 20, **t 94 562 11 75, *www.mayordemigueloa.com* (€€€). In a 17th-century mansion with antique furnishings; also has an excellent restaurant (€€€) and wine cellar.

Antigua Bodega de Don Cosme Palacio, Ctra Elciego, **t 94 562 11 95 (€€). Delightful little hotel with a fine restaurant in the original *bodega* of this renowned wine-producer. Rooms are prettily decorated with rustic furnishings and each is named for a different grape.

Hotel Palacio de Samaniego, 16km west of Laguardia in Samaniego, C/Constitución 12, **t** 94 560 91 51,

www.palaciosamaniego.com (€€). Well-restored 18th-century mansion, with personalized rooms and a restaurant where the emphasis is on primary ingredients and local wines.

Hotel Castillo El Collado, Paseo El Collado, **t** 94 562 12 00, *www.hotel collado.com* (€€). The pick of the hotels: a 1920s palace full of antiques and luscious fabrics, with an incredibly welcoming owner (if you're lucky he'll tell you the story of the 'Love and Madness' suite). The restaurant (€€) serves Basque and Navarrese dishes, and magnificent roasts.

Palacio Rural Larrain, 14km east of Laguardia in Lanciego, C/Mayor 13, **t** 94 562 82 26, *www.hotellarrain.com* (€€). Refurbished 18th-century mansion, with nine spick-and-span rooms and a warm welcome.

*Pachico Martinez, C/Sancho Abarca 20, **t** 94 160 00 09, *www.pachico.com* (€€). In the same family since 1806 and still doing fine.

*Marixa, C/Sancho Abarca 8, **t** 94 560 01 65, *www.hotelmarixa.com* (€€). The best dining in town, with air-conditioning and expensive meals. You might try an unlikely local favourite – *acelga rellena* (stuffed Swiss chard).

****Hotel Viura, C/Mayor, Vilabuena de Álava, **t** 94 560 90 00, *www. hotelviura.com* (€€). Spectacular contemporary design hotel in a series of dramatic cubes overlooking a medieval village west of Laguardia. There are beautiful views over the wine country, a magnificent restaurant, and the staff can organise wine tours.

Elciego ✉ 01340

Hotel Marqués de Riscal, C/Torrea 1, **t** 94 518 08 80, *www.starwood hotels.com* (€€€€€). The owners asked Frank Gehry to design a 'château for the 21st century' but even they couldn't have envisaged this futuristic construction with its glittering titanium exterior. Even if you can't stay (and there are special deals if you plan way in advance), you can savour some of the surreal ambience at the fine gourmet restaurant.

ⓘ Haro >>

Plaza Hermanos F. Rodríguez, t 94 130 33 66, www.haro.org

⭐ Casa de Legarda >>

Haro ✉ 26200

****Hospedería Señorío de Casalarreina, Plaza Santo Domingo de Gúzman 6, Casalarreina (5km from Haro), t 94 132 47 30 (€€€). A charming rural hotel in part of the 16th-century monastery, with luxurious rooms and a pool.

****Los Agustinos, Plaza de San Agustín 2, t 94 131 13 08, *www. hotellosagustinos.com* (€€€). Superbly restored, occupying a former Augustinian monastery that later served as a prison. Fabulous restaurant, **Las Deulas** (€€€).

*Hostal Aragón, C/La Vega 9, t 94 131 00 04 (€). Basic, but very well priced, and centrally located.

Asador Jose Mari, Ctra de Peñacerrada s/n, Rivas del Tereso, t 94 133 40 61 (€€). Typical, delightfully old-fashioned spot specialising in roasts.

Beethoven I and II, C/Santo Tomás 3–5 and Plaza de la Iglesia 8, t 94 131 11 81 (€€). Traditional dishes at these neighbouring establishments.

Briñas ✉ 26290

***Hospedería Señorío de Briñas, Travesía de la Calle Real 3, t 94 030 42 24 (€€). A carefully restored mini-palace, decorated with antiques.

Casa de Legarda, C/ Real 11, t 94 131 21 34, *www.casadelegarda.com* (€€). A rural hotel outside Briñas in a beautiful 17th-century townhouse, with a restaurant down the street.

Inland: Bilbao to Donostia-San Sebastián

If you drive from Bilbao to San Sebastián along the coast, the narrow, twisting roads will take you nearly half a day. The more common routes east are the A8 (also signposted, confusingly, as the E5/E70 and E80) motorway, with its exorbitant tolls, and the slower, parallel N634, both of which follow some of the more somnolent landscapes of Euskadi before hitting the coast near Deba.

If you avoid the tolls and follow the latter, the first stop is the biggest town in the area, **Durango**, a name that conjures up cowboys and Westerns in the New World (besides the Durango in Colorado, there is another in Mexico, which in colonial times was capital of the province of 'Nueva Vizcaya' – there must have been a lot of Basques about). The original, sadly, has nothing to detain you long; in 1937 the German Condor Legion used it for target practice in a March prelude to Gernika. Colonel Wolfram von Richthofen, a cousin of the Red Baron flying ace, was one of the masterminds behind this new method of warfare, which he promised would terrorize the local population and undermine morale. The *Luftwaffe* razed Durango's cobblestoned streets and churches, just when the latter were filled for early Mass. In half an hour, 238 civilians were killed. When questioned, Franco claimed that Communist Basque church-burners were responsible for the destruction. What surprised him and the German theorists was that Durango's martyrdom only stiffened the Basques' resolve.

Getting around Inland from Bilbao to Donostia-San Sebastián

Durango and Elorrio are both served by **BizkaiBus** from Paseo del Arenal in Bilbao, and slow but scenic **EuskoTren** services between Bilbao and Donostia-San Sebastián call at Durango.

Somehow the bombs missed Durango's attractive Baroque centre behind the **Portal de Santa Ana**, an ornate survival from the old walls. Note the brightly painted **Ayuntamiento**, and the stone mosaic maze under the portico of **Santa María de Uribarri**. The most unusual monument is the 19th-century sculpted **Kurutziaga Cross**, just outside the centre in a neighbourhood of the same name.

😊 Parque Natural Urkiola

South of Durango, the **Duranguesado massif** juts abruptly out of rolling green hills, creating Vizcaya's most dramatic mountain scenery. Protected as the **Parque Natural Urkiola**, the range offers plenty of opportunities for sweaty assaults on the high peaks or leisurely ambles through birch forest (the park's name means 'place of birch trees' in Basque). Local legends tell that the goddess Mari haunts these hills; one mountain, Amboto, is especially famous for its witches, perhaps as a confused survival of Mari's mountain rituals. More earthly residents include goshawk, peregrine falcon and merlin, all of which can be spotted regularly, as well as two creatures especially associated with witches in Basque, the dragonfly (*sorginorratz*, or 'witch-needle') and butterfly (*sorginoilo*, or 'witch-hen').

North of Durango, in the heartland of old Basque traditions, are the minute village and valley of **Bolívar**, from whence came the family of the great liberator of South America, Simón de Bolívar. His Art Deco monument dwarfs the village square and, down the village's one lane, the site of his ancestral house has been fixed up as a **Museo Bolívar**. Near the old parish church of **Santo Tomás**, you can see the 'cattle trial yards' and the huge stone weights hauled by oxen at festivals.

Museo Bolívar
t 94 616 41 14; open July and Aug Tues–Sun 10–1 and 5–7, Sat–Sun 12–2; Sept–June Tues–Fri 10–1, Sat–Sun 12–2; closed Mon

Markina (Marquina), further north, is nicknamed the 'University of Pelota'; its historic *frontón* has produced champions who have made their mark around the world. The town is also famous for its craftsmen, especially those who weave *chisteras*, the handsome elongated wicker baskets used in *cesta punta*, or *jaï-alaï*.

Take the little bridge over the Río Artibay to visit the hexagonal church of **San Miguel de Arretxinaga**, built around an enormous altar constructed by the giant *jentillaks* (or, according to some, fallen from heaven) that consists of three massive rocks propped against one another. Probably a work of Neolithic times, it now shelters a statue of St Michael, who is almost inevitably associated with old weird places (*see* Aralar, pp.x216–17). Another 'cattle trial yard' next to the church only adds to Stone Age ambience.

Continuing along the N634, you'll get an object lesson in the life of the average Basque, passing through tidy, grey little industrial splotches like **Ermua** and **Eibar**, a typically peculiar Basque factory town stuffed into a narrow valley; **Elgoibar**, the next village up the road, is much the same.

South of the N634, on the BI632, **Elorrio** is an attractive village of grand palaces and impressive little squares adorned with a set of unique crucifixes from the 15–16th centuries. The façade of the **Ayuntamiento** bears a curious verse from Matthew 12:36: 'I tell you, on the Day of Judgement men will render account for every careless word they utter.' From the centre, it's a lovely walk out to the hermitage of **San Adrián de Argiñeta**, where you can see the 9th- and 10th-century tombs of Argiñeta, carved out of rock, some adorned with Latin inscriptions or pinwheel-like stars that may be sun signs. Nobody knows to whom these sarcophagi belong; some speculate they are the tombs of some leftover Visigoths or believe the tombs represent pre-Christian burial practices – not one bears a cross. From Elgoibar the road joins the coast.

Where to Stay and Eat Inland from Bilbao to Donostia-San Sebastián

Unlike the coast, this is definitely not tourist country, and you'll tend to find only simple accommodation.

(i) **Durango ›**
Askatasun Etorbidea 2,
t 94 603 39 38, www.
durango-udala.net

Durango ✉ 48200

★★★★ Gran Hotel Gran Durango, Gasteiz Bidea 2, t 94 621 75 80, www. granhoteldurango.com (€€€). A 19th-century mansion converted into a hotel with gardens, pool, restaurant.

★★★Hotel Kurutziaga, C/Kurutziaga 52, t 94 620 08 64, www.kurutziaga.com (€€). Central 18th-century mansion, transformed into a modern hotel.

Hotel O Camiño, C/Ollería 8, t 94 621 60 36 (€€). Modern, basic, with a restaurant serving Galician food.

Txacoli Larrinagatxu, C/Larrinagatxu Auzoa 4, t 94 681 49 66 (€€). This family-run restaurant offers some delicious local dishes.

Pedro Juan, C/San Antonio 1, in Bérriz, t 94 682 62 46 (€€). In a lovely stone

★ Jauregibarria >

ⓘ **Alto de Urkiola**
Caserio Toki-Alai,
t *94 681 41 55*

house, serving fine regional dishes and fabulous home-made desserts.

Jauregibarria, Barrio Bideaur 4, Amorebieta-Etxano (12km west of Durango), **t** 94 630 16 32, *www. jauregibarriajatetxea.com*(€€€). A superb restaurant, serving traditional and modern cuisine prepared with outstanding local ingredients. There's

a cheaper café. *Closed Mon, eves except Fri and Sat.*

Markina ✉ **48200**
Vega, Abesúa 2, **t 94 686 06 15 (€). Central place, with large, airy rooms overlooking the main *plaza*. The **Niko** restaurant (€) downstairs is good, and serves a good-value set lunch.

Along the Coast: Bilbao to Donostia-San Sebastián

Bilbao to Zumaia

When passing through the Bilbao suburbs of Getxo (*see* p.134) on the way to Plentzia, turn east to reach the best castle remaining in the vicinity, the 11th-century **Castillo de Butrón**, rebuilt in fairy-tale style in the 19th century and located in the wooded hills. Butrón can only be seen from the outside since it was sold to a property developer; it's Disneyland's Sleeping Beauty's castle on a bad trip, an incredible pile of towers and corbelled ramparts in a gloomy dark stone, built in a style that other countries in the Victorian era generally saved for prisons and asylums.

The main route along the coast beyond Plentzia passes close to **Lemoiz**, near the mouth of the Deba river, which for local fishing collectives and the million residents of Greater Bilbao only 17km away was the site of a real-life bad trip for decades. In 1972, work was begun here on a nuclear reactor, pushed through by Franco, just at a time when nuclear protests were growing around Europe. The usual fears of radiation pollution and an accident, however, went hand in hand with concerns over who would be in charge of it – and there was no doubt in the Basques' minds that it wouldn't be them.

Although the project was supported by the PNV and the tycoons of Bilbao (whose companies had been contracted for the work), democracy had no sooner returned than petitions and mass demonstrations showed the depth of opposition to the project, culminating in a 1977 protest in Bilbao that gathered an estimated 150,000 to 200,000 people, said to be the largest anti-nuclear demonstration in history. Appeals for a referendum on the plant, however, were ignored by Prime Minister Suárez, who claimed the matter was out of his hands.

Soon after, ETA became involved, carrying out 300 attacks in all that resulted in a dozen dead, among them workers at the plant, ETA militants and special targets (mostly engineers). In 1979, the Basques started to refuse to pay their electric bills, and in 1980,

Getting from Bilbao to Zumaia

Lemoiz was declared a military zone. In 1982, ETA kidnapped the director of the project and offered to exchange his life for the demolition of the plant; he was killed. When it happened again, the government threw in the towel. Later in the year Lemoiz became one of the few nuclear plants in Europe to be abandoned at such a late stage in its construction, and the whole project was finally scuttled, to great rejoicing, in 1994.

First stop on the coastal road proper is **Bakio**, a *txakoli*-producing new town tucked snugly into a little bay. *Txakoli*, a slightly effervescent and refreshingly tart wine, always flamboyantly poured at arm's length, is made of native hondarrabi zuri and hondarrabi beltza grapes, along with folle blanche and up to 25 per cent chardonnay, sauvignon blanc or cabernet sauvignon, and comes in white (the most common), rosé (or *ojo de gallo*, 'cock's eye') and red. Rated one of Spain's top wines way back in 1571, specialized *tabernas de txakolin* once flourished throughout the Basque country. Laws in many Basque towns banned the importation of other wines, while the General Assembly in Vizcaya took it upon itself to test the *txakoli* put up for sale, under the basic rating of 'drinkable'. Today the greenish, not-quite-ripe grapes are left in open steel vats from one to six weeks, sealed once they ferment, and bottled according to tradition after two February frosts.

Nearby, the islet of **San Juan de Gaztelugatxe** is linked to the mainland by a pretty arched bridge. In the old days, the isle supported a castle, but now the only building is a hermitage. On three dates in the summer – 24 June, 31 July and 29 August – big processions make their way there. According to legend, St John the Baptist, who must have been a first cousin to the *jentillaks*, took only three hops to get here from Bermeo; his footprint may still be seen near the top of the 232 steps to the sanctuary. The magnificent views along the dark coastal cliffs are worth expending the puff to get there.

Bermeo and Mundaka

Continuing round the coast from Bakio, **Bermeo** is Euskadi's largest fishing port, a colourful, working town that makes few concessions to tourism, especially since the fishing fleet has benefited from new EU fishing regulations. Bermeo and its neighbour Mundaka have the special distinction of racing in the first ever recorded regatta, in 1719, in a contest of fishing launches,

08

Euskadi | Along the Coast: Bilbao to Donostia-San Sebastián

or *traineras*, very like the popular regattas run today. Nor do seamen here waste any time with mermaids: the town is famous for the burning of an effigy of one named Xixili on 16 September, the day of its patron saint, Nuestra Señora de Alboniga.

Bermeo celebrates the long history of Basque seafaring in the **Museo del Pescador**, located in the imposing Torre de Ercilla, which relates stories of whaling expeditions from the Bay of Biscay, where the Basques first nabbed the so-called Basque whale (*Eubalaena glacialis*) – beginning with the ones who ran aground or came too close to shore – and then by the year 1000 pursuing them to the Arctic, perhaps reaching North America long before Columbus, although there is no solid proof. For centuries, whale-hunting was a great Basque secret, and in the early Middle Ages Bermeo and other whaling ports made fortunes trading the ivory from the teeth, the oil rendered from the blubber, and the meat, which was red yet permitted during Lent and on the many other fast days on the Church calendar, as it came from the sea. The better cuts (most notably the tongue, which the local bishops claimed as their tithes) were eaten fresh or preserved in salt, while the less prestigious bits were dried and exported around Europe. In the 13th century, Bermeo incorporated this seagoing gold mine on its seal. Whale-hunting expanded to cod, and by the early 16th century the Basques were fishing around the mouth of the St Lawrence to such an extent that pidgin Euskera became an important trading language, remembered for generations among the native people.

Museo del Pescador
open Tues–Sat 10–2 and 4–7, Sun 10–2.15; closed Mon

The route from here skirts the broad, flat Ría de Gernika estuary, and takes a detour south along the Río Oka to Gernika. Near the mouth of the inlet lie the Pedernales and **Mundaka**, the latter famous among surfers for having one of the longest left-hand breaks in Europe. If this means nothing to you, there's plenty of enjoyment to be had in wandering Mundaka's labyrinthine alleys and soaking up the views from its charming waterfront promenade – this is one of the prettiest working ports on the Basque coast. In the estuary's mouth, the tiny island of **Izaro** used to be home to a band of hardy monks. On the opposite shore are two more pretty beaches at **Laida** and **Laga**.

⭐ **Mundaka**

Gernika (Guernica)

Guernica is without doubt the most powerful and driving symbol in the entire Basque political culture. For an American, it would be Pearl Harbor, the Alamo and Bunker Hill combined in a single, searing metaphor.

Robert Clark

Beautifully set in the Mundaka valley, the ancient, sacred city of the Basques is mostly rebuilt now, and the majority of the inhabitants are too young to remember the horror that occurred one market day in 1937, when some 1,645 people were killed in a concentrated three-hour aerial bombardment by state-of-the-art German aircraft (*see* box, overleaf).

The **Tree of Gernika**, the seedling of an ancient oak by the 19th-century Basque parliament building (*La Casa de Juntas*), is the symbol of Basque democracy; under it the representatives of the Basque provinces met in assembly from the early Middle Ages on, and proclaimed the laws that governed them. After 1300, the kings of Castile would come to Gernika's oak to swear to uphold Basque *fueros* and ancient laws. The tree is the subject of one of the best-loved Basque songs, *Gernikako Arbola*, written in 1853 by José Maria Iparragirre, a veteran of the first Carlist War and itinerant folk singer. The song was so successful in the Basque country that Iparragirre was sent by Madrid into exile to Argentina. In 1876, after the Basque *fueros* were abolished, a community group demanded Iparragirre's return. The first verse goes:

Gernikako arbola
da bedeinkatua,
euskaldunen artean
guztiz maitatua.
Eman da zabal zazu
munduan frutua;
adoratzen zaitugu,
arbola santua.

(*The tree of Gernika/is a blessed symbol,/held dear by all the Basque people/with deep love./Let your fruit fall/over all the world;/we adore you,/sacred tree.*)

When the tree died in 1860, it was immediately replanted with a sapling from one of its acorns; the stub of the original's 300-year-old trunk can be seen under a nearby pavilion. The young tree somehow survived the bombing, and serves as a potent symbol of freedom and hope, not only for the Basques but for everyone – Gernika shocked the world because it was the first time modern technology was used as a tool of terror, a prelude to our own greatest nightmares.

Gernika was rebuilt in the Franco era, though neither the planning nor the architecture win any prizes. However, the hilltop area near the Tree of Gernika survived the onslaught comparatively unscathed and the regal 18th-century Palacio Alegría, built on the remnants of a much older fortified mansion, now contains the **Museo Euskal Herria**, dedicated to the history of the Basque

Museo Euskal Herria
t 94 625 54 51; open Tues–Sat 10–2 and 4–7, Sun 10.30–2.30; closed Mon; adm

08 Euskadi | Along the Coast: Bilbao to Donostia-San Sebastián

Country from prehistoric times. It's an engaging little museum, describing Basque language, customs and traditions. Behind it spreads the **Parque de los Pueblos de Europa**, a shady green expanse with lofty trees and a pretty wooden bridge. Cross it to find a pair of modern memorials: *Gure Aitaren Etxea (Our Father's House)*, an eloquent contribution by Eduardo Chillida, dedicated to peace, and a piece by Henry Moore, *Large Figure in a Shelter*. Behind, another palace contains the information centre for the Urdaibai Biosphere Reserve (*see* opposite). Near the park entrance, there's a ceramic copy of Picasso's masterpiece; the Basques, who not surprisingly feel that they are the rightful owners, have been lobbying Madrid to send them the original to hang in the Guggenheim, so far without result.

Parque de los Pueblos de Europa
open summer daily 10–9; winter daily 10–7

Down the hill, on the edge of the tiny pedestrianized old quarter, full of boutiques and cafés, you'll find Gernika's modern **Museo de La Paz**, focusing on the 1937 bombing. The centrepiece is a moving audiovisual exhibit (in Spanish and English) recounted by a local woman musing on her life just before her home is reduced to rubble. A gallery contains documents, uniforms and shocking photos, and there are several exhibits related to peace around the

Museo de La Paz
Foru Plaza 1, t 94 627 02 13; open July–Aug Tues–Sat 10–8; Sept–June Tues–Sat 10–2 and 4–7, Sun 10–2; call in advance for guided visits in English; adm

Experiments in Saturation Bombing

Gernika in 1937 became the kind of symbol for its times that Sarajevo was for the 1990s, a civilized little place that a band of thugs had chosen to flatten. Almost as soon as it happened, the Nationalist propaganda machine began sending out stories that the Communists had really destroyed the town by placing bombs in the sewers. It may have been the only time in his life that Francisco Franco was actually embarrassed. Just how much responsibility the Generalísimo had for Gernika will probably never be known, but there is nothing in his long, shabby career that suggests he was capable of such a stunt – Franco could massacre prisoners and stuff prisons with priests and professors, but Gernika, and Durango, which preceded it (*see* pp.165–6), were evil on a Nazi scale.

Hitler had sent his 'Condor Legion' to Spain not only to give Franco a hand, but to test the new *Luftwaffe*'s theories of terror bombing, and his commanders coldly determined Gernika to be the site of lesson number two (on a market day too). Though the town had no military significance whatsoever, as a symbol of Basque nationhood it was the perfect spot for a bombing designed especially to destroy the enemy's morale – by breaking their hearts, perhaps. While Gernika had little effect on the Civil War – the isolated Basque pocket was bound to fall anyhow – the Nazis were pleased enough with the results and the notoriety they gained from them to make such bombing the centre of their strategy; after Gernika came Warsaw, Rotterdam and Coventry, among many others.

Picasso's famous great painting, resting safely in New York during the Franco years, did as much as the bombing itself to catch the world's attention when it was displayed the following year in the Republic's pavilion at the Paris World Fair. Since 1981 it has been proudly displayed in Madrid, perhaps the ultimate exorcism of the War and the General. The *Guernica* that seemed so mysterious and revolutionary in its time now seems quite familiar and eloquent to us, so much have our ways of seeing changed since that distant age. The black and white gives it the immediacy of a newspaper photo. Picasso's preliminary sketches show that the central figures in the painting, the fallen horse and rider, were in his mind from the beginning. We can see in them the image of Gernika's destroyers: the eternal bully on horseback, the *caudillo*, the conqueror. In a way, *Guernica* may have been Picasso's prophecy – with such an atrocity as this, the man on horseback may finally have gone too far.

world, highlighting the absurdity of the destruction that continues in other lives and cities worldwide.

Urdaibai Biosphere Reserve
Parque de los Pueblos de Europa, t 94 625 71 25, www.urdaibai.org; open Mon–Thurs 9–1.30 and 3–5, Fri 9–2

Surrounding Gernika is the 220 sq km **Urdaibai Biosphere Reserve**, created in 1984 to prevent the destruction of habitats in the Ría de Mundaka. The reserve is hardly a pristine wilderness – besides Gernika it counts 18 towns within its boundaries – but the sympathetic interaction between inhabitants and their environment is an embodiment of that most elusive of eco-ideals: sustainable development. Farms and factories share Urdaibai with wetlands and lush oak forests; greenshank and bar-tailed godwit stalk the mud flats, while observers may get a glimpse of the nocturnal genet, an odd mixture of raccoon and tabby cat with huge eyes. For more information, stop by the Reserve's headquarters. About 5km northeast of Gernika, the **Cueva de Santimamiñe** has Euskadi's best Upper Palaeolithic art: two rooms with engravings of bison, horses, arrows, a bear and a deer, and geometric designs; they are rather faint, as only some of the black paint of the outlines has survived. It is said that these caves are also the home of the Beigorri, a huge, hairy red bull with a militant stare, the protector of the goddess Mari (*see* pp.45–6). A path leads from the cave entrance into the **Forest of Oma**, where local artist Agustín Ibarrola has fused art with nature by painting luminous multicoloured bands and symbols on the trees, to achieve an array of perspective tricks.

Cueva de Santimamiñe
t 94 406 77 37; guided tours Mon–Fri 10 and 11.15am, 12.30, 4.30 and 6pm; note that, owing to the fragility of the art, tours don't include the painting gallery, but visit the surrounding cave system; book in advance

From Gernika, a detour off the main road to Lekeitio leads northwards to **Elantxobe**, huddled beneath sheer cliffs, an immaculate little fishing village that funnels down to a bijou harbour, so steep in fact that the bus has to be spun around on a mobile turntable, like a San Francisco cable car. Geographical challenges have helped the village retain its remote atmosphere – there's only one way in, down the serpentine main street – and traditional fishermen's houses adorn the narrow lanes down to the little port. Above loom the cliffs of **Cabo Ogoño**, the highest on the Basque coast.

Lekeitio to Deba

Next along the coast is **Lekeitio** (**Lequeitio**), with its promenade flanked by restaurants and lovely beaches, **Isuntza** and **Cerraspio**, further out. Isabel II preferred these beaches to San Sebastián; she was holidaying in Lekeitio in September 1868 when rebellion broke out under Marshal Prim, whose *pronunciamento* deposed the dynasty, forcing Isabel into exile in France. The well-preserved palaces in Lekeitio's old quarter stand as testimony to its *belle époque* popularity, but the elegant old port still catches more fish than tourists. Don't miss the early 16th-century Gothic church of Santa María and its impressive Flemish *retablo mayor*, an intricate explosion of gilded wood and polychrome carvings. Lekeitio is famous for its *antzareguna*, which takes place during the *San Antolines* festival in early September. This goose rodeo, however, is not an event for the faint-hearted. A rope is stretched over the port, held on either side by strong tug-of-war veterans. In the middle a goose, liberally smeared in grease, is suspended by its feet over the port. Competitors, not allowed to weigh more than 70kg, are rowed to a point beneath and, one by one, they try to grab the slippery bird by the neck and tuck its head under their arms. Mercifully, these days they use a dead goose.

Crossing into Guipúzcoa province at **Ondarroa** used to mean paying duty at the provincial customs house near the medieval stone Puente Vieja. The village is another pretty fishing port, one of Vizcaya's busiest and a popular spot on sunny weekends, though quieter than Lekeitio. **Mutriku** is a quiet village set back on a narrow inlet 3km from the quiet beach at **Saturrarán**. Mutriku is linked with Deba and Zumaia by a clifftop path which passes through green fields and tiny hamlets, affording magnificent views. The coastal scenery between Deba and Zumaia is the best in Euskadi: cliffs arc gracefully from a choppy ocean, in great vertical bands of pink and golden sandstone, and the path is a good way to explore it. The local church, **Santa María la Real**, is of late Gothic construction and has a painted portal; somewhat older are the Palaeolithic scratchings in the nearby **Cueva de Ekain**.

Cueva de Ekain
t 94 342 29 45; accessible only to groups of max 6 people, by prior appointment, tours in Spanish

ⓘ **Bermeo**
C/Lamera, t 94 617 91 54, www.bermeo.org

ⓘ **Mundaka >>**
Plaza Lehendari Aguirre, t 94 617 72 01, www.mundaka.org; open Tues–Sun

⭐ **Atalaya >>**

Market Days from Bilbao to Zumaia

Bermeo: Tuesday.
Gernika: Monday, one of the biggest markets in Euskadi (*see* p.172).

Where to Stay and Eat from Bilbao to Zumaia

Bakio ✉ 48130
Hotel Joshe Mari, C/Bentalde 31, t 94 619 40 05, *www.bakio.com* (€€). This unusual little hotel has only a handful of rooms, each individually decorated with locally gathered antiques; the restaurant offers good food in a relaxing atmosphere.

**Hotel Arimune, C/Bentalde 95, t 94 619 40 22, *www.arimune.es* (€). Right on the beachfront, this is a delightfully old-fashioned place, furnished with antiques, with two terraces, one shaded by trees, the other overlooking the sea.

Gaztelu-Begi, Gibelorratzagako San Pelaio 86, t 94 619 49 24, *www.bakio. com* (€). Just beyond Bakio, this pretty hotel and restaurant is on the rocky headland with sweeping lawns overlooking the sea, and a rustic brick and beam interior.

Mundaka ✉ 48360
**Atalaya, Itxaropen Kalea 1, t 94 617 70 00, *www.atalayahotel.es* (€€€). One of the loveliest hotels in the region, on the river in one of those glorious Basque buildings of a century ago, with glass galleries all around. Small, comfortable rooms and a large terrace restaurant.

*Mundaka, Florentino Larrínaga 9, t 94 687 67 00, *www.hotelmundaka. com* (€€). More down-to-earth, but with bar and Internet facilities. A sign in the lobby asks surfers to knock the sand off their feet.

*El Puerto, Portu Kalea 1, t 94 687 67 25, *www.hotelelpuerto.com* (€€). Pretty, whitewashed hotel with bright rooms overlooking the port.

Camping Portuondo, Carretera Amorebieta-Bermeo, Km.2, **t** 94 687 77 01, *www.campingportuondo.com* (€). A very well equipped and beautifully located campsite, with steps leading down to the main surfing beach and a pretty terraced site. If you don't fancy being under canvas, there are several bungalows to let, which sleep up to four and have kitchens.

Asador Zaldua, Sabino Arana 10, Pedernales, **t** 94 587 08 71 (€€). Serves a wonderful array of fresh fish and succulent steaks grilled to perfection. *Lunch only Sun–Thurs during Nov–June; closed all day Sun in July–Sept.*

Bar Txopos, Kepa Deunaren , **t** 94 493 79 51 (€). This friendly bar has a shady terrace, harbour views and a tasty selection of burgers, sandwiches, and tortillas, filled with peppers, cheese and ham.

Gernika ✉ 48300

***Gernika, Carlos Gangoiti 17, **t** 94 625 03 50, *www.hotel-gernika.com* (€€). Good location but little charm at this comfortable, modern hotel.

Boliña, C/Barrenkale 3, **t** 94 625 03 00, *www.hotelbolina.net* (€). In the heart of the pedestrian area, this offers simple rooms with or without bath and a good restaurant with a *menú de degustación* for €32.

Akelarre Ostatua, Barrenkale 5, **t** 94 627 01 97 (€). Brightly painted rooms with private bathroom at this friendly and central *pensión*.

Baserri Maitea, Ctra. BI 635 (near Forua, on the way to Mundaka), **t** 94 635 34 08 (€€€). A wonderful restaurant in a 300-year-old farmhouse with wooden beams; the fish is particularly good. Book in advance. *Closed Sun eve in May-Oct; Sun–Thurs eves in Nov–April.*

Zallo Berri, C/Juan Calzada 79, **t** 94 625 18 00, *www.zallobarri.com* (€€). A delightful restaurant serving excellent regional cuisine with innovative touches (excellent value *menú del día* €20; *menú degustación* €40). *Closed eves Sun–Wed.*

Lekeitio ✉ 48280

***Zubieta, Portal de Atea, **t** 94 684 30 30, *www.hotelzubieta.com* (€€€). Charming hotel on the grounds of a castle, in the former gatehouse, with lovely rooms and lovely owners. Atmospheric café-bar too. *Closed mid-Nov–early Feb.*

***Emperatriz Zita, C/Santa Elena Etorbidea s/n, **t** 94 684 26 55, *www.aisiahoteles.com* (€€). A plush modern palace of a place, complete with a thalassotherapy centre, built over the ruins of the home of the last Austro-Hungarian empress.

Beitia, Avda Abaroa 25, **t 94 684 01 11, *www.hotelbeitia.com* (€€). Good value, adequate accommodation situated in a modern block.

Piñupe, Avda Abaroa 10, **t** 94 684 29 84 (€€–€). Simple rooms, but a really handy location, just five minutes from the beach.

Méson Arropain, Ctra Marquina, Ispaster, **t** 94 684 03 13 (€€). Five km from Lekeitio, this friendly restaurant serves fish dishes that are smothered with bubbling salsas, and has good *txakoli* to wash it down with. *Closed Sun eve and Wed.*

Kaia, Txatxo Kaia 5, **t** 94 684 02 84, *www.lekeitiokaia.com* (€€€–€€). Best in summer, with terrace dining and harbour views. Good seafood and salad choices, including *ensalada de alcachofa* (artichoke salad).

Bar Lumentza, Buenaventura Zapirain Kalea 3, **t** 94 684 20 70 (€). Popular local tavern, lauded for its wonderfull array of *pintxos* and fine hams.

ⓘ **Lekeitio** >>
Independentzia Enparantza, t 94 684 40 17, www.learjai.com; open summer only

ⓘ **Gernika** >
C/Artekale 8, t 94 625 58 92, www.gernika-lumo.net

⭑ **Méson Arropain** >>

Museo Zuloaga
t 94 386 23 41, open mid-April–mid-Sept Wed–Sat 4–8; for visits rest of year call to arrange an appointment; adm

Zumaia to Donostia-San Sebastián

Zumaia

Zumaia is a pleasant town set at the mouth of the Urola river. A kilometre on the other side, keep an eye out for the town's chief attraction, the **Museo Zuloaga**, a cosy villa set in a small park of

Getting around from Zumaia to Donostia-San Sebastián

The coast is served by frequent **buses** from Bilbao. The narrow-gauge **EuskoTren** stops 4 or 5 times a day at Durango, then Deba, Zumaia and Zarautz on the way to Donostia-San Sebastián.

ancient trees, surrounded by a wall. This was the home of the Basque painter Ignacio Zuloaga (1870–1945), and it holds a selection of his own works and masterpieces he collected over the years: El Grecos, Goyas, Moraleses, two saints by Zurbarán and a collection of medieval statues and *retablos*. Adjacent, the 12th-century church and cloister of **Santiago Etxea** was a stop for pilgrims taking the coastal route to Compostela.

There's more art in the centre of Zumaia, in the 15th-century church of **San Pedro**: two triptychs on either side of the altar, the one on the right Flemish, and a dark, Gothic *St Christopher* on the back wall. There's another beach to the west at **San Telmo**, a dramatic swath of sand under sheer red cliffs, known for its pounding surf.

Getaria

Getaria

East of Zumaia, the N634 ascends dramatically over the sea before reaching **Getaria**. The shipbuilders of Zarautz, the next fishing town to the east, built the *Vitoria*, the first ship to circumnavigate the globe; Getaria, now a petite and utterly charming resort, produced the man who captained it, Juan Sebastián Elcano.

From the coastal road, you wouldn't think there was much to Getaria at all, but once you're there you will find one of the loveliest villages of Euskadi, hugging the steep slope down to the harbour, sheltered by a narrow peninsula and an islet known for its shape as El Ratón, 'the mouse'. Whenever the Getarianos go to mass in the church of **San Salvador**, in the centre of the old town, they step on Elcano's grave, located just inside the door, though Elcano died of scurvy in the Pacific in 1526, so there probably isn't much of him in there anyway. Once you're beyond Elcano's tomb, this church has other surprises up its sleeve. Founded in the 13th century, it was rebuilt in 1429 in a curious off-kilter fashion: the wooden floor lilts as if on rough seas and the choir vaulting is just as tilted. No one knows why. Along the right wall, near the suspended *ex voto* of a ship, is something you rarely see in a church: a menorah. The crypt contains the remains of the ancestors of the same Queen Fabiola who made nearby Zarautz a resort. Getaria doesn't mind; although it has two small beaches of its own, it picked up all of Zarautz's fishing business. From the port, with its brightly painted boats and seafood restaurants, a path leads up to the top of **Mount San Antón**, better known as the *Ratón de Getaria* ('the Getaria Mouse'), a pretty wooded natural area with flitting birds and fine views.

The First Man to Sail Around the World

In the Age of Discovery, no Spanish or Portuguese captain worth his salt would set out without a Basque pilot, heir of centuries of experience in whaling boats off Europe's westernmost shores, and who may actually have found the American coast in the Middle Ages, but kept the knowledge a closely guarded secret. Basques were deeply involved in all four of Columbus' voyages, from building the ships to outfitting them and providing the crews. One Basque who accompanied Columbus, Juan de la Cosa (or Juan Vizcaíno) later explored the Caribbean on his own and in 1500 drew the first world map showing America.

Juan Sebastián Elcano, like many seamen in Getaria, started off as a deep-sea fisherman and smuggler to French ports, but he sought even greater adventures, and went on to fight with the Gran Capitán of Córdoba against Naples and explore some of the coast of Africa. He was in Seville in 1519, and got a job on an expedition backed by Charles V to send Portuguese navigator Ferdinand Magellan on what they hoped would be a quick western shortcut to the Indies by sailing southwest around America to the spice-laden Molucca Islands. Charles supplied five ships and 239 men, and in August they set out. As they wintered on the coast of Brazil there was a mutiny against continuing any further. By then Magellan and Elcano avidly hated one another, and most of the blame fell on Elcano, who was chained up and forced to do hard labour. One ship turned back before attempting the turbulent straits that took Magellan's name (October 1520).

If already dismayed by the distances involved just crossing the Atlantic, the expedition must have been appalled at the extent of the Pacific. Even worse, by the time Magellan's little fleet made it to the Philippines in 1521, a civil war had just broken out, which soon numbered Magellan among its dead. After several other Portuguese leaders fell victim to the intrigues of the war, Elcano took over the helm of the expedition and sailed halfway around the world from the Moluccas to Seville in the only surviving ship, the *Vitoria*, with the 17 surviving members of the crew. He arrived in October 1522, some 1,124 days after setting out (Elcano was surprised to find he had lost a day somewhere according to the ship's log, the first inkling of an international date line). Charles V later received Elcano, granting him a pension of 500 *ducados* and a coat of arms with the legend *primus circumdedisti me*. It was a feat that no one would try to equal for a long time; the one lesson of the expedition was that the eastern route around the Cape was in fact much quicker.

In spite of his singular feat, Elcano was destined to remain forever in Magellan's shadow – except of course in the eyes of his fellow Basques. The Getarianos erected a statue of Elcano just outside the gate of the old town, and stage a historical re-enactment of his landing every four years on 7 August.

Besides hauling in the fishy ingredients for a *marmitako*, Getaria is also the epicentre of *txakoli* production in Euskadi (*see* p.60). Demand for the tangy wine, which is closely identified with the Basques, has soared since autonomy; whereas in 1981, Getaria had a mere 16 hectares of vines, there are now over a hundred, especially since *Txakoli de Getaria* was given its *Denominación de Origen* credentials in 1989.

Zarautz and Orio

Big waves and a mile and a half of sand draw surfers to nearby **Zarautz**. Whaling and shipbuilding in the Middle Ages put Zarautz on the map, while more summering royalty – this time Belgium's King Baudouin and Queen Fabiola – inaugurated its international reputation as a resort in the 20th century. Now the second biggest resort in Euskadi after Donstia-San Sebastián, Zarautz is especially popular among well-to-do Basque nationalists – hence summer courses in Basque language and folklore events, to go with the golf course, riding stables and good food (with some harder-to-swallow prices). In the historic centre of Zarautz, look for its trio of tower houses, especially the **Torre Luzea** in Calle Mayor and the one incorporated into the 16th-century **Palacio de Narros**. The most important church, **Santa María la Real**, has a half-Plateresque, half-Renaissance *retablo*; the campanile was added atop yet another medieval tower house in the 18th century. The last stop on the coast before the cliffs take all roads inland is **Orio**, a venerable fishing village that looks like an industrial town at the mouth of the Río Orio, once one of the most polluted rivers in Spain but now considerably cleaner and once again teeming with fish.

Where to Stay and Eat from Zumaia to San Sebastián

(i) **Zumaia >**
Plaza Zuloaga,
t 94 314 33 96, www.
zumaiaturismo.com;
open summer only

Zumaia ✉ 20808

Some of the bars in the main square have inexpensive rooms, and cheaper food can be found on C/Erribera.

***Zelai**, C/Itzurun, t 94 386 51 00, *www.talasozelai.com* (€€€). A modern thalassotherapy centre with functional rooms in an unbeatable location high up on the cliffs.

Agroturismo Jesuskoa, Barrio de Oikia, t 94 314 32 09, *www.jesuskoa.net* (€€–€). Six rooms in a restored farmhouse outside town; also has an apartment to rent.

Landarte, Ctera Artadi 1, t 94 386 53 58, *www.landarte.net* (€). A beautifully restored country house, offering B&B in pretty rooms with bright prints.

★ **Kaia >>**

Marina Berri, Puerto Deportivo, t 94 386 56 17, *www.marinaberri.com* (€€€–€€). Elegant restaurant, café-bar and *sidrería* in one, with splendid views. Excellent *menú del día* for around €10. *Closed Mon–Thurs eves, and Jan.*

(i) **Getaria >**
Parque Aldamar 2,
t 94 314 09 57, www.
paisvasco.com/getaria;
open summer only

★ **Saiaz Getaria >**

Getaria ✉ 20808

Saiaz Getaria, Roke Deuna 25, t 94 314 01 43, *www.saiazgetaria.com* (€€). Exquisite guesthouse, with seventeen individually decorated rooms, many with beautiful sea views, in a magnificent 15th-century *torre* in the historic heart of Getaria. In the evenings, sit out on the terrace with a drink and listen to the waves.

(i) **Zarautz >>**
Nafarroa Kalea,
t 94 383 09 90, www.
turismo.zarautz.com

**Pensión Guetariano, C/Herrerieta 3, t 94 314 05 67 (€€–€). In the cheerful green and yellow house at Getaria's main crossroads; a friendly place with magazines in the lounge.

**Pensión Iribar, C/Aldamar 23, t 94 314 04 51 (€€–€). Four simple rooms in a great location near the port. Has a good restaurant (€€).

Agote Aundi, Askizu (3km from Getaria), t 94 314 04 55, *www.agoteaundia.com* (€). Overlooking the sea, this lovely country farm offers a well-priced, intimate stay and good home cooking.

Elkano, C/Herrerieta 2, t 94 314 00 24, *www.restauranteelkano.com* (€€€). This traditional *asador* serves superb grilled fish and meat and is justly considered one of the finest restaurants in the the Basque lands. *Closed Sun and Mon eves in Nov–May.*

Kaia, Gral. Arnao 10 (upstairs), t 94 314 05 00, *www.kaia-kaipe.com* (€€€). Spectacular Basque seafood, elegant surroundings, charming staff and beautiful harbour views. The ground floor has a cheaper grill house (**Kai-Pe**), where you can dine outside on fresh seafood. *Closed Mon and Wed eve in winter.*

Itxas-Etxe, Kaia 1, t 94 314 08 02 (€). Prime position on the harbour. Has a daily fish menu and a great lunch menu for €13.

Zarautz ✉ 20800

Zarautz can be as pricy as Donostia-San Sebastián in summer.

****Karlos Arguiñano, C/Mendilauta 13, t 94 313 00 00, *www.hotelka.com* (€€€€). A lavish mock castle on the beach owned by the eponymous celebrity chef. The restaurant (€€€–€€) is one of the best along this stretch of coast, with a great tasting menu (*menú de degustación*) for a surprisingly modest €32.

*Olutu, C/Ipar 10, **t** 94 300 55 22, *www.olatuhotela.com* (€€–€). A small, modern hotel in a 19th-century townhouse a short walk from the beach, with tasteful rooms.

Camping Talai-Mendi, Monte Talai-Mendi, **t** 94 383 00 42, *www.campingeuskadi.com* (€). Quiet campsite, on a hillside with sea views. *Summer only*.

Otzarreta, C/Santa Klara 5, **t** 94 313 12 43, *www.restauranteotzarreta.com* (€€€). An elegant and traditional

establishment set in beautiful gardens. Popular for weddings. *Closed Sun eve and Mon*.

Aiten-Etxe, C/Elkano 3, **t** 94 383 18 25 (€€€). Fine, uncomplicated seafood dishes and magnificent views along Zarautz's main beach. *Closed Sun eve*.

Argoin-Txiki, Argoin Auzoa s/n, **t** 94 389 01 84 (€€–€). Friendly cider house that offers different variations of traditional home cooking washed down with fine cider or *txakoli*. They also offer good value rooms.

Txiki Polit, Musika Plaza s/n, **t** 94 383 53 57, *www.txikipolit.com* (€€–€). Great tapas bar, with a huge variety of tasty treats. They also rent out comfortable and cheap rooms in the *pensión* upstairs.

Donostia-San Sebastián

Sebastian bat ba da zeruan
Donosti bat bakarra munduan

(There's only one St Sebastián up in heaven
And there's only one Donostia here on earth)
from *The March of St Sebastian*, 1861

⭐ Donostia-San Sebastián

At the beginning of the 21st century, it is difficult to imagine that a place like San Sebastián (now officially called Donostia-San Sebastián, but still usually called simply San Sebastián by non-Basque-speakers) could ever exist. The *belle époque* may be a hundred years away, but in San Sebastián the buildings still seem to be made of ice-cream, with trims in Impressionist colours and florid brass streetlights; people still dress up instinctively for the evening *paseo*. This confection embraces one of the peninsula's most enchanting bays, the oyster-shaped Bahía de La Concha, protected from the bad moods of the Atlantic by a wooded islet, the Isla de Santa Clara, and by Monte Urgull, the humpbacked sentinel on the easternmost tip of the bay. It looks a bit like Rio de Janeiro, and it's a movie set when the sun's shining, which is most of the time.

San Sebastián has probably been around as long as the Basques, but the earliest mention of it is as a Roman port called *Easo*. The town resurfaced in the Middle Ages; in the 12th century, when the Navarrese controlled this part of the coast, they built the first fortress on Monte Urgull, one that has been rebuilt and reinforced many times since. The first recorded tourist came against his will – François Ier, king of France, was locked up in the fortress for a time

Getting to and around Donostia-San Sebastián

By Air

Donostia-San Sebastián's airport (t 91 321 1000, www.aena.es), 22km to the east near Hondarribia, has connections to Madrid, Barcelona, Palma de Mallorca, Brussels and Rome. The bus to the airport, Hondarribia and Irún (t 94 364 13 02) departs from Plaza Gipúzkoa every hour, and takes about 30 mins.

By Train

RENFE trains depart from the **Estación del Norte** (t 902 320 320, www.renfe.com), on Paseo de Francia. There are frequent connections with Irún and Hendaye, Burgos and Madrid; and less frequent trains to Paris, Barcelona, Pamplona, Salamanca, Vitoria-Gasteiz, Zaragoza and León. *Talgos* whizz all the way to Madrid, Málaga, Córdoba, Algeciras, Valencia, Alicante, Oviedo and Gijón.

EuskoTren (t 902 543 210, www.euskotren.es) runs services to Hendaye and Bilbao from **Amara** station on Plaza Easo: trains stop everywhere on the way (journey time to Bilbao is 2hrs 40mins).

By Bus

A bewildering number of buses leave from the station on Plaza de Pio XII at the southern end of town. The ticket office for **Pesa** (t 902 101 212, www.pesa.net), which runs the services to Bilbao, Biarritz and Bayonne, is nearby at C/Sancho el Sabio 33, though some lines (including **La Roncelesa**, t 94 346 10 64, www.conda.es, for buses to Pamplona and Vitoria) have their offices on Paseo de Bizkaia. There are five buses daily to Oviedo, seven to Burgos and five to Galicia.

Within Euskadi, buses depart every half-hour to Bilbao and Vitoria, and up to 10 times a day to Pamplona. For information on buses in Donostia-San Sebastián itself, call t 94 328 71 00. No.16 goes to Igueldo and the funicular (*daily in summer 10–10, every 15mins*).

By Car

Car hire is available at the following:
Avis, t 94 364 45 16.
Atesa, t 94 364 02 14.
Europcar, t 94 366 85 30.
Hertz, t 94 366 85 26.

By Taxi

Radiotaxi Donosti, t 94 346 46 46, www.taxidonosti.com.
Vallina Teletaxi, t 94 340 40 40, www.vallinagrupo.com.

By Bike

Cycling is a great way to explore Donostia-San Sebastián, especially along the 12km seafront promenade: it's possible to get from one end of the city to the other without having to cross a road. Bikes can be hired from **Bici Rent Donosti**, Avenida de la Zurriola 22, t 639 016 013 (mobile).

Motor Boats

Boats (t 94 300 04 50), including a glass-bottomed catamaran, make excursions out to the Isla de Santa Clara every hour (*June–Sept only*) from the pier (*muelle*), where you can also rent a rowing boat to do the same yourself.

Tours

Walking, cycling, running tours: The tourist office (*see* p.180) run several themed tours, including gourmet and cinema walking tours, a bike tour – and even a running tour, if you want to keep fit and see the sights at the same time. Prices range from €10–12 per person. The tourist office has a list of other companies which can arrange sporting activities, cooking lessons and guided visits.

Bus tour: An open-topped tour bus, the **Bus Turistikoa**, t 696 429 847, www.busturistikoa.com, departs for hour-long circuits from the tourist office, picking up and dropping off at all the major sights.

---

by Charles V after being captured at the Battle of Pavia in 1527. In the 19th century, the city found a new role as the cynosure of fashion: a century before there were any such thing as '*costas*',

*Sebastian bat
ba da zeruan

Donosti
bat bakarra
munduan*

*(There's only one
St Sebastián
up in heaven
And there's only
one Donostia
here on earth)*
from *The March of
St Sebastian*, 1861

wealthy Spaniards were coming here to spend their summers bathing. In the 1850s it was blessed by the presence of Queen Isabel II, who brought the government and the court with her in summer. It was during her reign that San Sebastián was made capital of the province and the Paris–Madrid railway was completed, making the city convenient to holidaymakers from both capitals.

Queen Regent María Cristina again made San Sebastián the rage in 1886 – following the example of Empress Eugénie of France, who had popularized nearby Biarritz. The sister city of Reno, Nevada, it's still a classy place to go: a lovely, relaxed seaside resort in a spectacular setting. And the Donostiarrak, as the inhabitants are known, know how to throw a party. The wild 24-hour nonstop *Tamborrada*, beginning at midnight on 19 January, honours the town's patron saint with a mad tattoo of drums and barrels, recalling how the town's laundresses mocked the occupying Napoleonic troops by following their drummers about, banging away on their washtubs; now the roles are played by the *txokos*, or gastronomic societies (*see* p.56), who dress up as soldiers and chefs. Carnival here is Rio-style, with plenty of transvestites. A major jazz festival takes place in July, followed by a week of city-wide partying for the *Semana Grande* (8–15 August), coinciding with an International Fireworks Festival. Spain's answer to Cannes, the International Film Festival, takes place in September.

Playa de la Concha and the Comb of the Winds

Sheltered within the bay is the magnificent golden crescent of the **Playa de la Concha**, San Sebastián's centrepiece and its largest beach, beautifully hemmed by the Paseo de la Concha, an elegant promenade with flouncy balustrades, dotted with creamy *belle époque* cafés and the matronly **bath house** (now a modern thalassotherapy centre offering health and beauty treatments, with a seafront restaurant; *see www.la-perla.net*). On its western end stands a promontory topped by the mock-Tudor **Palace of Miramar of María Cristina**, built as a summerhouse for the royal family, and the scene of a raging battle on the day the Spanish Republic was declared in 1931. It is now owned by the city and used for receptions and special exhibitions, but you can sit in the gardens. A tunnel under the Miramar leads to the **Playa de Ondarreta**, a traditional society retreat, with a smart tennis club and graceful old villas. Ondarreta beach itself comes to a dead end at seaside **Monte Igueldo**, crowned by a Parque de Atracciones. You can get to the top by road or by the delightful, rickety old funicular from the end of the beach, and the reward is a spectacular view over San Sebastián, the Bay of Biscay (Bizkaiko Golkoa) and the Cantabrian mountains.

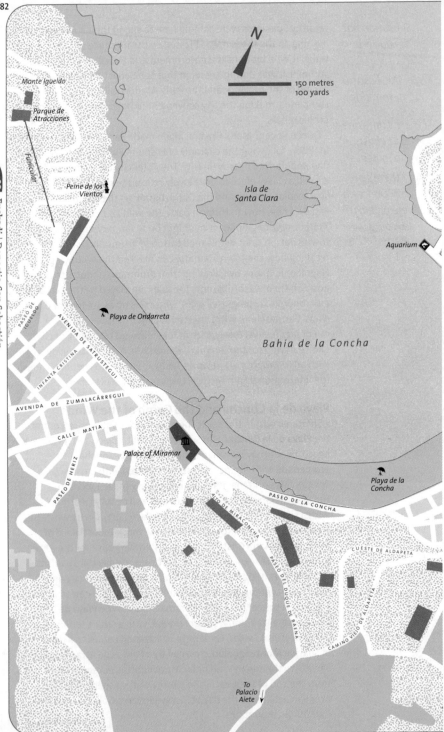

N

150 metres
100 yards

Monte Igueldo

Parque de Atracciones

Funicular

Peine de los Vientos

Isla de Santa Clara

Aquarium

PASEO DE IGUELDO

AVENIDA DE SATRUSTEGUI

INFANTA CRISTINA

AVENIDA DE ZUMALACÁRREGUI

CALLE MATIA

PASEO DE HERIZ

Playa de Ondarreta

Bahia de la Concha

Palace of Miramar

ALTO DE MIRACONCHA

PASEO DE LA CONCHA

Playa de la Concha

CUESTE DE ALDAPETA

PASEO DEL DUQUE DE BAENA

CAMINO VIEJO DE ALDAPETA

To Palacio Aiete

Mar Cantábrico

British Cemetery

Monte Urgull

🏛 Castillo de Santa Cruz

PASEO NUEVO

Museum of
San Telmo

Santa María
del Coro

🏛 Museo Naval

✝ PLAZA DE
LA TRINIDAD CALLE 31 DE AGOSTO

✝ San Vicente

PASEO DE SALAMANCA

LA PARTE VIEJA

CALLE MAYOR

PUERTO

CALLE SAN JERÓNIMO

MARI

PLAZA
DE LA
CONSTITUCIÓN

ÍÑIGO

ALDAMAR

CALBETÓN FERMÍN

El Muelle

PUENTE
DE
ZURRIOLA

Playa de Gros ☂

*Playa de
Zurriola* ☂

Palacio de Congresos
Kursaal y Auditorio

AVENIDA DE LA ZURRIOLA

ALAMEDA DEL BOULEVARD 🛈

PASEO DE COLÓN

CALLE DE ZABALETA

BERMINGHAM

GEN

Ayuntamiento

*Parque de
Alderdi Eder*

PEÑA FLORIDA

PLAZA DE
GIPÚZKOA

CALLE ANDÍA

CALLE OQUENDO

PASEO REPÚBLICA ARGENTINA

C NUEVA

CALLE DE SAN FRANCISCO

SECUNDINO ESNAOLA

CENTRO ROMÁNTICO

CALLE MIRAMAR

AVENIDA DE LA LIBERTAD

PUENTE
DE SANTA
CATALINA

PLAZA DE
EUSKADI

GROS

CALLE MIRACRUZ

✉

PLAZA DE
CERVANTES

PASEO DE LA CONCHA

CALLE LOIOLA

CALLE DE SAN MARCIAL

FUENTERRABIA

ETXAIDE

PASEO DE LOS FUEROS

PLAZA DE
ZUBIETA ZARAGOZA

CALLE DE SAN MARTÍN

CALLE DE SAN BARTOLOMÉ

CALLE DE EASO

CALLE DE URBANETA

✝ Catedral del
Buen Pastor

CALLE URDANETA ✉

CALLE REYES
CATÓLICOS

CALLE DE PRIM

PASEO DEL ÁRBOL DE GUERNICA

PASEO DE FRANCIA

Mercado de la
Brecha 🧺

PUENTE
DE MARÍA
CRISTINA

Estación
del
Norte

PASEO DEL DUQUE DE MANDAS

PLAZA
EASO

CALLE MORAZA

Río Urumea

Estación de
Amara

*To
Bus Station*

*Parque de
Cristina Enea*

Río Urumea

Río Urumea

Back on the shore, beyond the beach and the funicular, stands one of the most talked-about monuments of modern Spanish sculpture, Eduardo Chillida's *Peine de los Vientos* (the *Comb of the Winds*). The work is a series of terraces, built into the rocks that guard the entrance to the bay, decorated with cast-iron constructions, the 'teeth' of the comb that smooths the winds coming from the sea towards the city. Chillida was a native of San Sebastián (he was once goalie for the local football side), and lived in a house on the cliffs above the monument.

Centro Romántico

Nearly all the city behind the beaches of La Concha and Ondarreta dates from the 19th century. San Sebastián is an ancient place, but it has been burned to the ground twelve times in its history, lastly by Wellington's drunken soldiers, who celebrated their conquest with their accustomed murder and mayhem. The city was rebuilt and even expanded soon after, in a neat neoclassical grid now called the **Centro Romántico**, with the **Catedral del Buen Pastor**, completed in the 1880s, at its centre. The **Mercado de San Martín** squats nearby, with stalls packed with fresh produce from the sea and the surrounding mountains. At the heart of this district is the arcaded Plaza de Gipúzkoa, sternly overlooked by the neoclassical **Palacio Foral**.

Heading towards the river, the Plaza de Okeando is flanked by the grand María Cristina hotel, with its pretty swaths of colourful tiles, and the prim **Victoria Eugenia Theatre**, inaugurated in 1912 and host to the *Quincena Musical*, a fortnight-long programme of classical music. This trim neighbourhood is the main shopping district of the city, with several swanky designer shops and classy teashops.

A promenade-lined river, the Urumea, divides 19th-century Sanse (as the city is affectionately known) from the newer quarter of Gros, once the working men-student-bohemian enclave, a lively place full of bars and restaurants and endowed with its own beach, the **Playa de Gros**, which is always less crowded but lies outside the sheltered bay, subject to the wind, waves and filthy debris. Still, it's great for surfers, who come in droves. Of the three charming bridges that span the Urumea, the **María Cristina** (near the station) most resembles a cream pastry.

With its imposing main façade facing the Cristina-Enea Park and its back to the north railway station is the old tobacco factory, **Tabakalera**, which is fast becoming one of the region's most important contemporary art centres. The vast factory is currently being dramatically remodelled, but continues to host exhibitions, talks, debates and workshops while works are under way.

Tabakalera
for updates, info and current exhibitions, see www.tabacalera.eu, and the tourist office, or call **t** *943 011 311*

Parte Vieja and Monte Urgull

Most of the action in town takes place under Monte Urgull in the narrow streets of the Parte Vieja, or old town (also known as the Casco Viejo). From La Concha beach, its entrance is guarded by a beautiful, well-manicured square, the **Parque de Alderdi Eder**, and the enormous 19th-century **Ayuntamiento**, or town hall, formerly the casino that María Cristina built (the new one is on Calle Mayor). Behind it, the swanky yacht club (*members only*), set in a slightly battered white rationalist building from the 1930s, looks like something from an Agatha Christie novel. What remains of the city's fishing fleet may be seen in the harbour behind the Ayuntamiento, a picturesque tumble of whitewashed cottages rimmed by souvenir shops, pricy tourist restaurants – although it's worth trying the freshly grilled sardines – and a pair of salty museums. The **Museo Naval** is set in the 18th-century consulate and is devoted to the Basques' proud naval history, with models, photographs and biographies of famous Basque seafarers. At the far end of the port, the **Aquarium** is stuffed with model ships, the skeleton of a Basque whale that went belly-up in San Sebastián's port and, downstairs, tanks of fish and other sea creatures from around the world.

From here you can stroll along the outer edge of **Monte Urgull** on the Paseo Nuevo, a splendid little walk between turf and surf. In the late afternoon, when the light is best, stroll up one of the numerous paths to the summit of the rock; Monte Urgull is really the city's park, closed to traffic and including surprises along the way, such as a peaceful British cemetery from Wellington's campaign and some of the old bastions and ancient cannons of the city's defences. Up at the top is the half-ruined **Castillo de Santa Cruz de la Mota** (16th-century), topped with an ungainly kitsch statue of Christ (from the Franco era) called the **Sagrado Corazón**, which keeps an eye on the holiday-makers on La Concha beach below.

The centre of the Parte Vieja is the arcaded **Plaza de la Constitución**, which once did double duty as the local bullring, when spectators would cram onto the crisply painted (and still numbered) balconies for the best view. Within a few blocks of this local centre of Basque nationalism stand San Sebastián's three best monuments. From Calle Mayor, the distant neo-Gothic spires of the **Catedral del Buen Pastor** outstare the hyper-ornate façade of **Santa María del Coro** (18th century) on Vía Coro, topped with a writhing statue of St Sebastián full of arrows. It's gloomy inside, with dark, monstrous *retablos* half-hidden in shadows, but the main altarpiece is well lit and surmounted by the church's treasure: a statue of the Virgin which is said to have been found

Museo Naval
open Tues–Sat 10–1.30 and 4–7.30, Sun 11–2; closed Mon; adm

Aquarium
www.aquariumss.com, open July–Aug daily 10–9; Oct–Easter Mon–Fri 10–7, Sat and Sun 10–8; Easter–June and Sept Mon–Fri 10–8, Sat and Sun 10–9; adm; note last admission is 1hr before closing; feeding sessions Tues, Thurs, Sat 12pm

up the sleeve of a priest who was trying to smuggle it out, and placed in its present position to discourage further attempts. Don't miss, at the back of the church, a limpid alabaster Greek cross by Eduardo Chillida in a pale arc of light. Dense cubes interlock, and the shape of the cross is formed by the central hollow. Next to the church is the **Plaza de la Trinidad**, focus of the city's celebrated jazz festival in July and a popular spot for skateboarders during the rest of the year.

At the other end of the Calle 31 de Agosto, the only street left standing after the great fire of 1813, is the solid Gothic church of **San Vicente** (16th century), the oldest building in the city. Inside, there's a dramatic *retablo* by Basque painters Bengoechea and Iriarte, but the moving *Pietá* (1999) by Oteiza and José Ramon Anda on the exterior walls is infinitely more affecting. Nearby, the old Dominican monastery of San Telmo is now the fascinating

Museum of San Telmo
t 94 348 15 80, www. santelmomuseoa.com; open Tues–Sun 10–8; closed Mon; adm, free Tues

Museum of San Telmo, which reopened in 2011 after a massive expansion and remodelling programme. The monastery's church is adorned with golden murals by the Catalan artist Josep Sert (1930) on the history of the Basque people. Old Basque discoidal tombstones are lined up in the cloister; upstairs, the museum contains three El Grecos, two bear skeletons, Basque lucky charms and amulets, Basque sports paraphernalia, the interior of a Basque cottage and more. Excellent temporary exhibitions are hosted, along with a full programme of complementary activities.

Isla de Santa Clara
ferry from El Muelle, the dock behind the Ayuntamiento; summer 10–8.30

The main attraction of the Parte Vieja is its countless bars, where the evening crowds hasten to devour seafood *tapas* and Basque goodies. Here, in the homeland of the Basque *txokos* (*see* p.56), eating is the greatest obsession. A fun excursion is to gather up some of that good food and row it out to **Isla de Santa Clara** for a picnic.

Around Donostia-San Sebastián

There are several lovely parks in the hills around the city. The **Parque Monte Ulía** (climb up from Sagües station on the edge of Gros) for dramatic views of the thrashing Cantabrian Sea; this is

Museo Chillida Leku
take the N1 from San Sebastián and turn off on to the Gl 2132 to Hernani, or get the half-hourly G2 bus from C/Okendo, t 94 333 60 06, www.museo chillidaleku.com; closed indefinitely, call for updates

where sailors once watched for whales. A couple of kilometres inland from La Concha is the graceful **Aiete Palace** (private, but gardens always open), built in the late 19th century for the duke and duchess of Bailén, and surrounded by breezy woods and pretty landscaped gardens with a lake.

About 8km from town, the open-air **Museo Chillida Leku** (Chillida Museum) is devoted to the works of San Sebastián's favourite son. Eduardo Chillida restored this 16th-century farmhouse with its old oak beams, lit by a sheet of natural light which pours in from a glass wall and illuminates works spanning half a century. The lawns, shaded by huge old trees, are dotted with more than

Eduardo Chillida (1924–2002)

Creator of a slew of monumental sculptures adorning boulevards and museums across the world, Chillida was the international standard-bearer of the Escuela Vasca (Basque School) founded by Jorge de Oteiza (*see* p.119), who exhorted Basque artists to define an aesthetic rooted in the Basque character. Chillida's use of iron, granite and wood follows the same tradition as the Basque ironworkers and shipwrights, and their predecessors who worked in stone, leaving dolmens and cromlechs in the mountains and finely worked tools in the caves.

Born in San Sebastián, Chillida studied architecture in Madrid for four years before abandoning his studies for sculpture, and the Spanish capital, then ruled by the repressive Franco, for the French one. Chillida's earliest works were figurative, including sculptures in clay or plaster, but he soon rejected them in favour of purely abstract pieces forged from iron, 'drawings in space' reminiscent of the work of the great Catalan sculptor Julio González. These early pieces were often spiky, penetrating or spearing, and yet retained an impression of lightness, fluidity and airiness. Chillida was interested in the contrast 'between the solidity of the iron and its sudden endings in space', an interest which became clearer after his return to Hernani (near San Sebastián) in 1951. The later works are often solid pieces, created from interlocking cubes of iron or granite; others are formed entirely from a single strip of metal, the flow of form unbroken. He constructed a series of monolithic sculptures, hewn from Galician granite, their massiveness and weight deliberately counterbalanced by a sense of airy grace, so that stone can sometimes seem liquid and weightless. He was notoriously prolific, and few Basque towns can't boast of a Chillida or two – if only on the plaques at their local branch of the Kutxo bank. Chillida designed the logo.

40 massive pieces, sculpted mostly from iron and granite, yet light and graceful. Unfortunately, the museum closed in 2011, a victim of the global recession, and its future remains uncertain, so call in advance before making the trip out of town.

Tourist Information in Donostia-San Sebastián

San Sebastián ›
C/Reina Regente 3,
t 94 348 11 66,
www.donostia.org,
www.sansebastian
turismo.com

The **tourist office** sells the **San Sebastián Card**, which offers free public transport plus discounts on museums and attractions, and is valid for three days (€14). They also run walking and bike tours (€8–12), including a special cinema route.

Post office: C/Urdaneta, behind the cathedral.

Internet access: Like many Spanish cities, Donostia-San Sebastián offers free WiFi access, provided by the city council. There are several hotspots throughout the city, including at the bus station, on the Boulevard, and along the Paseo de la Concha. Most hotels and guesthouses, and several restaurants and cafés also offer free WiFi access, or you could ask the tourist office for a list of *ciber cafés*.

Shopping in Donostia-San Sebastián

Along with the tourist shops in the Parte Vieja, there are a number of more original places that sell a range of items, from surf-punk paraphernalia to exquisite home-made chocolates. The Centro Romántico has a wide range of fashionable boutiques, from chains like Zara and Mango to chic individual establishments selling creations by Spanish designers.

Trip, C/31 de Agosto 33, t 94 342 94 43. Small, intriguing shop selling everything from snazzy bags to scented candles.

Casa Ponsol, C/Narrica 4. An institution in the world of Basque berets, established in 1832.

Barrebnetxe, Plaza de Gipúzkoa 9, t 94 342 44 82. Fabulous Basque pastries, cakes and chocolates, and wonderful bread. Café area.

Villa Sora >>

Hontza, C/Okendo 4. If you're inspired by all the seafood you've been eating, this place sells books in English on Basque cooking.

Saski-naski, Boulevard 24, t 94 342 28 91. Delightful boutique run by kindly staff specializing in hand-made Basque gifts, including ceramics, sculpture, linens and jewellery.

Solbes, Aldamar 4, t 94 342 78 18, www.solbes.com. Pristinely presented delicatessen and wine shop that has been run by the same family since 1894.

Markets in Donostia-San Sebastián

The central **Mercado de la Bretxa** now houses upmarket shops with designer boutiques, cinemas and cafés, but the basement contains a fresh produce market with countless stalls. Don't miss the spectacular fish counters. The **Mercado de San Martín** in the Centro Romántico is of the traditional fruit and vegetable variety. Just follow all those shopping baskets!

Where to Stay in Donostia-San Sebastián

San Sebastián ⌧ 20000

San Sebastián is not the place to look for bargains – many of the cheaper *hostales* and *fondas* are packed full of university students most of the year. In general, the farther back you are from the sea, the less expensive the accommodation is likely to be.

Luxury–Very Expensive

*****María Cristina**, C/Okendo 1, t 94 343 76 00, www.westin.com. For a touch of *belle époque* elegance, this old *grande dame* is one of Spain's best hotels; it looks onto the Río Urumea's promenade, a short walk from La Concha.

****Hotel Londres y Inglaterra**, C/Zubieta 2 (on La Concha beach), t 94 344 07 70, www.hlondres.com. The city's other most luxurious

address, with splendid views, first-class service,and plenty of charm, as well as one of the city's best restaurants.

****Villa Sora**, Avda Ategorrieta 61, t 94 329 79 70, www.villasoro.com. A 19th-century villa surrounded by gardens, with sumptuous rooms which fashionably combine contemporary and antique furnishings. Superb service and a romantic restaurant.

Expensive

****Mercure San Sebastián**, Paseo del Faro 134, on the top of the mountain, t 94 321 02 11, www.monteigueldo.com. Modern rooms, now rather in need of an update, with stunning views over the bay (and a funfair). Great deals often available online which can drop a price category – or even two, outside the high season. Note that guests still have to pay for the funicular up the hill.

****Gudamendi Park**, Plaza de Gudamendi, Barrio de Igueldo, t 94 321 40 00, www.hotelgudamendi.com. Quiet, comfortable and attractive, located amid gardens halfway up Monte Igueldo; the best rooms have sea views.

Moderate

The best you'll find will be at the higher end of the moderate range, and there are a fair number of them both in the Parte Vieja and in the centre.

***Hotel Niza**, C/Zubieta 56, t 94 342 66 63, www.hotelniza.com. A good central choice, near the beach, with a Modernista lobby and an old-fashioned lift. The best rooms have sea views. There's also a decent restaurant.

La Galería, C/Infanta Cristina 1–3, t 94 321 60 77, www.hotellagaleria. com. A couple of minutes from Playa Ondarreta on a lovely quiet street, this French-inspired *palacete* has rooms full of antiques, art and individuality.

Pensión Bikain, C/Triunfo 8, t 94 345 43 33, www.pensionbikain.com. Top-notch facilities at a very good price, close to the beach and Parte Vieja, as well as spotless rooms, parking facilities and a helpful owner.

Pensión Alameda, Alameda del Boulevard 16, **t** 94 342 64 49, *www.pensionalameda.com*. The charming owners of this central *pensión* have kitted out the rooms with all kinds of thoughtful extras including hairdryers, free WiFi, and small fridges. Triples available.

Pensión Donostiarra, C/San Martin 6, **t** 94 342 61 67, *www.pension donostiarra.com*. Light, airy rooms with either a little balcony of flowers or a glassed-in *solana* full of plants. Drops a price category outside the summer months.

Pensión Gran Bahía, C/Embeltrán 16, 2°, **t** 94 342 02 16, *www.pension granbahia2.com*. Run by delightful, chatty Teresa, this friendly *hostal* is cosy and comfortable.

*Pensión Urgull, C/Esterlines 10, **t** 94 343 00 47. Delightful choice; just five immaculate rooms with two shared bathrooms. The charming owners are kind, friendly and more than happy to help with local information.

(★) **Pensión Bellas Artes** >

Pensión Bellas Artes, C/Urbieta, 64, 1°, **t** 94 347 49 05, *www.pension-bellasartes.com*. Leire and her mother Carmen could well win the competition for most friendly hosts, more than compensating for the smallish rooms. If you are sensitive to street noise, ask for an interior-facing room.

Inexpensive

*Hotel Record, Calzada Vieja de Ategorrieta, **t** 94 327 12 55, *www.hotelrecord.com*. A little family-run hotel in a quiet residential neighbourhood in Gros. Good family rooms available.

Pension Lorea, Alameda del Boulevard, 16, *www.pensionlorea.com*. An intimate choice (only six doubles and one single) in a centrally located part of town. Rooms are decorated in white and pink traditional style. In summer, prices nudge up a bracket.

*Pensión Amaiur, C/31 de Agosto 44, **t** 94 342 96 54. Covered in flowers, this is a charming little spot in the Casco Viejo, with simple rooms (shared bathrooms), some with pretty balconies. There's even a small kitchen for guests to use.

Pensión Anne, Esterlines 15, 2nd floor, **t** 94 342 14 38, *www.pensionanne.com*.

Also centrally located, with clean rooms. There is a bathroom for every two rooms.

*Pensión Easo, C/San Bartolomé 24, **t** 94 345 39 12, *www.pensioneaso.com*. A good, economical choice.

fridge and kettle) and friendly owners.

Camping Igueldo, Paseo Padre Orkolaga 69, **t** 94 321 54 02, *www.campingigueldo.com*. Close to the Ondarreta beach and Monte Igueldo (5km from the centre), this large campsite is open year-round.

Eating Out in Donostia-San Sebastián

As eating is the local obsession, it's not surprising the city claims several of Spain's most renowned, award-winning restaurants – cathedrals of Basque cuisine. Be sure to book weeks if not months in advance. For cheaper dining, follow the crowds through the *tapas* bars of the Parte Vieja.

Expensive

Arzak, Alcade Elosgui 273, **t** 94 328 55 93, *www.arzak.com*. Often described as the finest restaurant in Spain; offers a constantly changing menu of delights. Chef Juan Mari Arzak or his equally gifted daugher Elena are often at hand to make suggestions, as dishes change with the seasons and availability. Book weeks in advance. *Closed Sun and Mon; Jan–June also closed Tues; closed 2 weeks in June and 3 weeks in Nov.*

Akelarre, Paseo Padre Orkolaga 56 (in the Barrio de Igueldo), **t** 94 331 12 09, *www.akelarre.net*. This restaurant is celebrated for its mixture of some of the most remarkably innovative New Basque cuisine with a delicious array of traditional local dishes – look out for the wonderfully prepared langoustines. Beautiful mountainside setting with views over the sea to boot. *Closed Sun eve and Mon, Tues Jan–June, Feb and first fortnight in Oct.*

Urepel, Paseo de Salamanca 3, **t** 94 342 40 40, *www.urepel.net*. This is another of San Sebastián's most eminent restaurants, serving classic Basque cuisine with original touches. The house speciality is the *sopa de* *pescados* (fish soup). *Closed Sun, Tues, Christmas, Easter and 3 wks in July.*

Rekondo, Paseo de Igueldo 57, **t** 94 321 29 07, *www.rekondo.com.* A superb choice, this classic *mesón*-style restaurant specializes in grilled fish and meat and has a huge wine cellar. Come here for superb dining at around €50. *Closed Tues eve and Wed.*

Martín Berasategui, C/Loidi Kalea 4, Lasarte (8km from San Sebastián), **t** 94 336 64 71. Berasategu's temple to New Basque cuisine at its finest. The *menú de degustación* is a hefty €165, but this is a dining experience you won't forget. *Closed Sun eve, Mon and Tues, plus mid-Dec–mid-Jan.*

⭐ **Mugaritz** >

Mugaritz, Aldura Aldea, 20, Errenteria, (10km from San Sebastián), **t** 94 352 24 55, *www.mugaritz.com.* Book well in advance for a table at this enchanting Basque *caserio* on top of a hill. Voted one of the world's top five restaurants, it serves dazzling

⭐ **Gandarias** >>

contemporary Basque cuisine, presented in a choice of two set menus (€110 or €140). *Open April to mid-December, but check website for exact dates. Closed Sun eve, Mon and Tues; open Tues eves from May–Sept.*

Beti Jai, C/Fermín Calbetón 22, **t** 94 342 77 37, *www.restaurantebetijai.com.* Bang in the middle of 'Restaurant Walk', this is one of the city's liveliest seafood restaurants, although there are plenty of other things on the menu and a hectic bar if you don't want to sit (*see* p.192). The *salpicón de mariscos* (a refreshing seafood salad) is excellent. *Closed Mon, Tues, 3 weeks around Christmas and end June–early July.*

Izkiña, C/Fermín Calbetón 4, **t** 94 342 2562. Perfectly prepared, fresh seafood, excellent steaks, and a superb tapas bar piled high with *pintxos. Closed Mon, Tues eve and Wed.*

Moderate

Bodegón Alejandro, C/Fermín Calbetón 4, **t** 94 342 71 58, *www.bodegonalejandro.com.* This is where famed chef Martín Berasategui started out; excellent traditional cuisine with innovative touches. The house speciality is a *succulent marmita de bonita* (tuna stew), and there's a great lunchtime deal at €15.

Branka, Paseo Eduardo Chillida 13, **t** 94 331 70 96, *www.branka-tenis.com.* This restaurant has a marvellous location near Chillida's sculpture *Peine de Los Vientos* at the far end of La Concha beach; go for the elegant Basque fare in the dining room, or lighter and cheaper meals and *pintxos* in the café. There's also a terrace for post-prandial cocktails.

Chomin, Avda Infanta Beatriz 16, **t** 943 31 73 12, *www.restaurante chomin.info.* Pretty villa (plus a handful of delightful rooms) housing this local favourite by the Ondarreta beach. Delicious Basque specialities on a splendid terrace in summer. *Closed Sun eve and Mon.*

La Fábrica de Iñigo Bozal, C/Puerto 17, **t** 94 343 57 01, *www.restaurante lafabrica.es.* By the port; serves deft, modern cuisine from a promising young chef. A good set menu is served for €23. *Closed Sun eve.*

Gandarias, C/31 de Agosto 23, **t** 94 342 63 62, *www.gandarias.com.* As well as the spectacular bar, with its dazzling array of tapas, this also serves excellent traditional Basque meat and seafood accompanied by a good wine selection.

Urbano, C/31 de Agosto 17, **t** 94 342 04 34, *www.restauranteurbano.com.* Elegant, white-painted restaurant with modern art on the walls and a delicious menu which mixes traditional and modern Basque dishes. *Set lunch menu €22; set dinner menu €27.*

Inexpensive

Portaletas, C/Puerto 8, **t** 94 342 42 72. Fronted by a hugely popular tapas bar, the restaurant has an excellent set lunch menu.

La Zurri, C/Zabaleta 9, Gros, **t** 94 329 38 86. Near the Kursaal in the Gros neighbourhood, this lively local hang-out has a good selection of fresh daily specials (including a set lunch).

Tedone Jatetxea, C/Corta 10, **t** 94 327 35 61, *www.tedone.eu.* This restaurant in Gros offers two menus – one traditional and one vegetarian– using fresh, usually organic produce. Lovely staff, and a relaxed atmosphere. *Closed Sun eve, Mon.*

Tapas/*Pintxos* in Donostia-San Sebastián

Parte Vieja

The Parte Vieja is proud of its reputation for having more bars per square metre than anywhere else in the world. Every street is lined with dozens of bars, with groaning counters.

Perhaps the gastronomic heart of the Parte Vieja is Calle Mayor and C/31 de Agosta, the only streets to withstand the destruction of the city in 1813, and filled with the most traditional bars, restaurants and the famous secret gastronomic societies or *txokos* (*see* p.56).

Plaza de la Constitución, with its freshly painted balconies and cool arcades, is a lovely place to while away an hour or two, and the C/Fermín Calbetón is sometimes known as 'Restaurant Walk', thanks to the virtually unbroken string of busy establishments.

A Fuego Negro, C/31 de Agosto 31, **t** 650 135 373, *www.afuegonegro.com*. This, bright modern bar is famous for its exquisite, creative concoctions, all beautifully presented: go for one of the tasting menus to try a selection of their best tapas.

Clery, Plaza de la Trinidad 1, **t** 94 342 34 01. One of San Sebastián's most-loved restaurants, with an attractive bar and terrace where you can sample tasty *pintxos* like little fried balls of cod with a green pepper sauce. A great place to eat during the spring jazz festival, when concerts take place in the Plaza de la Trinidad.

La Cepa, C/31 de Agosto 7–9, **t** 94 342 63 94. With a ceiling dripping with cured hams and a liberal splashing of taurine memorabilia, this is one of the most down-to-earth of the local bars. Among its classic *pintxos* are the *gildas*, anchovies with tuna and mild green chillies, a perennial favourite.

Martínez, C/31 de Agosto 13, **t** 94 342 49 65. A brightly polished bar with a broad counter piled staggeringly high with delicious *pintxos*. Try the *champis*, wild mushrooms sometimes stuffed with a pungent slice of cured sausage, or the delicious fresh prawns tossed in breadcrumbs and fried.

Ormazábel, C/31 de Agosto 22, **t** 94 342 99 07. A family-run *bodega* with an excellent selection of local wines to accompany the unusual spinach *croquetas*, or *chipirones*, baby squid, which have been everyone's favourite for half a century.

Gaztelu, C/31 de Agosto 22, **t** 94 342 14 11. Next to the Ormazábel, this friendly, neighbourhood bar where everyone seems to know everyone else has got a big reputation for its *cazuela de caracoles* (snail stew). Even a simple dish like *tortilla de patatas* is mouth-wateringly rich and buttery. *Closed Wed.*

La Cuchara de San Telmo, C/31 Agosto 28, **t** 94 342 08 40, *www.lacucharade santelmo.com*. You'll have to squeeze your way inside to sample some of the immaculately presented *pintxos*, including stuffed peppers, tortilla with *bacalao* (cod) and much more; there's a lovely summer terrace.

Bideluze, Plaza de Guipúzcoa, 14, **t** 94 342 28 80. Given its key location and reputation, you'll be hard pushed to find a table. But the long wait will all be worth it when you try '*El Tigre*' ('The Tiger') a *pintxo* based on mussels, green pepper and onion.

Gambara, C/San Jeronimo 21, **t** 94 342 25 75. A tiny bar with a big reputation for its wide array of *pintxos*: excellent prawns, fresh asparagus in season, a good selection of cured meats, all washed down with some of the best *txakoli* (the sharp, local wine; *see* pp.60–61) in town.

Astelena, Plaza de la Constitución, **t** 94 342 52 45 . This is the city's hot spot on the feast of St Tomás in December, when the *plaza* fills up with revellers. A great selection of *pintxos*, including freshly prepared hot delicacies which are ordered from the day's specials marked up on a blackboard. *Closed Sun.*

Txepetxa, C/Pescadería 5, **t** 94 342 22 27. This bar has become a 'temple of anchovies', and you can get them prepared in every imaginable way, from classic anchovies with black olives to an exotic dish prepared with coconut and Polynesian spices.

⭐ La Cuchara de San Telmo >>

Tamboril, C/Pescadería 2, **t** 94 342 35 07. All kinds of *banderillas* (mini-tapas skewered on toothpicks) are on offer here, but the house speciality is the stuffed mushrooms (*champis*), which are served up on a slice of crusty bread. There's a much sought-after terrace in summer. *Closed Mon eve and Tues*.

Borda Berri, C/Fermín Calbetón 12, **t** 94 342 56 38. An elegant, historic bar with a range of innovative *raciones* – stuffed peppers with tuna and a light red capsicum mousse among them – and, unusually for this part of town, a refined cocktail list.

Bar Beti Jai, C/Fermín Calbetón 22, **t** 94 342 77 37. If you can't manage a big splurge in the restaurant (*see* p.190), try some of the exquisite seafood specialities as *raciones* in the bar. The food is all so fresh that it doesn't require any fancy sauces; try the sublimely simple marinated anchovies or the baby squid (*chipirones*). *Closed Mon eve and Tues*.

Casa Alcade, Calle Mayor 19, **t** 94 342 62 16. Lined with bullfighting memorabilia and hanging hams, this bar has remained virtually unchanged for almost a century. Wafer-thin slices of cured ham make a fine accompaniment to the excellent Riojas on offer.

Gros

Surprisingly few tourists make it across the river to this pleasing neighbourhood, which has plenty of its own lively bars and nightlife.

Bodega Donostiarra, C/Peña y Goñi 13, **t** 94 301 13 80. An old-fashioned classic near the Kursaal, serving a huge array of classic favourites.

⭐ **Bar Bergara >**

Bar Bergara, C/General Arteche 8, **t** 94 327 50 26. Spacious, attractive bar with lightly fried titbits skewered on

cocktail sticks and an excellent selection of wines and spirits. Try *txalupa*, langoustine gratinéed with wild mushrooms, or the cod baked with garlic and herbs (*bacalao ajoarriero*). *Closed Oct*.

Joxean, C/Secundino Esnaola 39–41, **t** 94 332 30 00. A lively bar with a small restaurant. The *pintxos* are imaginative twists on old favourites, like *mollejas encebolladas*, a rich sweetbread dish, or *hojaldre de pimientos rellenos*, flaky pastry with stuffed peppers.

Entertainment and Nightlife in Donostia-San Sebastián

The centre of the party action is the streets of the Parte Vieja. Late-night bars and clubs are also found around the end of Ondarreta beach. For listings, check out the back pages of *El Diario Vasco*, the local newspaper.

Bataplán, C/Paseo de la Concha 6, *www.bataplandisco.com*. Hugely popular seafront disco with outdoor terrace. Electro-pop and dance.

Be Bop, Paseo de Salamanca 5, **t** 94 342 98 69. One of several bars in the area with live music. This one's a jazz venue.

Casino Kursaal, C/Mayor 1, **t** 94 342 92 14. The place to hit if you fancy a flutter.

La Kabutzia, Paseo de la Concha, *www.lakabutzia.com*. The sleek Real Club Náutico is the setting for this crowd-pleasing disco, which offers everything from salsa to pop.

Altxerri Bar & Jazz, Reina Regente, 2, **t** 94 342 16 93. An emblematic haunt for jazz-lovers, not just in Donostia but in the Basque country.

Inland from Donostia-San Sebastián

Tolosa and Ordizia: Beans and Cheese

Guipúzcoa, San Sebastián's province, is the most densely populated rural part of the Basque country, where plenty of fat villages bear unpronounceable, unimaginable names. To see them, you'll have to invest a lot of time on some lovely, lazy back roads, and stay off the motorways from Donostia-San Sebastián to Tolosa and to Pamplona. Despair will probably set in at a corner with signs pointing you to Aizarnazabal, Azpeitia, Azkoitia, Azkarate or Araiz-Matximenta; you'll think the Basques are doing this just for you.

One of the first Basque towns to join the Industrial Revolution, **Tolosa** (named after Toulouse) is the largest town on the Oria river and still fairly industrial, although most of the paper mills have now closed. Tolosa also makes wicker *chisteras* for *pelota*, and sweets, especially *tejas* (almond biscuits) and *delicias*. You can learn all about them in the **Museo de Confitería** at C/Lechuga 3, next to the Plaza del Ayuntamiento, run by Tolosa's *pastelería* of renown, Gorrottxategui, in the Plaza Zarra. Dining out is the main reason to stop, though, as the town itself is fairly drab.

To a Basque, however, Tolosa means beans, or more precisely, *Tolosako Babarruna Elkartea* or *alubias de Tolosa*, a native of Venezuela introduced in the 18th century by the Real Compañia Guipúzcona de Caracas. Even the method of planting them between rows of maize is continued here by the 40 official bean growers; like *txakoli*, red peppers, sheep's cheese and so on, they are strictly *Denominación de Origen*. Dry beans are almost black, oval and plump, but once cooked they turn red. The proper way to cook them is in an earthenware crock with garlic, onion and olive oil, which conjures up a delicious thick sauce. For a truly filling meal, the Basques pile them on top of boiled cabbage and serve them with ribs and blood sausage.

Southwest of Tolosa on the E5/E80, there's **Ordizia**, a medieval new town founded as Villafranca de Oria in 1256. Ordizia's special privileges, designed to promote the production of ewe's milk cheese (*ardi gasna*), were ratified by Juana the Mad in 1512, and ever since then it has been the cheese capital of Euskadi. The cheese, more precisely, is Idiazabal, made with the milk of an ancient race of Basque sheep, the *laxta*, a handsome, black-faced breed with curling horns and dainty grey dreadlocks. Since Neolithic times, shepherds have herded them up to summer pastures in the mountains, then down the paths of transhumance into the valleys each winter; some 800 shepherds still keep up the good work, a quarter of them producing their own cheese and, since 1904, competing in Ordizia's September cheese contest, the focal point of the village's *Fiestas Vascas*.

The pretty mountain village of **Segura**, farther south, has a main street lined with the palaces of a locally powerful family, the Guevaras, and other nobles. Up in the mountains beyond Zegama, bits of the original Roman road to Vitoria are still visible, and traditionalist pilgrims to Santiago de Compostela still ascend the

Aizkorri massif through the narrow, pedestrian-only San Adrián tunnel, before descending into the dry ochre plains of Álava.

Oñati and the Sanctuary of Arantzazu

For leisurely motorists, however, this valley has become something of a dead end. Before Segura, at Beasain, a road branches westwards off the motorway for **Oñati** (**Onate**), beautifully set in a rich, rolling valley, dominated in the distance by the bluish pointed peaks of Mount Amboto and Udalaitz. It served as the capital of the pretender Don Carlos in the Carlist Wars and was one of the few towns in Euskadi to be ruled by a noble; it retained a degree of independence until 1845. For many years the town had the only Basque **university**, founded in 1540; Oñati's landmark, it has a beautiful Plateresque façade and a Mudéjar-style arcaded courtyard. The parish church of **San Miguel** (15th-century) contains a number of treasures, including the alabaster tomb of the university's founder, Bishop Zuázola de Ávila, attributed to Diego de Siloé, and an attractive Plateresque cloister. Other noteworthy buildings include the baroque rococo-style **Ayuntamiento** and the Franciscan **Convento de Bidaurreta**.

University
Universidad Sancti Spiritus; open Mon–Thurs 9–5, Fri 9–2; adm, includes guided visit; to book, call t 94 378 34 53

Oñati is known also for its well-preserved Renaissance palaces, one of which saw the birth in 1511 of the *conquistador* Lope de Aguirre, perhaps best known these days as the deranged 'Wrath of God' in the film by Werner Herzog. The limping, mad-eyed Klaus Kinski was perfectly cast for the real man, who sailed from Seville at the age of 21, not long after Pizzarro arrived with the first fabulous shipments of treasure from the New World. Aguirre fought up and down South America in all the wars of the day, with a rare obsessiveness; at one point, after a judge had him publicly whipped for a minor infraction, Lope pursued the judge for 6,000km, barefoot through Peru, to kill him in revenge. Some-where along the way he acquired a daughter, and in 1560 the two of them accompanied Pedro de Ursúa's expedition down the Amazon in search of El Dorado. Aguirre mutinied, had Ursúa killed and, although he remained the real power, proclaimed Guzmán, the ranking nobleman of the expedition, the Prince of Peru in an act signed by 186 soldiers, 'the first act of American Independence'. Although in the film Herzog has the members of the expedition die one by one on their raft, the real expedition reached the Atlantic in July. Aguirre took the port there by surprise and wrote a famous letter to King Philip II – surely the most astonishing the royal bureaucrat ever received – informing him that he was going straight to hell for the misdeeds of his vassals in the New World, signing it 'Son of your loyal Basque vassals, and I, rebel until death against you for your ingratitude, Lope de Aguirre, the Wanderer.' Although the Spaniards in Venezuela were terrorized by Aguirre's approach, by this time his men had had enough and deserted him. When the troops of the governor of Venezuela closed in, Aguirre killed his daughter to keep her from being captured, and was cut to pieces.

Sanctuary of Arantzazu
www.arantzazuko santutegia.org; open daily 8.30–8

A scenic road up from Oñati climbs 9km to the **Sanctuary of Arantzazu**, usually filled with tour buses and pilgrims. Here, in 1469, a shepherd found an icon of the Virgin by a thorn bush and a cow bell, and the Virgin of Arantzazu became the patron saint of Guipúzcoa. The church that houses the icon has been rebuilt innumerable times since, lastly in 1950. This curious temple of Basque modernism is striking in its lonely and rugged setting, its two towers covered with a distinctive skin of pyramidal concrete nubs, creating a waffle-iron effect – a reference to an eccentric Renaissance conceit popular in Spain, seen in many buildings from Salamanca to Naples. Some of the best-known Basque artists contributed to the church: there are sculptures on the facade by Jorge Oteiza, the main doors are by Eduardo Chillida and the crypt holds paintings by Nestor Basterretxea.

Arrasate (Mondragón) and Bergara

The only town of any size in the region has two names: Basques call it **Arrasate**, Spaniards **Mondragón**. Though a nondescript industrial town these days, Arrasate used to be a spa – a Spanish prime minister, Antonio Cánovas del Castillo, was murdered here by an anarchist in 1897 while taking a cure. Arrasate still has some of its medieval walls and gates, along with the 14th-century Gothic church of San Juan. It's under the name of Mondragón that the town has made its mark, synonymous with one of the most successful, innovative cooperative ventures in the world; one that's often pointed out as proof that the hard-working, egalitarian virtues of the Basques are still a force to be reckoned with. It all started with a young, inspired priest, José María Arizmendiarrieta, who arrived in town in 1941 to find it, like the rest of Euskadi, severely depressed both economically and emotionally after the Civil War. A firm believer in the ability of people to control their own destiny, no matter how hard the circumstances, in 1943 he founded the Mondragón Eskola Politeknikoa, open to any young person in the area who wanted to attend and learn a useful skill. In 1956 five graduates formed the first co-operative manufacturing company. In 1959, they helped to create the Caja Laboral Popular savings bank, a co-operative credit company that became the keystone in the creation of scores of new co-operatives in the area. During the 1970s a technological research centre was founded, in the 1990s a private business university. Now the seventh largest firm in Spain, Mondragón has since gone international, and employs almost 84,000 workers.

Farther north, as a contrast, pretty **Bergara** offers a step back in time, with its palaces, churches and other monuments from the 16th and 17th centuries. Note the **Palacio Arrese**, with its cut-out corner window in the best Spanish Renaissance style. Bergara is closely linked with another great Basque initiative, the *Real Sociedad Bascongada de Amigos del Pais* (Royal Basque Society of Friends of Bascongadas), founded by aristocrats in Azkoitia in 1764 to 'cultivate the learning and the taste of the Basque nation for the sciences, the fine arts and the arts; to correct and refine its customs, banish idleness, ignorance and their fatal consequences, and further tighten the union of the Three Basque Provinces of Álava, Vizcaya, and Guipúzcoa'. Its motto was *Irurak Bat*, 'the Three are One' (the inspiration for the nationalist slogan, *Zazpiak Bat* – 'the Seven are One'), and it became the model for similar societies in Spain under the one enlightened king, Charles III (1759–88). In 1767, the Real Sociedad Bascongada founded the University of Bergara, the first secular university in Spain. It taught experimental physics, chemistry, mineralogy, humanities, mathematics, philosophy, ethics, religion, poetry, design, statistics, the history of the Basque country and the *fueros*, Euskera (taught as a museum-piece even back then, a telling sign of 18th-century bourgeois attitudes), Latin, Spanish, French, English, Italian, vocal and instrumental music, gymnastics, fencing and dance. Were it not for the University of Bergara, in fact, you would be reading this by candlelight: here, in 1783, the Elhuyar brothers from the French Basque country isolated tungsten, the element used in the filaments of light bulbs.

East of Bergara, near the village of Zumárraga, is the unusual 15th-century fortress church of **Santa María**, popularly known as La Antigua. The hewn-oak interior is rustic and spartan, with carved geometric patterns running along the balustrades and beams, punctuated by the occasional female bust.

Loyola: St Ignatius' Home Town

From Zumárraga the GI631 heads north, passing through Azkoitia before reaching the ancient village of **Azpeitia** and the nearby hamlet of **Loyola** (**Loiola**), birthplace in 1491 of Ignatius or Iñigo López de Loyola, and now home of the **Santuario de Loyola** (Sanctuary of St Ignatius). The actual birth house, built by the saint's grandfather after his four-year exile among the Moors, is a fortress-like Mudéjar structure, redesigned inside as a museum with solemn chapels and over-the-top gilded ceilings. Next to it stands the **basilica**, one of the outstanding Baroque works in all Spain. Carlo Fontana, a student of Bernini who had worked on many of the great Baroque building projects in Rome, was the main architect, and the costs were borne by a Habsburg queen of

Santuario de Loyola
t 94 302 50 00; open daily 10–1 and 3–7; adm free, charge for audioguide

The First General

Among the most Catholic of Catholics, the Basques are very proud that 'their' saint's Company of Jesus is today the largest of all religious orders (unless you count their new rivals for the pope's affections, Opus Dei; see p.207). In the past, however, the Loyolas weren't always so popular, at least locally: not only were they exceptionally warlike, but they fought for Castile against their fellow Basques, and were ennobled by Alfonso XI in 1331. From their castle in Azpeitia, they got into the habit of raiding their neighbours, even the Church. Iñigo's grandfather wasn't very good at it, and got caught and sentenced to fight the Moors in Andalucía. His son, Iñigo's father, fought for Ferdinand and Isabella.

Iñigo was the last of 13 children born into this family of warriors. His mother died when he was an infant, and there was a vague idea of raising him to be a priest, although he would have none of it. At 16, he was made a page to Juan Velázquez, the treasurer of Castile, where he adopted all the vices of court life – womanizing, gambling and brawling – with great gusto. In a family feud, he and his one brother who actually became a priest ambushed some clerics belonging to the rival family, killing one. When they were finally brought to justice, Iñigo argued that he too had a right to clerical immunity; the case dragged on, and the Loyolas seem to have been influential enough to get the charges dropped. But by all accounts Iñigo was a strong-minded, persuasive force to be reckoned with.

After his patron died, he went to Pamplona to serve the viceroy of Navarra, his cousin. In 1521, when François I's huge army marched into Navarra and was welcomed in Pamplona as liberators from Castile, Iñigo got into the citadel and convinced the commander to hold out against all the odds for the honour of Spain. Just when Iñigo was ready to fight to the finish, a cannon ball hit him in the legs, breaking one. The French, in honour of his bravery, set his leg and carried him back to the family home in Loyola on a litter.

Iñigo suffered all the tortures 16th-century medicine had in its little black bag. His leg failed to heal, so the surgeons rebroke it and reset it. He nearly died, the leg finally healed, but the bone protruded below the knee and one leg was shorter than the other. Wanting to continue to wear the high boots of the courtier, Iñigo ordered the doctors to saw off the offending knob of bone and lengthen his shorter leg by stretching it on a kind of rack. The pain was excruciating, and it didn't work. During the long weeks of recovery the patient became so bored that he asked for romances to read. All they had in the house was the *Lives of the Saints*, so he read that. He was especially impressed by St Francis, who like himself had fought and been wounded in battle. And, like Francis, as he recuperated, he found a new calling.

In March 1522, when he was well enough to walk, he went to Barcelona and its otherworldly holy of holies, Montserrat, where he knelt all night in vigil before the Virgin's altar, according to the rites of chivalry. He would be her knight, and, leaving his sword at the altar, he gave away all his fine clothes and dressed himself in rough clothes with sandals and a staff. He had his first mystical experience, living as a hermit in a nearby cave. He sailed to Rome, had an audience with the pope, went to the Holy Land and returned to Spain determined to become a priest.

First, however, he had to go back to school to learn Latin. While there, he began to preach; the Spanish Inquisition arrested him twice, questioned him for weeks, and finally banned him from holding forth. So he went to Paris, where he attended university, and gathered his first followers. In an old crypt in Montmartre, seven of them took vows of poverty and chastity and to travel to Jerusalem, where Ignatius (as he now called himself) hoped they could be hospital porters. Discussions with the pope and the Inquisition in Italy led in another direction, to forming a community, the Company of Jesus, which began to teach in Rome. Well educated and disciplined to total obedience, the Company was like no other religious order: it had no routine of offices to perform, no special dress or habits. In its military-style hierarchy, its General was answerable only to the pope.

For Pope Paul III, this middle-aged Basque soldier of Christ, with his special skills of persuasion and organization, was exactly the right man in the right place at the right time, the undaunted warrior he needed to lead the counter-attack at the front lines of dogma. The Reformation was in full swing and the rest of Europe was in danger of sliding into the Protestant camp. As bullying had failed to do the job, education seemed to be the answer and, for the first time ever, the Catholic church began to take it seriously. Ignatius had his orders: teach the people.

> The Jesuits, in fact, would turn the tide and become the Church's greatest single weapon in the Counter-Reformation. By the time of Ignatius' death in 1556, they had 100 establishments throughout Europe and over 1,000 members, talented, educated and ready to go wherever they were called to set up seminaries and advise on religious issues – somewhat like a modern consultancy firm. Although the original intention was to serve the poor, they were so successful that they soon became closely associated with the élite (purely for practical reasons, it was claimed, as the élite decided which church their subjects attended).
>
> 'Obey and you will be saved,' was the brunt of the Jesuit message, nicely linking the secular and sacred, and all beautifully packaged with grandeur and pageantry in their vast new 'Jesuit-style' or Baroque churches, offering tempting previews of heaven's delights.

Austria; her family's coat of arms in stone hangs over the main door. Begun in 1689, this circular temple with its 211ft-high dome took almost 50 years to complete. To give an Italian building the proper Spanish touch, the ornate rotunda is flanked by two plain, broad wings of monastery buildings, making a façade almost 500ft wide – creating the sharp contrast of vast, austere surfaces and patches of exuberant decoration that marks so many of the best Spanish buildings. At the entrance, a monumental stairway guarded by stylized lions leads up to a porch under three arches; in it are five niches with statues of early Jesuit heroes, including Ignatius' fellow Basque St Francis Xavier (*see* pp.232–3). Nothing on the exterior, however, prepares you for the overwrought stone carving that covers every part of the dome inside, designed by a group of masters that included Joaquín de Churriguera, one of the three brothers whose taste for ornament gave Spanish architecture the word *churrigueresque*. As in most Jesuit monuments, no expense was spared, from the fine Carrara marble frieze around the rotunda to the elaborate pavement in coloured stone. Over the main altar, a life-size statue of St Ignatius is covered with silver sent by the Basques of Caracas, Venezuela.

On the way back east to Tolosa, the twisting GI2634 passes through **Errezil** (Régil), a pretty little town with beautiful, far-reaching views from a nearby mountain pass nicknamed the 'Balcón de Guipúzcoa'.

Market Days Inland from Donostia-San Sebastián

ⓘ **Tolosa** >>
Santa Maria Plaza 1,
t *94 369 74 13,*
www.tolosaldea.net

Tolosa: Saturday around the Plaza Foruen.
Ordizia: Wednesdays, Plaza Mayor and around.

Where to Stay and Eat Inland from Donostia–San Sebastián

Tolosa ✉ 20400

*Oria, C/Oria 2, **t** 94 365 46 88, *www.hoteloria.com* (€€). Central, modern hotel with a pretty annexe in a garden villa on the edge of the old town.

⭐ Pensión Karmentxu ›

Pensión Karmentxu, C/Korreo 24, **t** 943 673 701, *www.pension karmentxu.com*, (€). Ten fresh, pretty rooms in the old town, all with bath.

Casa Julián, Santa Klara Kalea 6, **t** 94 367 14 17 (€€€). Tolosa's oldest restaurant, still one of the best, specializing in grilled steaks, *pimientos del piquillo* and *tejas de Tolosa*, with a good list of Rioja wines. *Closed Mon–Thurs eves.*

Frontón, Paseo San Franciso 4, **t** 94 365 29 41 (€€). Longstanding classic from the 1930s with an Art Deco interior and New Basque cuisine. Also likely to have the town's famous beans on the menu. Fantastic lunch menu. *Closed Sun eve, Mon.*

Nicolás, Zumalacárregui 6, **t** 94 365 47 59 (€€). A classic, traditional *asador*, serving succulent grilled meats; try the *chuletas de buey*. They also have an extensive wine list featuring some unusual Riojas. *Closed Sun and Aug.*

Sausta, Belate Pasealekua 7–8, **t** 94 365 54 53, *www.sausta.com* (€€). For some of the finest modern cuisine at very decent prices, this is a must. Try the sautéed baby squid with sesame, and top it all off with an almond pastry with chocolate mousse. *Closed Sun eve and Mon, plus last 2 weeks Feb and first 2 weeks Aug.*

ⓘ Oñati ›
Foru Enparatza 11,
t *94 378 34 53,*
www.oinati.org

⭐ Borda Aranzazu ›

Oñati ✉ 20400

Borda Aranzazu, Barrio Aranzazu 11, *www.bordaaranzazu.com*, **t** 94 378 13 03 (€€€). Spectacular rural hotel set amid beautiful countryside, with three self-catering suites (sleeping up to 4) in a strikingly converted stone barn near the Sanctuary of Arantzazu.

***Hotel Santuario de Arantzazu, **t** 94 378 13 13, *www.hotelsantuario dearantzazu.com* (€€–€). An elegant, modern hotel at the Sanctuary of Arantzazu, with well-equipped, designer rooms and lovely views.

Etxe Aundi, Torre Auzo 10, **t 94 378 19 56, *www.etxeaundi.com* (€€–€). Traditional, stone-built hotel with charming rooms and a fine restaurant.

*Ongi Ostatua, Kale Zaharra 19, **t** 94 371 82 85, *www.hotelongi.com* (€). Cheerfully decorated, modern rooms in the centre, with a café-bar.

Casa Rural Annegi, Garagaltza Auzoa 19, **t** 94 378 08 24 (€). Located 2km from Oñati and 9km from the Sanctuary of Arantzazu *(see p.195)*, this newly built house looks older than it is, as it has been built in the traditional stone and wood combination of the area. The set-up is cosy with six double bathrooms and two living areas with chimney and TV, as well as parking space and a garden.

Txopekua, Barrio Uribarri, **t** 94 378 26 98 (€). A good restaurant in a Basque homestead on the road to Arantzazu. Tasty dishes; fresh local ingredients.

Iturritxo, Atzeko Kale 32, **t** 94 371 60 78 (€). A well-loved local establishment serving superb regional cooking at reasonable prices.

Etxeberria, Kale Barria 15, **t** 94 378 04 60 (€). Reliable bar/restaurant in the middle of town.

Azpeitia ✉ 20730

Loiola, C/Loioaka Inazio 47, **t 94 315 16 16, *www.hotelloiola.com* (€). Modern hotel with reasonable rooms.

Trintxera, Ctra. Tolosa-Azpeitia Km 10, Errezil, **t** 94 368 12 06, *www.trintxera. com* (€). Simple country hotel on the Balcón de Gipuzkoa, with a traditional restaurant and a large terrace offering splendid mountain views.

Larrañaga, Elosiaga 392, **t** 94 381 11 80, *www.hotel-larranaga.com* (€). A charmingly old-fashioned hotel with a good, local restaurant.

Along the Coast: Donostia-San Sebastián to France

If you're driving to France, there is a choice of routes: either the A8 motorway, which is expensive though occasionally dramatic, or the old routes through Hondarribia to Hendaye. Just east of

Getting along the Coast from Donostia-San Sebastián

It's only 20mins by **bus** from Donostia-San Sebastián to Irún or Hondarribia on the frontier; connections are frequent by bus and train, and not a few people watching their euros stay in Irún (or in France) rather than in the more pricy resort. If you're not in a hurry, take the narrow-gauge **EuskoTren** for a leisurely ride through fine scenery.

Donostia-San Sebastián on the coastal road, the long ribbon town of **Pasai Donibane** (**Pasajes de San Juan**)) lines the east bank of an estuary, with picturesque old houses. Victor Hugo lived in one for a while, and the Marquis de Lafayette lodged in another before sailing off to aid Britain's American colonists in their revolution. Philip built part of the Invincible Armada here, although now all such business affairs are handled by San Juan's ugly stepsister on the San Sebastián side of the estuary, **Pasai San Pedro** (**Pasajes de San Pedro**). From here the road goes along Monte Jáizkibel, offering superb views over the **Bay of Biscay** and the Pyrenees.

Hondarribia and Hendaye stand either side of the sandy ford of the Río Bidasoa, which has endowed it with a spacious protected sandy beach. **Hondarribia** (**Fuenterrabía** in Spanish), with an aspirated 'H' that apparently neither the French nor Spanish can get right, often gets overlooked with all the border confusion, but this is one of the most agreeable destinations on the coast; the historic walled part of town glows with colour – in its brightly painted houses, especially along Calle San Nicolás and Calle Pampinot, in its balconies loaded with flowers, and in its fishing fleet, which has not been afraid to take on France in the EU's battles over fishing rights. The town has had its share of sieges – you can still see the ancient walls and a castle of Charles V, now a *parador* – and every summer sees an invasion of French tourists (the local defensive measure of raising prices has had little effect in repelling them). In the evening, head out towards the lighthouse on **Cabo Higuer** – the northeasternmost corner of Spain – for views of the sunset over the bay.

A Border Anomaly

In the Río Bidasoa between Hondarribia and Hendaye, there is a small island called the Isla de la Conferencia, or Ile des Faisans. This was a traditional meeting place for French and Spanish diplomats from the 15th century. In 1659 the Treaty of the Pyrenees was signed here, ending the long wars between France and Spain; the following year, representatives of both sides returned to plan the marriage of Louis XIV and the Spanish infanta (*see* p.251). A special pavilion was erected for the occasion, and the king of Spain sent his court painter, Velázquez, to decorate it. Unfortunately, the artist caught a bad cold here that eventually killed him.

Even today, the island is owned jointly by both countries, and there is a solemn agreement in a cabinet somewhere that details how the Spanish police shall look after it from April to October, and the French for the other six months. But really, there isn't anything to watch over; the island at present is uninhabited and completely empty.

If you come on Good Friday, the old streets around the church of the Assumption are the scene of an atmospheric procession after the symbolic entombment of Christ: Roman soldiers, the Archangel Michael and the Apostles, each bearing their attributes (in real life, most of them are old fishermen). On Easter Day they gather again, and when the priest declares '*Gloria in Excelsis Deo*', the Romans all fall over at once, as if struck by a bolt of lightning.

Take the faster N1, which runs alongside the A8 from San Sebastián, and you end up in **Irún**, further up the Bidasoa and formerly known to all as the grim border stop of endless, pointless waits. This sad state comes courtesy of Franco and his German friends, who bombed it to smithereens in the Civil War after Gernika. These days there is no border stop at all. One thing to do in Irún is visit the Porcelenas Bidasoa, at Avenida Elizatxo 60, makers of prestigious ceramics. Inland you can climb **Monte San Marcial** for a memorable view over the Bay of Biscay (there is a road to the top), or else flee the bustling coast for the serene **Valley of Oyarzun**, one of Euskadi's rural beauty spots, with the pretty villages of Oyarzun, Lesaka and Vera de Bidasoa. There are plenty of Neolithic monuments all through this region, on both sides of the border; the place where the Pyrenees meet the sea seems to have been a particularly holy spot. A site called **Oianleku**, off the main road near Oyarzun, includes some small stone circles among the dolmens.

Where to Stay and Eat along the Coast from Donostia-San Sebastián

Hondarribia ✉ 20280

In the moderate and inexpensive ranges there are few choices (actually, rooms are a better bargain across the border in Hendaye, though Hondarribia makes a more pleasant stay). If you like staying in converted historic buildings, however, Hondarribia also has more choices than any town in the Basque country.

★★★★Parador de Hondarribia, Plaza de Armas 14, t 94 364 55 00, *www.parador.es* (€€€). Prettily situated at the very top of town, in the castle of Charles V. The decoration is medieval, including fine tapestries.

★★★Hotel Obispo, Plaza del Obispo, t 94 364 54 00, *www.hotelobispo.com* (€€€). A 14th-century mansion, in the old residence of the Bishop of Hondarribia, built on the Bastión San Felipe, with sumptuously refitted rooms and splendid views.

★★★Hotel Jauregui C/Zuloaga 5, t 94 364 14 00, *www.hoteljauregui.com* (€€). Excellent value in the centre of town, boasting an excellent restaurant serving mouthwatering seafood dishes. Also has self-catering apartments for rent.

★★San Nikolas, Plaza de Armas 6, t 94 364 42 78 (€€–€). A little blue-and-pink hotel with attractive rooms right on the *plaza*, with sea views.

★Hotel Palacete, Plaza Guipuzkoa 5, t 94 364 08 13, *www.hotelpalacete.net* (€€–€). In a medieval mansion, with simple, but well-equipped rooms and friendly staff; breakfast is served on a flower-filled terrace.

Pension Zaragoza, Javier Ugarte 1, t 94 364 13 41 (€). Clean rooms in the old centre, many with a sea view.

Txoko Goxoa, C/Margolari Etxenagusia, t 94 364 46 58 (€).

⭐ Hotel Palacete >>

Delightful, welcoming *hostal* in the Casco Histórico.

Restaurant Sebastián, C/Mayor 11, t 94 364 01 67, *www.sebastian hondarribia.com* (€€€). Offers intimate dining in an ancient grocery store; try the wonderful pheasant stuffed with wild mushrooms. *Closed Sun eve, Mon and Nov.*

Alameda, C/Minasoreta 1, t 94 364 27 89, *www.restalameda.com* (€€€). Rustically furnished, this is the best restaurant in the region, serving imaginative, award-winning New Basque cuisine with a strong local flavour: roast scallops with vichysoisse, or a tender suckling pig. *Menú Alameda €80; other set menus €35–50. Closed Sun eve, Mon, and Tues eve.*

Ramon Roteta, Villa Ainara, C/Irún 1, t 94 364 16 93 (€€€). Gracious dining in a lovely villa with a garden; grand cuisine and superb desserts. *Closed Sun eve and Tues, plus Feb.*

Beko Errota, C/Barrio de Jaizubia, t 94 364 31 94 (€€€–€€). Traditional Basque dishes are on offer here, with a good selection of seafood. An elegant restaurant surrounded by beautiful gardens, it's everyone's favourite spot to celebrate family occasions at the weekends, so book ahead. *Closed Sun eve and Mon.*

Arraunlari, Butroi Pasealekug 3, t 94 364 15 81 (€€). The best bet next to the sea. Offers fine, traditional fish dishes and picture-postcard views. *Closed Sun eve and Mon, plus mid-Dec–mid-Jan.*

Restaurant Danontzat, C/Las Tiendas 6, t 94 364 56 63 (€). Budget snack/tapas bar downstairs, with cheap but tasty *platos combinados*. More formal dining upstairs and outdoor summer terrace.

Irún ✉ 20300

***Atalaia, Aritz Ondo 69, t 94 362 94 33, *www.hotelatalaia.com* (€€). Pretty, quiet rooms on the edge of town, private parking and a good restaurant.

***Alcázar, Avda Iparralde 11, t 94 362 09 00, *www.hotelalcazar.net* (€€). Central, old-fashioned and friendly.

**Lizaso, C/Aduana 5, t 94 361 16 00 (€). Possibly the best deal in Irún, with decent rooms. Triples available.

Labeko Etxea, Barrio Olaberria, t 94 363 19 64 (€€€–€€). In a rural setting, offering Basque dishes prepared with a knowing touch. The adjoining *sidrería* offers cheaper but delicious fare. *Set menus from €30–48. Closed Sun eve and Mon.*

Larretxipi, Larretxipi 5, t 94 363 26 59 (€€). Excellent fish, though a number of places nearby are cheaper. *Gourmet menu €17. Closed Sun eve, Tues, last 2 weeks Mar, last 2 weeks Nov.*

Arano, C/Mayor 15, t 94 362 08 59 (€). Serves tasty Basque dishes and a well-priced *menú del día*.

Bar Izartxo, C/Mayor 17, t 94 362 61 81 (€), t 94 363 86 30. A good place to fill up on tapas. Gets livelier as the night wears on.

Navarra

Europe's traditional front door to Spain, Navarra (Nafarroa in Basque) combines a sizeable, often national-istic, Basque minority up in the misty western Pyrenees with a conservative, non-Basque Navarrese majority tending the sunny vineyards and gardens of the Ebro valley flatlands to the south. The combination hasn't always been comfortable, and only now that much of the population has abandoned the countryside have tensions between the two groups loosened up.

As everyone must know by now, much of this 'loosening up' is concentrated in Pamplona, the capital both groups share, into an ecstatic week-long bacchanalia of inebriated recklessness, bull running and partying known as Los Sanfermines. *There is plenty to see at other times, much of it old and strange, and much of it up in the Basque strongholds of the Pyrenees or along the* camino francés *to Santiago de Compostela.*

09

Don't miss

1 Running the bulls
Pamplona **p.206**

2 The atmospheric 'town of the star'
Estella **p.220**

3 Striking Wild West scenery
Bardenas Reales **p.227**

4 Haunting Gregorian chants
Leyre Monstery **p.233**

5 A beech and yew forest
Forest of Irati **p.236**

See map overleaf

Bay of Biscay

BIARRITZ

SAN SEBASTIÁN
(DONOSTIA)

Vera (Bera)

Zugarramurdi

Lesaka

Etxalar

PAYS

Guipúzcoa

Ituren

Arizkun

Elizondo

Leitza

Zubieta

EUSKADI

Betelu

Aspirotz

Beruete

Lanz

Sierra de Aralar
Errazquin

Lekunberri

Auritzberri

Roncesvalles

Sanctuario de
San Miguel in Excelsis

Huarte Arakil

Auritz

Orbaitzeta

BASQUE

Altsasu

Uriz

Sierra de Abodi

Ochagavía

Berrioplano

Nagore

Oronz

Baquedano

PAMPLONA
(IRUÑA)

Isaba

Zudaire

Monasterio
de Iranzu

Urroz

Vidángoz

Roncal

Noaín

NAVARRA

Aoiz

Estella

Cirauqui

Puente la
Reina

Artaiz

Navascués

Ayegui

Obanos

Lumbier

Burgui

Basílica de
San Gregorio

Monasterio
de Irache

Santa María
de Eunate

Sierra

de

Leyre

Sorlada

Artajona

Yesa

Monasterio
de Leyre

Los Arcos

Javier

Viana

Torres
del Río

Tafalla

San Martín
de Unx

Sangüesa

Embalse de Yesa

Logroño

Olite

Ujué

Lodosa

LA RIOJA

Calahorra

Las

Ermita de Nuestra
señora del Yugo

Alfaro

Bárdenas

Corella

Arguedas

Reales

Cintruénigo

Fitero

Tudela

Cascante

Camino de Santiago

20 km

10 miles

N

FRANCE

PORTUGAL

SPAIN

Don't miss

p.350

p.246

History: Navarra, the Flea Between Two Monkeys

Navarra (perhaps the name of the ancient Basque tribe that lived here; no one knows) has played a standoffish, James Dean role in history since 605, when the Franks tried to harness it as part of the duchy of Vasconia, a huge untenable territory that extended from the Garonne to the Ebro. Charlemagne himself came down in 778, either to discipline the unruly duchy or to force it to join his fight against the Moors, and after razing the walls of Pamplona he went stomping back to France – except for his rear guard, which the furious Basques of Pamplona ambushed at the pass of Roncesvalles.

Charlemagne taught the Navarrese (who were all Basque back then) that the best policy was to owe nothing to anybody, and within a few years of his unlamented passing they created the independent kingdom of Navarra. It was the generally democratic Basques' one experiment in monarchy, and for a brief period it was a wild success under the gifted Sancho III 'the Great' (c. 1000–34). Sancho worked hand in hand with Cluny's abbots to establish the *camino francés* to Santiago de Compostela through Navarra. He controlled much of the French Basque country, appointing his relatives as viscounts and inviting in French Gascon settlers to boost the population (and beginning the long trend towards diluting Navarra's Basqueness), and he ruled Galicia itself, at the end of the pilgrims' road, and then pocketed Castile and León after the death of its last count, setting up his son Fernando I as the first to take the title of 'King of the Spains'. Sancho's creation was too precocious to hold, and by the time of Sancho IV (1054–76) Navarra was once again a fierce rival of Castile, but avoided entanglements – marital or martial – by playing the French card.

'The Flea between Two Monkeys', as it became known, was ruled by three different French dynasties from 1234, when the Basque line died out. The last dynasty was the d'Albrets of Foix, one of whom, Germaine, married Ferdinand the Catholic after the death of Isabella. This link, however, did not keep Ferdinand from slyly demanding that Navarra's rulers, Jean and Catherine d'Albret, let his armies march through to France in 1512. His request, as he expected, was refused, and he used the refusal as an excuse to grab Navarra south of the Pyrenees and annexe it to Castile. Ferdinand kept the Navarrese happy by maintaining their *fueros*, which in practice gave the region an autonomy enjoyed by no other in Spain; it was ruled by a viceroy, minted its own coins and had its own government. But the Basques, who remembered their centuries of true independence, soon grew restless, and wanted the Castilians out.

Meanwhile, the d'Albrets were left with only Basse-Navarre, a thimble-sized realm north of the mountains. When François Ier became king of France and arch-rival of Ferdinand's grandson Charles V, he took on the cause of Henri d'Albret and sent a huge French and German army through Roncesvalles. After taking Pamplona (much of the population of which welcomed the French as liberators), the army marched on to take Castile. It stopped along the way to sack the Navarrese town of Los Arcos, and in revenge the Basques and Castilians united to defeat the French. The d'Albrets would never rule a united Navarra, but they went on to give France a long line of kings with the accession of Henri IV (1589–1610).

Napoleonic and Liberal attempts to do away with the *fueros* turned the Navarrese into fierce reactionaries and the most ardent of Carlists who thoroughly distrusted the Left, so much so that in the 1930s Navarra rejected the Republic's offer of autonomy. Instead, the Navarrese *requetés* in their distinctive red berets became some of Franco's best troops, fighting for their old privileges and Catholicism – just as the Basques were, only on the Republican side. Franco rewarded Navarra by leaving the *fueros* intact, making it the only autonomous region in Spain until his death, while culturally oppressing the Basques in the northern valleys. Today, Navarra is officially the Comunidad Foral de Navarra, all on its own; the fact that a referendum was never held in Navarra, allowing it to vote on whether it wanted to join with the other three Basque provinces, remains a bone of contention with nationalists to this day.

Pamplona (Iruña)

⭐ Pamplona

Whether you call it Pamplona, the town founded by Pompey in 75 BC, or by its older name of Iruña, which means simply 'the city' in Basque, the capital of Navarra sits on a strategic 1,400ft pimple on the beautiful fertile plain, its existence as inevitable as its nickname, the 'Gateway of Spain'. For a few years in the 730s, the Arabs used it in reverse, as the gateway to France, until their dreams of Europe were hammered at Poitiers.

Over the next decades, the Basques regained control of Pamplona, clobbered Charlemagne after he burnt their walls, and set up their own king. In 918 the Moors came back and razed Pamplona to the ground again. To encourage rebuilding, Sancho the Great invited his subjects over the Pyrenees, in what is now Basse-Navarre, to come and start trades in what became the two new districts of Pamplona, San Cernín and San Nicolás. The fact that the three districts of the city were practically independent and

Getting to and around Pamplona

By Air

Pamplona's **airport** (**t** 91 321 10 00, *www.aena.es*) is 6km south of the city, with regular connections to Madrid and Barcelona. The cheapest way to get to the airport is to take no.16 bus opposite the bus station, which drops you 800m from the airport.

By Train

The RENFE **train station** (**t** 902 320 320, *www.renfe.com*) is 2km out of town on Avda San Jorge. Local bus nos.9 and 3 link it to the centre.

By Bus

The **bus station** (**t** 902 023 651, *www.estaciondeautobusesdepamplona.com*) is in town, near the citadel, at C/Yanguas y Miranda 2. Besides provincial connections, there are several buses daily to Vitoria-Gasteiz, Bilbao, Donostia-San Sebastián and Zaragoza. There are fewer services at weekends, particularly on Sundays. Local bus timetables are available at *www.mcp.es* (Spanish only).

---

had their own privileges led to violent rivalry between them, so much so that in 1521 the French, coming to the rescue of the French Navarrese, unsuccessfully besieged Pamplona in an effort to regain San Cernín and San Nicolás. Wounded while fighting for Castile was a certain Captain Iñigo López de Recalde (or Loyola), who got religion in a militant way and founded the Jesuits (*see* pp.197–8).

Pamplona seems to have been naturally conducive to that sort of thing, with a reputation for being crazily austere, brooding and puritanical. To anyone who knows the city only for throwing the wildest party in Europe, this comes as a shock of *desfase*, or maladjustment, a word that means (and gleefully celebrates) the unresolved contradictions that coexist in post-Franco Spain. Stern Catholicism ('*Qui dit basque, dit catholique,*' say the French) is part of the city's fabric. 'From the top to the bottom of Pamplonese society, I have found the whole place poisoned by clerical alkaloid,' grumped Miguel de Unamuno. 'It oozed out of every corner... One drop in the eye is enough to infect you forever.' In the 1950s, the shadowy Opus Dei, Christianity's ultra-conservative fifth column (known as Octopus Dei or the Holy Mafia by detractors), chose Pamplona to build their Universidad de Navarra, their most important educational institution in Spain, especially since the late Pope John Paul II's beatification of the founder, Josemaria Escrivá. Today, the head prelate of the order is a Basque, Bishop Javier Echevarria.

In the 1960s, Pamplona's new tennis club still built separate swimming pools for men and women. Half a century on, the city prides itself on having set up Spain's first shelter for battered women, the first city workshops for training disadvantaged youths and the first urban rubbish recycling programme. It is also the seat of the Udako Euskal Unibertsitaea (Basque Summer University), which has led the way in higher education in Euskera and has

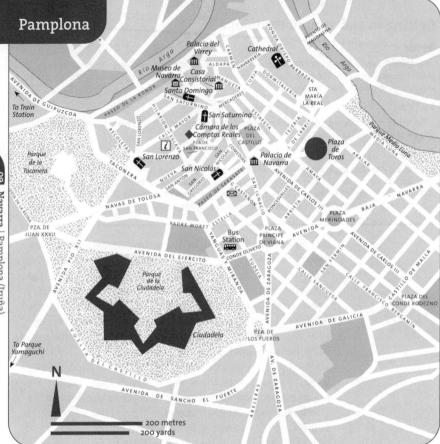

promoted the printing of over 180 university textbooks in Basque. 'Pamplona is a city that gives much more than it promises,' said Victor Hugo. It certainly will if you come in the second week of July for *Los Sanfermines*, but expect it also to take your money, your sleep and a lifetime's supply of adrenaline.

A Walk through the Casco Viejo

Pamplona was squeezed into a tight girdle of walls until the early 1900s, when the city spread in all directions and accumulated around 185,000 inhabitants in the process. But for all its 20th-century flab the vital organs in the historic Casco Viejo remain intact, curled tightly around the city's heart, the spacious **Plaza del Castillo**. Off the southwest corner extends the **Paseo de Sarasate**, populated by stone kings and queens and the overwrought **Monumento a los Fueros**, erected by popular subscription after Madrid tried to mess with Navarra's privileges back in 1893. The bronze allegory of Navarra holds a copy of the *Ley Foral*, or *Fueros'*

Law, surrounded by the broken chains from the Battle of Las Navas de Tolosa, symbolizing freedom; these also feature on Navarra's coat of arms. Historical frescoes decorate the neoclassical **Palacio de Navarra** at one end of the Paseo (which today hosts temporary art exhibitions); its archives contain one of the best caches of medieval documents in Spain and the garden boasts a massive sequoia.

Off the eastern end of Plaza del Castillo, the narrow streets jammed with shops and bars were once the **Judería**, where Pamplona's Jews, 'a gentle and reasonable race' according to the king of Navarra, lived unmolested until Navarra was gobbled up by the intolerant, Inquisitor-infested Spain of Ferdinand and Isabella. Behind these, tucked up near the ramparts, the gracious 14th–15th-century Gothic **cathedral** hides behind a dull neoclassical façade, slapped on in the 18th century by a misguided do-gooder; a shame, because the original front, according to travellers' descriptions, was ribald and lusty, almost verging on the obscene.

Cathedral
cathedral open Mon–Sat 10–7, Sun 10–2 and 6.30–9; museum open mid-Mar–mid-Oct Mon–Sat 10–7, mid-Oct–mid-Mar Mon–Sat 10–5; adm, includes Museo Diocesano

When completed, this was the second-largest cathedral in Spain after León's, and suitable shelter for the beautiful alabaster tombs of the cathedral's sponsors, big-nosed Charles III 'the Noble' and his big-nosed queen Leonora de Trastámara, sculpted in the 15th century by Jean de Lomme of Tournai. The kings of Navarra were crowned before the Romanesque statue of Santa María La Real, carved and gilded in silver in the 12th century, who peers out from beneath a spidery neo-Gothic canopy in the presbytery. The cathedral was at the cutting edge of ecclesiastical fashion: the Renaissance choir benches are the work of the region's finest sculptors and the lacy Gothic grille was one of the first of its kind in Spain. The door to the cloister, the Puerta del Amparo (Gate of Succour, 1335), has a sad but busy little polychrome gathering mourning the Virgin's death in the tympanum, and a host of miniature carvings depicting scenes of succour encrusting the door frame.

The delicacy of the Gothic **cloister** (1280–1472) approaches gossamer in stone and reaches a climax of decorative bravura in the justly named Puerta Preciosa (1350–60), carved with a superb *Dormition of the Virgin*. The Garro family are buried in the northeast corner beneath a jolly band of cavorting musical angels. Off the cloister, the vain archbishop of Barbazán built the Barbazana Chapel in the 14th century to house his tomb, and now lies contented beneath a star-strewn vaulted roof and a Gothic carving of the Virgin of Consolation. The **Museo Diocesano** occupies the kitchen and refectory where pilgrims once dined; the refectory is filled with sweet-faced 12th–15th-century carvings of the Madonna and Child, while the kitchen is remarkable for its enormous chimneys, one in each corner with a huge lantern chimney in the middle. The Cillería (behind the ticket desk) contains two remarkable reliquaries – the 1258 *Relicario del Santo Sepulcro* and the 1401 *Relicario del Lignum Crucis*, adorned with precious stones, and the cathedral's glittering 16th-century silver shrine and processional monstrance.

The narrow old lanes around the cathedral belong to the **Navarrería**, the original Basque quarter, populated in the Middle Ages by cathedral-builders and farmers who tilled the bishop's lands. Here, on the promontory on the Rincón del Caballo Blanco, you'll find the most impressive segment of the surviving **walls** built by Philip II, with a reputation for impregnability so powerful that no one challenged it until the French tried to hole up here against Wellington; the views stretch for miles over the plain. Just west, the 13th-century **Palacio del Virrey** started out as the royal palace and is now being restored.

Past the attractive **Portal de Zumalacárregui** (16th-century, but renamed after the heroic Carlist general who died at the siege of Bilbao), the **Museo de Navarra** occupies a huge 16th-century hospital and contains everything from Navarrese prehistory to contemporary art, with Roman mosaics, Gothic wall paintings, carved capitals from Pamplona's original Romanesque cathedral (minus the naughty bits), an ivory coffret from Leyre made in Córdoba in the 11th century and a fine portrait of the *Marqués de San Adrián* by Goya. A pretty courtyard with Roman mosaics offers views of a stretch of the old city walls.

Museo de Navarra
t 94 842 64 92, www.navarra.es; open Tues–Sat 9.30–2 and 5–7, Sun and hols 11–2; closed Mon; adm

Just below the museum, wooden barricades remind you that this is the beginning of the *encierro*; the bulls leave their corral near Plaza Santo Domingo and head up C/Mercaderes and C/Estafeta. Follow their route and you'll come to Plaza Consistorial and the colourful Baroque **Casa Consistorial**, topped with jaunty allegorical figures. Pamplona's nobles built their finest escutcheoned palaces just off this square, along C/Zapatería and C/Mayor. Plazas de Consejo and San Francisco, set diagonally opposite each other, are also worth a look, the latter with a Modernista (Art Nouveau) hotel converted into a bank. Nearby in C/Ansoleaga, the well-preserved Gothic **Cámara de los Comptos Reales**, the king's mint in the 12th century, has a magnificent porch opening onto a vault and patio with some original decorations intact.

Cámara de los Comptos Reales
open Mon–Fri 8–3

The not always tremendously popular *francos* invited to Pamplona by Sancho the Great lived just to the east in their two rival quarters named after, and defended by, 13th-century churches that doubled as fortresses when their fellow citizens went on the warpath. These are **San Saturnino** (or San Cernín) in C/San Saturnino and **San Nicolás** in lively, bar-lined C/San Nicolás; a plaque by the former marks the site where the first Pamplonans were converted by San Saturnino. To the west, **San Lorenzo** is best

San Saturnino/ San Nicolás/ San Lorenzo
all churches open roughly 8.30–12 and 6.30–7.30

Pamplona's Annual Meltdown: *Los Sanfermines*

Before Hemingway there was Fermín, son of a Roman senator and first bishop of Pamplona. His family had been converted by San Saturnino (or Sernin, or Cernín) of Toulouse, who was martyred by being dragged about by a bull. Fermín, for his part, travelled as a missionary to the Gauls and was beheaded in Amiens for his trouble. Some time between then and 1324, when Pamplona held its first fiesta, Fermín decided to take bullfighters under his saintly cape; by 1591 his festival had found its current dates and form.

Although it's the insanely dangerous running of the bulls that has made *Los Sanfermines* world-famous, this is only a tiny portion of the nine days of non-stop revelling when 'Pamplona becomes the world capital of happiness', a state of hyper-bliss fuelled by three million litres of alcohol. Each year.

There is some order to the madness. The *Sanfermines* officially start at noon on 6 July, when thousands of Navarrese in their festival attire (white shirts and white trousers or skirts, red sashes and red bandanas) gather in front of the town hall to hold their bandanas aloft as a rocket called El Chupinazo is fired off the balcony and a city councillor cries in Spanish and Basque: 'People of Pamplona! Long live San Fermín!' The city explodes with a mighty roar, while popping tens of thousands of champagne corks (and smashing the bottles on the pavement, usually causing the first casualties).

In the afternoon, the giants and big heads (*gigantes y cabezudos*) – as essential to the fiesta as the bulls – leave their 'home' in the bus station. The eight 13ft plaster giants supported by dancers date from 1860 and represent kings and queens, whirling and swirling to the minuet, their sweeping skirts flowing in the air. They are accompanied by the *cabezudos* and *kilikis*, big-headed figures in tricorn hats, with names like Napoleon and Patata, who wallop children on the head with foam rubber balls tied to bats. This is also the prerogative of the *zaldikos*, the colourfully dressed men wearing cardboard horses around their waists; all are accompanied by dancers, *txistularis* and *gaiteros*.

At four o'clock a massive scrum, the *Riau Riau*, begins when members of the Corporación de San Fermín dressed in all their finery try to proceed 400m down the Calle Mayor to the chapel of San Fermín at San Lorenzo for vespers, but everyone else tries to prevent them in a gung ho defiance of authority, to the extent that it's often late at night before the Corporación achieves its goal. The mayor of Pamplona has tried for several years to ban the chaotic *Riau Riau*, but it seems to be unbannable. After a first night of carousing and dancing in the streets, the dawn of 7 July and every following day is welcomed with the *dianas*, a city-wide wake-up call performed on screeching pipes.

The *encierro*, or *zezenketa*, the running of the bulls, begins daily at 8am, but, if you want a good place to watch, wedge yourself into a spot along the route – Cuesta de San Domingo, Mercaderes and Estafeta – at least an hour earlier. Before running, the locals sing a hymn to Fermín and arm themselves with a rolled-up newspaper to distract the bull's attention, since the animals – 1,200lbs of muscle and fury – charge at the nearest moving object, ideally at a flung newspaper instead of a falling runner. A rocket goes up as the first bull leaves the corral; a second rocket means that all are released, and a third signals that all have made it to the bullring – on a good run the whole *encierro* only lasts three minutes. The most dangerous moments are when the runners and bulls have to squeeze into the runway of the bullring, or when a bull gets loose from his fellows and panics. People (and not all of them tourists) get trampled and gored every year; if you run you can hedge your bets by running on weekdays, when it's less crowded, and by avoiding the *toros* of the Salvador Guardiola ranch, which have the most bloodstained record.

The spirit of abandon is so infectious that, even if you come determined not to run, you may find yourself joining in on a self-destructive spur of the moment. Women do defy the authorities and run, although the police try to pull them out. During the *encierro* the lower seats of the bullring are free (again, arrive early), except on Sunday; from here you can watch the bulls and runners pile in and, afterwards, more fun and games as heifers with padded horns are released on the crowd in the ring. The traditional breakfast is huge (bull stews, lamb's sweetbreads, ham and eggs in tomato sauce, washed down with gallons of chilled rosé and *patxaran*).

The bullfights themselves take place daily at 6.30 in the evening – tickets sell out with the speed of lightning and are usually only available from scalpers. The *sombra* seats are for serious aficionados, while members of the *peñas* (clubs devoted to making noise and in general being as obnoxious as possible) fill up the *sol* seats and create a parallel fiesta if the action in the ring isn't up to snuff, or create pandemonium if it is. Afternoons also see other bull sports that are bloodless (for the bull, at any rate): the dodging, swerving *concurso de recortadores* and leaping *corrida vasca-landesa*.

Between the bullfights there are concerts, Navarrese dance (*jotas*) and Basque dances, processions of the relics of San Fermín and other religious services, parades and activities for young children and senior citizens. At night, fireworks burst over the citadel and the *toro de fuego*, or 'fire bull', carried by a runner and spitting fireworks, chases children down the route of the *encierro*. Then there's the midnight *El Estruendo de Irún*, led by an enormous drum called the *bomba*, in which hundreds of people – just about anyone who can lay their hands on anything that makes a sound – gather and let loose in an ear-bashing sonic disorder.

At midnight on 14 July, Pamplona winds down to an exhausted, nostalgic finale, a ceremony known as the *Pobre de mí*; everyone gathers in front of the town hall (or in the Plaza del Castillo for the livelier, unofficial ceremony), with a candle and sings: 'Poor me, poor me, another San Fermín has come to an end.' As the clock strikes 12 everyone removes their red scarves and agrees, like Hemingway, that it was 'a damned fine show' and promises to do better and worse next year. Die-hards party on until 8am the next day, and perform one last feat, the *encierro de la villavesa*: the bulls are all dead so they run in front of a bus.

known for its chapel dedicated to San Fermín, built by the city in 1717, where his bust reliquary quietly resides 51 weeks of the year, presiding over weddings; so many Pamplonese want to be married under his protective eye that there's a two-year waiting list.

Pamplona is well endowed with parks. The oldest, the French-style **Parque de la Taconera**, closes the west end of the Casco Viejo and has one of the city's nicest cafés, the **Vienés**. Just south, the star-shaped **Ciudadela**, built on the orders of Philip II, now has a green park inside and outside the steep walls. The immaculate **Parque Yamaguchi** is named after Pamplona's Japanese 'twin' and has a neat Japanese garden complete with lakeside wooden house for the tea ceremony. Also here is one of Pamplona's newer attractions, a tall, fat red-and-blue tower containing the **Planetario**.

The city's prettiest garden, **Parque Media Luna**, lines the river east of the city and has a path ending at the medieval bridge, the Puente de Magdalena, used by the pilgrims. The park in front of the **Plaza de Toros** was renamed Paseo Hemingway and has a grizzled bust of the writer whose novel *The Sun Also Rises* (1926) made Pamplona into a household word.

The influential sculptor Jorge Oteiza (1908–2003; *see* p.119) is remembered in the **Museo Oteiza**, close to the village of Navarra de Alzuza. The museum is set in the sculptor's former home, linked to a bold, boxy new building, and includes more than 1,600 pieces.

Planetario
t 94 826 26 28, www. pamplonetario.org; open Aug–Sept Mon–Sat 11–1.30 and 5–8; Oct–June Mon 9.30–1.30, Tues–Fri 9.30–1.30 and 4–7.30, Sat 11 –1.30 and 5–8.30; closed Sun and July; adm

Museo Oteiza
t 94 833 20 74, www.museooteiza.org; open Oct–May Tues–Fri 10–3, Sat–Sun and hols 11–7; June–Sept Tues–Sun 11–7; adm, free on Fri

Tourist Information in Pamplona

ⓘ **Pamplona >**
C/Eslava 1, Plaza San Francisco, t 84 842 0420, www.turismode pamplona.es

For up-to-date info on *Los Sanfermines*, see *www. sanfermin.com*.
Cultural/historical walking tours:

The **tourist office** runs themed tours of the city, including tapas and wine-tasting tour and night tours. See *www.turismodepamplona.com*, or ask at the tourist office. Other tour companies include **Incoming**, t 94 822 15 06, *www.incomingnavarra.net*, who offer a range of tours in Pamplona and around.

Post office: Paseo de Sarasate 9, **t** 94 820 72 17.

Internet access: The city provides free WiFi at hotspots throughout the city, including the Parque de la Ciudadela. For a cybercafé, try **Kuria Net**, C/Curia 15, **t** 94 822 30 77

Shopping in Pamplona

Abárzuza, C/Santo Domingo 29, **t** 94 821 32 13. Local bookshop with titles covering all aspects of Navarrese and Basque culture.

La Vinoteca, C/Chapitela 15, **t** 94 822 10 92, *www.vinotecanavarra.com*. An excellent range of local, national and international wines. They also arrange special tasting events.

Casa Casla, C/Calceteros 8. Justly famous for its *chorizo de Pamplona*; you can't miss this old-fashioned little shop bristling with cured sausages.

Markets in Pamplona

Mercado de Santo Domingo, next to the town hall in Plaza de los Burgos. The oldest and most popular market in the city, with an array of fresh local produce on offer (*Mon–Sat*).

Mercadillo de Landaben, Polígono Landaben. This Sunday-morning open-air market (*not July and Aug*) has everything from clothes to fruit.

Sports and Activities in Pamplona

All kinds of adventure sports are on offer in the surrounding mountains and valleys. Tour agencies offer a range of different trips:

BKZ, **t** 94 859 23 22, *www.navarra aventura.com*. Mountain-biking, rock-climbing and hiking.

Nattura Naturaleza y Aventura, **t** 94 813 10 44, *www.nattura.com*. Rafting, potholing and hiking.

Ordoki, **t** 94 845 30 26, *www.ordoki.com*. Horse-riding and trekking in the Baztán valley.

Where to Stay in Pamplona

Pamplona ✉ 31300

During *Los Sanfermines*, hotel prices double and often triple, supplemented by scores of overpriced rooms in *casas particulares*, advertised weeks ahead in the local newspaper, *Diario de Navarra*. If you end up sleeping outside, any of the gardens along the walls or river are preferable to the noisy, filthy, vomit-filled citadel. Keep a close eye on your belongings (petty criminals, unfortunately, go into overdrive along with everyone else during the fiesta) and check in what you don't need at the *consigna* in Plaza San Francisco, next to the tourist office; everyone else does too, so get there early. Two free campsites are set up along the road to France, but again, don't leave anything there you might really miss. If you stay outside Pamplona and drive into town, beware that theft from cars is widespread.

*****La Perla**, Plaza del Castillo, **t** 94 822 30 00, *www.granhotellaperla.com* (€€€€€–€€€). Hemingway always stayed at this, Pamplona's oldest hotel, with its high ceilings and plaster mouldings. It was lavishly restored and reopened as a luxury hotel a few years ago; Woody Allen counts among its more recent celebrity guests.

****Hotel Palacio Guendulain**, C/Zapateria 53, **t** 94 822 55 22, *www.palacioguendulain.com* (€€€€–€€€). A luxury hotel in a sumptuously restored 18th-century palace, with a fine restaurant, and a garden with a collection of vintage cars. Bedrooms are classically elegant.

****Alma Pamplona**, Beloso Baja, **t** 948 29 33 80, *www.almapamplona. com* (€€€€–€€€). Bold, contemporary architecture and 21st-century design meet in this smart hotel on the edge of the city. It has a gym, spa, and restaurant.

****Iruña Palace Los Tres Reyes**, C/de la Taconera, **t** 94 822 66 00, *www. hotel3reyes.com* (€€€). Conveniently located a short walk from the old town, this big modern hotel pampers its well-heeled guests with every possible convenience, including an indoor heated pool and tennis.

***Yoldi, Avda San Ignacio 11, t 94 822 48 00, *www.hotelyoldi.com* (€€). A bland, modern business hotel that offers great deals at weekends and in August.

***Maisonnave, C/Nueva 20 (next to Pza San Francisco), t 94 822 26 00, *www.hotelmaisonnave.es* (€€€). This gleaming modern edifice offers comfort, prestige and a peaceful garden at the back. It also has a restaurant.

***NH El Toro, Berrioplano (5km from Pamplona on the Guipúzcoa road), t 94 830 22 11, *www.nh-hotels.es* (€€). Quiet rooms in a traditional-style stone mansion, overlooking a statue group of the *encierro*.

***Hotel Blanco de Navarra, Avda Pio XIII 43, t 94 817 10 10, *www.hotelblanca denavarra.com* (€€). A boxy, modern hotel on the edge of town near the Parque de la Ciudadela, with comfortable if rather bland bedrooms at very reasonable prices. It's about a 15-minute walk through the park to the centre.

(★) Josetxo >>

Arriazu, **Comedias**, 14, t 94 821 02 02, *www.hostalarriazu.com* (€€–€). Located next to the Plaza del Castillo and a popular eating area, this is a good bargain as long as you avoid San Fermín.

Casa Otano, San Nicolás 5, t 94 822 50 95, *www.casaotano.com* (€). Popular for years for its nice rooms with baths, and a good, inexpensive bar and restaurant. Discounts for pilgrims.

(★) **Hostal Navarra >**

**Hostal Navarra, C/Tudela 9, t 94 822 51 64, *www.hostalnavarra.com* (€). Next to the bus station, this offers immaculate cream-painted rooms with sage-green furnishings and all the conveniences. Five minutes' walk from the Casco Viejo.

*Castillo de Javier, San Nicolás, 50–52, t 94 820 30 40, *www.hotelcastillo dejavier.com* (€). A delightful and well-priced hotel in a central location. Rooms are stylish, comfortable and clean. The street-side rooms can get noisy, so, if you are a light sleeper, insist on a back room.

**Hotel Eslava, Plaza Virgen de la O, t 94 822 22 70, *www.hotel-eslava.com*

(€). A modest, family-run hotel tucked next to the old city walls, with clean, simple rooms and park views.

Mesón del Barro, C/Acella 2, t 92 825 63 66, *www.mesondelbarro.com* (€). Good-value rooms, with or without bath, above a restaurant close to the Parque Yamaguchi. They also offer self-catering apartments.

***Hs Bearán, San Nicolás 25, t 94 822 34 28, *www.hostalbearan.com* (€). The doubles here come with baths, TV, and air-conditioning.

Pensión Sarasate, Paseo Sarasate 30, t 94 822 30 84 (€). Small and personal; the decent but unspectacular rooms all have a private bath.

Ezcaba, t 94 833 03 15, *www.campingezcaba.com*. A good campsite, 7km north of the city and linked by a bicycle path.

Eating Out in Pamplona

Josetxo, Plaza Príncipe de Viana 1, t 94 822 20 97, *www.restaurante josetxo.com* (€€€). A local gourmet institution in Pamplona for more than half a century, serving contemporary updates of classic Navarrese cuisine. Try the artichokes with crayfish or the venison with a nut sauce. *Closed Sun and Aug*.

Alhambra, C/Francisco Bergamín 7, t 94 824 50 07, *www.restaurante alhambra.es* (€€€). Look out for the more imaginative dishes at this fashionable place, a favourite with local gourmets: potatoes stuffed with truffles and scampi. *Closed Sun and mid-July–early Aug*.

Europa, C/Espoz y Mina 11, t 94 822 18 00 (€€€; *set menus €47 and €62*). Indulges diners with refined service and classic Navarrese meat and game dishes; try the monkfish with scallops or the incredibly tender roast kid. It's very popular for weddings and other big events. *Closed Sun*.

Rodero, C/Emilio Arrieta 3, t 94 822 80 35, *www.restauranterodero.com* (€€€). One of the best restaurants in the city, serving modern variations on Navarrese, Basque and French recipes prepared with the finest seasonal ingredients. Try the Baztán suckling pig with honey, pumpkin seeds and kumquat. *Closed Sun.*

Mertintxo, C/Irunbidea 1, Cizur Minor, (3km from the centre), t 94 818 00 20 (€€€–€). Locals flock to this traditional asador on the edge of town, which is famous for its perfectly prepared roast meats and fish. The adjoining *sidrería* is always lively and serves good, inexpensive local fare.

Enekorri, C/Tudela 14, t 94 823 25 47, *www.enekorri.com* (€€€). Stylish, contemporary restaurant serving exciting modern Navarrese cuisine.

Asador Olaverri, C/Santa Marta 4, t 94 823 50 63, *www.asadorolaverri. com* (€€). Come here for a big grilled-meat-and-wine feast. Good value and great atmosphere. *Closed Sun eve and last 2 weeks Aug.*

Casa Manolo, C/García Castañón 12, t 94 822 51 02, *www.restaurantecasa manolo.com* (€€). Traditional, good value and welcoming, with a range of set menus offering fine local cuisine.

El Colmado, C/Iturralde y Suit 24, t 94 824 21 99, *www.elcolmado.es* (€€). A modern, chic restaurant, shop and *pintxos* bar in one, serving excellent Navarrese cuisine prepared with the finest locally sourced produce. The shop has a fabulous range of wines, as well as oils and other delicacies, and there's a bar lined with fresh *pintxos*.

Bodegón Sarria, C/Estafeta 50, t 94 822 77 13, *www.bodegonsarria.com* (€€). Fronted by a wonderful old bar (with some of the best tapas in town) with black and white pictures of Hemingway and bulls on the walls, the restaurant here dishes up solid traditional fare.

La Chistera, C/San Nicolás 40, t 94 821 05 12 (€€). Another popular, if slightly pretentious, spot for local dishes; try the *solomillo ai roquefort* (fillet of steak with Roquefort sauce) and finish up with the divine fruit tarts. Also has a good bar for *pintxos* (try the award-winning *zamburiña con tomate raf y Roncal gratinado* – a scallop topped with tomato and Roncal cheese).

El Merca'o, C/Tafalla 5–7, t 94 829 25 88, *www.elmercao.com* (€€). Stunning designer restaurant and bar, with

superb *pintxos*, stellar contemporary cuisine and award-winning service.

Erburu, C/San Lorenzo 15, t 94 822 51 69 (€€–€). This is a quiet, wooden-beamed retreat in the middle of a buzzy bar-lined street. It serves tapas, traditional Navarrese dishes, and a good range of wines. *Closed Mon.*

Baserri, C/San Nicolás 32, t 94 822 20 21, *www.restaurantebaserri.com* (€€). Hard to beat for *cocina en miniatura*; this restaurant's fine creations have repeatedly walked away with the top honours at Pamplona's annual *Concurso de Pintxos*.

San Fermín, C/San Nicolás 44, t 94 822 21 91, *www.restaurantesanfermin.com* (€€). This is one of the best places to try Navarra's famous vegetables, all freshly prepared. They also offer tasty meat and fish, and there's a good lunch menu for €17 (including wine). *Closed Mon.*

Sarasate, C/San Nicolás 19, t 94 822 57 27 (€€). Come here for the best vegetarian meals in Pamplona. *Closed Sun and evenings, except Fri and Sat.*

Montón, C/Jarauta 29, t 94 822 11 41 (€). In the Casco Viejo, this simple restaurant serves regional fare including stews, game in season, along with a range of *pintxos*.

Casa Flores, C/Estafeta 85, t 94 822 21 75 (€€–€). Cheap and cheerful favourite on Pamplona's most celebrated street, with a daily lunch *menú*, sandwiches and snacks.

Tapas/*Pintxos* in Pamplona

As well as elegant cafés, Pamplona had some 700 bars at the last count, or one for every 280 inhabitants – many of whom seem to be always in them, day and night.

Café Iruña, Plaza del Castillo 44, *www.cafeiruna.com*. A famous 1888 Modernista place, with etched glass and chandeliers. It also boasts a wonderful summer terrace.

Baviera, Plaza del Castillo 10. The best of the old stalwarts on the *plaza*; plenty of atmosphere, delightful service, and one of the best selections of Navarrese *pintxos*.

★ El Colmado >

★ El Merca'o >

★ Baviera >>

⭐ La Botería >>

Mesón del Caballo Blanco, Rincón del Caballo Blanco (behind the cathedral), C/Redín s/n, **t** 94 821 15 04. An atmospheric old stone house with the best summer terrace in the city and a cosy fireplace in winter. Outdoor concerts in summer.

Café Roch, C/Comedias 6. One of the oldest cafés in the city, this is small, lively and usually packed; try the house special, pepper croquettes.

Letyana, Travesía de Bayona 2. Excellent, award-winning *pintxos*, and a great atmosphere.

El Molino, Avda Bayona 13. A much-loved classic, with fabulous *pintxos* and a regular crowd of locals.

Fitero, C/Estafeta 58. The best tapas bar on legendary C/Estafeta, with an array of mouthwatering *pintxos*.

Mesón del Pirineo, C/Estafeta 41. Set in a beautiful old building, a very lively spot located on the main bull-running street.

La Estafeta, C/Estafeta 54. Classic Pamplona bar offering local wines and a huge choice of *pintxos* despite its diminutive size.

Bar Gaucho, C/Espoz y Mina 7. Nothing traditional about the award-winning *pintxos* here. Try the *hojaldre de crema de paté de uvas al oporto* (paté in pastry with grape and port sauce). *Closed last 2 weeks July.*

Savoy, C/Francisco Bergamin 27. Delicious tapas, including platters of local hams, cured meats and cheeses. The house speciality are *pintxos* topped with *foie*.

El Molino, Avendia Bayona 2. A popular spot for a chilled *vermut* from the barrel, accompanied by a wide selection of freshly prepared traditional *pintxos*.

Bodegón Sarria, C/Estafeta 52. This traditional favourite on a bar-lined street specialises in *jamón Ibérico* – wafer thin slices of cured ham. Behind the modern façade is a traditional, wood-panelled bar.

La Botería, Avenida de Roncesvalles s/n, **t** 94 822 51 18. This has a terrace and good *pintxos* – good components for a full house.

La Cepa, C/San Lorenzo 2. One of the most popular bars in town for *pintxos*; also specializes in a vast range of *bocadillos* (filled baguettes).

Entertainment and Nightlife in Pamplona

Theatre

Teatro Gayarre, Avda de Carlos III, **t** 94 822 01 39, *www.teatro gayarre.com.* Besides drama, the theatre hosts music concerts, opera and *zarzuela* (Spanish operetta).

Cinema

For undubbed films (marked 'v.o.'), check local newspapers.

Cinés Saide, C/Cortes de Navarra 7, **t** 94 822 55 95, *www.saide.es.*

Golem Yamaguchi, Plaza Yamaguchi 9, **t** 94 822 23 33, *www.golem.es.* The city's main cinema for undubbed films.

Nightclubs and Bars

Marengo, Avda Bayona, 2, **t** 948 26 55 42. Hugely popular club, attracting a big student crowd.

Boulevard Jazz Bar, Plaza Félix Huarte 6. Live jazz and a mellow atmosphere.

Utopia, C/Nueva 117. Excellent cocktails and a buzzing atmosphere.

Kabiya, Cuesta del Labrit, *www.kabiya.com.* Popular haunt in the historic centre, with cushioned sofas on the terrace and a lively bar inside.

West of Pamplona I: Aralar and San Miguel in Excelsis

Navarra's magic mountain, **Aralar**, now a natural park, is a favourite spot for a picnic or Sunday hike from Pamplona, gracefully wooded with beech, rowan and hawthorn groves. It has been sacred to the Basques since Neolithic times, when they

Getting around West of Pamplona

Most Pamplona–Altsasu **trains** stop at Huarte Arakil. Daily **buses** go to Lekunberri and Aldatz from Pamplona (La Muguiroarra, t 94 850 40 66)

Sanctuario de San Miguel in Excelsis
open 9.30–8

erected 30 dolmens and menhirs in the yew groves around Putxerri, the biggest concentration of Neolithic monuments in all Spain. On top is Navarra's holy of holies, the **Sanctuario de San Miguel in Excelsis**, on a panoramic north–south road (NA751) that climbs over Aralar between Huarte Arakil and Lekunberri. The gloomy stone chapel built by the count of Goñi was consecrated in 1098. Traditionally guarded by mastiffs (although we didn't see any), the chapel has had an empty air ever since French Basques plundered it in 1797, when they knocked off St Michael's head (or so say apologists who find the crystal head too weird); the hands of the desecrators were chopped off before they were put to death, and nailed over the chapel door. You can see the chains worn by Teodosio de Goñi (*see* overleaf) and the hole through which the dragon appeared; pilgrims still stick their heads into it, although no one remembers why. A high-tech alarm system protects the enamelled Byzantine *retablo* (stolen and recovered in 1979) showing the Virgin on a rainbow in a mandorla with the Christ Child; the only comparable work in Europe is the great altarpiece in St Mark's in Venice. Tentatively dated 1028, it was probably originally stolen from Constantinople by a Crusader and sold to Sancho the Great, who donated it to the chapel.

Around Aralar

Beigorri
www.beigorri aventura.com; check opening times on the website; adm; not suitable for children under 8

Peru-Harri
open Sat–Sun 10.30–2.30; adm

Of the villages under the mountain **Lekunberri** is the most orientated to tourism; among its newest attractions is the **Beigorri** forest adventure park. **Leitza**, just north, is a prettier choice, besides being the home of Basque legend Iñaki Perurena, the *arrejazotzale* or champion heavy-stone weightlifter. Along with his son Iñaki, also a stone-lifter, he has established a museum, **Peru-Harri**, with a park full of sculptures and a traditional *caserío* displaying photographs and Basque sport memorabilia.

Zudaire, south of Aralar, is the head town in a broken terrain called **Las Améscoas**, the refuge of the Carlists and delight of speleologists: most of the caves are located above Zudaire around **Baquedano**, with its craggy ravine and streams.

Aralar is hardly the only mountain in Europe dedicated to heaven's *generalísimo*: there's Mont-St-Michel in France, St Michael's Mount in England and Monte Sant'Angelo in Italy, to name a few. In art, Michael is often shown with a spear, not slaying so much as *transfixing* dragons to the earth. A recurrent theme in the endless mysticism surrounding St Michael has it that his cult took over ancient religious centres concerned with water sources

The Knight, the Dragon and the Archangel

In the 9th century, Count Teodosio de Goñi went off to fight the Saracens with his Visigothic overlord King Witiza. He was returning home when he met a hermit (the devil in disguise) who warned him that his wife was unfaithful. Seething with rage, the knight stormed into his castle, saw two forms lying in his bed and without hesitation slew them both (this was endemic in the Middle Ages; the same thing happened to St Julian the Hospitaller). When Teodosio ran out he met his wife returning from Mass, who told him, to his horror, that she had given his own aged parents the bed. Horrified, Teodosio went to Rome to ask the pope what penance he could possibly do to redeem his soul, and after three nights the pope had a dream that he should wear heavy chains in solitude until God showed his forgiveness by breaking them.

Binding himself in chains, Teodosio went up to the top of Mount Aralar and lived as a hermit for years. One day, when he was sitting next to a cave, a scaly green dragon emerged, smoke billowing from its nostrils. Teodosio implored the aid of St Michael, who suddenly appeared with his sword in hand and spoke to the dragon in perfect Basque: '*Nor Jaunggoitkoa bezaka?*' ('Who is stronger than God?'). The dragon slunk back into its cave and the archangel struck off the knight's chains and left a statue of himself – an angelic figure with a large cross on its head and an empty glass case where the face ought to be. Every year between March and August the figure goes on a fertility-blessing tour through a hundred Navarra villages; and on Corpus Christi pilgrims walk or cycle up to the chapel to pay their respects.

and underground streams (and, if you like, 'telluric forces' within the earth); the act of fixing the 'dragon' symbolizes the capture and manipulation of these forces. Sure enough, the Sierra de Aralar is so karstic as to be practically hollow: under the sanctuary there's an immense subterranean river that makes moaning dragonish sounds, feeding an icy lake under a domed cavern.

Altsasu (**Alsasua**), below Aralar on the road to Vitoria-Gasteiz, is a typical Navarrese town for 364 days of the year, but on Carnival Tuesday it goes atavistic with one of the most spectacular rural carnivals to survive in modern Europe, suppressed under Franco but revived in 1982. As the light fails, men appear dressed as *momotxorroaks*, half-demonic creatures bearing sharp wooden pitchforks, dressed in sheepskins, with head-dresses that cover their faces, sprouting huge horns and white aprons. A vat of bulls' blood is brought out and they cover hands, arms and aprons with it, then set about each other with their pitchforks, while the *heriotsaks*, the 'deaths', join in with their sickles, and witches and sorcerers dance around the *akerbeltz*, a great black billy goat, all to the sound of the *gaïtas*. As the violence increases, the leader of the *momotxorroaks* blows a horn, and all dance a mad, frenetic, high-kicking dance. And then it's over, and all the creatures retire to the bar. Visitors are not welcome, however, and could get hurt.

Where to Stay and Eat West of Pamplona

(i) **Lekunberri**
Plazaola 21,
t 94 850 72 04,
www.lekunberri.net

**Hs Ayestarán I and II, C/Aralar 22, t 94 850 41 27, *www.hotelayestaran. com* (€€). A pleasant, old-fashioned atmosphere, with tennis, children's leisure facilities, a swimming pool and garden, and tasty local food. *Closed Oct–Mar.*

Hostal Elosta, C/Alde Zaharra 44, t 94 860 48 15 or t 626 177 915, *www.*

(i) **Alsasua**
Plaza de los Fueros,
t 94 846 83 43

hostalelosta.com (€). Seven simple rooms above a country café-bar in a traditional building in the old quarter.
Asador Epeleta, Aralar s/n, t 94 850 43 57, *www.asadorepeleta.com* (€€–€). Possibly the finest roast meats in Northern Spain, along with seafood. Book well in advance. *Closed Mon, second fortnight of June.*

Venta Muguiro, Autopista A15 (exit 123), **t** 94 850 41 02 (€). Old-fashioned 19th-century inn, with country cooking, including sturdy local stews and grills, and plenty of atmosphere.
Restaurant Iru-Bide, Avenida Vitoria 3, Alsasua, t 94 846 88 76 (€). Local bar with a *comedor* serving traditional dishes and well priced set menus.

West of Pamplona II: The Camino de Santiago

Few places in Europe can boast such a concentration of medieval curiosities as this stretch of the famous road (*see* **Basque Culture**, pp.49–51), where the mystic syncretism of Jews, Knights Templars, pagans and pilgrims was expressed in monuments with secret messages that tease and mystify today.

From Pamplona to Estella

Santa María de Eunate
open July–Sept Tues–Sun 10.30–1.30 and 5–8; Mar–June and Oct Tues–Sun 10.30–1.30 and 4–7; Jan–Feb and Nov Tues–Sun 10.30–2.30; closed Mon and Dec

A short turn off the N111 (about 15km from Pamplona) leads to the old village of **Obanos**, and 1.6km beyond that village to a lonely field and **Santa María de Eunate**, a striking 12th-century church built by the Templars. The Templars often built their chapels as octagons, but this one was purposely made irregular and is surrounded by a unique 33-arched octagonal cloister – hence its name 'Eunate' ('the hundred doors'). Many knights were buried here, and it's likely that its peculiar structure had deep significance in the Templars' initiatory rites. There are only a few carved capitals – some little monsters, and pomegranates on the portal, which, oddly, faces north. During the church's restoration, scallop shells were discovered along with the tombs – the church also served as a mortuary chapel for pilgrims. The lack of a central keystone supporting the eight ribs inside hints that Arab architects were involved in the building. The Romanesque Virgin by the alabaster window is a copy of the one stolen in 1974.

The *camino francés* from Roncesvalles (*see* pp.238–40) and the *camino aragonés* converged at the 11th-century bridge in pretty **Puente la Reina**, which hasn't changed much since the day when pilgrims marched down the sombre Rúa Mayor, where many houses preserve their coats of arms. The pilgrims traditionally entered Puente la Reina through the arch of another Templar foundation, **El Crucifijo**, a church with scallops and Celtic interlaced designs on the portal and two naves. The smaller one was added to house a powerful 14th-century German crucifix left by a pilgrim, where the Christ is nailed not to a cross, but the trunk and branches of a Y-shaped tree. Towards the bridge, the church of

Getting along the Camino de Santiago

By Bus

La Estellesa buses (t 94 832 65 09, *www.laestellesa.com*) from Pamplona stop at Puente la Reina and Estella (with a neo-Moorish station), en route to Logroño; timetables at *www.autobusesdenavarra.com*.

Tours

For **guided tours** in the Estella region – everything from cultural tours to active pursuits such as pot-holing, climbing, and cycling, see the website *www.turismotierraestella.com*.

Santiago has a weathered Moorish-style lobed portal and, inside, two excellent polychrome 14th-century statues.

From Puente la Reina, the path (although not the road) continues up to atmospheric old **Cirauqui** propped on its hill, where the church of **San Román** has another multifoiled portal framed in archivolts with geometric designs. The ancient road to the west of Cirauqui, paved with Roman stones, predates even the pilgrims.

Estella (Lizarra): the Town of the Star

⭐ Estella

A stop at Estella, known as Estella la Bella for its beauty, was much looked forward to by the pilgrims. It owes its foundation in 1090 to a convenient miracle: nightly showers of shooting stars that always fell on the same place on a hill intrigued some shepherds, who investigated and found a cave hidden by thorns, sheltering a statue of the Virgin. Returning from the siege of Toledo the same year, King Sancho Ramírez founded Estella on the opposite bank of the Río Ega from the old settlement of Lizarra (coincidentally the Basque word for 'star') and populated it with *francos*, or freemen: artisans, merchants and others who owed allegiance to no feudal lord (although, confusingly, most of these *francos* were also Franks from Gascony, who fought in the Reconquista for pay or piety's sake). Thanks to them, Estella has numerous fine medieval buildings; if many have been cropped, thank the Grand Inquisitor of Castile, Cardinal Cisneros, whose troops literally cut Navarra down to size in 1512 for Ferdinand the Catholic. The most exciting time to visit Estella is the Friday before the first Sunday in August, when it holds one of very few *encierros* which attract as many men as women – even if the bulls are really heifers with padded horns.

The arcaded **Plaza Fueros** is the town's bustling main square, full of terrace cafés and overlooked by the Gothic church of San Juan, with a dour early 20th-century façade and bells which ring ear-splittingly on the hour. To the west is the **Basílica de Nuestra Señora de Puy**, a must on the pious pilgrim route, being built on the point where the stars fell on Navarra that night. The 14th-century Virgin is still there, but the old basilica was replaced in 1951 with a concrete and glass star-shaped church, and a *mirador* offering lovely views across the old town. South of Plaza Fueros, the highlight for art pilgrims is 12th-century **San Miguel**, the parish church of the *francos*, set on a craggy rock atop its original set of steps (which lead up from C/Chapitel). Don't hesitate: march right up to them for the magnificent portal, where Christ in Majesty holds pride of place among angels, Evangelists and the Elders of the Apocalypse, the favourite theme on church tympanums all along the *camino francés* in both France and Spain. On the left, St Michael pins the dragon and weighs souls; on the right, an angel shows the empty tomb to the three Marys. The top, sadly, fell to the Cardinal's tower-bashing squad, but the brackets are good, especially the man-eating wolf.

Near San Miguel you'll find a faithful 19th-century copy of Estella's medieval bridge, which pilgrims crossed to the Lizarra side to visit the 12th-century **San Sepolcro**, with a fascinating façade added in 1328 but again truncated by Cisneros. The tympanum has an animated Last Supper, Crucifixion, Resurrection and what looks to be the Harrowing of Hell; statues of the 12 Apostles flank the door; one of them appears to be holding a stack of pancakes. To the right of the bridge is the piquant centre of old Lizarra, with churches and palaces bearing proud coats of arms, most now occupied by antiques shops, along Calle de la Rúa ('street of the street'). The finest palace is the Plateresque brick **Casa Fray Diego**, now used as the Casa de Cultura.

Off to the left was the Judería, or ghetto, its 12th-century synagogue converted into **Santa María Jus del Castillo**, where the apse is decorated with a rich assortment of Romanesque modillions. The church is dwarfed by the adjacent 13th-century, wonderfully austere **monastery of Santo Domingo**, now a retirement home. Further up, near the new bridge, a 16th-century fountain under a canopy of linden trees in **Plaza de San Martín** is a delightful place to linger.

A curving flight of stairs leads up to the 12th-century **San Pedro de la Rúa**, defended by a skyscraper bell tower. The Moorish-inspired foiled arch of the portal is crowned by a relief of St James in a boat with stars, blessed by a giant hand emerging from the water. Inside, the church has its share of curiosities: a unique column made of three interlaced 'serpents', and the black *Virgen de la O*, a cult figure of the masons, who left their marks all over the church. The Baroque chapel to the left houses St Andrew's shoulderblade; the story goes that the bishop of Patras took it with him for good luck while making the pilgrimage in 1270. Luck failed him in Estella, where he died and was buried in San Pedro's cloister, along with his relic. The holy shoulderblade wasn't going to have any of this and made itself known by a curious light that appeared over the tomb; in 1626, the day when Andrew was proclaimed

Casa Fray Diego
open Tues–Fri 6.30pm–8.30pm, Sat 12–2 and 6.30–8.30, Sun 12–2; closed Mon

San Pedro de la Rúa
open for Mass or guided visits only; see tourist office

patron of Estella, a burning vision of his X-shaped cross hovered over the church. Of the cloister, only two galleries survive, reconstructed after the castle above was blown up in 1572 and crashed down on top of it. The capitals are carved with the Lives of the Saints and the Apocalypse: the twisted column is a copy of a famous one in Santo Domingo de Silos in Burgos.

Over the years, Estella became a favourite residence of the kings, whose 12th-century **Palacio de los Reyes de Navarra**, opposite San Pedro, is one of the best-preserved civic buildings from the period. Prominent at street level, a capital bears the oldest known depiction of Roland (*see* p.239), clad in scaly armour, fighting the equally scaly giant Ferragut; further up, another capital shows a scene of devils and animal musicians, including a donkey playing a harp. The palace now houses the **Museo Gustavo de Maeztú**, devoted to works by Estella's best-known painter (1887–1947).

Museo Gustavo de Maeztú
t 94 854 60 37; open Tues–Sat 11–1 and 5–7, Sun 11–1.30; closed Mon

Around Estella

Estella is an important producer of DO Navarra wine, and the most interesting *bodega* to visit just happens to be the Benedictine **Monasterio de Irache**, 2km south at Ayegui. First recorded in 958, it later received a generous endowment from Sancho the Great, who helped finance one of the very first pilgrims' hospitals here. In 1569, Philip II moved the university of theology here from Sahagún (near Léon), where it remained, enjoying the same privileges as Salamanca until it closed down with the expropriation of monasteries in 1824. The complex is a handsome mix behind an eclectic façade. The entrance is through an elegant Plateresque door, leading into an austerely beautiful Romanesque church with three apses under a Renaissance dome, stripped of centuries' encrustation of altarpieces. The original Romanesque north door is decorated with hunting scenes, while the sumptuous Plateresque cloister has a bevy of grotesque and religious capitals. The small wine museum preserves Irache's 1,000-year-old custom of offering free drinks to pilgrims.

Monasterio de Irache
monastery open summer Tues 10–1.30, Wed–Fri 10–1.30 and 5–7, Sat–Sun 9–1.30 and 4–7; winter Tues 10–1.30, Wed–Sun 10–1.30 and 4.30–6; closed Mon; wine museum open Sat–Sun 10–2 and 4–8

Twelve kilometres up the Donostia-San Sebastián road in Abarzua, the **Monasterio de Santa María de Iranzu** was founded in the 11th century by Cistercians, who chose to live in a dramatic ravine true to their preference for wild, remote settings. It was restored by the government of Navarra and given to the Theatine order. The monks will show you the Romanesque-Gothic cloister with a hexagonal fountain, the medieval kitchen, and church.

Monasterio de Santa María de Iranzu
open summer daily 10–2 and 4–8; winter daily 10–2 and 4–6; adm; to arrange guided visits call t 94 852 00 47

South of Estella on the Ebro, **Lodosa** is famous for its red peppers, *pimientos del piquillo* (similar to the *piments d'Espelette, see* p.58), which are dried in long garlands over the white façades of the houses. Its church, **San Miguel**, has an immense rococo *retablo*.

Los Arcos, Sorlada and Torres del Río

After Estella, the pilgrims walked to **Los Arcos**, where, tucked off the N111, there is an arcaded *plaza* and a 16th-century church, **Santa María**, with a pretty cathedral-size Gothic cloister, carved choir stalls and frantic Baroque *retablos*. Seven kilometres north of Los Arcos at **Sorlada**, a grand 18th-century Baroque basilica belongs to **San Gregorio Ostiense**, a once immensely popular saint who lost much of his influence to modern fertilizers. His story is told in the basilica's naïve paintings: back in 1039 locusts plagued the region so badly that a group of farmers walked to Rome and asked the pope for help. The pope had a dream that Cardinal Gregory of Ostia was the man for the job, and off he was sent to Navarra, where he preached and dispersed the locusts, an exertion that killed him after five years. He was buried at Sorlada and forgotten, until a light redirected farmers to his tomb. Remembering his good juju against the locusts (and their ancestral Celtic head cult), they would cart his skull reliquary around their fields, pouring water through the hole which made it into 'holy Gregory water'. Philip II had gallons of it sent down to water the orchards of the Escorial. Farming is so big here that you can take an **agricultural tour** of the local *bodegas*, ostrich farm, preserve-makers and distilleries.

Agricultural tour
t 94 864 00 21,
Los Arcos tourist office

West of Los Arcos, **Torres del Río** has a striking, tall octagonal church, **Santo Sepolcro**, built in the late 12th or early 13th centuries by the Knights of the Holy Sepulchre, or some say the Templars; like **Santa María de Eunate** (*see* p.219) it may have been a mortuary chapel for pilgrims. The rather majestic cross-ribbed vaulting in the dome, with additional ribs springing from the four corners of the building, is exactly like that in the churches built in Córdoba under the Caliphs, all said to be ultimately modelled on the second mihrab in the Great Mosque there.

Viana: where Cesare Borgia Bit the Dust

Viana, the pilgrims' last stop in Navarra, fits a lot of monument-ality into a small space. Founded by King Sancho VII 'the Strong' in 1219 to defend his frontier with Castile, it became the hereditary principality of the heir to the throne of Navarra in 1423. Although its once-proud castle fell to Cardinal Cisneros' demolition programme, nobles and courtly hangers-on stayed on and built themselves splendid mansions with big coats of arms, the elegant 17th-century **Casa Consistorial**, crowned with an escutcheon the size of an asteroid, and the 13th–14th-century church of **Santa María**, hidden by a magnificent concave Renaissance façade based on a triumphal arch, with a coffered ceiling designed and carved by Juan de Goyaz (1549). Inside, the Gothic interior is quite airy and lovely, culminating in an intricate gilded Baroque *retablo*.

The façade could be considered the tombstone of Cesare Borgia (1475–1507), whose memorial, all that is left of his desecrated remains, lies buried under the marker in front of the church. Now, how did Pope Alexander VI's son and Machiavelli's hero end up in Viana? With the papacy and central Italy in his pocket by 1502, married to Charlotte, sister of the king of Navarre, and supported by France, Cesare had embarked on a brilliant career as a ruthless Renaissance prince-assassin. When his father pulled the rug out from under him by dying suddenly in 1503, Cesare himself was too ill to get to the Vatican and influence the conclave to elect a Borgia candidate; according to Machiavelli's *The Prince*, it was the only political mistake he ever made. It proved to be fatal. Once Julius II, arch-enemy of the Borgias, was elected in late 1503, Cesare's conquests in Italy were frittered away in anarchy, the French turned against him, and he went from being on top of the world to a man whose life was in danger. He fled to Aragón, the cradle of the Borgias, only to be imprisoned by Ferdinand. The still-independent kingdom of Navarra proved to be his only refuge, and he died in a skirmish in Viana, fighting Castilian rebels.

From here, the pilgrim's road continues to Logroño in La Rioja.

Where to Stay and Eat on the Camino de Santiago

(i) **Puente la Reina >**
C/Mayor 105,
t 94 834 08 45;
www.puentelareina-gares.es

Puente la Reina ✉ 31100

**Hotel El Peregrino, on the Pamplona road, t 94 834 00 75, www.hotelelperegrino.com (€€€). This stone and timber place isn't as old as it looks, but it has luxurious, air-conditioned rooms, lush gardens, and a pool, and serves up excellent meals with a French gourmet touch in a split-level dining room. *Closed Sun eve and Mon.*

Hotel Rural Bidean, C/Mayor 20, t 94 834 11 56, www.bidean.com (€€). A pretty stone building with a cosy, country atmosphere, this provides a comfortable stay along the old pilgrims' route to Santiago.

(i) **Estella >**
C/San Nicolás 1,
t 94 855 63 01,
www.turismotierra estella.com

Estella ✉ 31200

Estella isn't known for its dining; consider a picnic by the banks of the river instead.

****Hospederia Chapitel, C/Chapitel 1, t 94 855 10 90, http://hospederia chapitel.com (€€). Opened in 2011, this is a very comfortable choice, right in the heart of the old quarter.

*Hôtel Yerri, Avenida Yerri 35, t 94 854 60 34, www.hotelyerri.es (€€–€). Another modern and well-equipped if rather bland establishment, next to the bullring.

*Pensión San Andrés, Plaza Santiago 58, t 94 855 41 85 (€). Excellent value, clean and central, with family-size rooms overlooking the square (ask for a top-floor room).

*Hs Cristina, C/Baja Navarra 1, t 94 855 07 72 (€). Simple, clean and central.

Fonda Izarra, C/Caldería, t 94 855 06 78 (€). The cheapest doubles in town.

La Cepa, Plaza Fueros 15, t 94 855 00 32 (€€€–€€). Specializes in Basque and Navarrese cuisine, with a good value menu and terrace. *Closed Sun eve.*

La Navarra, C/Gustavo de Maeztú 16, t 94 855 00 40 (€€). Another good bet, perhaps more for its medieval atmosphere than food, which is good if a bit pricy. *Closed Sun eve and Mon.*

Restaurante Richard, Avda Yerri, 10, t 94 855 13 16, www.barrestaurante richard.com (€€). Traditional cooking using fresh local produce. *Closed Mon and first week Sept.*

ⓘ Los Arcos ›
*in the Ayuntamiento,
Plaza de los Fueros 1,
t 94 864 00 21*

ⓘ Viana ›
*Bajos Ayuntamiento,
t 94 844 63 02*

Los Arcos ✉ 31210

Hotel Monaco, Pza del Coso 1, **t 94 864 00 00, *www.hotelmonaco.es* (€). A modest hotel in the centre, with crisp modern rooms.

Hs Ezequiel, Avda General Uda s/n, **t 94 864 02 96 *www.hostal ezequiel.com* (€). A friendly, family- run hotel, with large restaurant/bar.

Viana ✉ 31230

Hôtel Casa Armendariz, C/Navarro Villoslada 19, **t** 94 864 50 78 (€). A cosy little spot in the centre of town; the rooms are small, but the management is charming. They offer a mix of traditional and modern cuisine in their good-value *sidreria* (€€–€).

Borgia, C/Serapio Urra 1, **t** 94 864 57 81 (€€). A classic, serving modern interpretation of traditional Navarrese specialities, all prepared with the freshest local produce. The cellar is excellent, with a particularly good range of unusual regional wines. *Closed Sun and Aug.*

South of Pamplona to Tudela

The green Basque hills are a distant memory south of Pamplona; here the skies are bright and clear, the land arid and toasted golden brown after the winter rains, except for the green swaths of vineyards in La Ribera, cradle of Navarra's finest, freshest rosés.

Tafalla and Olite

In the 17th century, a Dutchman named E. Cock described Tafalla and Olite as the 'flowers of Navarra', and both have determinedly crowed Cock's sweet nicknames ever since. Old **Tafalla** has wilted a bit over the centuries and grass grows between the cobbles, but it still has an impressive Plaza Mayor and claims one of the finest and biggest *retablos* in the north: a masterpiece by Basque artist Juan de Ancheta tucked away in the austere church of **Santa María**.

Northwest of Tafalla, **Artajona** has the air of an abandoned stage set: majestic medieval walls with startlingly intact crenellated towers defend little more than the 13th-century fortress church of **San Saturnino**. This has a tympanum showing the saint exorcizing a woman, watched by Juana the Mad and Philip the Fair of France, while the lintel shows Saturnino's martyrdom with the bull (*see* pp.211–12). The Hispano-Flemish *retablo mayor* dates from 1515. This is the second church on the site. Artajona's walls, redone in the 14th century, were first built between 1085 and 1103 by the Templars and canons of St-Sernin (San Saturnino) of Toulouse, at a time when the counts of Toulouse were among the chief players in Europe, leading the First Crusade and fighting alongside the Cid.

Near Artajona, the **Ermita de la Virgen** shelters a bronze and enamel 13th-century Virgin holding a bouquet of roses. There are two megalithic gallery tombs nearby.

Palacio Real de Olite
open July and Aug 10–8; spring and autumn 10–7; winter 10–6; adm

Olite, south of Tafalla, is a fabulous medieval town dwarfed by its bewitching, lofty-towered **Palacio Real de Olite** built for the king of Navarra in 1407. Each of its 15 towers and turrets has its own character, and restorers have made the whole thing seem

Getting around South of Pamplona

Trains linking Pamplona and Zaragoza call at Tafalla, Olite and Tudela.
Conda **buses** (t 94 822 10 26, *www.conda.es*) stop at Tafalla, Olite and Tudela on the way to Zaragoza.
Hire a **bicycle** or mountain bike from Chiqui-bike in Tudela and Arguedas (for the Bardenas Reales), t 94
882 52 01, *www.chiquibike.com*.

startlingly new. Inside, the décor is Mudéjar; hanging gardens were
suspended from the great arches of the terraces, and there was a
leonera, or lion pit, and a very busy set of dungeons; the Navarrese
royal families led messy, frustrated lives. At night the whole
complex is illuminated with a golden light, creating a striking
backdrop to performances in the summer Festival of Navarra.

**Santa María
la Real**
open 9.30–12 and 5–8

San Pedro
open 9.30–12 and 5–8

The castle's Gothic chapel, **Santa María la Real**, has a gorgeous
13th-century façade, and the Romanesque church of **San Pedro**
has an octagonal tower and portal adorned with two large stone
eagles, one devouring the hare it has captured (symbolizing force)
and the other, more friendly, representing gentleness.

Eastwards, the village of **San Martín de Unx** has a superb crypt
under its 12th-century church. From here a by-road branches south
for the spectacular medieval village of **Ujué**, set on a hill
corrugated with terraces, where a shepherd, directed by a dove
(*ujué*), found the statue of the black Virgin now housed in the
powerful 13th-century Romanesque-Gothic church of **Santa María**.
The doorway has finely carved scenes of the Last Supper and the
Journey of the Magi, and the altar preserves the heart of King
Charles II of Navarra. Every year since 1043, on the first Sunday after
St Mark's day (25 April), the Virgin has been the object of a solemn
pilgrimage that departs from Tafalla at 2am.

Tudela

Founded by the Moors, Tudela, the second city of Navarra and
capital of La Ribera region, was the last town in Navarra to submit
to Ferdinand the Catholic, and it did so most unwillingly. Before the
big bigot, Tudela had always made a point of welcoming Jews,
Moors and heretics expelled from Castile or persecuted by the
Inquisition, and it was no accident that its tolerant environment
nurtured three of Spain's top medieval writers: Benjamin of Tudela,
the great traveller and chronicler (1127–73); the poet Judah Ha-Levi
of the same period; and doctor Miguel Servet (1511–53), one of the
first to write on the circulation of the blood.

Don't be disheartened by Tudela's protective coating of dusty,
gritty sprawl, but head straight for its picturesque, labyrinthine
Moorish-Jewish kernel, around the elegant 17th-century **Plaza de
los Fueros**; the decorations on the façades recall its use as a
bullring in the 18th and 19th centuries. The Gothic **cathedral** was
built over the town's Great Mosque in the 12th century and topped

Cathedral
*open Tues–Sat 9–1
and 4–7, Sun and
Mon 9–1; adm*

with a pretty 17th-century tower. It has three decorated doorways: the north and south portals have capitals with New Testament scenes, while the west portal, the Portada del Juicio Final, is devoted to the Last Judgement, depicted in 114 different scenes in eight soaring bands. The delightful choir, behind its Renaissance grille, is considered the finest Flamboyant Gothic work in Navarra, carved with geometric flora, fauna and fantasy motifs; note, under the main chair, the figures of two crows picking out the eyes of a man – the dean who commissioned the work but refused to pay the sculptors the agreed price. The main altar has a beautiful Hispano-Flemish *retablo* painted by Pedro Díaz de Oviedo, and yet more chains from Las Navas de Tolosa. There's an ornate Gothic *retablo* of Santa Caterina and a chapel of Santa Ana, patroness of Tudela, with a cupola that approaches Baroque orgasm. The cool, plant-filled 13th-century cloister, with twin and triple columns, has capitals on the Life of Jesus and other New Testament stories, while the Escuela de Cristo, off the east end of the cloister, has Mudéjar paintings and decorations. The square, pedestrianized and filled with a sea of tables spilling out from terrace cafés, is a favourite with locals.

Among the best palaces are the 16th-century **Casa del Almirante**, near the cathedral, and, in the C/de Magallón, the lovely Renaissance **Palace of the Marqués de San Adrián**. An irregular, 17-arched, 13th-century **bridge** spanning the Ebro still takes much of Tudela's traffic, with help from an ultramodern suspension bridge.

Around Tudela: a Desert, Water and Wine

Bardenas Reales
www.bardenas reales.es; open 8am–1hr before dusk; visitor centre: north of Tudela, just off the NA-134, Ctra del Polígono de Tiro, Km.6, t 94 883 03 08, turismo@ bardenasreales.es

Just east of Tudela is a striking desert straight out of the American Far West known as the **Bardenas Reales**, where erosion has sculpted steep tabletops, weird wrinkled hills and rocks balanced on pyramids. You might recognize it, since it's a popular location for everything from Bond films to pop videos. The best way to see it (and not get lost) is by the GR13 walking path, which crosses its northern extent from the Ermita de Nuestro Señoro del Yugo. An easier way, however, is to go on an organized excursion, by horse, mountain bike or 4x4 (*see* p.228).

South of Tudela, **Cascante** is known for its wines and the lofty church of the **Virgen del Romero** (Our Lady of the Rosemary Bush), built in the 17th century and reached by way of an arcaded walkway from the village below. The small spa town of **Fitero** (the waters are used in treating tuberculosis) grew up around the 11th-century Cistercian monastery of **Santa María la Real**, whose abbot, San Raimundo, founded the famous Order of the Knights of Calatrava in 1158. Don't miss the Romanesque Sala Capitular, a monumental *retablo* from the 16th century, the ornate 18th-century chapel of the Virgen de la Barda and, among the treasures, a 10th-century ivory coffer from the workshop of the Caliph of Córdoba. **Cintruénigo** and **Corella**, just north, are important producers of DO Navarra wine, with a good dozen *bodegas* in the environs.

Market Days South of Pamplona

Tafalla: Friday, Plaza Navarra.
Olite: Wednesday, Paseo del Portal.
Fitero: Tuesday and Friday, Plaza San Raimundo.

Sports and Activities South of Pamplona

A number of firms offer excursions into the Bardenas Reales, in a 4x4 or on horseback. For more info, see *www.bardenasreales.com*, which has a list of tour operators. Turismo Bardenas, *www.turismobardenas.com*, **t** 94 841 23 96, brings together professional guides offering a range of different tours, including wine and gourmet tours; active tours (4x4, quad biking, horse-riding and hiking).

Where to Stay and Eat South of Pamplona

Tafalla ✉ 31300

★★**Hs Tafalla**, on the Zaragoza road, **t** 94 870 03 00, *www.hostaltafalla. com* (€€€–€€). Modern roadside hotel. The food is delicious, especially when the dishes involve asparagus, lamb and hake. *Closed Fri.*

Túbal, Plaza de Navarra 6, **t** 94 870 08 52 (€€€–€€). Chef Atxen Jiménez draws in diners from Pamplona and beyond with her delicious variations on classic Navarrese themes. Book well in advance. *Closed Mon and late Aug.*

Olite ✉ 31390

★★★**Parador de Olite**, Plaza de los Teobaldos 2, **t** 94 874 00 00, *www. parador.es* (€€€). Next to the castle of Carlos III in the converted 13th-century Castillo de los Teobaldos. A garden, air-conditioning and beautiful furnishings make castle-dwelling a

★ Hotel de Aire de Bardenas ≫

ⓘ Tudela ≫
C/Juicio 4,
t 94 884 80 58,
www.tudela.es

ⓘ Olite ≫
Plaza de los Teobaldos
10, **t** 94 874 17 03,
www.olite.es

delight, as do Navarrese gourmet treats in the dining room.

La Joyosa Guarda, C/de las Medios 23, **t** 94 874 13 03, *www. laoyosaguarda.com* (€€€). Stylish country hotel in a renovated mansion, with a mix of antiques and contemporary furnishings and a very elegant restaurant.

★★**Hotel Merindad de Olite**, Rúa de la Judería 11, **t/f** 94 874 07 35 *www.hotel-merindaddeolite.com* (€€–€). In a restored old building, which incorporates part of the 12th-century walls. The restaurant, which boasts a huge fireplace, serves particularly good fish dishes, and a tasty lamb with *chilindrón*, a kind of Navarrese ratatouille.

★★**Casa Zanito**, Rúa Revillas 16, **t** 94 874 00 02, *www.casazanito.com* (€€). A modern hotel in a historic building with cheerful rooms and excellent meals, based on market availability, topped off with home-made desserts.

Ujué ✉ 31390

Casa El Chofer I and **II**, **t** 94 873 90 11 (€). Simple rooms in a charming old house, plus a cottage to rent.

Mesón las Torres, **t** 94 873 90 52 *www.mesonlastorres.com* (€€). Has long been the place to eat, with Navarrese treats and Ujué's special *migas*, once a shepherd's dish.

Tudela ✉ 31500

★★★★**Hotel de Aire de Bardenas**, Ctra de Ejea, **t** 94 811 66 66, *www.airedebardenas.com* (€€€). Award-winning contemporary design and luxurious amenities unite in this low, boxy hotel set amid gardens on the edge of the desert. Perfect base for exploring the Bardenas Reales.

★**Hs Nueva Parrilla**, C/Carlos III el Noble 6, **t** 94 882 24 00 (€€–€). A friendly, basic choice with functional rooms.

★★**Hs Remigio**, C/Gaztambide 4, **t** 94 882 08 50, *www.hostalremigio.com* (€).

Simple *hostal*, not far from the Plaza de Fueros, decorated with an old-fashioned rusticity.

Restaurante 33, C/Capuchinos 7, **t** 948 82 76 06 (€€€). Widely regarded as the best in Navarra when it comes to local produce – they even offer a *menú* entirely of vegetable dishes. Carnivores will be more than satisfied with lamb and country stews. *Closed Sun and first 3 weeks Aug.*

Casa Ignacio, C/Cortaderos 11, **t** 94 882 10 21 (€€). Long-established favourite: try the famous *menestra de verduras*: asparagus, artichokes, peas, celery and lettuces. *Closed Mon eve.*

Iruña, C/Muro 11, **t** 94 882 10 00 (€€). Another great place to try the local *menestra de verduras. Closed Thurs.*

Bar Aragón, Plaza de los Fueros 2 (€). Café/restaurant with good tapas.

La Estrella, C/Carnicerías 14, **t** 94 882 18 58 (€). Serves up good home cooking and wonderful *pintxos. Closed Sun eve and 2 wks in Sept.*

Cintruénigo ✉ 31592

Hotel Restaurante Maher, C/La Ribera 19, **t** 94 881 11 50, *www. hotelmaher.com* (€€€). One of Navarra's best restaurants. Delicious Navarrese dishes with an imaginative nouvelle cuisine touch.

⭐ Restaurante 33 >

East of Pamplona: Sangüesa, Javier and Leyre

Pilgrims to Santiago from Mediterranean lands would cross the Pyrenees at Somport in Aragón and enter Navarra at Sangüesa, home of one of the very best Romanesque churches and one of the craziest palaces in all Spain, but these days, if the wind's wrong, the pong of the nearby paper mill hurries visitors along; note that if you go by bus from Pamplona (*see* overleaf), there are only three a day and you'll be stuck with the stink for longer than you might like. If you have a car, there's enough of interest in the area to fill a day out.

Agoitz (Aoiz)

The area due east of Pamplona, crossed by the Río Irati, gets few tourists, but, if you're driving, the undulating landscapes and nearly deserted villages make an interesting alternative to the more direct N240 to Sangüesa. Agoitz itself has fine old houses, a medieval bridge and the 15th-century church of **San Miguel Arcángel**, worth a look for its excellent *retablo mayor* (1580) by Basque master Juan de Achieta and for its unusual 12th-century painted stone font. Romanesque connoisseurs should go out of their way to **Artaiz**, a tiny blip to the southwest (due south of Urroz), where the church of San Martín has the finest sculpture in rural Navarra.

Sangüesa

Sangüesa was a direct product of the pilgrimage, purposely moved from its original hilltop location in the 11th century to the spot where the road crosses the Río Aragón. In 1122, Alfonso el

Getting East from Pamplona

Around three **buses** a day are run by La Veloz Sangüesina, **t** 94 887 02 09, from Pamplona to Sangüesa.

Batallador, king of neighbouring Aragón, sent down a colony of *francos* to augment Sangüesa's population, and 10 years after that ordered the Knights of St John to build a church well worth stopping for: **Santa María la Real**. This possesses one of the most intriguing and extraordinary portals anywhere (unfortunately the street in front is quite busy, so you have to look at it between the cars), so strange that some writers believe that its symbols (knotted labyrinths, mermaids, two-headed beasts symbolizing duality, etc.) were sculpted by Agotes (*see* box, opposite), or by a brotherhood of artists, into something deeper than orthodox Catholicism. Even the damned are laughing in the *Last Judgement* on the tympanum, presided over by a Christ in Majesty with a secret smile and vigorous Evangelists almost dancing around the throne. Below, the elongated figures on the jambs show stylistic similarities to Chartres cathedral, although again the subjects are unusual: on the left the three Marys (the Virgin, Mary Magdalene and Mary Salome, mother of St James), on the right Peter, Paul and Judas, hanged, with the inscription *Judas Mercator*. The upper half of the portal is by another hand altogether, crossed by two tiers of Apostles of near-Egyptian rigidity and another Christ in Majesty, surrounded by symbols of the four Evangelists. If the church is open, ask the sacristan to show you the capitals in the apse, hidden behind the Flemish Renaissance *retablo*, and note the well in the corner. Walk around to see the beautiful carved corbels on the apse and the octagonal tower.

When Sangüesa came to be part of Navarra, the kings made it one of their several residences. Sangüesa's arcaded Rúa Mayor is lined with palaces, including the **Casa Consistorial**, built over the old royal patio of arms, today a charming leafy square; behind this is the austere 12th-century, twin-towered **Palacio del Príncipe de Viana**. The 12th-century **church of Santiago** has a huge battlemented tower and carved capitals, and conserves a large stone statue of St James, discovered buried under the floor in 1965. The slightly later, Gothic **San Salvador** has a pentagonal tower and a huge porch, sheltering a carved portal; its Plateresque choir stalls come from Leyre. Just around the corner, in C/Alfonso el Batallador, the brick **Palacio Vallesantoro** catches the eye with its corkscrew Baroque portal and the widest, most extraordinary wooden eaves in Spain, carved with a phantasmagorical menagerie that makes the creatures on Santa María look tame.

Europe's Untouchables: the Agotes

Some of Europe's best-known outcasts, the Agotes (Cagots in French) lived in the valleys of Navarra and especially across the Pyrenees in Basse-Navarre and Gascony. People believed the Agotes to be lepers and forced a stringent code of apartheid on them: by law they had to marry only amongst their own kind, and they could not farm, or enter a mill or a tavern, or drink out of public fountains save the ones reserved for them. Although what remains of their houses does not differ much from other dwellings, they were constrained to live apart, either in closed-off quarters of towns or in separate hamlets on the outskirts. They had to enter church only by a certain door, use a holy-water stoup reserved for them alone, and hear Mass in a special corner. Often they had their own church, and they were always buried in separate cemeteries. In some localities they were forced to wear distinctive clothing, such as a goose foot sewn on to the backs of their coats.

There was an elaborate etiquette in everyday life to stop the Agotes coming into close contact with anyone else (in Navarra they had to play castanets at all crossroads and public places to warn people of their presence). Although exceptions are recorded, almost all of them worked with wood; besides the master carpenters, they chopped trees for firewood, and made furniture, wooden plates and utensils. Back then it was believed that wood did not transmit diseases (a notion born out by modern science: bacteria survive much longer on plastic, for example). Most were carpenters by trade, and wherever you see a really old market *halles*, or a wooden church steeple or a half-timbered house, chances are it was they who built it.

Small communities of Agotes were reported in obscure corners of the Basque country as late as 1902, but even as this mysterious people was fading away, French, Spanish and Basque writers and scientists were becoming interested in the strange story of these outcasts and who they really were. Under a number of different names, they are mentioned in documents dating back to the 11th century: Crestias, Capots, Agots (in Basque), Ladres (Gascon for lepers), Gafets, Gézitains. But one thing is certain – lepers they were not. Leprosy, though a continuing scourge in the Middle Ages, is not a hereditary disease, and the Agotes made up a caste that lived its separate life for centuries, without any evidence of chronic ill health – even though country people believed that even the touch of one would burn your skin. Plenty of guesses have been put forward as to their origins. Some people held them to be descendants of Visigoths, caught behind after the Frankish conquests and reduced to servitude. Others claimed the first Agotes were Moorish slaves, brought back by the many Gascon lords who went to Spain to hire themselves out in the battles of the Reconquista. Miscellaneous conjectures include refugee Cathar heretics after the Albigensian crusade, Jews, religious excommunicates, Gypsies – and even dwarves, or albinos covered with a blond down.

Others believe, using Sangüesa's church as a prime example, that the Agotes were only symbolic lepers, kept at a distance for the stigma of their heresies (curiously, one of their alternative names, Crestias, or Christians, seems only to emphasize that they were still, really, in the fold). This heresy may have been a highly contagious kind of universal mysticism practised by the Templars or the Order of the Knights of St Lazarus, an order founded in the East before the Templars and devoted to the care of lepers, using Lazarus as their symbol of death within life.

The most reliable contemporary accounts of Agotes suggest they really didn't look much different from anyone else. And as for their origin, the correct answer might be 'all of the above, among others'. The most plausible hypotheses have the children of lepers still living apart, by habit or by force, in the old leper colonies that were once found all over the region. Over the centuries, they were possibly joined by any and every sort of vagabond and refugee seeking a new life in this more tolerant, semi-autonomous, out-of-the-way corner of Europe. The main pilgrimage routes to Compostela converged in Navarra – the last stop before the difficult crossing over the mountains – and a huge number of people made the trip each year (many of them forced to do it as penance or punishment for crimes); more than a few would be likely to stay. To these, add the people attracted by the huge land-clearing and building programmes of the 13th century (most of which welcomed criminals and anyone else willing to work) and it is easy to imagine all the loose ends of Europe piling up here on the Pyrenees.

Neighbouring French-controlled Languedoc had no Agotes, but it did see several massacres of Jews and vagabonds in the 14th century (in medieval times, the lands of the king of France were never a very healthy place for minorities of any sort). Perhaps the stigma of being an Agote was a worthwhile trade for a peaceable life for some people. Still, the mystery will probably never be solved. Why, for example, were they called Crestias (Christians), and why, in the Middle Ages, were they exempt from civil law and taxes, and subject only to Church laws and courts?

The end of the story is as remarkable as the beginning. On the French side, the Cagots seem to have undertaken an epic civil rights struggle and, incredibly enough in the context of *ancien régime* France, they eventually won. Although in 1479 a medical inquest by the *Parlement* of Toulouse concluded that they were not diseased in any way, it still took until 1627 to get the *Parlement* to publish an ordinance prohibiting local officials from persecuting the *maîtres charpentiers* (as they preferred to be known). From 1680 onwards, they fought for the right to be buried in common ground; decades later, men began marrying Cagot women, and finally a prototypical Rosa Parks, a man named Michel Legaret, got fed up one Sunday and stepped right up to the front of the church. He got a hundred days in the jail for that, an outrage that finally moved the Bordeaux *Parlement* to outlaw all segregation.

Winning in court proved much easier than raising the consciousness of their fellow men. Throughout the 18th century, *Parlements* and church officials had to intervene in remote villages, where peasants resisted the new laws and sometimes resorted to violence. By then the Cagots' numbers were on the decrease, as men found they could take their skill and make a living elsewhere or move to the colonies where no one had ever heard of a Cagot, let alone knew how to discriminate against one. The definitive end came with 1789 and the *Declaration of the Rights of Man*; in return, grateful Cagots signed up for the army in large numbers to defend the Revolution. After that, there were no more Cagots, only Frenchmen.

Javier

Sangüesa is the base for visiting two of Navarra's holy sites. **Javier**, 13km away, is topped by a picturesque if over-restored battlemented castle, the birthplace in 1506 of Francisco de Javier (Xavier). In the complicated politics of Navarra, the Javiers were Basques who had supported the French d'Albrets and fought against the Castilians and Basques; Francis's father had died in battle and he went to live in exile, attending the University of Paris, where he met and roomed with a much older, war-scarred fellow Basque named Iñigo from Loyola, whose family had fought against his. Nevertheless, the two got along, at least socially; the charming, athletic Francisco found his roommate's religious ardour ridiculous and argued with him for two years before Iñigo won him over, and he became one of the seven founders of the Company of Jesus in 1534 (*see* pp.197–8). Francisco was the most talented of the early Jesuits, and in 1540, Iñigo sent him on a mission to the Indies and Japan, where in the face of all obstacles (notably from European traders) he became the Church's most successful missionary since St Paul. He died en route to China in 1552, was canonized at the same time as St Ignatius, in 1622, and was later declared the apostle of Japan and the Indies, the patron saint of missionaries.

Although the **castle** is now a Jesuit college, you can take the tour and learn a lot, about both St Francis and castles – this one dates back to the 11th century, was wrecked in 1516 by Cardinal Cisneros'

Javier castle
t 94 888 40 24, www. santuariodejavier.org; open for guided visits daily 10–1.30 and 3.30–6.30; adm

troops, and was restored after 1952. Perhaps most fascinating is the fresco of the *Dance of Death*, a grim reminder that the Pyrenees were especially hard hit by the plague.

Leyre

Just north of Javier, at **Yesa**, the Río Aragón has been dammed to form the vast **Yesa Reservoir**. A road from Yesa leads up into the Sierra de Leyre and to the **Monasterio de San Salvador de Leyre**.

⭐ **Monasterio de San Salvador de Leyre**
t 94 888 41 50; www.hotelhospederia deleyre.com; open Mar–Oct Mon–Fri 10.15–2 and 3.30–7; Sat and Sun 10.15–2 and 4–7; Nov–Feb Mon–Fri 10.15–2 and 3.30–6; Sat and Sun 10.15–2 and 4–6.30; adm

Leyre in Basque means 'eagerness to overcome'. The monastery's foundation predates the Moors, and its abbots served as the first bishops of Pamplona. In the 8th century its most famous abbot, San Virila, so constantly prayed to heaven for a peek into infinity that he was granted his wish, by the lovely warbling of a bird. To the abbot, the vision was a sublime moment, but when he went down to tell his monks about it he found that his eternal second had lasted 300 years. He missed the precarious 9th century, when Leyre temporarily served as a refuge for the king of Pamplona from the Moors; the first kings of Navarra were buried there.

Located on the pilgrimage road branching in from Aragón, Leyre essentially dates from the 11th century, when Sancho the Great reformed the rule according to that of Cluny and declared it 'the centre and heart of my realm'. Abandoned in the 19th century, the monastery was reoccupied in 1950 by the Benedictines, who began a restoration programme that unfortunately obscures much of the older building. Visits begin in the startling, 11th-century crypt, where the first impression is that the church is sinking into the ground. The columns are runty little stubs of columns of unequal height weighed down by heavy block capitals, carved with simple geometric designs that stand at about chest level. The architect, it appears, was torn between the desire for ennobling capitals and columns and the need to provide the vaulting to support the chancel area above; a compromise perhaps only possible for an architect who never studied his classical proportions, although to us it may look like some postmodernist Romanesque Expressionist having fun with our perceptions. The chancel above was consecrated in 1057, modelled on a French Romanesque design from the Limousin, and supplemented two centuries later with a single-aisled nave; the effect is harmonious, light and austere, providing the perfect setting for the Benedictines' beautiful 7th-century **Gregorian chants**, still sung at matins and vespers. The bones of the first 10 kings of Navarra lie in a simple wooden casket behind a fine grille; the 13th-century statue of the Virgin of Leyre sits on the altar. The west portal, the **Porta Speciosa**, is finely carved with a mix of saints and monsters.

Gregorian chant
t 94 888 41 50; call to confirm times, but usually daily 7 pm and 9.15pm, plus at noon on Sun and special feast days

If Rip van Winkle legends don't faze you, it's a 10-minute walk up to the **Fountain of San Virila** for the magnificent view of the

09

Navarra | East of Pamplona: Sangüesa, Javier and Leyre

Where to Stay and Eat East of Pamplona

ⓘ **Agoitz >**
C/Nueva 22,
t 94 8 33 60 05,
www.aoiz.es

⭐ **Xabier >>**

ⓘ **Sangüesa >**
C/Mayor 2, t 94 887
14 11, www.sanguesa.es

Agoitz (Aoz) ✉ 31430

*****Hs Beti Jai**, C/Santa Águeda 2, t 94 833 60 52, www.beti-jai.com (€). A rural delight, with classically decorated rooms, an excellent restaurant (€€), and a traditional café-bar for drinks and tapas. You can also enjoy riverside views. *Closed Mon.*

Sangüesa ✉ 31400

**Yamaguchi, on the road to Javier, t 94 887 01 27, www.hotelyamaguchi.com (€€). A modern hotel with a pool, *frontón*, and a pleasant restaurant.

**Hostal Rural JP, Avda Padres Raimondo Lumbier 3, t 94 887 16 93, www.hotelruraljp.com (€). A handful of basic but spotless rooms and a café-bar. They also rent apartments.

Mediavilla, C/Alfonso El Batallador 15, t 94 887 02 12 (€). A Basque *asador* serving delicious charcoal-grilled fish and meat with local wine. *Closed Mon.*

Javier/Leyre ✉ 31411

****Hotel Señorio de Monjardín, Ctra de Leyre 4, t 94 888 41 88, www.hotelsenoriodemonjardin.com (€€). Large, modern hotel, 3km from Leyre on the N240, with some luxurious suites and a restaurant featuring Navarrese cuisine and game dishes.

***Xabier, Plaza de Javier, t 94 888 40 06, www.hotelxabier.com (€€). You can stay and eat next to the castle at this charming, historic hotel-restaurant, with balconies peeking through the ivy.

**El Mesón, t 94 888 40 35, www.hotelmeson.com (€€). Also next to the castle; pretty, but rather more basic. *Closed mid-Dec–mid-Feb.*

**Hospedería de Leyre, t 94 888 40 11, www.hotelhospederiadeleyre.com (€€). This charming former pilgrims' *hostal* at Leyre is the perfect antidote to stress; its restaurant specializes in traditional Navarrese cuisine.

artificial lake and the Navarrese countryside that the abbot contemplated during his prayers, although the warbling birds have been replaced by hang-gliding Spaniards. Nature is a big attraction in eastern Navarra. The Sierra de Leyre divides the Roncal and Salazar valleys (*see* pp.235–7), but there are two splendid gorges quite close at hand. The **Foz de Lumbier**, formed by the Irati river, has a pleasant riverside trail, and is a breeding site for griffon vultures and the rare red-beaked variety of chough. The even more spec-tacular, sheer-sided, 6km **Foz de Arbayún** (*see* p.237) lies further to the north along the Río Salazar, with more griffon and a few Egyptian vultures; both gorges are accessible from Lumbier.

Routes into France: Up the Valleys of the Pyrenees

The Navarrese Pyrenees don't win altitude records, but they're green, wooded and shot through with legends, many lingering in the mists around Roncesvalles, for centuries the pass most favoured by French pilgrims to Santiago. Much of Navarra's Basque population is concentrated in the three valleys of Roncal, Salazar and Baztán (divided in the *ley del vascuence*, or 'Basque law', of 1986 into three different linguistic zones). Seemingly every house in

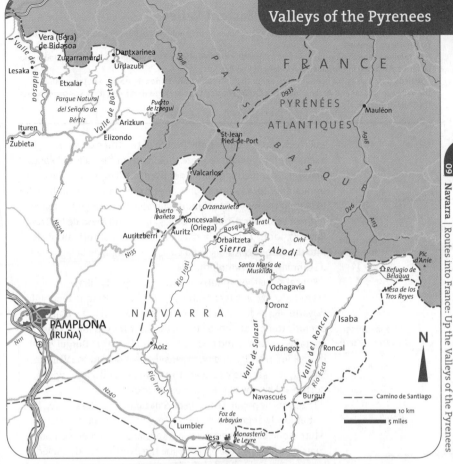

every hamlet is emblazoned with a coat of arms – for the Basques have traditionally considered themselves all equal and all noble.

The Eastern Valleys: Valle del Roncal and Valle de Salazar

Like many Pyrenean valleys, the Roncal was so remote for centuries that the central authorities were content to let it run its own show. Time has changed a few things: timber logged on its thickly forested slopes now travels by truck instead of careering down the Esca river, and the valley's renowned sheep's cheese, *queso de Roncal*, is now made in a factory (but according to farm traditions). Mist often envelops **Isaba**, the Valle del Roncal's biggest town, gathered under its fortress-church of San Cipriano (1540). Every 13 July since 1375, at stone frontier-marker no.262, the mayor of Isaba and his colleagues don traditional costume, march up to meet their counterparts from the Vallée de Barétous in France, and

Getting to and around the Eastern Valleys

There are no **trains** here, and in most cases the **buses** from Pamplona go only once a day; there is usually no service on Sundays.

La Tafallesa (**t** 94 870 09 79) buses go to the Valle del Roncal, with stops at Burgui, Roncal, Urzainqui and Uztárroz. For a **taxi** in the valley, call Vidángoz **t** 94 847 70 13.

Artieda (**t** 94 830 35 70) operates the service to Roncesvalles, and **Conda** (**t** 902 422 242) runs buses to the Valles de Salazar and Aezkoa, including Ochagavía and Orbaitzeta. **La Baztanesa** (**t** 94 858 01 29) serves the Valle de Baztán.

Refugio de Belagua
t 94 839 40 02

Casa-Museo Julián Gayarre
www.julian gayarre.com; open April–Sept Tues–Sun 11.30–1.30 and 5–7; Oct–Mar Sat–Sun 11.30–1.30 and 4–6; adm

✪ **Forest of Irati**

ask them three times for the 'Tribute of the Three Cows' in exchange for the right to graze their herds in the Valle del Roncal in August – something both sides used to kill for before the annual tribute was agreed on. Isaba provides an excellent base for exploring the magnificent mountain scenery: hike up the region's highest peaks, **Pic d'Anie** (8,200ft/2,500m) and **Mesa de los Tres Reyes** (7,900ft/2,408m), or make the most beautiful walk of all, into the Parque Natural Pirenaico to the **Refugio de Belagua**, set in a stunning glacial amphitheatre.

Roncal, once the capital of the valley, is a pretty village surrounded by pine forests. The great, amiable Basque tenor Julián Gayarre (1844–90) was born here and lies buried in a suitably high-operatic tomb just outside town; the **Casa-Museo Julián Gayarre** contains costumes and photos from his glory days. **Burgui**, south, has a Roman bridge and two roads that cut over to the Valle de Salazar: an easy one westward to Navascués and a narrow one northward by way of the remote village of Vidángoz.

The sparsely populated **Valle de Salazar** is much less visited but just as lovely, abubble with trout streams, beech forests and old white stone Basque *caserones*, or mansions, with their pompous coats of arms. The best of them line the riverfront and cobbled lanes in **Ochagavía**, the local metropolis and another good base for walks. An easy one is up to the 13th-century chapel of **Santa María de Muskilda**, topped by an unusual square tower with a round roof: its *romería* (pilgrimage) on 8 September is celebrated with some of Navarra's most ancient dances.

To the north, a road twists through the Sierra de Abodi to the snow-white hermitage of **Nuestra Señora de las Nieves** (1954): from here, trails of varying length and difficulty lead into the vast beech and ancient yew **Forest of Irati** (Bosque de Irati), the largest primeval forest in Spain, with majestic Mount Orhi (6,618ft/2,017m) as a backdrop. This is one of the richest wildlife habitats in the Pyrenees, full of red squirrels, deer and wild boar, with lesser populations of wild cat and beech marten. The area also contains a couple of real rarities: the white-backed woodpecker, found only where there are plenty of insect-ridden beech trees, and the endemic Pyrenean desman, an aquatic shrew with a nose like a dragon's snout. Besides the usual Basque fairy folk, the forest is haunted by a rather unexpected ghost: that of Jeanne d'Albret, queen of French Navarre and mother of Henri IV, a nasty, die-hard Protestant fanatic. Poisoned in 1572, Jeanne tours her old domain on windy nights with an escort of lovely Basque *lamiaks*, the mischievous nymphs with whom she never would have been caught dead while still alive. On the other side of the forest, the picturesque village of **Orbaitzeta** makes a good base; nearby, a dolmen called **Azpegi I** is surrounded by a circle of 123 stones.

In the south of the valley, the spectacular 1,000ft sheer-sided limestone gorge, the **Foz de Arbayún**, extends for 10km below the road, home to Spain's largest colonies of rare griffon vultures (*buitres leonados*), with their 8ft wing span, and an assortment of smaller eagles; you can nearly always spot them floating majestically around the roadside belvedere between Navascués and Lumbier.

Where to Stay and Eat in the Eastern Valleys

Navarra as a whole has made efforts to improve the provision of reasonably priced accommodation in rural areas: many are listed online at *www.turismonavarra.es*.

(i) **Roncal >**
Centro de Interpretación de la Naturaleza, **t** *94 847 52 56, www.roncal.es*

(★) **Casa Tetxe >>**

(i) **Ochagavía >>**
Centro Interpretación de la Naturaleza, on the main road, opposite the river, **t** *94 889 06 41, www.ochagavia.com*

Valle del Roncal ✉ 31680

There are several *casas rurales* in and around Roncal: visit the website *www.roncal-salazar.com* (Spanish only) or contact the tourist office. The website *www.toprural.com* is available in several languages. Most accommodation here is concentrated in Isaba, the largest village.

***Isaba, C/Bormapea 51, Isaba, **t** 94 889 30 00, *www.isabaha.com* (€€). A modern 'apart-hotel', offering apartments with kitchenettes for 2–4 people. Ideal for families.

*Hs Lola, C/Mendigatxa, Isaba, **t** 94 889 30 12, *www.hostal-lola.com* (€). Welcoming little place with comfy rooms, flower-filled balconies, and a decent restaurant.

Pensión Txiki, C/Mendigatxa 17, Isaba, **t** 94 889 31 18, *www.pensiontxiki.com* (€). Plain rooms in a pretty, white-washed building in the centre of the village. The traditional restaurant (€) serves good local cuisine.

*Hotel Ezkaurre, C/Garagardoia 14, Isaba, **t** 94 889 33 03, *http://*

hotelezkaurre.es (€).This classic mountain *hostal* has basic rooms and serves dinners to non-guests during the summer months.

Casa Estanislao, C/Izarjentea, Isaba, **t** 94 889 34 50, *http://casaestanislao. com* (€). Pintxos, regional dishes, *platos combinados*, and set menus.

*Hs Zaltua, C/Castillo 23, Roncal, **t** 94 847 50 08 (€). A friendly whitewashed *hostal* with simple rooms and a lovely dining room.

Casa Tetxe, C/Iriondoa 63, Roncal, **t** 94 847 50 98 (€). A charming *casa rural* in a traditional stone-built house, with B&B accommodation and a small organic farm. Meals are served with two days' notice.

Ochagavía ✉ 31680

Most accommodation in the Salazar valley is in *casas rurales*.

Auñamendi, Plaza Gurpide 1, **t** 94 889 01 89, *www.hostalauniamendi.com* (€€–€). As well as offering rooms, this place serves good local cuisine. *Closed mid-Sept–mid-Oct.*

Hs Salazar, C/Mayor s/n, Oronz, **t 94 889 00 53, *www.hostalsalazar. com* (€). Traditional chalet-style hotel just south of Ochagavía, with an outdoor Jacuzzi and pretty views.

*Hs Orialde, C/Urrutia 6, **t** 94 889 07 42, *www.hostalorialde.com* (€). A welcoming 12-room inn in a former farmhouse by the river.

Casa Ballent, t 94 889 03 73 (€). One of the best, with just three cosy bedrooms, a welcoming owner and views from the terrace over the Pyrenees and the vegetable patch.
Casa Sarbide I and **II, t** 94 889 03 42, *www.casasarbide.com* (€). A guest room with private bathroom and lots

of character; they also rent out a *casa rural* which sleeps four.

Orbaitzeta ✉ 31670
Casa Sastrarena, C/San Juan, **t** 94 876 60 93 (€). Offers modern rooms with private bath and a little garden in the heart of this pretty village.

Roncesvalles (Orreaga)

Of all the passes over the Pyrenees, introverted Roncesvalles ('Bramble Valley') is the most renowned, thanks to the *camino francés* to Compostela (*see* pp.49–50). French pilgrims would mumble verses from the *Chanson de Roland* as they paid their respects to the sites associated with Charlemagne and his nephew Roland, then say their first prayer to another gallant knight, Santiago. From Roncesvalles' Colegiata it's 781km to Santiago, a distance the fittest pilgrims could cover in 20 days.

Not so long ago the Colegiata had a sad, has-been look. Although in the 18th century, Roncesvalles still counted 30,000 passing pilgrims a year, numbers fell dramatically in the 19th century. Most of the monasteries and churches along the route were closed forever with the national confiscation of church lands in 1837; many were converted into stables or pillaged for their building stone. By the 1970s, the medieval floods of pilgrims had dried to a trickle of eccentrics.

But just when it seemed that the pilgrimage was ready to be pushed into Europe's closet of forgotten traditions, it came roaring back. A number of factors seem to be involved – modern disillusionment with conventional religion, the restless search for something beyond the routine of over-organized day-to-day lives and, more prosaically, the growth of ecological and alternative tourism. In 1982, John Paul II became the first pope ever to visit Santiago, followed in 2010 by Benedict XVI; in 1985, UNESCO declared this the 'Foremost Cultural Route in Europe', helping to fund the restoration of the churches that punctuate the trail. Although modern roads have changed the face of the *camino francés* for ever, efforts have been made to create alternative paths for pedestrians, marked with scallop shells, and *hostales* have sprouted along the way for walkers or cyclists. No one predicted that the number of pilgrims who stopped to have their documents stamped in Roncesvalles would grow by thousands each year. The pilgrims' quest is back in business; Shirley MacLaine has done it and written a book about her experience, and it has even been the subject of a 2011 Hollywood movie, *The Way*.

The three main pilgrims' routes through France converged at Saint-Jean-Pied-de-Port and then continued up to the busy frontier

Roland the Rotter

All over the Pyrenees you'll find memories of Roland – from the Brèche de Roland in the High Pyrenees, hewn with a mighty stroke of his sword Durandal, to a menhir on Mount Aralar that he tossed like Obelix. From here, his fame spread across Europe, remembered in everything from Ariosto's Renaissance epic *Orlando Furioso* to the ancient, mysterious statue of 'Roland the Giant' that stands in front of Bremen city hall.

But who is this Roland really? Outside of the *Chanson de Roland*, information is scarce. The chronicler Einhard, writing c. 830, mentions a certain Roland, duke of the Marches of Brittany – who perished in the famous ambush in the Pyrenees in 778 – without according him any particular importance. But two hundred years later this obscure incident had blossomed into one of the great epics of medieval Europe. Here is the mighty hero, with his wise friend and companion-in-arms Oliver. Here is the most puissant knight in the army of his uncle Charlemagne, come down from the north to crusade against the heathen Muslims of Spain. Charlemagne sweeps all before him, occupying many lands south of the Pyrenees and burning Pamplona to the ground before coming to grief at the unsuccessful siege of Zaragoza. On their return, Roland and Oliver and the peers of the rearguard are trapped at the pass of Roncesvalles, thanks to a tip from Roland's jealous stepfather Ganelon. Numberless hordes of Muslims overwhelm the French; though outnumbered, they cut down Moors by the thousands, like General Custer or John Wayne against the savage Injuns. Finally Roland, cut with a thousand wounds, smites his sword Durandal against the rock, meaning to keep it from the hands of the infidels (although in the *Chanson* he ends up heaving it into the air, whereupon it finally ends up stuck in the cliff at Rocamadour, a major site on the pilgrims' road in southwest France). He then sounds his horn Oliphant to warn Charlemagne, alas too far away to rescue them, puffing so hard that he blows his brains out, as Michael and Gabriel appear to escort his soul to heaven.

History says it wasn't a Muslim horde at all, but rather the Navarrese Basques who did Roland in. And why shouldn't they get their revenge on these uncouth Franks who were devastating their land, trying to force this democratic nation to kneel before some crowned foreign thug who called himself their king? We might excuse a people who did not even have a word in their language for 'king' if they were not much impressed with Charlemagne.

How this affair metamorphosed into an epic at the turn of the last millennium, or how the caterpillar Roland of history re-emerged as the mythological butterfly in the *Chanson*, is murky, but as with most epics it involved a modicum of propaganda. The immediate source of the *Chanson* is said to have been a famous vision of Roland given to an 11th-century archbishop of Pamplona, which transformed Basque farmers into infidel knights (just in time for the Crusades). For the French there was another bonus: glorification of Carolingian imperialism provided poetic justification for the expansionist dreams of the Capetian kings.

town of **Valcarlos**, the 'carlos' in its name referring to Charlemagne, who was camped here when he heard the dying Roland's horn blast. From here, the road winds up through lush greenery to Roncesvalles, where the 12th-century **church of Sancti Spiritus** (the 'Silo de Charlemagne',) is said to have been first built as Roland's tomb. According to legend, by the time the emperor arrived, not only were Roland and the peers dead, but so were all the Saracens; since he couldn't tell who was who (poor Charlemagne – his legends always make him seem as thick as a pudding), he asked heaven for a sign to make sure he gave all the Franks a Christian burial, and all at once the Christian corpses looked up to heaven, with red roses sprouting from their lips. Equally unlucky pilgrims were laid in the 7th-century **ossuary** underneath the church; according to Aymery Picaud (*see* p.50), many were done in by 'false

Santiago
open summer daily 10–2 and 3.30–7; winter except Jan daily 10–2 and 3.30–5; Jan Thurs–Tues 10.30–2.30, closed Wed; adm

pilgrims', mostly locals. Adjacent, the tiny church of **Santiago** is a plain Gothic chapel from the 13th century.

Set back from the road, at the foot of the pass, the **Colegiata de Roncesvalles** is a French-style Gothic church consecrated in 1219, which replaced the first Colegiata, built up at Puerto Ibañeta in 1112 and abandoned by the frostbitten monks after five ghastly winters. What was originally the frzont of the Colegiata caved in under the snow in 1600 (hence the incongruous corrugated zinc roof on the rest) and was replaced by a **cloister**, from where you can pop into the 14th-century **chapterhouse** to see the stained glass (1960) showing a scene from the 1212 Battle of Las Navas de Tolosa, where Sancho VII 'the Strong' led the Navarrese to their great victory over the Moors. The chains in the chapel are among those that bound 10,000 slaves at the ankle and wrist, forming a human shield around the emir's tent, a scurvy tactic that failed to prevent the Christians from leaping over and carrying off the tent as booty. The chapterhouse holds the tomb of Sancho the Strong. Apparently, in life the king was exactly as tall as his 7ft 4in effigy: pilgrims used to think that his battle maces, now in the museum, belonged to Roland. Sancho financed the Colegiata, which over time has been stripped of its costly gifts, with the exception of a much revered 13th-century image of the Virgin under her baldachin. Its jumbled, anachronistic, pious legend goes that after the battle at the pass, Charlemagne founded a monastery up at Ibañeta. When the Moors poured through to attack France in 732, the monks hid the statue, and it remained hidden until 1130, when the hiding place was revealed to a Basque shepherd by a red stag with a star shimmering between its antlers.

Museum
open daily 10–2 and 3.30–7; adm

The fascinating **museum** contains such rarefied medieval treasures as the emerald which fell from the emir's turban when giant King Sancho burst into his tent at Las Navas de Tolosa (surely a sight enough to scare the emerald off anybody); an 11th-century *pyx*, or golden box used to hold the Host; and a reliquary of gold and enamel (*c.* 1350) called 'Charlemagne's chessboard' for its 32 little cases, each designed to hold a saintly fingertip or tooth. Among the paintings there's an excellent 15th-century Flemish triptych and a *Holy Family* by Morales, and two books on Confucianism, purchased in India in the time of St Francis Xavier.

An easy and beautiful path from the monastery leads up in half-an-hour to the **Puerto Ibañeta** (3,150ft/960m), from where the Basques, hidden on Mounts Astobizkar and Orzanzurieta, dropped boulders on the heads of the Franks. A modern chapel replaces the monastery of San Salvador, where the monks would toll a bell to guide pilgrims through the mists and snowstorms. Heading south, the pretty villages of **Auritz** (**Burguete**) and **Auritzberri** (**Espinal**) were the pilgrims' next stops and are still good places to stay.

Where to Stay and Eat in Roncesvalles

(i) **Roncesvalles >**
Antiguo Molino,
t 94 876 03 01,
www.roncesvalles.es

Roncesvalles ✉ 31650

If you have no luck at any of the places listed below, then try one of several *casas rurales* in the vicinity.

Hs Loizu, Avda Roncesvalles 7, in Auritz (3km from Roncesvalles), **t 94 876 00 08, *www.loizu.com* (€€). A pretty, two-hundred-year-old hotel-restaurant with plenty of atmosphere.

Hostal Burguete, C/Única s/n, Auritz, **t 94 876 00 05, *www. hotelburguete.com* (€). Whenever Hemingway decamped to the Pyrenees, he stayed here. Though its elegance is mostly faded, this antique-bedecked old place is still a great choice for slumming it in style.

*Hs Casa Sabina, **t** 94 876 00 12, *www.casasabina.es* (€). By the monastery, with four pleasant rooms and good Navarrese cooking. They also run the **Hotel Roncesvalles** (€€).

Hs La Posada, **t 94 876 02 25, *www.laposadaderoncesvalles.com* (€). Charming, with spacious rooms in the Colegiata, and a fine **restaurant** (€€) in the medieval inn which formerly served the pilgrims.

Western Valleys: Valle de Baztán and Valle de Bidasoa

Frequent rains off the Atlantic make these valleys so lush that they're called the 'Switzerland of Navarra'. Both are dotted with well-preserved, unspoiled white Basque villages, trout streams and quietly beautiful scenery. One of the best-known smugglers' routes ran from the caves of Sare, just over the border in France, to the caves of Zugarramurdi; it still makes a pretty and easy walk today.

But what **Zugarramurdi** is most famous for is its role as the Salem of the Basque lands. The **Valle de Baztán** once had Spain's largest Agote population (*see* pp.231–2) and perhaps not entirely coincidentally a supposed colony of witches in the early 17th century, based in Zugarramurdi, 'the Hill of Elms', a pretty place just in from the French frontier. As in Salem, the witchcraft scare began with the dubious confessions of a young woman in 1608, and spread like wildfire from denunciation to denunciation in a kind of mass hysteria. It wasn't long before 10 witches had confessed to a whole slew of heinous crimes, taking responsibility for nearly every death and trouble in Zugarramurdi that had occurred over the past 50 years. According to Basque law, they were tried and pardoned. Then the Inquisition, based in Logroño, got wind of it. Thirty-one hapless souls, mostly women and children, were arrested and 'put to the question' in 1609; of those condemned, 13 died under torture, and six, who refused to confess, survived to be burned alive at an *auto-da-fé*. Another 11 were burned the following year. That year, the Inquisition claimed to have discovered 1,590 witches in Navarra alone. No one really knows how many died. The village's **Museo de las Brujas**, in a restored hospital, tells their tale.

Museo de las Brujas
Behitiko Karrika 22,
t 94 859 90 04;
mid-July–mid-Sept
Tues–Sun 11–7.30;
mid-Sept–mid-July
Wed–Fri 11–6.30,
Sat–Sun 11–7; adm

Cuevas de Zugarramurdi
www.turismo zugarramurdi.com,
t 94 859 91 70;
open summer daily
9–dusk; adm

Just outside the village, carved out of the mountain by the *Infernuko Erreka* ('Hell's Stream'), the vast **Cuevas de Zugarramurdi** were the scene of black sabbaths, or *akelarres*, in which the participants smeared themselves with an unguent made of human brains and bones – mixed with belladonna, toads, salamanders and snakes – and flew through the night to join in outrageous orgies with a Satanic black billy goat, *akerbeltz* – at least according to the confessions extracted by the Inquisitors.

Basque witchcraft enjoyed a revival in the post-Franco 1970s, when the cult was seen either as a feminist revolt against an oppressive male-dominated society and religion, or as an instance of pocket survivals of the old pagan beliefs, demonized by the Church, perhaps even practised as underground rituals of Basque solidarity. Whatever the case, the inhabitants of Zugarramurdi have decided that it was all a splendid excuse for a hugely popular *Sorginak Besta* (Fiesta of Witches), to dress up and party on the Saturday closest to the summer solstice, and thousands still gather in the caves for an old-fashioned re-enactment of an *akelarre*, complete with all kinds of philtres and magic potions.

Even older magic was built into the **cromlechs**, dedicated to the Basque goddess Mari, reached by a path from the village. There are other caves, including the lovely stalactite **Cuevas de Urdax** just south at Urdazubi/Urdax, where fish-tailed *lamiaks* once frolicked in the stream, or perhaps still do when no one's looking; guided tours run roughly every 20 minutes in the summer.

Elizondo, one of the prettiest villages in the Baztán valley, has an informal tourist office where you can pick up a map that pinpoints the historic houses: those along the river are especially impressive. **Arizkun**, 7km northeast, has the fortified stone house of one of Spain's busiest *conquistadores*, Pedro de Ursúa, leader of the search for El Dorado up the Amazon in 1560 when he was killed by rebel leader Lope de Aguirre (*see* pp.194–5). The parish church has a striking Baroque façade. Further north a road turns east to France by way of the spectacular **Izpegui pass**.

Izpegui pass
Accessible during summer only

Navarra's westernmost Pyrenean valley, the **Valle de Bidasoa**, embraces streams filled with salmon and trout and, more prosaically, the main San Sebastián–Pamplona road. Bus services in the area offer a chance to visit charming old Basque villages such as **Bera (Vera) de Bidasoa**, only a couple of miles from the French frontier, with the former summer home of Basque novelist and doctor Pío Baroja (1872–1956). A member of the Generation of '98, Pío Baroja was a firm supporter of the Republic from the beginning (*Memorias de un hombre de acción*), but he was also fascinated by Basque witchcraft, and made it a feature of one of his novels, *La Dama de Urtubi*. **Lesaka**, equally pretty, claims one of the best-preserved fortified feudal houses in Navarra. Tiny **Etxalar (Echalar)**, a hamlet that time forgot, is on a stream on the pretty, seldom-used road to Zugarramurdi – seldom used except in October, during the annual wild pigeon and woodcock holocaust. The church at Etxalar is surrounded by 100 Basque funerary steles with their distinctive solar symbol discs.

Parque Natural del Señorío de Bértiz
t 94 859 24 21, www. parquedebertiz.es; open summer daily 10–8; winter daily 10–6

Farther south, the **Parque Natural del Señorío de Bértiz**, a former private estate, has foot, bicycle and riding paths through thousands of acres of oak, beech and chestnut forests; the gardens near the manor boast over 120 species of exotic trees. Note the coat of arms of the lord of Bértiz, showing a mermaid holding a mirror and comb; Charles III ordered her to be placed there in 1421 in honour of his ambassador, Micheto de Bértiz.

Two villages just west of here, **Zubieta** and **Ituren**, are famous for a late-January ritual ushering in spring that could have been invented by Dr Seuss: young unmarried men and boys (starting as young as five) called *joaldunaks* dress up in dunce's caps and lacey smocks or sheepskins and fasten a pair of copper *polunpaks* (giant bells) to their backs with an intricate network of laces. Thus arrayed, for two days the *joaldunaks* make a *zanpantzar*, a group of 20 or so, who dance and march from village to village across the frosty land, their *polunpaks* clanging with deep resonance as they go along. It is all very serious, and this is one of those occasions when the Basques show their great age. The *joaldunaks* with their sheepskins and bells have a very close counterpart in the *Mamuthones* of Mamoiada, who perform a similar function in Sardinia, the Italian island whose people are nearly as long in the tooth.

Sports and Activities in the Western Valleys

ⓘ **Zugarramurdi »**
in the Museo de las Brujas, t 94 859 90 04, www.turismo zugarramurdi.com

Sports and Activities in the Western Valleys

The old **smugglers' path** to Sare is easy to follow and waymarked with silhouettes of the little Basque horse, the *pottok*.

Orbela, at the Albergue Beintza, Beintza-Labaien ✉ 31753, t 94 845 00 14, *orbela@alberguesnavarra.com*. Treks, mountain-biking, potholing and other activities.

BKZ, at the Albergue Bertiz Aterpea in Narbarte, t 94 859 23 22, *bkz@navarraaventura.com*. White-water rafting and canoeing trips, suitable for all levels.

Where to Stay and Eat in the Western Valleys

Zugarramurdi ✉ 31710

Alzatenea, C/Basaburua 3, t 948 59 91 87 (€). Charming restaurant: roast meats cooked over a wood fire.

Urdazubi ✉ 31711

Hostal Irigoienea, C/Salvador, t 94 859 92 67, *www.irigoienea.com* (€€). This old, whitewashed Navarrese farmhouse furnished with a handful of antiques is a charming place to stay.

Restaurante La Koska, C/San Salvador, 4, t 94 859 90 42 (€€). Traditional Navarra fare is served in this long-established, family-run restaurant. *Closed Mon, and mid-Dec to mid-Jan.*

Elizondo ✉ 31700

ⓘ **Elizondo »**
Palacio de Arizkunenea, t 94 858 12 79

Señorío de Ursúa, Caserio Ikazatea, Arizkun, t 94 845 35 00, *www.hotelursua.com* (€€). Sumptuous rooms and a fine restaurant in this beautifully renovated 17th-century Basque farmhouse.

***Baztán, on the main road, **t** 94 858 00 50, *www.hotelbaztan.com* (€€). Modern, with panoramic views, two pools (one for children) and a garden.

Hs Saskaitz, C/María Azpilijueta 10, **t 94 858 04 88 (€€€–€€). Cosy and calm, despite being in the centre of town.

 Casa Rural Urruska >

Casa Rural Urruska, 10km away in Barrio de Bearzún, **t** 94 845 21 06, *www.urruska.com* (€€). This B&B is a real charmer. Simple but solid home cooking is served, and kids can help feed the livestock and collect eggs.

Casa Galartza, C/Santiago 1, **t** 94 858 01 01 (€). A rival to Roncal's offerings, this haven of traditional Baztánian cuisine and cheese serves tender lamb chops and local vegetables.

Bera (Vera) de Bidasoa⊠ 31780

Hotel Churrut, Plaza de los Fueros 2, **t** 94 862 55 40, *www.hotelchurrut.com* (€€). A chic rural hotel, with antique-filled rooms in a rosy-pink 18th-century building surrounded by woods and gardens. It also has a great restaurant.

The Pays Basque

Of all the départements of France, number 64 is the one with the most remarkable split personality. Béarn, occupying the eastern half of the département, is a resolutely Gascon province, redolent of garlic and castles and good Jurançon wine; it has personality enough of its own. But cross the Gave d'Oloron, a national boundary that does not appear on any map, and you enter an entirely different world: specifically, the Pays Basque, or North Euskadi as the Basques prefer to call it.

10

Don't miss

⭐ **A delicious medieval town**
Bayonne **p.263**

⭐ **Belle Epoque and beaches**
Biarritz **p.254**

⭐ **Sun, sand and seafood**
St-Jean-de-Luz **p.249**

⭐ **The high mountain gateway to Spain**
St-Jean-Pied-de-Port **p.277**

⭐ **Isolation and tradition**
Ste-Engrâce **p.280**

See map overleaf

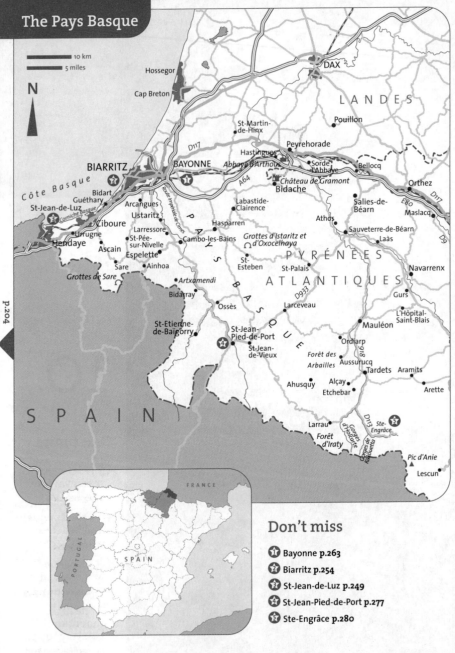

Don't miss

The three little provinces in France are laid out in vertical stripes across the western half of the Pyrénées-Atlantiques: first, coastal Labourd (from Lapurdum, the Roman name of Bayonne), a delightful land full of beautiful villages, which also includes Bayonne and Biarritz, where Basques have long been a minority, and with a string of resorts that the French tourist office has dubbed the Côte Basque; next, inland, Basse-Navarre (Behe-Nafarroa), with Pyrenean valleys in the south and hard-working farmers in the humble lowlands; and finally, the even humbler Soule (Zuberoa) around Mauléon, the most isolated Basque province, with a mere 16,000 inhabitants, last guardian of a unique dialect and old folk ways lost elsewhere.

The Basques, whose territory once extended to Bordeaux, have been losing ground in France ever since Roman times, and they worry that unless drastic measures are taken, especially in teaching Euskera to the young, they may vanish altogether. If the results of a recent survey, taken after the government's unprecedented proposal to grant an autonomy statute to Corsica, are any indication, two centuries of centralization policies and the comforts of the French social system have succeeded in dividing opinion on the future direction of the Pays Basque. A majority still favour their own *département basque* (as promised by Mitterrand over three decades ago) and mandatory bilingual schooling, yet the survey also found that only 22 per cent of the Basques considered themselves Basque first, before French or European.

Whether this might change, thanks to the recent revival of Basque culture and media inspired by the renaissance over the border, remains to be seen. Nationalist feeling remains strongest in the countryside, where the percentage of Euskera-speakers remains high. We met one nationalist supporter in Basse-Navarre, a young mechanic on his way to a ping-pong tournament. With an earnest look in his eyes, he told us: 'They'll never let the Basque lands unite, because together we would be stronger than either France or Spain.' A marvellous people.

The Côte Basque

Hendaye (Hendaia) and Urrugne

A booming resort and the border crossing-point into Spain, **Hendaye** is divided into two distinct units, the old town, and **Hendaye-Plage** on the coast. Hendaye's border location on the River Bidassoa puts it in the news every century or so. There is a small, uninhabited island in the Bidassoa called the **Ile des Faisans** (also known as Ile de la Conférence) that belongs to neither country; a traditional meeting place for kings and ministers since the 1400s, it is still under an unusual joint administration – the Spanish watch over it from February to July, the French the rest of the year. Here in 1526, King François Ier was returned after a year of imprisonment, when he was captured in battle at Pavia, Italy, by the Spanish king and Holy Roman Emperor Charles V. In 1659, the

Treaty of the Pyrenees was signed here, and the following year representatives of both sides came back to plan the marriage of Louis XIV and María Teresa. A special pavilion was erected for the occasion and decorated by Velázquez – who caught a bad cold doing the job, which eventually killed him. And then in October 1940, Hendaye's train station was the scene of the famous meeting between Hitler and Franco. Hitler had come down in his private rail car to bluster the Caudillo into joining the war; later he said he would rather have his teeth pulled out than talk to such a stubborn character again.

The **beach** is long and broad, though as a resort Hendaye can't match the charm of the other towns along the Côte Basque. The old town offers nothing particularly special to draw you out of your way, and the beach area is a bland place lined with old villas, gradually being replaced by concrete hotels, the preserve of family vacations. Occasionally, tours are offered at the **Château Antoine d'Abbadie**, an eccentric Disneyland-Gothic castle set on a hill at the southern end of the beach. It was built by Viollet-le-Duc for an Irish-born traveller son of a Basque family named Antoine d'Abbadie who spent a lot of time in Ethiopia; there's a large collection of mementos from that country, an observatory and **Le Domaine**, an exotic 110-acre park. The villa is covered with inscriptions in Amharic and Gaelic.

Château Antoine d'Abbadie
t 05 59 20 04 51, www.chateau-abbadia.fr; open for guided visits 24 Jan–April Mon–Sat 2–6 (also Sun during school holidays); May–3 July Mon–Fri 10–12 and 2–6, Sat–Sun 2–6; 3 July–28 Aug daily 10–6 (until 9pm 18 July–21 Aug); 29 Aug–2 Oct Mon–Fri 10–12 and 2–6, Sat–Sun 2–6; 3 Oct–Dec Mon–Sat 2–6 (also Sun during school holidays); adm; last visits depart one hour before closing

Heading into the Pays Basque from Hendaye, you have a choice of either the coastal road, the scenic Corniche Basque (the D912), or else the more inland N10 or the motorway; these two pass through **Urrugne**, where the church of **St-Vincent** has a Renaissance portal with some excellent reliefs, which were damaged somewhat by English artillery in 1814. Note the famous if somewhat gloomy inscription on the tower's sundial: *vulnerant omnes*, *ultima necat*, referring to the hours – 'each one wounds, the last one kills'. Inside, there is more good sculptural work, notably on the bishop's chair, supported by a figure the locals call 'Samson'; they say if you pull his nose you will grow strong, and you can bet all the aspiring Basque barrel-lifters and wagon-pullers stop in to visit. The **Château d'Urtubie** was the home of the medieval viscounts of the Labourdan. The castle in its present incarnation dates from the 1340s, though each century until the Revolution added its bits and pieces; Wellington made it his headquarters briefly in 1814. The interior has some impressive 17th–18th-century furnishings, and a fine set of Flemish tapestries. There's a tea room and restaurant.

Château d'Urtubie
t 05 59 54 31 15, www.chateaudurtubie.net; open mid-July–Aug daily 10.30–6.30; April–mid-July and Sept–Oct daily 10.30–12.30 and 2–6.30; adm

From the village, a winding road leads up to the pilgrimage chapel of **Notre-Dame-de-Socorri**, with views over the mountains; it's a lovely spot for a picnic (though it may be disconcerting to know that nearly all the souls sleeping in the chapel's oak-shaded cemetery were victims of cholera epidemics).

Market Days in Hendaye

Hendaye: Wednesdays and Saturdays.

Where to Stay and Eat in Hendaye and Urrugne

(i) **Hendaye** >
12 Rue des Aubépines,
t 05 59 20 00 34,
www.hendaye-
tourisme.fr

Hendaye ✉ 64700

Rather less attractive than Biarritz or St-Jean, Hendaye is correspondingly less posh.

***Hôtel Serge Blanco, Bd de la Mer, t 05 59 51 35 35, www.thalassoblanco.com (€€€). Named for the famous Basque rugby star, with a thalasso-therapy centre (complete with doctors and beauticians), gym, pool and restaurant on the beach.

***Hôtel Villa Goxoa, 32 Avenue des Magnolias, t 05 59 20 32 43,

(★) **Hôtel Villa Goxoa** >

http://villa-goxoa.com (€€). Elegant little villa, with just nine charming rooms furnished with contemporary design, and a pool.

**Lafon, 99 Bd de la Mer, t 05 59 20 04 67, www.hotel-lafon.com (€€). Friendly, family-run option facing the sea. With restaurant and café-bar.

**Santiago, 29 Rue Santiago, t 05 59 20 00 94 (€). One of the least expensive hotels, with a garden, bar and restaurant.

Lieu Dit Vin, Route de Behobie 3, t 05 59 20 67 09, www.eguiazabal.com (€€). Stylish, bottle-lined French bistro and wine bar, with inventive dishes prepared with market-fresh ingredients: they can also be served as *pintxos* with a glass of wine.

Urrugne ✉ 64122

***Chez Maïté, Place de la Mairie, t 05 59 24 95 50 (€€–€). Comfortable village inn with seven rooms on the main square with a good restaurant.

Ecoparc
t 05 59 54 84 95, www.
ecoparc-urrugne.com;
open July and Aug daily
10–7; April–June and
Sept–Oct Tues–Sun
10–7; adm

Just outside Urrugne, no one who likes gardens will want to miss the **Ecoparc**, which has opened in a corner of the sadly neglected old Parc Florénia (once one of the loveliest gardens in southeast France). The Ecoparc currently covers 18 hectares of verdant countryside, although there are plans to extend it further, and contains more than three kilometres of trails through woodland groves and elegant gardens. Note that picnics are not allowed, which seems a shame, although there is a café-bar (and a little shop selling organic products) on site.

St-Jean-de-Luz

St-Jean-de-Luz

For those who do not naturally gravitate towards the sun and fun of the beach, a seaside resort needs a certain special, intangible quality. Like the theatre, a good resort must be able to make one suspend one's disbelief. In all of southern France there are very few places that can do this: one is Collioure on the Mediterranean, another St-Jean-de-Luz. The name is perfect. Light and colour can be extraordinary here, illuminating an immaculately white Basque town and acres of glistening rose-silver seafood that its restaurants roll out on tables to lure in customers. Even in the Basque Lands, St-Jean's cooks are renowned for their skill and imagination. The beaches are fine and, best of all, this is not the sort of town to have entirely succumbed to the tourist tide; the fishermen on the quay still strut around as if they own the place. What more could you ask?

Getting around St-Jean-de-Luz

There is a **tourist train** that leaves from the Rond Point du Port, **t** 05 59 41 96 94.
Free **shuttle buses** ply the streets in summer, and link St-Jean-de Luz with Ciboure.

Unfortunately, the name really has nothing to do with light (*luz* in Spanish). Gradgrind etymologists have traced it back to a Celtic or Latin word *louth* or *lutum*, meaning mud, the same as Paris's original name, Lutetia – Mudville. St-Jean, or rather Donihane Lohitzun, as the Basques know it, grew up in a swampy nowhere that just happened to have a good harbour. It began to thrive as a fishing port when the River Adour started silting up the harbour of Bayonne in the Middle Ages. The Luziens shared fully in the French Basques' whaling and buccaneering adventures until the Revolution. It's tuna and sardines they're after now – and tourists.

The Port

A casual visitor could walk around St-Jean all day and never spot it had a beach, but it's a good one, long and deep, tucked away on the northern side of town; it is protected by a jetty, and very safe for swimming. At its centre is the lavish **casino**, built in 1924.

St-Jean naturally turns its face to the port, lined with blue, red and green fishing boats, and a broad quay where the fishermen spread their nets; St-Jean is home to the biggest tuna fleet in France. There will be boats offering excursions around the area, or to the Spanish coast. Some, like the *Nivelle*, also offer deep-sea-fishing trips. Behind the port is the town hall and the adjacent **Maison de Louis XIV**, where the Roi Soleil stayed for his wedding. It is a typical Basque townhouse, built in 1643. You can also visit the nearby **Maison de l'Infante**, where the Infanta stayed.

From the port, the main stem, pedestrian Rue Gambetta, takes you to **St-Jean Baptiste**, largest and greatest of all the Basque churches to be found in France, where Louis XIV and María Teresa were married. The church is a lesson in Basque subtlety, plain and bright outside, and plain and bright within; any Baptist or Methodist would feel at home here. The aesthetic is in the detail, especially the wonderful wooden ceiling formed like the hull of a ship, and the three levels of wooden galleries around both sides of the nave, carved with all the art and sincerity the local artisans could manage. The church was begun in the 1300s, but such wooden galleries do not last for ever, no matter how well made; this latest version, probably much like those that preceded it, was completed in the 1860s. Another feature, also typical of Basque churches such as this, is the ornate gilded altarpiece, dripping with Baroque detail. The main door of the church was sealed up after Louis and María Teresa passed through it on their wedding day.

Nivelle
http://croisiere-saintjeandeluz.com; trips between April and mid-Oct

Maison de Louis XIV
Place Louis XIV, t 05 59 26 01 56, www.maison-louis-xiv.fr; open for guided tours only; July and Aug daily 10.30–12 and 2.30–6.30; June and Sept–mid-Oct visits at 11, 3, 4 and 5; Easter week and last week of Oct (Toussaint) visits at 11, 3 and 5; adm; last tour departs 30mins before closing

Maison de l'Infante
open mid-June–mid-Oct and 25 Oct–11 Nov Mon 2.30–6.30, Tues–Sat 11–12.30 and 2.30–6.30; closed Mon am, Sun

St-Jean – Petit Paris

It was a party to remember, and without its tourists St-Jean would be left only with the memory of that one glorious month when it seemed the centre of the world. In 1659, Spain and France signed the Treaty of the Pyrenees, putting an end to a century and a half of almost continuous hostility. To ice the deal, a marriage was arranged between Louis XIV and the Spanish infanta, María Teresa. Preparations went on for a year, and this obscure whaling and fishing port, roughly halfway between Paris and Madrid, was chosen as the venue. In May 1660, *everybody* came to St-Jean, including nearly the entire French court. 'Monsieur' (Louis's neurotic brother) and Cardinal Mazarin were there; the 'Grande Mademoiselle' (Louis' flamboyant cousin) and her lover floated down, and all the dandies and popinjays of Versailles followed in their wake. Louis himself arrived last, in a gilded carriage. One observer, Madame de Motteville, marvelled at how everyone was covered in lace and feathers and tassels. So were the horses. It reminded her of King Cyrus and ancient Persia.

Years before, a gypsy fortune-teller had predicted that peace between France and Spain would finally come 'with a whale'. And, on the day that María Teresa and the Spaniards arrived in St-Jean, a great whale was sighted just off the harbour. The courtiers rushed to the shore to watch the town's seamen give chase. Young Louis, however, took the opportunity to barge in on his future bride in her chambers; he surprised her *en déshabillé* and they had an intimate lunch together. For the wedding, there were Basque dancers, mock naval battles offshore, a bullfight and a grand ball in the main square, now Place Louis XIV, illuminated with thousands of candles and torches. Louis and his bride lived happily ever after (though the France Louis ruled suffered greatly); when the queen died, Louis remarked that her death was 'the only chagrin she ever caused me'. The peace with Spain has lasted up to the present, save for the unfortunate interlude of Napoleon. As for the whale, they caught it, and the bishop of Bayonne, who performed the wedding ceremony, took the tongue and fat of it back to Bayonne.

Messe des Corsaires
the tourist office has the dates

These days, on special occasions the church hosts a *messe des Corsaires* – a service sponsored not by pirates, but by St-Jean's confraternities dedicated to 'the defence of the sardine, tuna and anchovy'. There's nothing fishy about the Mass, however, which is famous for the beauty of its Basque choral music.

Ecomusée de la Tradition Basque
t 05 59 51 06 06; open July–Aug daily 10–6.30; April–June and Sept–Oct Mon–Sat 9.30–11.30 and 2.30–5.30, Sun 2.30–5.30; adm

On the edge of the town, just off the RN10, you can find out about Basque traditions, language, costumes, music and crafts at a Basque theme park, the Ecomusée de la Tradition Basque. Among its most curious exhibits is a section dedicated to Basque lingerie, sponsored by a local firm. Visits finish with a tasting of the local herb-based liqueur, Izarra.

Ciboure

Right across the port from St-Jean, over a little bridge, this is the less-touristy, working member of these twin towns. Ciboure is the home of the composer Maurice Ravel, who was born at No.12 Quai Ravel, and who once started a concerto based on Basque themes and rhythms (called *Zaspiak Bat*), but never finished it.

The town has a mirror-image of St-Jean's picturesque port, though this side is mostly used by pleasure boats. Behind the port, there are pretty streets of old Basque houses such as **Rue de la Fontaine**, and the simple Eglise St-Vincent, a 16th-century fortified church with an octagonal tower. On the northern end of town, facing the coast, is the quarter of **Socoa** with its **castle**, begun by Henri IV, which today houses a surfing and windsurfing school.

(i) **St-Jean-
de-Luz >**
*Pl Maréchal Foch, t 05
59 26 03 16, www.saint-
jean-de-luz.com; open
July and Aug daily
9–7.30; Sept–mid-Nov
and Feb–June Mon–Sat
9–12 and 2.30–6.30*

(★) **L'Ephémère >>**

(★) **Hôtel Les
Almadies >>**

Market Days around St-Jean-de-Luz

St-Jean-de-Luz: Markets are held on Tuesdays, Fridays, and also Saturdays in summer. There are also markets all year round in Les Halles from Monday to Saturday, and on Tuesday, Friday and Saturday in summer there are local producers around Les Halles. **Ciboure**: Sundays.

Where to Stay around St-Jean-de-Luz

St-Jean-de-Luz ✉ 64500

If St-Jean has one unfortunate drawback, it's finding a reasonably priced place to stay – the rates here are even higher than in Biarritz – although, unexpectedly, the top spots are not always by the beach.
****Parc Victoria**, 5 Rue Cèpe, t 05 59 26 78 78, *www.parcvictoria.com* (€€€€€). A gracious mansion on the outskirts of town set in large luxuriant gardens. It's a beautifully decorated, intimate place (20 rooms and suites). It has a pool, a shady terrace and gourmet restaurant (€€€).
****ZazpiHotel**, 21 Boulevard Thiers, t 05 59 26 07 77, *www.zazpihotel.com* (€€€€€). Ultra-chic boutique hotel, with a stunning contemporary interior behind a classic façade. The rooftop sun terrace with plunge pool offers splendid views.
****Chantaco**, Route d'Ascain, t 05 59 26 14 76, *www.hotel-chantaco.com* (€€€€€–€€€). The emphasis is on golf, with Chantaco golf course, the area's most famous, next door. The hotel, in a 1930s-style Andalucian villa, with a patio covered in vines, is set in a lovely park, and offers tennis courts and a pool in addition to golf. *Closed Nov–April.*
***Hôtel de la Plage**, 33 Rue Garat, t 05 59 51 03 44, *www.hoteldelaplage.com* (€€€). With spacious, bright, modern bedrooms (some with private terraces) overlooking the beach. There's a good restaurant and a car park (for a fee).
***Hôtel Les Almadies**, 58 Rue Gambetta, t 05 59 85 34 48, *www.hotel-les-almadies.com* (€€€–€€). A lovely hotel in the heart of town in the main pedestrian zone. Seven good-sized bedrooms with balconies. The hotel has been renovated and has a clean, crisp and modern design. Very light and airy. The owners are friendly and helpful.
****Grand Hôtel de la Poste**, 83 Rue Gambetta, t 05 59 26 04 53, *www.grandhoteldelaposte.com* (€€). Right in the centre of town (and with its very own snooker table). *Open all year.*
***Bakea**, 9 Place Camille Julian, across the harbour in Ciboure, t 05 59 47 34 40, *www.hotel-ciboure-bakea.com* (€€). Modest hotel with spotless rooms and an arty café-restaurant.
***Ohartzia**, Rue Garat, t 05 59 26 00 06, *http://hotel-ohartzia.com* (€€–€). Very pretty, family-run hotel, situated in the middle of St-Jean, with a lovely terrace and garden on the first floor. Neat as a pin.

Eating Out around St-Jean-de-Luz

Everyone knows St-Jean as the capital of Basque cuisine in France, and there is a marvellous collection of restaurants around the centre. Competition keeps the quality high.

Rue de la République, just off main Rue Gambetta near the port, must be counted among the sights of the Basque coast no one should miss. It's almost entirely lined with seafood restaurants, each one with its beautifully arranged table of *fruits de mer* out front.

Le Kaïku, 17 Rue de la République, t 05 59 26 13 20 (€€€). A pair of ancient mansions (one dating back to 1540) rolls out a fine marine repast. Service can be slow when busy. Very atmospheric, but hugely popular.

L'Ephémère, 15 Quai Maurice Ravel, Ciboure, t 05 59 47 29 16, *www.lephemere-ciboure.fr* (€€€). Exciting contemporary cuisine and bold modern design unite at this chic address, which overlooks the port. The set lunch is a bargain at €22 for two courses, €28 for three, or you could splash out on the *menu gourmandise* at €58. This may be your most memorable meal in the region. *Closed Tues and Wed, exc. public hols and school holidays.*

Ferme Lizarraga, Chemin de Lizarraga, 3km from Saint-Jean-de-Luz, **t** 05 59 47 03 76 (€€). Beautiful, Basque country farm set amid rolling fields, with delicious local cooking served out on the terrace in summer and by a roaring fire in winter. *Menus from €17.*

Chez Pantxua, Port de Socoa, **t** 05 59 47 13 73 (€€). A long-established local favourite, decorated with Basque paintings, serving *fruits de mer* and fish according to the catch of the day. *Closed Tues in winter, and all of Jan.*

Pasaka, 11 Rue de la République, **t** 05 59 26 05 17 (€€). A cosy interior and two terraces, where you can feast on freshly caught local grilled sardines, or *ttoro*, a satisfying Basque fish soup with potatoes and saffron. *Menus from €17. Closed Mon and Tues in winter.*

Le Peita, 21 Rue Tourasse, **t** 05 59 26 86 66 (€€). All the Basque seafood favourites, with good value *plats du jour* at lunchtimes. *Closed Tues.*

Le Portua, 18 Rue de la République, **t** 05 59 51 01 12 (€€). Oysters, salmon for starters, a satisfying *ttoro* and grills. *Menu €20–30. Open daily.*

Restaurant Chez Maya, 2 Rue St-Jacques, **t** 05 59 26 80 76 (€€). This place is very popular with the locals and tourists alike for its simple and authentic Basque cuisine. Good value. *Menus from €22–32.*

Vieille Auberge, 22 Rue Tourasse, **t** 05 59 26 19 61 (€€). For a filling Basque meal in the company of Luziens that usually includes grilled fish and sometimes paella. *Menus from €20. Closed Tues, Wed and Jan–Mar.*

Le Brouillarta, Rue Garat, **t** 05 59 51 29 51 (€€–€). A busy brasserie (part of the Hôtel de la Plage) with sea views. Good for a light lunch. *Closed Sun eve and Mon.*

Guéthary and Bidart

If St-Jean-de-Luz is too frenetic and Biarritz is too big and cosmopolitan, you've got two very amiable choices in between: Guéthary and Bidart. Both are perfect Basque villages, with church, *mairie* and *fronton* right in the middle, and both have good beaches. If they do get a bit crowded at the height of summer, it's much too early to call them spoiled yet.

Leaving Biarritz on the coastal N10, **Bidart** comes first, with a grand view across the coast from the pilgrimage chapel of Ste-Madeleine. Bidart's parish church, in the centre, has some painted altarpieces and a quite unusual Slavic baptismal font – a gift of Queen Natalie of Serbia, who spent a lot of time here before the First World War, in a palace called the Pavillon Royal above the beach. You can visit an 18th-century flour mill in **Bassilour**, where they make *gâteau basque*.

Sleepy **Guéthary** has been a resort as long as Biarritz, though it never made it big. It has a Basque-style *mairie*, which must get a window broken every now and then from the *fronton* in front of it, along with a tiny port and a beach. In an early 20th-century house in the village's park, the **Musée de Guéthary** is full of sculpture by Polish artist Georges Clément de Swiecinski, and there are temporary exhibitions across a range of genres.

Bassilour mill
t 05 59 41 94 49; open July–mid-Sept daily; mid-Sept–June Wed–Mon, closed Tues

Musée de Guéthary
www.musee-de-guethary.fr; open July and Aug 2–6.30; May–Oct Mon and Wed–Sat 2–6

Where to Stay and Eat in Bidart and Guéthary

ⓘ Guéthary >>
Rue du Comte Swiecinski, t 05 59 26 56 60, www.guethary-france.com

⭐ Hôtel Villa Catarie >>

⭐ Harotzen Costa >>

Bidart ✉ 64210

Hôtel Elissaldia, Place de la Mairie, t 05 59 54 90 03, *www.hotel-elissaldia.com* (€€). A handsome, authentic place to stay within a *pelote* ball's throw of the church and *fronton* court. All rooms were refurbished in 2011. There's also a bar and restaurant. *Menus €13–28. Open daily all year.*

Table des Frères Ibarboure, Chemin de Italiénèa, t 05 59 54 81 64, *www.freresibarboure.com* (€€€). One of the region's most celebrated restaurants. It's a family establishment, but the cuisine is predictably perfect and abstrusely *soignée*, from the roast lobster with crystallized fennel to the rich and extravagant desserts. *Menus €38–105.* There are a handful of rooms, too, part of the Relais du Silence. *Restaurant closed Mon lunch in July and Aug, Mon and Wed in low season.*

Guéthary ✉ 64210

★★★★Hôtel Villa Catarie, Av du Géneral de Gaulle, opposite the *mairie* and *fronton*), t 05 59 47 59 00, *www.villa-catarie.com* (€€€€–€€). This old Basque villa has been beautifully restored. Comfort, romance and luxury, classically done.

Restaurant Madrid, right in the village centre on Av du Général de Gaulle, t 05 59 26 52 12, *www.lemadrid.com* (€€). Cheery and homey and serves mostly seafood, with a panoramic terrace; also has delightful rooms (€€).*Closed Mon, Tues, Jan and Feb.*

Harotzen Costa, Jetée des Alcyons, t 05 59 47 19 74, *www.harotzencosta.com* (€€). Beautiful wooden kiosk at the foot of the cliffs, where you can dine on freshly grilled fish and local specialities as you watch the waves. *Closed Nov–Mar.*

Biarritz

🔟 Biarritz

Les vents, les astres et la mer me sont favorables

The winds, the stars and the sea are favourable to me

town motto

For their 1959 season, the designers at Cadillac came up with something special: a sleek and shiny convertible, nearly 25ft (7.5m) long, with the highest tail-fins in automotive history (22 inches/ 56cm). They called it the *Biarritz*, a tribute to the Basque village that was chosen by fortune, for a few decades at the end of the 19th century, to become the most glittering resort in Europe. Nowadays, there's still enough Ritz in Biarritz to support six luxury hotels (among 65 more modest establishments). But, freed from the burden of being the cynosure of fashion, the resort has become a pleasantly laid-back place, where anyone, wealthy or not, can have an unpretentious good time.

A recent article by the economic journal *Les Echos* confirms that the population of the BAB (Bayonne/Anglet/Biarritz) conurbation is growing rapidly thanks to workers following the companies moving in and the influx of retired people from across France. There are also many holiday homes in the area. The mayor of Biarritz, Didier Borotra, is quoted as saying that, out of 23,000 houses, 8,000 are second homes. After September, Biarritz seems to decline into an overgrown village. Then everybody knows everyone else; they shake hands and exchange pleasantries on street corners, or lounge in the bar talking about how nice and quiet it is.

Getting to and around Biarritz and Bayonne

By Air

Biarritz's airport, the Aérogare de Parme (t 05 59 43 83 83, *www.biarritz.aeroport.fr*) has regular flights to Paris with Air France and easyJet. Ryanair flies from London Stansted, and also in summer from Birmingham, Dublin and Shannon. EasyJet fly from London Heathrow and (summer only) Bristol.

The no.6 **bus** from Biarritz goes to the airport Mon–Sat; on Sundays, take bus C.

By Train

Biarritz is a stop on the main rail line from Paris through Bordeaux to the Spanish border. Bus no.2 connects the station with Biarritz and Bayonne city centres. There are plenty of trains along this run; most of them also stop at Bayonne, including a few TGVs each day.

SNCF information, t 36 35, *www.voyages-sncf.com*. Other lines from Bayonne go up the Gaves to Orthez and Pau in Béarn, and down the valley of the Nive to St-Jean-Pied-de-Port.

By Bus

There is a parallel and equally convenient bus service down the coast run by the **ATCRB** line (timetables online at *www.transdev-atcrb.com*) – about a dozen a day from Biarritz and Bayonne to St-Jean-de-Luz and Hendaye. The Spanish bus line, **PESA** (*www.pesa.net*), runs a twice-daily service (except Sundays) along the coast to St-Jean-de-Luz and on to Donostia-San Sebastián, leaving from just outside Bayonne's tourist office (which holds timetable info; buy tickets on the bus).

Public Transport

Public transport in the Biarritz–Bayonne area is very efficient. The useful website *www.chronoplus.eu* has information and plans of all bus routes, or call t 05 59 52 59 52.

Buy single, 24hr or 7-day **tickets**, or get a good-value *Ticket 10 Voyages* for 10 rides. Regular city buses connect the two cities, from the Hôtel de Ville in Biarritz to the Hôtel de Ville in Bayonne – line 1 or 2.

Biarritz's SNCF **station** is far from the city centre; take bus A1. Both Biarritz and Bayonne operate a free *navette* (shuttle) bus which makes circuits around the city centres (timetables are on the website).

Tours

Walking tours can be arranged through the tourist office and are available during July and August only, unless pre-booked. Tours leave at 10am on Mondays and 6pm on Fridays.

Petit train: every tourist town in France seems to have one, and Biarritz is no exception. If you simply can't take another step, hop on for a guided tour of the town from near the casino (t 06 07 97 16 35, *www.petit-train-biarritz.fr*, runs April–Oct).

History under the Palms

Local historians claim that both Biarritz and its landmark, the Atalaya, are names bestowed by the ancient Phoenicians, who may well have used the port as a stage on their trade routes to Britain. Biarritz is said to mean something like 'safe harbour', and Atalaya a kind of tower (like the *talayots* of Menorca), an important landmark visible to the early, coast-hugging sailors.

Before the 1860s, Biarritz was never more than a simple fishing village. But, in the Middle Ages, even more than Bayonne it was the heart of the Basque whaling fleet. Cachalots and other species of whales were once common in the Bay of Biscay. A permanent watch was kept on the Atalaya, and whenever one was sighted the entire village would row out and try to nab it; the Biarrots were probably the inventors of the harpoon, and a harpooner once figured on the village's coat of arms. When the whales caught on and started avoiding the area, the Biarrots and the other Basque whalers bravely sailed out into the open sea after them.

There doesn't seem to be any conclusive evidence for it, but the Basques will tell you they discovered Newfoundland in the 14th century, and probably other parts of the Americas as well (Columbus did after all take a Basque along to be his navigator). By 1800, Basque whalers couldn't keep up with the British and Americans, but Biarritz was beginning to make part of its living from a new and unprecedented phenomenon, the desire of northerners to come and spend a holiday beside the sea.

Eugenia Maria de Montijo de Guzmán, to whom Biarritz owes its present status, came from a minor Spanish noble family rather down on its luck. But, even when she was a young girl, fortune-telling gypsies and nuns forecast a brilliant future for her; 'an eagle will carry you to the heavens and then drop you,' one of them supposedly said. Eugenia also had a scheming, social-climbing mother, who got her daughter as far as the court of the new Emperor Napoléon III in Paris in 1852. This striking 26-year-old was more than capable of doing the rest of the job herself. A brilliant horsewoman who liked to smoke a cigar now and then, she made quite an impression. But there was a cold, unapproachable side to her too, and she used it to win the emperor's heart by being the only girl in Paris the old rogue couldn't have. It is claimed he found his way into her bedroom one night; meeting a chilly reception, he asked the way to her heart. 'Through the church,' she replied.

As Empress Eugénie, she helped inaugurate the cult of fashion in Paris, making the fortune of Worth, the first of the celebrity couturiers. With a political outlook somewhat to the right of Attila the Hun, and a near-total control over Napoléon, she was able to exert a tremendous influence over the policies of the government, presiding gloriously over the orgy of greed, corruption, décolletage and waltzes that was the Second Empire. It took a woman historian, Edith Saunders, to notice this strangely significant bit of the world's secret history. In her book, *A Distant Summer*, she wrote:

...Eugénie had risen like a brilliant star, to create not only new fashions but a new taste in beauty, a new type of woman. The old type, which had lingered on in England and was represented in the pages of Dickens, belonged to Europe's Romantic period and was open-mouthed, angelic and mawkish. The new type, with its predilection for blonde hair and its hard expression, is still with us. The Empress set the modern standard of highly polished perfection which is maintained today by Hollywood film stars and mechanically transmitted to entranced millions who follow in the measure allotted by their circumstance. To look like a film star is the dream of the present day woman of the industrial age; in 1855 everyone dreamed of looking like Eugénie.

As a girl, Eugénie and her mother had often vacationed at the 'just-discovered' village of Biarritz. As empress, she dragged Napoléon back down with her and established the summer court on the beach. Having invented the new woman, Eugénie now made some great contributions to the modern concept of the seaside resort. The imperial couple didn't stay in a hotel; Eugénie had a palace – the Villa Eugénie – built on the most prominent spot along the beach in 1854. Everybody who was anybody in Paris soon followed, along with grand dukes, *petits* dukes, every sort of count and baron, and plenty of factory owners with marriageable daughters. The royal families of Spain and Belgium came; the English were already here, laying out golf courses, while Count von Bismarck canoodled with the wife of the Russian ambassador.

The Fall of France in 1870 put an end to the Second Empire, and to Eugénie's fairytale. In 1881, the government of the Third Republic demolished the Villa Eugénie after a fire, and divided the estate into building lots. But you can't keep a good princess down; Eugénie lived a romantic if somewhat melancholy life in exile, an object of fascination wherever she travelled. She died in Madrid in 1920, at the age of 94.

Even without her, Biarritz carried on. The Belle Epoque brought a tidal wave of building: grand hotels, the casino, a salt-water spa and acres of wealthy villas in every imaginable style. More Russian princes and even Queen Victoria came to visit (in 1889); the Prince of Wales left so much money in the casino that they named two different streets after him. It wasn't a wild scene like the Côte d'Azur in the 1920s: the swells followed a respectable and rather bland daily schedule, starting with a morning promenade past the shop windows on Rue Mazagran at 10, followed by an hour on the beach, dressing for lunch at 11.30, and so on. The First World War started Biarritz's fall from fashion; in the '20s everybody started shifting to Nice and Cannes, where life promised more excitement.

Now Biarritz has begun to shake off its dusty image with dramatic refurbishment of its hotels and fine buildings, in architectural styles ranging from Belle Epoque to Art Deco and Art Nouveau. These include the splendid Municipal Casino, which dominates the Grande Plage, with its restored casinos, entertainment centres and an old-style grand café overlooking the beach.

Despite its hordes of retirees, Biarritz is hardly behind the times. France Telecom made it their experimental city for the communications of the future, wiring up the town with a single fibre optic cable to provide cable TV, telephone, '*visiophone*', '*télétel*' and broadband. And plenty of young people still come in the summer for one unexpected reason – surfing. Stuck in its odd angle of coastline, Biarritz provides what many claim are the only perfect waves on the Atlantic; French hot-doggers and surf bunnies have

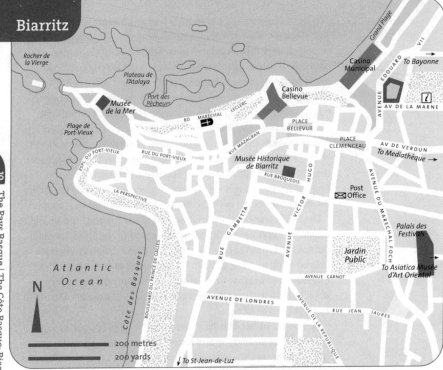

made it the modest Malibu Beach of Europe. And lots of good Frenchmen who have never heard of surfing, and who would never dream of sitting on a beach, know Biarritz for its crack rugby squad – the great Serge Blanco played here until his retirement in 1992, and Imanol Harinordoquy, who plays number 8 for Biarritz, is also a member of the French national rugby team.

The Atalaya

Here, on the tip of old Biarritz's little peninsula, is the height where in the old days the watch would send up smoke signals when whales were sighted. To the right, the Port des Pêcheurs now holds only pleasure craft. To the left is the old fishing port, long ago unusable and filled up with the beach of Port-Vieux, and the best place in Biarritz for a stroll, the **Rocher de la Vierge**. Napoléon III and Eugénie are responsible for this system of causeways and tunnels, connecting a number of crags and tiny islands into a memorable walk just above the pounding surf; the biggest rock carries a marble statue of the Virgin Mary.

Up on top of the Atalaya, the **Musée de la Mer**, in a clean Art Deco building, contains an imaginatively decorated old aquarium for a look at what's down below the surface of the Bay of Biscay, along with exhibits on the natural history of the sea, whales and

Musée de la Mer
t 05 59 22 75 40,
www.museedelamer.
com; open July and Aug
daily 9.30–12; Easter,
June and Sept daily
9.30–7; Oct daily
9.30–12.30 and 2–6;
Nov–Mar Tues–Sun
9.30–12.30 and 2–6;
Jan–Feb Sat–Sun and
hols 9.30–6, closed two
weeks Jan; adm

whaling, navigation, and so on. Audioguides are available in English. Descending eastwards from the Atalaya, the Bd Maréchal Leclerc takes you to the church of **Ste-Eugénie**, another modest contribution from the empress; the big organ inside won a prize at the 1900 Paris World's Fair. It faces one of the centres of resort life in the old days, the beautifully restored Casino Bellevue, now converted to residences and exhibition and conference rooms.

Not far away, by the city marketplace on Rue Broquedis, is the **Musée Historique de Biarritz**; set in a former Anglican church, this is a small exhibition of photos and mementos of the good old days. There is also an interesting museum of oriental art, **Asiatica**, with a collection which includes jades, bronzes and porcelain from China, Nepal and India, and many Tibetan *thangkas* (paintings on silk); an audioguide is available in English. Finally, there is a **chocolate museum**, including tastings.

Musée Historique de Biarritz
*t 05 59 24 86 28;
open Tues–Sat 10–12.30
and 2–6.30; adm*

Asiatica
*1 Rue Guy Petit,
t 05 59 22 78 78,
www.museeasiatica.com;
open Mon–Fri 10.30–
6.30, Sat and Sun 2–7*

Musée du Chocolat
*Av Beaurivage, t 05 59
41 54 64, www.planete
museeduchocolat.com;
open Mon–Sat 10–12.30
and 2–6.30 (daily 10–7
during school holidays);
adm; ticket office
closes 5.30*

Beaches and Villas

Below this, the shore straightens out northwards into the long, luscious expanse of the Grande Plage, which, before Eugénie, was called (for reasons not entirely clear) the Plage des Fous, dominated by the magnificent casino. Farther up the beach, behind the wrought-iron fences, is Biarritz's stately landmark, the sumptuous Hôtel du Palais. This is the spot where Eugénie built her palace, destroyed by fire in 1881. The present hotel, begun in 1905, is the successor to an even grander one that also burned down. Across the street, the Russian aristocrats built their onion-domed church of St-Alexandre-Nevsky (1908).

Avenue Edward VII, which becomes Avenue de l'Impératrice further on, was the status address of Belle Epoque Biarritz, lined with ornate hotels and residences now largely converted to other uses. In the shady streets behind them, all originally part of the imperial estate, scores of wealthy villas still survive, in a crazy quilt of styles ranging from Art Nouveau to neo-Moorish to Anglo-Norman. Some of the best can be seen on and around Avenue Reine Victoria. Also in this area, you can have a look at what passed for piety in the Second Empire – another creation of Napoléon and Eugénie, the 1864 **Chapelle Impériale**, on Avenue Reine Victoria at Rue Pellot. Dedicated to the Black Madonna of Guadaloupe, it boasts a lavish neo-Byzantine interior.

Chapelle Impériale
*t 05 59 22 37 10; open
July–Aug Tues, Thurs
and Sat 3–7; at other
time, call first*

There is an enjoyable walk along the Plage Miramar to the most visible landmark on this stretch of the coast, the 143ft (43m) **Phare St-Martin**, a rare example of an old-fashioned lighthouse: built in 1834, and little changed since. It has only 249 steps to climb; at the base there is a giant sundial.

Phare St-Martin
*t 05 59 22 37 00;
open July and Aug
Tues–Sun 10–12 and
3–7; mid-April–June Sat,
Sun and hols, 3–7*

As for beaches, there is a wide choice of places to plant your towel, and you should be able to find a spot that's not too crowded even at the height of summer. From south to north: at Biarritz's southern limits is the broad expanse of the Plage de la Milady, Plage Marbella and the Côte des Basques, a favourite of the surfing set. Under the old town is the tiny but pleasant Plage du Port Vieux. The Grande Plage and Plage Miramar, the centre of the action, are lovely if often cramped, but further out, stretching miles along the northern coast in the suburb of **Anglet**, there are plenty more. In summer, a free *navette* (shuttle bus) links the Port Vieux with the Plage de la Côte Basque (the most central of the city's beaches). Or you could go north and take your pick among the Plage de la Chambre d'Amour, the Plage des Corsaires, de la Madrague, de l'Océan, des Dunes, and Plage des Cavaliers. The first one takes its name from a number of caves, now mostly submerged, that served as lovers' trysts long ago. Plenty of different stories have grown up around the place – about pairs of lovers who took refuge here and were tragically drowned with the tide – but the notorious French witch-hunter De Lancre, who wrote a report on witchcraft in the Labourd in 1609, said that this was known locally to be none other than the birthplace of Venus, where the goddess rose up from the foam of the sea.

Navette
*t 05 59 41 59 41;
summer only*

Around Biarritz: Arcangues

For a break from the city, in 10 minutes you can drive from the beach to Arcangues, a lovely village on a height south of Biarritz. In the centre, a fine 16th-century church shares space with the *fronton* and a bust of Arcangues's son Luis Mariano, celebrated singing star of some really excruciating French film musicals of the 1940s and '50s.

Shopping in Biarritz

Arosteguy, 5 Avenue Victor Hugo, t 05 59 24 00 52, *www.argosteguy.com*. Celebrated grocer selling the finest Basque products and lots of imported delicacies as well. Great selection of wines.

Bijoux Rodon, 1 Rue Mazagran, t 05 59 24 74 30, *www.bijoux-basques-rodon.com*. In business since 1939, selling excellent Basque jewellery.

Bookstore, 27 Place Clemenceau, t 05 59 24 48 00. A small selection of books in English if you finish your holiday reads too soon.

Cazaux Céramistes, 10 Rue Broquedis, t 05 59 22 36 03, *www.cazauxbiarritz.com*. This ceramics workshop has been going since 1750, and in the last century produced some of France's

top Art Deco pieces. Guided visits of the workshop can be arranged in advance but the shop is open all year.

Chailla, Halles Centrales (central market), t 05 59 24 21 08. For a wide range of local cheeses, Bayonne hams, and other cured meats – this is just one of many amazing stalls.

Chocolat Henriet, Place Clemenceau, t 05 59 24 24 15. Delicious chocolates in gorgeous packaging – try the ones filled with oranges and almonds.

Ophite, 44 Avenue Edouard VII, t 05 59 24 58 55. A stylish little boutique with designer clothes and accessories.

Pariès Confiseur, 27 Place Clemenceau, t 05 59 22 07 52, *www.paries.fr*. For marzipan fantasies, *mouchous* (macaroon kisses), and their very own *Kanougas* – chocolate-covered caramels, flavoured with walnuts, hazelnuts, coffee and vanilla.

Sports and Activities in Biarritz

ⓘ Biarritz >>

Place d'Ixelles, Javalquinto (next to the town hall), t 05 59 22 37 00, www.biarritz.fr and www.ville-biarritz.fr; open July and Aug daily 8–8; Sept–June Mon–Sat 9–6, Sun 10–5

Golf

Golf thrives in Biarritz. There are 10 courses within a 20km radius of the town and several more in St-Jean-de-Luz, ranging from lush, professional-length links with an ocean view to dinky par-3 places to practise your iron shots. At least one important tournament is held in Biarritz each season. Serious courses include the **Golf de Chiberta** in Anglet, Bd des Plages; **Golf d'Arcangues** in Arcangues, south of Biarritz; **Golf de Chantaco**, Rte d'Ascain, St-Jean-de-Luz; and **Golf de la Nivelle**, Place Sharp, Ciboure.

Water Sports

If you should feel a sudden desire to take up **surfing**, there are more than a dozen schools in Biarritz and Anglet, and plenty of places to hire equipment. Some useful contacts are **Biarritz Surf Training**, 102 Rue Pierre de Chevigné, t 05 59 23 15 31, *www.surftraining.com*, and **Ecole de Surf Moraiz**, Bd Prince de Galles, t 05 59 41 22 09, *www.jomoraiz.com*.

For other water sports, you might do better in some of the smaller resorts down the coast. St-Jean-de-Luz has plenty of places that offer deep-sea fishing excursions or hire out sailing boats, including the **Yacht Club Basque**, *www.ycbasque.org*, at Socoa, Ciboure, t 05 59 47 18 31.

Thalassotherapy

You may not have heard of the use of sea water for helping with stress, fitness or recovery from diseases – but in France it is big news; Biarritz has two of the most up-to-date places, the **Thalassa Sea & Spa**, 13 Rue Louison Bobet, t 05 59 41 30 01, and **Les Thermes Marine**, 80 Rue de Madrid, t 05 59 23 01 22, *www.biarritz-thalasso.com*.

Gambling

You can fritter away your money on the *tiercé*, *quarté* and *quinté* at the **Hippodrome des Fleurs**, *www.hippodrome-biarritz.com*, on Av du Lac Marion, still one of France's premier racing venues.

Where to Stay in Biarritz

Biarritz ✉ 64200

Don't let Biarritz's past fool you into thinking there's no place for the likes of you and me here. In fact the vast majority of people who come these days are looking for a bargain, and they have little trouble finding it, although Biarritz is somewhat lacking at the lower end of the scale – if you arrive without a reservation in July or August you might get pushed up into the higher brackets. The tourist office on Place d'Ixelles can help you find a suitable room.

Luxury–Very Expensive (€€€€€–€€€€)

*****Hôtel du Palais**, 1 Av de l'Impératrice, t 05 59 41 64 00, *www.hotel-du-palais.com*. Probably the most prestigious address on France's west coast. Built in Biarritz's glory days on the site of Napoléon and Eugénie's villa, this compound on the beach has a circuit of old wrought-iron fences to separate you from the rest of the world. For a while in the 1950s, the Palais was closed, but the city got it fixed up and reopened, under a determined mayor who had campaigned under the simple slogan: 'No Palace, No Millionaires.' Some of the rooms are palatial, many with period furnishings. There is also a spa with pool, gym, sauna and beauty treatment centre. There are several restaurants, of which **La Rotonde** (*see* overleaf) is the swankiest.

*****Le Beaumanoir**, 10 Av de Tamamès, t 05 59 24 89 29, *www.lebeaumanoir.com*. Chic, luxurious boutique hotel in a sumptuous villa on the fringes of town. There are just eight rooms, suits and apartments, superb service (a free transfer in a Rolls-Royce is included in the booking), with every amenity including a huge pool in the gardens.

****Sofitel Le Miramar Thalassa**, 13 Rue Louison Bobet, t 05 59 41 30 00,

★ Le Beaumanoir >>

www.thalassa.com. The younger contender for the luxury prize. Modern and up-to-date, this hotel may not have the panache of the Palais, but compensates with very high standards in every respect: one of Biarritz's best restaurants and another serving simpler meals (€€€–€€), two pools, sauna and even its own thalassotherapy centre. *Open all year.*

Expensive (€€€)

***Hôtel du Clair de Lune**, 48 Av Alan Seeger, **t** 05 59 41 53 20, *www. hotelclairlune.com*. A charming alternative far from the centre. It's in a Belle Epoque château in a delicious park, with tranquillity assured, and lovely rooms shared between the *château* itself and the hunting lodge. Drops a price category out of high season, and offers fabulous bargains in winter. There is a restaurant, located in an old Basque farmhouse.

Hotel 7B, 7, Rue de Gascogne, **t** 05 59 50 07 77, *www.hotel7b.com*. Chic, central boutique hotel filled with contemporary designer furnishings. Fabulous service and just a short walk to the beach.

Hôtel de Silhouette, 30 Rue Gambetta, **t** 05 59 24 93 82, *http://hotel-silhouette-biarritz.com*. Elegant villa set amid a pretty garden in the centre of town. The bedrooms boast original interior design, and it has its own bar and restaurant.

Moderate (€€)

***Maison Garnier**, 29 Rue Gambetta, **t** 05 59 01 60 70, *www.hotel-biarritz. com*. Set in a 19th-century Basque house. There are seven exquisitely restored rooms, all with antique furniture.

***Louisiane**, Rue Guy Petit, **t** 05 59 22 20 20, *www.louisiane-biarritz.com*. Worth a try despite its unprepossessing modern exterior. This is a conveniently located, well-managed chain hotel with its own swimming pool in the garden.

Inexpensive (€)

Arima Biarritz, 16 Rue Larrepunte, **t** 05 59 24 08 21, *www.arima-biarritz.com*. There are just three

pretty bedrooms at this friendly B&B located on the edge of town.

Villa Vaureal, 14 Rue Vaureal, **t** 0610 11 64 21, *www.villavaureal.com*. Four-poster beds and a garden make this B&B a standout.

***Palym**, 7 Rue du Port-Vieux, **t** 05 59 24 16 56, *www.le-palmarium.com*. A family-run, old-style place above a restaurant-pizzeria; popular with surfers.

Camping

While every other town on the coast has a huge choice of places to pitch your tent, Biarritz doesn't. You'll do better looking in nearby Bidart, which has several options.

Biarritz Camping, 28 Rue Harcet, **t** 05 59 23 00 12, *www.biarritz-camping.fr*. About a ten-minute walk from the beach, with a pool. Mobile homes available. *Closed mid-Sept–early May.*

Eating Out in Biarritz

Expensive (€€€)

La Rotonde, Hôtel du Palais, **t** 05 59 41 64 00. May be the southwest's ultimate trip in luxurious dining: a magnificent domed room with its original decoration, and views over the beach and sea. There is a formidable wine list. *Menus from €58.*

Café de Paris, 5 Place Bellevue, **t** 05 59 22 19 53. Stylish brasserie and restaurant specializing in southwestern cuisine, with excellent crab and lobster. *Closed 15 Nov–15 Mar.*

Campagne et Gourmandise, 52 Avenue Alan Seeger, **t** 05 59 41 10 11, *www.campagneetgourmandise.com*. In a Basque farmhouse in the grounds of the Château du Clair de Lune (*see* 'Where to Stay', above). You can dine on a terrace with breathtaking panoramic views of the Pyrenees. Sample dishes might include *noisette* of Pyrenean lamb or sole with a mushroom cappuccino, or fresh anchovies with a tomato tart. *Closed Sun eve (except in Sun), Mon lunch, Wed.*

Le Moulin d'Alotz, Arcangues, 10km from Biarritz, **t** 05 59 43 04 54. Superb dining in a lovely 17th-century mill set amid verdant fields. Expect to pay around €60–80 per head.

Sissinou, 5 Av Foch, **t** 05 59 22 51 50. Wonderfully creative cuisine from a chef who has trained with France's best, and a delightfully unstuffy ambience at this highly recommended restaurant.

Moderate (€€)

Chez Albert, Port des Pêcheurs, **t** 05 59 24 43 84, *www.chezalbert.fr*. This may look like a typical tourist restaurant, but it's popular year-round with visitors and Biarrots alike for quality seafood at reasonable prices, including paella, grilled lobster and sardines. There are meat choices too.

La Goulue, 3 Rue E. Ardouin, **t** 05 59 24 90 90, *www.lagouluebiarritz.com*. A Belle Epoque-style restaurant with attentive service of classic local dishes; try a plateful of baby squid or monkfish cooked with bacon. *Menus from €13 at lunch; €25 in the evenings. Closed all Mon, and Tues lunch out of high season.*

L'Opale, 17 Av Edouard VII, **t** 05 59 24 30 30. An elegant seafood restaurant right on the seafront; try the simply grilled fish of the day. *Closed Mon.*

Le Clos Basque, 12 Rue Louis Barthou, **t** 05 59 24 24 96. An authentic little *bistrot* with stone walls and Spanish tiles inside, and a charming terrace outside. Local specialities such as squid with peppers are served. *Menu €24, plats du jour from €8. Closed Sun eve except July and Aug and Mon all year.*

Café de la Grande Plage, 1 Avenue Edouard VII, **t** 05 59 22 77 88. A 1930s-style brasserie-café, facing the ocean and overlooking the Grande Plage. Part of the casino, it has a range of drinks and light meals. *Open daily all year.*

⭐ Bar Jean >>

Blue Cargo, Villa Itsasoan, Av Ibarritz, Bidart, **t** 05 59 23 54 87, *www.bluecargo.fr*. In a villa perched right on the beach of Ibarritz on the outskirts of Biarritz. It's perfect for sunset-over-the-sea drinks or simple seafood meals. *A la carte only, €25–30.* Becomes a nightclub later.

Bistrot des Halles, Rue du Centre, **t** 05 59 24 21 22. Usually crowded for lunch and dinner. As in any French town, you won't go wrong looking around the market, and you won't do better than the daily special (usually a grilled fish or steak). *Menu €17. Closed Sun exc. for hols, plus 15–31 Oct.*

Le Pim'Pi, 14 Av Verdun, **t** 05 59 24 12 62. Atmospheric spot for dining on Basque classics including fresh fish, widely recommended by locals. *Menus from €12.50 (lunch), Closed Wed eve and Sun.*

Inexpensive (€)

The Players, Esplanade du Casino de Biarritz, **t** 05 59 24 19 60. Can't be beaten for good cheap fish and vast pizzas. It's right next to the Grande Plage, with views out to sea. *À la carte €25, pizza €10–12. Closed Nov.*

Bar Jean, 5 Rue des Halles, **t** 05 59 24 80 38, *http://barjean-biarritz.com*. A Biarritz classic; the place to go for superb fresh tapas, oysters and a good choice of wines in a traditional Spanish tiled *bodega. Closed Tues and Wed from Oct–April plus Jan and Feb.*

El Callejon, 15 Place Clemenceau, **t** 05 59 24 99 15, *www.elcallejon-biarritz.com*. A good tapas bar. *Open eves only exc. Sat and Sun.*

Pâtisserie Miremont, Pl Clemenceau, **t** 05 59 24 01 38. A Belle Epoque pâtisserie and tea room, which also serves light lunches. An essential Biarritz experience is to drop in at 4pm for a coffee and a little pastry.

Bayonne

🔵 Bayonne

Arthur Young, the famous English traveller of the 1780s, called it the prettiest town he'd seen in France. Young had a good eye; even today, Bayonne is as attractive and lively an urban setting as you'll find in the southwest. Despite a remarkable history, a

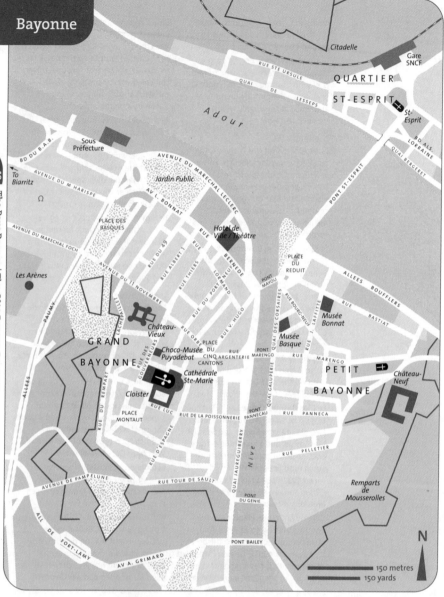

majestic cathedral and a delicious medieval centre full of brightly painted old half-timbered buildings, Bayonne doesn't attract much attention these days, lost as it is in the sprawling conurbation that includes Biarritz, the ports and industry of Boucau and the bedroom community of Anglet. Nevertheless, if you enjoy good cities or if you need a break from the beaches, spend a day in Bayonne.

Getting to and around Bayonne

See Biarritz, p.255.

If you want to discover the Adour **by boat**, take a cruise on *Le Coursic*, leaving from the *quai* near Allées Boufflers, **t** 05 59 25 68 89, *www.adour-loisirs.com*.

History

Bayonne began in the 3rd century AD as a Roman *castrum* called Lapurdum, home to the cohort that guarded Novempopulania. Nothing, however, is heard from it until the booming 12th century, when it adopted its present name and grew into an important port town. From the beginning, Bayonne was not Basque but in fact a predominantly Gascon town; the two peoples have been getting on well enough ever since.

From 1151 until 1452, the English ruled Bayonne. As in Bordeaux, it was an arrangement enjoyable to both sides; Bayonne gave the Plantagenets a strong base at the southern end of their continental empire, and the town enjoyed considerable privileges and freedom, not to mention a busy trade with Britain. At the same time, the intrepid Basques began sailing around the Atlantic in (as any reader of *Moby Dick* knows) the world's first whale fishery. They taught whaling to the Dutch, who taught the English, who, in turn, taught the Massachusettsans.

All that ended when King Charles VII marched in at the end of the Hundred Years War. Not long after, an even bigger disaster hit – the River Adour suddenly picked itself up and moved to a new bed, leaving the port high and dry. But Bayonne, close to the border with Spain, was important to the French; in 1578 they sent down engineers to dig a canal and redirect the Adour, and the port was back in business. A century later, Louis XIV dispatched his famous military engineer, Vauban, to make Bayonne an impregnable stronghold; the sprawling, state-of-the-art fortifications he designed, along with the Citadelle, are a striking feature of the cityscape even today.

Bayonne's military vocation flourished during the 18th century. An armaments industry grew up and gave the world the word 'bayonet', while Basque and Gascon corsairs, with letters of marque from the king, sallied out to snatch what they could from the Spanish, the English and the North Africans.

Besides weapons, the city's other passion was sweets. Jewish refugees from Spain introduced chocolate to Bayonne in the 1600s, and Louis XIV and his courtiers spread it across France when the king passed through on his way to marry the Spanish infanta in 1659. Bayonne's *chocolatiers* gradually built up a reputation as the best in France (*see* box, overleaf) – and there are still quite a few who keep up the tradition.

Chocolate City

While the Basques were among the first to recognize and profit from New World plants such as corn, tobacco and rubber (which put the bounce in their *pelota* balls), their history as *chocolatiers* came in a more roundabout way. The fad for drinking chocolate began with Hernan Cortés, who tried *xocoatl* during his conquest of Mexico in 1519 and brought back some beans and recipes. The Spanish court fell for the stuff, and so did the Basques, but the Spanish and Portuguese (who independently discovered chocolate in Brazil) were savvy enough to keep its secrets to themselves. Jewish refugees from the Spanish Inquisition who had settled in Portugal learned how to make it, and, when Philip II inherited Portugal and extended the Inquisition there, the *chocolatiers* took refuge in Bayonne's ghetto, the Quartier St-Esprit. When Louis XIV passed through on his way to marry the Spanish infanta María Teresa in 1659, he and his courtiers succumbed to the delights of chocolate; María Teresa herself was a cup-a-day girl, in spite of popular wisdom that condemned chocolate along with tobacco as evil and ruinous to the health.

In the 18th century, a Basque pirate captain named Sopite thoughtfully provided something to sprinkle on top of one's morning dose, bringing the first cinnamon from Sumatra to France in a daring trip ordered by royal command in the middle of a war (his ship, *La Basquaise*, met five English vessels on the way home and beat them all). After the Revolution put an end to discrimination, Bayonne's Jewish *chocolatiers* moved out of the ghetto into the centre and built up a reputation as the best in France. Two of the best keeping up the tradition in the old town are Daranatz and Cazenave, both located under the arcades of the Hôtel de Ville.

Bayonne lost its status as a free port, and most of its trade, with the Revolution, and there were more troubles to come. Vauban's walls proved their worth in the Napoleonic Wars. Coming up from Spain, Wellington's army twice besieged the city, in 1813 and 1814; it took it on the second try, by stringing a bridge of ships across the Adour and dragging artillery across it to bombard the city from both sides. Recovery came only with the arrival of the railway from Paris in 1854. Industrialization proceeded apace after that, and now Bayonne's little jewel of a historic centre is wrapped in the 'BAB' (Bayonne, Anglet, Biarritz), a metropolitan area of over 120,000 people, counting Biarritz and smaller towns.

Grand Bayonne and the Cathedral

Bayonne's main street is a river, the little Nive, and it is one of the most delightful centrepieces a city could ask for, lined on both sides with busy quays and old tall houses with trims painted in bright colours (mostly red and green, but no prizes for guessing that). The Nive also marks the division between the two old quarters of the walled town, Grand Bayonne and Petit Bayonne. The former is the business and retail end, jammed with animated, pedestrian-filled shopping streets. Right in the heart of Grand Bayonne, on Rue des Gouverneurs, you can learn more about chocolate at the **Choco-Musée Puyodebat**.

Cathédrale Ste-Marie

One of these streets, narrow Rue Argenterie, will take you from the quays to Bayonne's landmark and symbol, the Cathédrale

Choco-Musée Puyodebat
*t 05 59 59 48 42,
www.chocolats-
puyodebat-bayonne.fr;
open Mon–Sat 9.30–12
and 2–6; adm*

Cathédrale Ste-Marie
*t 05 59 59 17 82,
http://cathedrale-
bayonne.org; open
Mon–Sat 10–11.45 and
3–5.45, Sun and hols
3.30–6; no visits
during services*

Ste-Marie. It is also a symbol of the coming of French control – one of the few examples of the Northern Gothic style in the southwest, and certainly one of the best. Although construction was begun in the 12th century, most of the work was done in the 13th. Some was still going on in the 1500s, when the south tower went up, and the arms of the king of France were added to the sculptural decoration of the portal in honour of Bayonne's new rulers. Throughout, the building was largely financed by Bayonne's whalers. The bishops exacted a tenth of the profits from them, also claiming 'by divine right' the most prized parts of each whale for themselves – the tongue and the fat; nobody really knows what they did with them. Despite all the city's loot from cetaceans, piracy and chocolate, however, the cathedral still wasn't finished until the 1800s, when followers of Viollet-le-Duc oversaw a thorough restoration and added the matching north tower.

So far from the Ile-de-France is the cathedral, and so long in the building, it isn't surprising that there are no unusual stylistic departures here. What is surprising is how well it all fits together. Best of all, it still enjoys the sort of setting a Gothic cathedral should have – among narrow streets and tightly packed tall buildings, where its presence and verticality make exactly the impression its designers intended.

Individual details worth calling attention to are few; this cathedral was thoroughly trashed in the Revolution. Inside, there's no need for detail; the rise of the slender pilasters that carry the rib-vaulted nave permits a lofty interior that no church in the southwest save the Jacobins in Toulouse can match. There is some good Renaissance stained glass in the nave windows, heavily restored a century ago. Note the scene of Adam and Eve, where the serpent (with a female head) wears the bonnet of a medieval doctor of philosophy – just to show what a subtle argument she was capable of. In the left aisle, the **Chapel of St Jerome** has one of the best windows (1531), a scene of the Canaanite woman (from Matthew, 15:22), crowned by a salamander, the symbol of King François Ier. The **sacristy** shelters the only original 13th-century sculptures that survived the Revolution: one tympanum of the *Last Judgement*, with the Devil boiling a king and a bishop in his cauldron, and another of the *Virgin Mary*, surrounded by angel musicians. This leads to a lovely cloister, also much damaged in the Revolution.

Château-Vieux

Just behind the cathedral, on Rue des Gouverneurs, the Château-Vieux was the city's stronghold and the seat of its governors: first the English (parts of what you see are from the 12th century; one of the governors was the Black Prince), and then the French (the outworks were added in the time of Louis XIV to guard against revolts by the Bayonnais). Though it is usually closed to visitors, some of the tours organized by the tourist office will take you through here, and through the amazing expanses of underground chambers that underlie much of the city, some of them as properly vaulted as the cathedral's aisles. In medieval times they were used for storing wine.

Petit Bayonne

The smaller but livelier side of Bayonne, this is a *rive gauche* on the right bank of the Nive. The narrow back streets of Petit Bayonne are crowded with popular neighbourhood bars and restaurants – you won't see the likes of an old, unspoiled city neighbourhood like this in many places in southwest France. Right in the middle, on the Quai des Corsaires, is the **Musée Basque**. This 16th-century building facing the Nive started out as a convent, and later did long service as a customs house. In 1922 the city of Bayonne took it over as a museum that gradually turned into the largest collection of objects on Basque culture and folk life anywhere. Recently modernized and reopened after a long absence, the collection includes over 100,000 items covering every aspect of Basque life with interactive displays, from agriculture to seafaring, with special sections on the old Basque talent for wood and stone carving, religious and folklore traditions, and modern Basque art.

Musée Basque
t 05 59 59 08 98,
www.musee
basque.com;
open Tues–Sun
10–6.30; adm

Musée Bonnat

Bayonne's own Léon Bonnat was one of the best-known salon painters of late 19th-century France, the sort of happy Philistine who got rich painting celebrity portraits, collected prizes and sneered at the Impressionists when he served as a judge in the Salon competitions. When he died, in 1922, Bonnat left his own considerable collection of art to Bayonne, and it has become the nucleus of one of the finest museums in the southwest.

Musée Bonnat
www.museebonnat.
bayonne.fr;
currently closed for
refurbishment; check
the website for updates

Some of Bonnat's work takes pride of place in the museum's main hall: portraits of shiny bankers and blooming society ladies in corsets – another world. There's a portrait of Puvis de Chavannes, by Bonnat, and one of Bonnat himself – done by Degas, of all people. If you want to do the museum chronologically, however, start upstairs, with the late medieval and early Renaissance works that the French, ignorantly and infuriatingly, still call 'primitives'. Besides works of *quattrocento* masters Domenico Veneziano and Maso di Banco, there are some obscure delights: a *Christ* and *Virgin* of the Toulouse school, better than most of their work you'll see in any churches, and a number of Catalan-Aragonese paintings from the same age, with the Catalan love of extreme stylization and rich gold backgrounds. As always with this art, the works range from the really excellent, such as the *St Martin* of the unknown 'master of the Musée Bonnat', to some that are almost naïve – a bit of precocious Diego Rivera with halos and gold leaf.

There is a fine *Madonna* by Botticelli, from the late period when the artist renounced his magical mythological works and lapsed into extreme piety. It didn't always work; this one, despite the Christian trappings, is still plainly Botticelli's *Venus*. From the late Renaissance and Baroque there are some good Flemish tapestries, two El Greco portraits, and an entire room devoted to Rubens.

Almost all the great schools of 17th- and 18th-century painting are represented here. Standouts include a bit of chilly militarism from the time of the Thirty Years' War in Jan Bronkhorst's portrait of *General Octavio Piccolomini*; a Murillo, *Daniel in the Lions' Den*; and an equally disturbing untitled painting by Ribera of a distraught girl combing her hair. This work, in its weird intensity, seems to prefigure Goya, and there are some Goyas here in the museum to compare it with, including a fascinating self-portrait.

There's no telling whose face is going to turn up on the walls of this museum. Among the English paintings you will see Lawrence's portraits of the composer *Karl Maria von Weber* and *Johann Heinrich Füssli* – better known as Henry Fuseli, crazy painter and friend of William Blake. Ingres, one of the spiritual fathers of salon painting, was understandably a favourite of Bonnat's; among ten of his works here is an unspeakable portrait of the unspeakable last Bourbon, *King Charles X*.

An important part of Bonnat's collection were the 36 works by his friend Antoine Barye, the most popular sculptor of his day. Nearby, not always open, is the *cabinet des dessins*, a collection of almost 2,000 drawings and prints from the Renaissance up to the 20th century. Down in the basement is the museum's archaeological collection. Many of these works were Bonnat's: Greek pots and Roman glass, votive reliefs, and lovely statuettes of various goddesses that caught the painter's fancy.

Château-Neuf

Château-Neuf
ramparts open access

On the eastern edge of the walls, the Château-Neuf looms over the town, a stronghold begun in 1460 by the French to consolidate their control over the city. The adjacent parts of Vauban's walls, however, were tidied up by the city and opened to the public a decade ago. On these **Remparts de Mousserolles** you can see what was going through Vauban's mind, and what war was like in the late 17th and 18th centuries. To defend a city properly, it was usually necessary to destroy at least half of it for the fortifications. Baroque fortifications are notable for the space they take up: one or two rings of low-slung, zigzagging ramparts, with a complex of earthen salients and trenches beyond them, all designed to counter artillery rather than repulse a direct attack, which with the improved firearms of the age would have been suicidal. Today the Mousserolles ramparts are an attractive city park, with a lagoon and open-air theatre.

Quartier St-Esprit

The third district of Bayonne, cowering under Vauban's haughty Citadelle and half-demolished 150 years ago for the railway station, is the Quartier St-Esprit, reached by the long bridge across the Adour. At the end of the bridge, the **St-Esprit** church was a gift of Louis XI, that most excellent monarch who wore old clothes and kept a troupe of dancing pigs to entertain him. This 15th-century Gothic building retains from its original decoration an unusual wood sculptural group of the *Flight into Egypt* in the left aisle.

On the other side of the Citadelle, the working end of Bayonne, an impressive stretch of docks and factories follows the wide Adour down to the sea. At the northern edge of town, off Avenue Louis de Foix, is the **English cemetery** from Wellington's campaigns; Queen Victoria and other members of the royal family always came to visit when they were in Biarritz.

Market Days in Bayonne

Markets are held on Monday to Saturday mornings in Les Halles and all day on Friday. Place des Gascons holds a market on Wednesday and Saturday mornings; and Place de la République on Friday and Sunday mornings; Rue Ste-Catherine has one on Friday and Sunday mornings; and Polo Beyris holds one on Friday am.

Where to Stay in Bayonne

Bayonne ✉ 64100

If you're not too concerned about being very close to a beach, the animated streets of Bayonne might make a nice, cheaper alternative to staying in Biarritz.

****La Villa, 212 Chemin de Jacquette, t 05 59 59 62 00, *www.bayonne-hotel-lavilla.com* (€€€). An exquisite villa overlooking the river, with ten stylish rooms – the nicest of which have private terraces under the eaves.

***Best Western Grand Hôtel, 21 Rue Thiers, t 05 59 59 62 00, *www.bw-legrandhotel.com* (€€€). Rather bland but stately, and well-located.

***Hôtel Loustau, 1 Place de la République, t 05 59 55 08 08, *www.hotel-loustau. com* (€€€). Comfortable, well-run hotel, overlooking the Pont St-Esprit and the Adour. *Menus €17–25. Restaurant closed Sun eves in winter*.

**Hôtel Ibis, 44–50 Bd Alsace-Lorraine, Quartier St-Esprit, t 05 59 50 38 38 (€€). A functional chain hotel with a small garden and a restaurant.

*Hôtel des Arceaux, 26 Rue du Port-Neuf, t 05 59 59 15 53, *www.hotel-arceaux.com* (€€–€). One of the best reasonably priced options, near the cathedral. *Open all year*.

Le Poteau Rose, t 05 59 55 36 01, *www.lepoteaurose.com* (€€–€). Original, arty B&B, with three huge, loft-style rooms, filled with contemporary artworks.

*Monbar, 24 Rue Pannecau, t 05 59 59 26 80, *www.hotelmonbar.com* (€). Well-kept little hotel on a lively street in Petit Bayonne, across the Nive.

⭐ Hôtel des Arceaux >>

ⓘ Bayonne >
Place des Basques, t 05 59 46 01 46, www. bayonne-tourisme.com; culture website www.ville-bayonne.fr

⭐ La Villa >

Eating Out in Bayonne

Like other cities of the coast, Bayonne does much better with restaurants than with hotels. Many of the best inexpensive places can be found in Petit Bayonne, either on the quays along the Nive or in the back streets behind them.

Le Cheval Blanc, Rue Bourg Neuf, just around the corner from the Musée Bonnat, t 05 59 59 01 33 (€€€–€€). At the top of the heap, by popular acclaim. Even though the Tellechea family has been running this place for a long time, they never get tired of finding innovative twists to traditional Basque cooking: salmon from the Adour or *merlu croustillant parfum d'anis*. *Menus €30–85. Closed Mon, Sat lunch, Sun eve.*

Le Bayonnais, 38 Quai des Corsaires, t 05 59 25 61 19 (€€). Traditional Basque restaurant in the old town, with décor dedicated to local sporting heroes. Lovely terrace overlooking the Nive. *Closed Mon, Sun eve (all day Sun in winter).*

François Miura, 24 Rue Marengo, t 05 59 59 49 89 (€€). A stylish small restaurant with modern furniture and contemporary paintings, specializing in fish dishes but there are meat options too. *Menus €22–32. Closed Sun eves and Wed.*

Le Petit Chalut, 26 Quai Galuperie, t 05 59 46 17 84 (€€–€). Friendly bistrot with a shady terrace under the arcades, and a menu of fresh fish and local favourites. *Menus from €20. Closed Sun.*

★ Le Cheval Blanc >

The Labourd Interior: Around La Rhune

The name of La Rhune, westernmost monument of the Pyrenean chain, comes from the Basque *larrun*, or pastureland. It's full of cows and sheep all right, just as it has been for the last few millennia. The tracks around its slopes have been one of the main Basque smugglers' routes for centuries. A Basque tale has it that La Rhune was once covered in gold. Some evil men came to take it away; they cut down the trees and burnt them to get at it, but the gold all melted and flowed away. The mountain's summit also had a reputation as an *akelarre*, a ritual ground for witches and sorcerers; up until the 18th century the mayors of the villages around it always paid a monk to live on top as a hermit for a term of four years, to keep the witches away and to pray for good winds.

Ascain, La Rhune and Sare

Coming in from Hendaye or St-Jean, the first of the villages below La Rhune is **Ascain**, with its landmark three-arched medieval bridge over the Nivelle, and a 16th-century church on its lovely square. You can also learn about cider-making with tastings and visits to the cellars at **Cidrerie Txopinondo**. From here a hiking trail leads up to the 2925ft (892m) summit of La Rhune, or else you can take the D4 up to the Col de St-Ignace, where there is another trail and also an old, open tramway to the top, the **Petit Train de la Rhune**.

In Neolithic times, **La Rhune** was a holy mountain, as evidenced by the wealth of monuments around its slopes. The rites of the

Cidrerie Txopinondo
t 05 59 54 62 34, www.txopinondo.com; open mid-June–mid-Sept Tues–Sat 10–12 and 3–7

Petit Train de la Rhune
t 08 92 39 14 25, www.rhune.com; open mid-Feb–mid-Nov daily 9.30–11.30 and 2–4; adm; closed mid-Nov–mid-Feb; free shuttle buses (summer only) link La Rhune with the SNCF stations in St-Jean-de-Luz and Sare

ancient Basque religion were usually celebrated on mountain-tops, hence their reputation in Christian times as haunts of sorcerers. You'll need a *série bleue* map and a day's hiking (at least) to find the monuments; there are eight small stone circles around a place called the **Crête de Gorostiarria**, and several dolmens and circular tumuli on the northern and western slopes. On the slopes of La Rhune towards Sare, the easiest to find are the four dolmens at a farm called **Xominen**, just off the Col de St-Ignace; further away at the **Aniotzbehere** farm are two more. The northern side of the **Pic d'Ibanteli** has four of them.

Just beyond the pass lies **Sare**, one of the true capitals of the Basque soul. For its isolation and its traditionally independent ways, people jokingly call it the 'Republic of Sare'. Since the 1400s, the republic was one of the main centres for what the Basques call *gabazkolana*, or 'night work' – smuggling. Folks on both sides of the border never really saw the logic of paying duties on moving their flocks around to French and Spanish foreigners. Smuggling sheep and cows gradually led to other things too. The French authorities usually treated all this with commendable humanity. The story is still told of a zealous customs man, just arrived from Alsace in the 1920s, who shot a local man in the leg while he was taking some cows over the slopes of La Rhune. His superiors went to the mayor of Sare and to the man's family to explain the situation and express their regrets, and then sent their officer over to the hospital to make his apologies. In 1938 and '39, Sare's night workers found a more rewarding if less lucrative business – helping their countrymen from the Spanish side escape Franco's troops; a few years later, they were doing great work smuggling Allied pilots and spies back the other way.

Sare's **church** is a wonderful example of the traditional Basque style, with its three levels of wooden balconies; memorials inside include the tombs of one of the early figures of Basque literature, the 17th-century Pierre Axular. More than most villages, Sare has retained a number of fine **town houses** with carved lintels, both in

The *Pottok*

It has a face that would make you suspect there was a camel somewhere in the family tree – but a sweet face just the same, with big soft eyes and a wild shaggy mane. It is quite shy, hiding out on the remotest slopes of the western Pyrenees, but it's not afraid of you; come too close and you'll get a bite to remember. The *pottok* is the wild native pony of the Basque country. They've been around for a while; drawings of *pottoks* have been found in the prehistoric caves up in the Dordogne.

Though they're hard to catch, people have been molesting the poor *pottoks* for centuries. A century ago, they were shipping them to Italy to make salami, or to Britain to pull mine cars, a dismal task for which their strength and small size made them perfectly adapted. Annual horse fairs took place in the villages of Espelette and Hélette. Business was so good that the unfortunate *pottoks* were on the road to extinction only a few decades ago. Then, a famous mayor of Sare, the late Paul Dutournier, stepped in, and got the government to set up a reserve for them on the slopes of La Rhune.

Grottes de Sare
*t 05 59 54 21 88, www.
grottesdesare.fr;
open July and Aug
10–7; April–June and
Sept 10–6; Oct 10–5;
Nov–Mar Mon–Fri 2–5;
adm; guided tours and
sound and light show*

Animal park
*t 06 15 06 89 51, www.
parc-animalier-etxola.
com; open daily July–Aug
10–7; April– June 10–6;
Sept–Oct 10–5; adm*

**Musée du
Gâteau Basque**
*t 05 59 54 22 09,
www.legateaubasque.
com; open July–Aug
daily 11–3.15 and
4.30–5.30; Easter
weekend and May–June
Tues–Fri 11–3.15; adm*

Basque house
*t 05 59 85 91 92,
www.ortillopitz.com*

the village and in the *quartier* of **Lehenbizkai** to the south – in the Basque country, outlying hamlets are considered as 'quarters', or neighbourhoods of the main village.

South of town, a side road off the D306 takes you to the **Grottes de Sare**, with Palaeolithic drawings largely destroyed by vandals in 1918; it's said that you can go in here and find your way out at the Cuevas de Bruja, across the border in Spain, but no one has tried it lately. There's also a museum on site with mostly prehistoric finds, and outside there are reconstructed dolmens, cromlechs and tumuli. Sare also offers a domestic **animal park** for the kids; a **Musée du Gâteau Basque** – learning how it was made then and including tastings; and a traditional **Basque house** presenting the history and traditions of the Basque people.

The D306 continues on to the Col de Lizarrieta and the Spanish border on its way to Pamplona.

St-Pée-sur-Nivelle, Ainhoa and Espelette

In the late 1500s many gypsies and converted Muslims fleeing from Spanish persecution took refuge in the Labourd. In that most credulous of ages, all manner of stories about sorcerers and heathen rituals started circulating. The trouble began in 1609, started not by the Church's Inquisition, but by the Parlement de Bordeaux. A lawyer named **De Lancre** was sent, and like most professional witch-hunters this one revealed himself as a murderous psychotic. De Lancre installed himself in **St-Pée**'s château, and soon accused the baroness herself of forcing him to participate in a black mass, where the Devil himself was present. With authority from the king, De Lancre started a reign of terror that lasted three years. Relying largely on the testimony of children and tortured women, he had several hundred people condemned to the stake over the next three years. When he started barbecuing parish priests, too, the bishop of Bayonne finally put an end to it.

Ainhoa, one of the southernmost of all *bastides*, was founded in the days when the English were fighting against the Navarrese for control of this disputed region. A 13th-century Navarrese baron started it, not only to keep the English out, but with the intention of charging tolls and otherwise making money off pilgrims to Compostela. Despite the straight streets, Ainhoa is another lovely Labourd village with many old houses – note the lintel over the door of the **Maison Gorritia** on the main street, telling how a mother built it in 1662 with money sent home by her son in the West Indies. For a pleasant if steep walk, take the path up to the pilgrimage chapel of **Notre-Dame-de-Aranzazu**, with panoramic views over the valley.

From either St-Pée or Ainhoa, the next step is **Espelette**, the village famous for its red peppers (*see* p.58); in the late summer you'll see them hanging everywhere. You can learn all about them at a permanent exhibition in the **château**. Here too are many attractive old houses, a church with a Baroque altarpiece, and an interesting **cemetery** full of discoidal stones; you might note an odd modernistic one, marking the tomb of a local girl, Agnes Souret, who became the first Miss France. There is now an exhibition to her, again at the château, and also one to local naturalist Père Armand David, a regular traveller to China.

Where to Stay and Eat around La Rhune

Prices for both rooms and meals in the Labourd will be a relief after the coast.

(i) **Ascain >**
Rue Ernest Fourneau, **t** 05 59 54 68 30, www.mairie-ascain.fr

Ascain ✉ 64310

★★Hôtel du Pont d'Ascain, Route de St-Jean-de-Luz, **t** 05 59 54 00 40, http://charmhotel-du-pont.fr (€€). Rooms overlooking the Nivelle and its bridge and a delightful restaurant (€€) with a garden terrace: among the signature dishes is *pieds de porc croustillants with mushrooms*.

(i) **St-Pée-sur-Nivelle**
Pl du Fronton, **t** 05 59 54 11 69, www.saint-pee-sur-nivelle.com

★Achafla Baïta, Route d'Olhette, **t** 05 59 54 00 30, www.hotel-achafla-baita.com (€). Out in the peaceful countryside, this tradtional Basque hotel and restaurant is well-priced and friendly. Good choice for families, with gardens and a play area.

(i) **Sare >**
Mairie, **t** 05 59 54 20 14, www.sare.fr

Sare ✉ 64310

In the Labourd, hotels tend to be sweet and simple, with immaculate rooms in white traditional buildings with red shutters and oak beams. Sare provides a bewildering choice of these, all wonderfully inviting.

(★) **Arraya >**

★★★Arraya, Place du Village, **t** 05 59 54 20 46, www.arraya.com (€€€–€€). Beautiful, beamed hotel with rustic rooms (the best look over the garden), and with a memorable restaurant. Menus are reasonable; you might want to surrender a little more for specialities such as fried trout with ham and garlic vinegar and *ris d'agneau* (sweetbreads) with prawns. *Menus €20–35.*

(i) **Espelette >>**
www.espelette.fr

(★) **Euzkadi >>**

★★★Hôtel Lastiry, Place du Village, www.hotel-lastiry.com, **t** 05 59 54 20 07 (€€). A pretty hotel in an early 18th-century building, with a good restaurant (*closed Tues and Wed*).

★★Pikassaria, just outside Sare at Lehembiscay, **t** 05 59 54 21 51, www.hotel-pikassaria.com (€). Also has a good restaurant (€€). *Menus from €13.50; has a menu enfants for €7.50.*

Les Trois Fontaines, Col de St-Ignace, **t** 05 59 54 20 80 (€€–€). A country *auberge* near the cable car. There's a charming terrace and garden, serving Basque specialities. *Menus €13–25.*

Ainhoa ✉ 64250

★★★Hôtel Ithurria, Place du Fronton, **t** 05 59 29 92 11, www.ithurria.com (€€). A large Basque house with pool, sauna and gym, and a celebrated restaurant (€€€–€€), featuring dishes such as langoustine ravioli or roast pigeon with truffles (*menus €38 and €61*), plus a cheaper *bistrot. Restaurant closed Wed plus Thurs lunch except July and Aug.*

★★Oppoca, Place du Fronton, **t** 05 59 29 90 72, www.oppoca.com (€). On the main street of this pretty village, in a restored 17th-century post house. Lovely rooms, some furnished with antiques. There is also a fine restaurant (€€€–€€) with a terrace, serving seafood and meat (*menus €26–55*), plus a *bistrot* for simpler meals. *Closed mid-Nov–20 Dec; restaurant closed Sun eve and Mon.*

Espelette ✉ 64250

★★Euzkadi, 285 Karrika Nagusia, **t** 05 59 93 91 88, www.hotel-restaurant-euzkadi.com (€€). In the same family for five generations, with simple rooms, a pool, and a remarkable restaurant (€€) where the chef is passionate about traditional Basque recipes and traditions. House specialities include *axoa*, a stew of veal and peppers, and *tripoxa*, a black pudding in a pepper and tomato sauce. *Menus €18–35.*

The Valley of the Nive

The little river that comes to such a handsome end among the quays and half-timbered houses of Bayonne has a long way to go before it reaches that city. Starting in the Spanish Pyrenees, it opens out into a narrow valley that cuts a diagonal swath across the Basque country. The D932/D918 that follows it is the high street of the Labourd and Basse-Navarre.

Hasparren to St-Etienne

From Bayonne, an alternative route to the D932 into the heart of the Basque country is the D22, the **Route Impériale des Cimes**, a beautiful road over the hilltops built in the time of Napoleon. It will take you to **Hasparren**, a grey, hard-working town where there is an unusual Roman altar behind the church. Nearby **La Bastide-Clairence** was founded by the king of Navarre in 1314; settled by Gascons, it long remained an ethnic enclave among the Basques. Just outside the village is a Jewish cemetery, from the community of Spanish refugees that formed here in the 1600s.

Southeast of Hasparren, near the village of **St-Esteben**, the **Grottes d'Isturitz et d'Oxocelhaya** are one of the most important prehistoric sights of this region: tools, paintings and other relics, including a musical instrument, have been found here going back some 40,000 years. Most of these have been spirited off to museums, though, and visitors will have to content themselves with a look at the underground stretch of the River Arbéroue, and some exceptional cave formations.

On the main road, the D932 up the Nivelle valley, the first big village is **Ustaritz**, once the meeting place of the Biltzar. Next comes **Larressore**, known for the manufacture of *makilas* (see p.46) and then the biggest village of the interior, **Cambo-les-Bains**. The name of this genteel spa seems to come from a Roman army camp; locals called the site 'Caesar's camp' long ago. The spa grew up in the 16th century, and was fashionable when Napoléon III and Eugénie visited from Biarritz. The Prince of Wales (Edward VII) also liked to drop in during his Biarritz holidays to see a legendary *pelote* star named Chiquito de Cambo play. Cambo's main attraction is the **Villa Arnaga**, the home of dramatist Edmond Rostand, who came here in the 1900s to treat his pleurisy at the baths. The house contains mementoes from his life; the real attraction however is the 18th-century-style French garden.

After Cambo, the foothills begin rising steadily. Nearby off the D918 is the sweet tiny village of **Itxassou**, famous for cherries. From here, through the hamlet of Laxia, a steep and difficult road can take you to the summit of 918m/3,010ft **Artxamendi** on the Spanish border, another ancient holy place. Besides a number of

Grottes d'Isturitz et d'Oxocelhaya
*t 05 59 29 64 72,
www.grottes-isturitz.
com; open July and Aug
daily 10–1 and 2–6; June
and Sept daily 11–12 and
2–5; Mar–May plus
Oct–Nov daily 2–5; guided
tours and workshops on
Wed for adults and
children; adm*

Villa Arnaga
*t 05 59 29 83 92,
www.arnaga.com; open
July–Aug daily 10–7;
April–June and Sept–mid-
Oct daily 9.30–12.30 and
2.30–6.30; mid-Oct–Nov
daily 2.30–6; Mar Sat and
Sun 2.30–6; closed
Dec–Feb; adm*

Irouléguy

From the sunny Palaeozoic Basque highlands come the red, rosé and white wines of Irouléguy, the wine that 'makes girls laugh'. Tucked in sheltered pockets in the mountains, and trained on vertical espaliers to protect the vines from frost, the once vast number of grape varieties has been limited since 1952, when Irouléguy was given its AOC status: cabernet (or *acheria*, 'fox' in Basque) and tannat for reds, and courbu and menseng for whites. Try the generous, sombre red Domaine de Mignaberry, the leading label produced by the co-operative **Maîtres Vignerons du Pays Basque** in St-Etienne-de-Baïgorry (t 05 59 37 41 33, *open Mon–Sat 9–12 and 2–6, Sun also in summer*) or the co-operative's fine fresh rosé, Les Terrasses de L'Arradoy. Of the independent growers, **Domaine Brana**, 3 bis Av du Jaï Alaï, St-Jean-Pied-de-Port (t 05 59 37 00 44, *www.brana.fr, open July–15 Sept daily 10–12 and 2.30–6.30*), has bottled some excellent, peppery reds; **Domaine Ilarria**, in Irouléguy (t 05 59 37 23 38, *call ahead to visit*) produces a lovely rosy rosé.

natural wonders, including waterfalls, small herds of *pottok* and rock needles, this 'mountain of the bear' has evidence of occupation ranging from long-abandoned iron mines and shepherds' huts to Neolithic dolmens and cromlechs.

From here, you cross the ancient boundary from the Labourd into Basse-Navarre. The next villages down the valley are **Bidarray** and **Ossès**, centres of a rich rolling country known for its *pur brebis* cheese. Their prosperity 300 years ago has given both a number of fine houses, many with 17th-century inscriptions. Bidarray has a graceful medieval bridge, the Pont d'Enfer, and a rare 12th-century church. Ossès's church, St-Julien, was rebuilt by the villagers in the 1500s, with a built-in *fronton*, a later Baroque façade and a rich interior decoration. The hills around the nearby village of **St-Martin-d'Arossa** offer three examples of another peculiarity of the Basque country, the *gaztelu*. This is an earth- and rock-built hilltop fortress dating from the Iron Age.

St-Etienne-de-Baïgorry, the principal centre for the production of Irouléguy wine, is really a collection of villages around the Nive and its branch, the Nive des Aldudes. St-Etienne, the centre, has another lovely humpbacked medieval bridge, and the château of the feudal *seigneurs*, the Etxauz.

ⓘ **Cambo-les-Bains** >

Av de la Mairie, t 05 59 29 70 25, www.cambo-les-bains.net; open Mon–Sat 8.30–12.30 and 2–5; mid-July–mid-Sept also Sun 10–12.30

★ **Domaine de Xixtaberri** >

Market Days in the Valley of the Nive

Hasparren: Every other Tuesday, and Saturday for farm produce.

Where to Stay and Eat in the Valley of the Nive

Cambo-les-Bains ✉ 64250

***Domaine de Xixtaberri, Quartier Hegala in the hills above Cambo, t 05 59 29 22 24 34, *www.xixtaberri. com* (€€). Bright, colourful rooms. A *ferme-auberge* with stunning views. Meals, using their own organic produce, are reserved for guests.

**Bellevue, Rue des Terrasses, t 05 59 93 75 75, *www.hotel-bellevue64.fr* (€€). An old, pleasant establishment with a view, near the top of town. The restaurant (€€) serves a three-course *menu* for €20.

**Hostellerie du Parc, Place de la Mairie, t 05 59 93 54 54, *www.hotel-parc-cambo.co* (€€), in the lower part of town, offers 12 pretty rooms, a little

ⓘ **Ustaritz**
Centre Lapurdi, t 05 59 93 20 81, www.ustaritz-tourisme.com; open daily 9–12 and 2–5.30

ⓘ **Hasparren**
2 Place St Jean, t 05 59 29 62 02

★ **Hôtel Ostapé >>**

garden, and a reasonable restaurant for guests only. There is outside dining in summer.

Chez Tante Ursule, Bas Cambo, **t 05 59 29 78 23, *www.auberge-tante-ursule.com* (€). Small rustic hotel with a modern annexe. There is also an excellent restaurant (€€–€). Try the pimientos stuffed with *morue* or the *confit de canard*. *Menus from €16.*

Itxassou ✉ 64250

Fronton, Place du Fronton, **t 05 59 29 75 10, *www.hotelrestaurantfronton.com* (€€). The hotel of choice in the village. The restaurant has a room with a view, and specialities include *pipérade* and *filets de canard aux cerises* (menus €20–30).

Hôtel Txistulari, direction St-Jean-Pied-de-Port, **t** 05 59 29 75 09, *www.txistulari.fr* (€). Traditional Basque villa that has been modernized. Well run and neat. Nice terrace plus pool with lovely views. Regional cuisine (€€–€), popular with locals, which is served

out on the terrace in summer. *Menus €12–30; plats du jour €8.50, set dinner €16.*

Auberge Etchepare, Place de la Mairie, **t 05 59 29 75 14, *www.aubergeetchepare.fr* (€). The flower-filled balconies of this traditional inn overlook the village square; there's a good restaurant serving local dishes. *Menus €16–28.*

Bidarray ✉ 64780

Bidarray offers a perfect setting, nestled in rolling hills with mountain views, nothing but the odd bleat or sheep's bell to break the silence.

****Hôtel Ostapé, Domaine de Chahatoa, **t** 05 59 37 91 91, *www.ostape.com* (€€€€€). Luxurious, rural hotel with its own extensive *domaine*, with a glorious hilltop setting and magnificent views. There is a choice of rooms, suites, or secluded villas (access by golf cart), a heated pool in the gardens, and an excellent restaurant. *Menus €39–56.*

St-Jean-Pied-de-Port

✪ **St-Jean-Pied-de-Port**

This town's real name, in Basque, is Donihane Garazi. The French name is even more curious, but *port* is an old mountain word for a pass, and St-Jean, or Donihane, stands at the foot of the pass of Roncesvalles (Roncevaux in French), the 'Gate of Spain' of medieval French legend and poetry. The location has made it a busy place. From the 8th century, Arab armies must have passed this way many times on their way to raid France; Charlemagne and Roland (*see* p.239) came back the other way to raid Spain, and pass into legend along the way. Pilgrims from all over Europe came through on their way to Compostela, and another famous visitor, Richard the Lion-Heart, put the original town – now nearby St-Jean-le-Vieux – to siege in 1177. When he took it, that most pitiless and destructive of warriors razed it to the ground; the kings of Navarre refounded St-Jean on its present site soon after.

Though it still holds four big fairs each year, just as in medieval times St-Jean today makes more of its living from visitors; it's the main centre for mountain tourism in the Basque lands, and in summer it can be quite a crowded place. Bars, restaurants and souvenir shops pack the centre, along the D933 and the picturesque streets around the **Vieux Pont** over the Nive. Old houses with wooden balconies hang over the little river, and facing the bridge stands the church of **Notre-Dame**, originally built by Sancho the Strong of Navarre in commemoration of the battle of Navas de Tolosa (1212), where the Christian Spaniards finally put an end to Muslim dominance of the peninsula. The current building is Gothic, rare in these parts, though it has been much reworked since. The old streets climb up from here to the house which the St-Jeanais have called the **Prison des Evêques**, and turned into a tourist attraction with art exhibitions and so on. The house in fact seems to have belonged to a merchant, and the unusual vaulted underground chamber may have been for storing his wares, like the similar cellars in Bayonne. The bishops who lived in the mansion above it c. 1400 weren't exactly kosher – supporters of the Antipope at Avignon during the great Schism – and the chains and shackles in the cellar wall were probably used by local authorities in the 18th century to lock up poor peasants who didn't pay their salt tax. If you climb to the top of the town for the view, you'll find the **citadel**, a castle last remodelled in the 17th century by Vauban.

Prison des Evêques
41 Rue de la Citadelle, t 05 59 37 00 92; open July and Aug daily 10–12.30 and 2–6.30; Easter–June and Sept–Oct Wed–Mon 10–12.30 and 2–6.30, closed Tues

Just east on the D933 stands St-Jean's original, **St-Jean-le-Vieux**. The town destroyed by the Lion-Heart has only the Romanesque tympanum of its church to remind it of its former importance. There are also scanty remains of a large Roman camp, including baths. There is a **museum** on site with items found during excavations. North of St-Jean-le-Vieux, on a height above the D933, a venerable stone pillar with a cross on top is known as the **Croix de Ganelon**, supposedly the spot where Roland's treacherous stepfather was pulled apart by wild horses at Charlemagne's command.

Museum at St-Jean-le-Vieux
t 05 59 37 09 10; open July–Aug Mon–Fri for visits, special tours with demonstrations, costumed guides, etc

South of St-Jean, the D933 leads down to the Spanish border and, 16km beyond that, the cold, misty pass of Roncesvalles itself (*see* p.238). For an alternative, if you want to get really lost, take the D301 from St-Jean down to the pretty village of **Estérençuby**, hub of a wild maze of steep narrow roads and hiking trails around the border. With a good map, you can find your way to the abandoned **Château Pignon**, a battered old castle last rebuilt by Ferdinand of Aragon that saw trouble in every conflict up to the Napoleonic wars. Even better, take the D428 up to the Col d'Arnostéguy, passing the primeval beeches of the **Forêt d'Orion** in one of the remotest parts of the region; exactly on the border stands the mysterious **Tour d'Urkulu**, a circular platform of huge, well-cut stone blocks some 65ft (20m) in diameter. Some historians, for lack of a better explanation, suppose it to be the remains of a Roman victory monument, like the ones set up on the Mediterranean at La Turbie and Perthuis. It is just as likely, though, that it is far older; the surrounding slopes are littered with dolmens, cromlechs and other Neolithic remains, and arrowheads dated from the Bronze Age have been found on the site. Some have speculated that the name Urkulu, which has no meaning in Basque, might have something to do with Hercules.

Market Days in St-Jean-Pied-de-Port

St-Jean-Pied-de-Port: Mondays.

Where to Stay and Eat around St-Jean-Pied-de-Port

ⓘ **St-Jean-Pied-de-Port >**

Place Charles-de-Gaulle, t 05 59 37 03 57, www.saintjeanpieddeport-paysbasque-tourisme.com

St-Jean-Pied-de-Port ✉ 64220

As this is a popular tourist base, hotel prices are substantially higher than in the other villages nearby.

***Les Pyrénées, Place Charles de Gaulle, **t** 05 59 37 01 01, *www.hotel-les-pyrenees.com* (€€€–€€) has a restaurant that is one of the most esteemed culinary temples in all the Basque country. The hotel is a member of Relais et Châteaux and has a pool and Jacuzzi. People come from miles around for cooking that, while not notably innovative, brings the typical Basque-Gascon repertoire of duck, *foie gras* and game dishes to perfection; they're especially noted for their desserts. A gratifying menu (*Mon–Sat*) puts Les Pyrénées within the reach of most. *Menus €40–100. Closed 20 Nov–just before Christmas and most of Jan; restaurant closed Tues except in July–Sept.*

Hôtel Central, Place Charles de Gaulle, **t** 05 59 37 00 22 (€€). Old family hotel and restaurant with views over the River Nive, which according to the fishing season yields such delights as salmon and eels for the table. *Menus €19–44. Closed Dec–Feb.*

Ramuntcho, 1 Rue de France, **t 05 59 37 03 91 (€€–€). An old, half-timbered hotel, just inside the Porte de France. Rooms have balconies and a view. The restaurant (€€–€) serves good simple dishes. *Menus €15–35. Closed mid-Nov–Dec; restaurant closed Tues and Wed except in July and Aug.*

Hôtel des Remparts, Place Floquet, **t 05 59 37 13 79, *www.touradour.com/hotel-remparts.htm* (€). A historic building dating from 1643 offering less expensive rooms. *Menus €14–19. Hotel closed Nov–Mar; restaurant closed weekends Oct–April and Nov–mid-Jan.*

Pecoïtz, **t** 05 59 37 11 88, in Aincille, just south of St-Jean-le-Vieux on the D118, *www.hotel-pecoitz-pays-basque.com* (€). Rooms cheaper than anything in the town, a quiet and lovely setting, and a very good restaurant (€€–€) that specialises in pigeon. *Menus €15–34. Closed Thurs eve–Sat lunch out of season and Jan–Mar.*

Estérençuby ✉ 64220

Sources de la Nive, **t 05 59 37 10 57, *www.hotelsourcesdelanive.com* (€). In Estérençuby, 11km south of town. Set among the mountain forests, next to the river, it offers perfect tranquillity, as well as a restaurant (€€–€) that serves venison and wild boar and other rural treats. There is a pool. *Menus €14–25. Closed Jan; restaurant closed Tues in winter.*

The Haute-Soule

By now, the mountains are getting taller and so are the roofs: steep slate ones become more common than the Roman tiles of the coast. From St-Jean-le-Vieux, the D18 will take you deeper into the remotest corner of the French Basque country, the beautiful, seldom-visited Haute-Soule, a 50km stretch of Pyrenees with scarcely more than 1,000 inhabitants. From the village of Mendive, an alternative route is the D117, narrow but marvellously scenic, passing near several peaks of over 3,000ft (910m). The only settlement it passes is **Ahusquy**, a former spa; from here trails lead into one of the largest of Pyrenean forests, the **Forêt des Arbailles**.

The D18/D19 is just as good, though more difficult, crossing three mountain passes before it arrives at **Larrau**, the closest thing to a village the Haute-Soule can offer. The GR10, the hiking trail that runs the length of the Pyrenees, passes nearby, among many other trails, and if you have some time to spare there are a number of attractions: west of Larrau is a small ski station called **Les Chalets d'Iraty**, set amidst another lovely beech forest, the **Forêt d'Iraty** (*see* pp.236–7). This area is a major transit point for many kinds of migrating birds; serious birdwatchers come from all over to see them in autumn. Hunters come too, and some of them still follow the practice of trapping doves by the thousands in great nets – remarkably, this is still legal in France. Netting birds is turning into a hot issue, and considerable hostility surfaces each year between hunters, birders, environmentalists and the local authorities.

Gorges de Kakouetta
www.sainte-engrace. com; open mid-Mar– mid-Nov daily 8am until dark; buy tickets from the snack bar La Cascade at the entrance

🌟 **Ste-Engrâce**

East of Larrau, the GR10 leads you to the wild and spectacular **Gorges d'Holçarté**, a series of canyons explored for the first time only in 1908; now a trail runs along the top, with a giddy cable footbridge (erected in 1920) across the gorge. Further east the GR10 meets another, similar sight, the **Gorges de Kakouetta**, also accessible by car on the D113. Here too a trail has been laid out; there's a lovely waterfall at the end. The D113 continues to a dead end in the mountains, passing tiny Ste-Engrâce.

Ste-Engrâce is one of the most isolated and tradition-bound of all Basque villages; the twisting road up to it was only built a decade ago. It is also the unlikely setting for one of the most fascinating medieval churches in the Pyrenees. Built in the 12th century, this cock-eyed church sits on a slope, tilted and asymmetric; pilasters added a century ago keep it from sliding away. The Romanesque tympanum shows the chrism, the monogram of Christ, in a circle supported by two flying angels – a remarkable example of the persistence of symbolism. Replace the chrism with a laurel crown and you have the emblem of the Roman Empire from the time of Augustus. The carved capitals inside are painted in detail, as Romanesque sculpture was meant to be. One shows a pair of lovers; for lack of a better explanation they are said to represent Solomon and Sheba, accompanied by a medieval European's idea of what an elephant might look like; others seem to show Salome's dance and the three Magi. Behind the church is an old cemetery with some strange discoidal tombstones.

Heading north from the Haute-Soule, the D26/D918 follows the Valley of the Saison (or Gave de Mauléon, depending on who you're talking to), a stream popular with canoeists. The valley is a rich land, thick with tiny villages of which the largest is **Tardets-Sorholus**, with a lively market selling cheeses and other local produce on Mondays (every two weeks in winter). **Ordiarp** has an interesting Romanesque church and cemetery in a pretty setting. There are caves with prehistoric paintings around Ossas and Camou, still being explored and documented. The peculiarity of this area is its large number of *gaztelu*; good examples can be found near the villages of Aussurucq, Ideaux-Mendy, Etchebar (an especially impressive one with three circuits of fortifications), Alçay and Ordiarp; this must have been as hot a border region in the Bronze Age as it was in the time of Louis XIII. The interactive **Centre d'Evocation des Chemins de St Jacques** tells pilgrims' tales, has information on Romanesque architecture, and initiates visitors into Souletine legends, dances and songs.

Centre d'Evocation des Chemins de St Jacques
t 05 59 28 07 63; call for opening times

East of Tardets, the D918 takes you to the villages of **Aramits** and **Arette**. The former is the home of Dumas's musketeer Aramis; there have always been some people here who won't admit he's a fictional character. The latter is largely new, rebuilt after a surprise earthquake in 1967, and is close to the small **ski resort** of La Pierre St-Martin. At Aramits you can visit a reconstructed **shepherd's hut** and see how he spent his time in the mountains. Then, at the tourist office in Arette, there is a permanent exhibition on a shepherd's life and the forest, and at the **Moulin d'Arette** you can learn what the miller got up to.

La Pierre St-Martin ski resort
www.lapierrest martin.com

Moulin d'Arette
t 05 59 88 90 82; guided visits July and Aug Wed 6pm; otherwise call

The Inner Reaches of the Soule: Mauléon

At first glance, the temptation to leave this grey industrial town immediately might be irresistible. But hang around a while; Mauléon, the town of the evil lion (*mauvais lion*), has character. They make furniture, sheep's milk cheese and fabrics here, too, but everyone knows Mauléon as the world capital of the espadrille. And, even though most of these classic French summer sandals may be produced in Asia these days (what isn't?), Mauléon's little factories still do their best to keep competitive. The capital of the Soule is a proper Basque village with its working clothes on.

To prove its Basqueness, there is the busy and famous *fronton* right in the centre, on the park called Les Allées. Mauléon's château faces it, the **Château d'Andurain de Maytie**, also known as the Hôtel du Maytie. This stern yet graceful building was erected in the early 1600s by a local boy who became bishop of Oloron-Ste-Marie in nearby Béarn. It is still in the original family; highlights are the Renaissance fireplaces and the grand oaken carpentry that holds up the steep roof, designed by a shipwright.

Château d'Andurain de Maytie
1 Rue Jeu de Paume, t 05 59 28 04 18; open July–20 Sept Fri–Wed, visits 11–12 and 3–6; closed Sun am; adm

Old Mauléon climbs precipitously up to the town's other castle, the **Château Fort**. There has probably been a castle on this site for at least 3,000 years; this latest version dates from the 1300s, rebuilt after Richard the Lion-Heart chased out the French viscount and wrecked the place in 1261. Mauléon and the castle remained English until 1449, when the viscount of Béarn seized it. In 1642 Richelieu ordered it destroyed, but before the work was done he changed his mind and ordered it rebuilt, and sent a bill for 130,000 *livres* to the Mauléonais, causing a fierce but

Château Fort
for information call tourist office, t 05 59 28 02 37; open 15 June–15 Sept daily 11–1.30 and 3–7; adm

short-lived fracas called the Revolt of Matalas. A tour of the castle may be wonderfully evocative, but watch your step – parts of it could collapse at any minute.

St-Palais

The northeastern corner of the Basque lands is a humble country, where you'll see plenty of livestock and farming paraphernalia and little else. Its only centre is an equally humble though quite pleasant village with a memorable Friday morning market, St-Palais (*San Pelayo* in Basque). Once St-Palais had a viscount and a mint, and the village disputed with St-Jean-Pied-de-Port the honour of capital of Basse-Navarre; today it's best known as host to the annual *Festival de Force Basque* (*see* p.76) each August (and a lot of the farmers you'll see walking around on market day look as if they could be competitors).

From the old days all that survives is the mansion called the **Maison des Têtes** across from the chapel of St-Paul on Rue du Palais-de-Justice. A 17th-century house of a noble family, its façade is decorated with odd 'heads' including those of Henri IV and Jeanne d'Albret. Nearby, in the courtyard of the *mairie*, you can mull over St-Palais's history in the small **Musée de Basse Navarre**. You can see how Basque cotton and linen is made and buy some at the **Atelier de Tissage Ona Tiss**.

Musée de Basse Navarre
Pl Charles de Gaulle, t 05 59 65 71 78; open Mon–Sat 9.30–12.30 and 2–6, Sun 10–12.30

Atelier de Tissage Ona Tiss
23 Rue de la Bidouze, t 05 59 65 71 84; open July and Aug Mon–Sat 9–12 and 2–5; Sept–June Mon–Thurs 9–12 and 2–5

ⓘ **St-Palais** >>
Place Charles de Gaulle, t 05 59 65 71 78, www.tourisme-saintpalais.com

ⓘ **Mauléon** >
10 Rue J. B. Heugas, t 05 59 28 02 37, www.valleedesoule.com

Market Days in the Haute-Soule

Tardets: Every other Monday, and every Monday in July and August.
Mauléon: Tuesday and Saturday mornings.
St-Palais: Fridays.

Where to Stay and Eat in the Haute-Soule

Tardets-Sorholus ✉ 64470
Hôtel de la Poste, 25 Rue de la Navarre, t 05 59 28 51 30 (€). Recently renovated hotel in the old post office in the village centre, with a traditional restaurant serving local dishes.

Mauléon ✉ 64130
**L'Hostellerie du Château, 25 Rue de la Navarre, t 05 59 28 19 06 (€). This friendly, immaculate hotel across from the château has simple but comfortable rooms and a good local restaurant with a summer terrace.

Barcus ✉ 64130
***Chilo, t 05 59 28 90 79, www.hotel-chilo.com (€€). Way out in the middle of nowhere, some 15km east of Mauléon, and it's worth the detour. This hotel has been in the same family for generations. Some rooms are fancy and furnished with antiques and there's a lounge with an open fire for colder evenings. There is also a pool where you can relax and enjoy views of the hills. There's a fine restaurant (€€€–€€), with a garden terrace, which is especially good for fish, along with starters like a salmon terrine and a wide range of tempting desserts. *Menus €30–69. Closed Sun eve plus Mon and Tues lunch in winter, and 2 weeks Jan and 2 weeks Mar.*

St-Palais ✉ 64120
Hôtel Le Trinquet, t 05 59 65 73 13, www.le-trinquet-saint-palais.com (€). Traditional hotel in the central square of this market town, with a classic wood-beamed restaurant (€€–€). *Menus €10–28.*

Language

French

Even if your French is brilliant, the soupy southern twang of the Basque region may well throw you. Any word with a nasal *in* or *en* becomes something like *aing* (*vaing* for *vin*). The last vowel on many words that are silent in the north get to express themselves in the south (*encore* sounds something like *engcora*).

What remains the same as anywhere else in France is the level of politeness expected: use *monsieur, madame* or *mademoiselle* when speaking to everyone (and never *garçon* in restaurants!), from your first *bonjour* to your last *au revoir*.

Pronunciation

Vowels
a/à/â between *a* in 'bat' and in 'part'
é/er/ez at end of word as *a* in 'plate' but a bit shorter
e/è/ê as *e* in 'bet'
e at end of word not pronounced
e at end of syllable or in one-syllable word pronounced weakly, like *er* in 'mother'
i as *ee* in 'bee'
o as *o* in 'pot'
ô as *o* in 'go'
u/û between *oo* in 'boot' and *ee* in 'bee'

Vowel Combinations
ai as *a* in 'plate'
aî as *e* in 'bet'
ail as *i* in 'kite'
au/eau as *o* in 'go'
ei as *e* in 'bet'
eu/œu as *er* in 'mother'
oi between *wa* in 'swam' and *wu* in 'swum'
oy as 'why'
ui as *wee* in 'twee'

Nasal Vowels
Vowels followed by an *n* or *m* have a nasal sound.
an/en as *o* in 'pot' + nasal sound
ain/ein/in as *a* in 'bat' + nasal sound
on as *aw* in 'paw' + nasal sound
un as *u* in 'nut' + nasal sound

Consonants
Many French consonants are pronounced as in English, but there are some exceptions:
c followed by *e, i* or *y,* and *ç* as *s* in 'sit'
c followed by *a, o, u* as *c* in 'cat'
g followed by *e, i* or *y* as *s* in 'pleasure'
g followed by *a, o, u* as *g* in 'good'
gn as *ni* in 'opinion'
j as *s* in 'pleasure'
ll as *y* in 'yes'
qu as *k* in 'kite'
s between vowels as *z* in 'zebra'
s otherwise as *s* in 'sit'
w except in English words as *v* in 'vest'
x at end of word as *s* in 'sit'
x otherwise as *x* in 'six'

Stress
The stress usually falls on the last syllable except when the word ends with an unaccented *e*.

Spanish

Castellano, as Spanish is properly called, was the first modern language to have a grammar written for it. When a copy was presented to Queen Isabel in 1492, she understandably asked what it was for. 'Your majesty,' replied a perceptive bishop, 'language is the perfect instrument of empire.' In the centuries to come, this concise, flexible, expressive language would prove just that: an instrument that would contribute more to Spanish unity than any laws or institutions, while spreading itself effortlessly over much of the New World.

Among other European languages, Spanish is closest to Portuguese and Italian – and of course, Catalan and Gallego. Spanish, however, may have the simplest grammar of any Romance language, and if you know a little of any one of these, you will find much of the vocabulary looks familiar. It's quite easy to pick up a working knowledge of Spanish, but Spaniards speak colloquially and fast (and although the Spanish spoken in the Basque country is very close to standard Castilian, the intonation is Basque, making it sound sing-song to other Spanish speakers); expressing yourself may prove a little easier than understanding the replies. Spaniards will appreciate your efforts, and when they correct you they aren't being snooty; they simply feel it's their duty to help you learn. There are dozens of language books and CDs on the market; one particularly good one is *Complete Spanish*, by Juan Kattan-Ibarra (Teach Yourself, 2010). If you already speak Spanish, note that the Spaniards increasingly use the familiar *tú* instead of *usted* when addressing even complete strangers.

Pronunciation

Pronunciation is phonetic but somewhat difficult for English speakers.

Vowels
a short *a* as in 'pat'
e short *e* as in 'set'
i as *e* in 'be'
o between long *o* of 'note' and short *o* of 'hot'
u silent after *q* and in *gue-* and *gui-*; otherwise long *u* as in 'flute'

ü *w* sound, as in 'dwell'
y at end of word, or meaning *and*, as *i*

Diphthongs
ai/ay as *i* in 'side'
ei/ey as *ey* in 'they'
au as *ou* in 'sound'
oi/oy as *oy* in 'boy'

Consonants
c before the vowels *i* and *e*, it's a *castellano* tradition to pronounce it as *th*; many Spaniards and all Latin Americans, however, pronounce it as an *s*
ch as *ch* in 'church'
d often becomes *th*, or is almost silent, at end of word
g before *i* or *e*, pronounced as *j* (see below)
h silent
j *ch* in 'loch' – a guttural, throat-clearing h
ll *y* or *ly* as in 'million'
ñ *ny* as in 'canyon' (the ~ is called a tilde)
q *k*
r usually rolled, which takes practice
v often pronounced as *b*
z *th*, but *s* in parts of Andalucía

Stress

If the word ends in a **vowel**, an *n* or an *s*, then the stress falls on the penultimate syllable; if the word ends in any other consonant, the last syllable is stressed. Exceptions are marked with an accent.

If all this seems difficult, consider that English pronunciation is even worse for Spaniards. Young people in Spain all seem to be madly learning English these days; if your Spanish friends giggle at your pronunciation, get them to try to say 'squirrel'.

Useful Vocabulary

English | French | Spanish

General

English	French	Spanish
hello	*bonjour*	*hola*
good evening	*bonsoir*	*buenas tardes*
good night	*bonne nuit*	*buenas noches*
goodbye	*au revoir*	*adiós*
please	*s'il vous plaît*	*por favor*
thank you (very much)	*merci (beaucoup)*	*(muchas) gracias*
yes	*oui*	*sí*
no	*non*	*no*
good	*bon*	*bueno*
bad	*mauvais*	*malo*
excuse me	*pardon, excusez-moi*	*disculpe*
Can you help me?	*Pourriez-vous m'aider?*	*¿Me puede ayudar?*
My name is...	*Je m'appelle...*	*Me llamo...*
What is your name?	*Comment t'appelles-tu?* (informal), *Comment vous appelez-vous?* (formal)	*¿Cómo te llamas?* (informal), *¿Cómo se llama usted?* (formal)
How are you?	*Comment ça va?*	*¿Cómo estás?*
Fine	*Ça va bien*	*Bien*
I don't understand	*Je ne comprends pas*	*No entiendo*
I don't know	*Je ne sais pas*	*No sé*
Speak more slowly	*Pourriez-vous parler plus lentement?*	*¿Podría hablar más despacio?*
How do you say ... in French/Spanish?	*Comment dit-on ... en français?*	*¿Cómo se dice ... en español?*
Help!	*Au secours!*	*¡Socorro!*
WC	*les toilettes*	*los servicios/aseos*
men	*hommes*	*señores/hombres/caballeros*
ladies	*dames/femmes*	*señoras/damas*
doctor	*le médecin*	*el doctor*
hospital	*un hôpital*	*el hospital*
Accident & Emergency (Casualty)	*la salle des urgences*	*la sala de emergencias*
police station	*le commissariat de police*	*la comisaría de policía*
tourist information office	*l'office de tourisme*	*la oficina de turismo*
No smoking	*Défense de fumer*	*Prohibido fumar*

Shopping & Sightseeing

English	French	Spanish
Do you have...?	*Est-ce que vous avez...?*	*¿Tiene usted...?*
I would like...	*J'aimerais...*	*Quisiera...*
Where is/are...?	*Où est/sont...*	*¿Dónde está/están...?*
How much is it?	*C'est combien?*	*¿Cuánto vale eso?*
It's too expensive	*C'est trop cher*	*Es demasiado caro*

English	French	Spanish
Shopping & Sightseeing *(cont'd)*		
entrance	*l'entrée*	*la entrada*
exit	*la sortie*	*la salida*
open	*ouvert*	*abierto*
closed	*fermé*	*cerrado*
push	*poussez*	*empujar*
pull	*tirez*	*tirar*
bank	*une banque*	*el banco*
money	*l'argent*	*el dinero*
traveller's cheque	*un chèque de voyage*	*los travelers*
post office	*la poste*	*correos*
stamp	*un timbre*	*un sello*
phonecard	*une télécarte*	*una tarjeta de teléfono*
postcard	*une carte postale*	*una tarjeta postal*
public phone	*une cabine téléphonique*	*un teléfono público*
Do you have any change?	*Avez-vous de la monnaie?*	*¿Tiene cambio?*
shop	*le magasin*	*la tienda*
central food market	*les halles*	*el mercado*
tobacconist	*le tabac*	*el estanco*
pharmacy	*la pharmacie*	*la farmacia*
aspirin	*l'aspirine*	*la aspirina*
condoms	*les préservatifs*	*los preservativos*
insect repellent	*l'anti-insecte*	*el repelente de insectos*
sun cream	*la crème solaire*	*la crema solar*
tampons	*les tampons hygiéniques*	*los tampones*
beach	*la plage*	*la playa*
booking/box office	*le bureau de location*	*la taquilla*
church	*l'église*	*la iglesia*
museum	*le musée*	*el museo*
sea	*la mer*	*el mar*
theatre	*le théâtre*	*el teatro*
Accommodation		
Do you have a room?	*Avez-vous une chambre?*	*¿Tiene usted una habitación?*
Can I look at the room?	*Puis-je voir la chambre?*	*¿Podría ver la habitación?*
How much is the room per day/week?	*Quel est le prix de la chambre par jour/semaine?*	*¿Cuánto cuesta la habitación por día/semana?*
single room	*une chambre pour une personne*	*una habitación para una persona*
twin room	*une chambre à deux lits*	*una habitación con dos camas*
double room	*une chambre pour deux personnes*	*una habitación doble*
... with a shower/bath	*... avec douche/salle de bains*	*...con ducha/baño*
... for one night/one week	*... pour une nuit/une semaine*	*...por una noche/una semana*

English	French	Spanish
Accommodation (*cont'd*)		
bed	*un lit*	*una cama*
blanket	*une couverture*	*una manta*
cot (child's bed)	*un lit d'enfant*	*una cuna*
pillow	*un oreiller*	*una almohada*
soap	*du savon*	*el jabón*
towel	*une serviette*	*una toalla*
Directions		
Where is...?	*Où se trouve...?*	*¿Dónde está... ?*
left	*à gauche*	*a la izquierda*
right	*à droite*	*a la derecha*
straight on	*tout droit*	*todo recto*
here	*ici*	*aquí*
there	*là*	*allí*
close	*proche*	*cerca*
far	*loin*	*lejos*
forwards	*en avant*	*adelante*
backwards	*en arrière*	*hacia atrás*
up	*en haut*	*arriba*
down	*en bas*	*abajo*
corner	*le coin*	*la esquina*
square	*la place*	*la plaza*
street	*la rue*	*la calle*
Transport		
I want to go to...	*Je voudrais aller à...*	*Quisiera ir a...*
How can I get to... ?	*Comment puis-je aller à... ?*	*¿Cómo puedo llegar a... ?*
When is the next... ?	*Quel est le prochain... ?*	*¿Cuándo sale el próximo... ?*
What time does it leave (arrive)?	*A quelle heure part-il (arrive-t-il)?*	*¿A qué hora sale (llega)?*
From where does it leave?	*D'où part-il?*	*¿De dónde sale?*
Do you stop at... ?	*Passez-vous par... ?*	*¿Para en... ?*
How long does the trip take?	*Combien de temps dure le voyage?*	*¿Cuánto tiempo dura el viaje?*
A single (return) ticket to...	*un billet aller or un billet aller simple (aller et retour) pour...*	*Un billete (de ida y vuelta) a...*
How much is the fare?	*Combien coûte le billet?*	*Cuánto cuesta el billete?*
Have a good trip!	*Bon voyage!*	*¡Buen viaje!*
airport	*l'aéroport*	*el aeropuerto*
aeroplane	*l'avion*	*el avión*
berth	*la couchette*	*la litera*
bicycle	*la bicyclette/le vélo*	*la bicicleta*
mountain bike	*le vélo tout terrain, VTT*	*una bicicleta de montaña*
bus	*l'autobus*	*el autobús*
bus stop	*l'arrêt d'autobus*	*la parada*
car	*la voiture*	*el coche*
coach	*l'autocar*	*el autocar*
coach station	*la gare routière*	*la estación de autobuses*

11

Language

English	French	Spanish
Transport (cont'd)		
flight	le vol	el vuelo
on foot	à pied	a pié
port	le port	el puerto
railway station	la gare	la estación de tren
ship	le bateau	el buque/barco/embarcadero
subway/underground	le métro	el metro
taxi	le taxi	el taxi
train	le train	el tren
delayed	en retard	con retraso
on time	à l'heure	puntual
platform	le quai	el andén
date-stamp machine	le composteur	la fichadora
timetable	l'horaire	el horario
left luggage (locker)	la consigne (automatique)	la consigna (automática)
ticket office	le guichet	la taquilla
ticket	le billet	el billete
seat	la place	el asiento
Driving		
breakdown	la panne	la avería
car	la voiture	el coche
danger	le danger	el peligro
driver	le chauffeur	el conductor/chófer
entrance	l'entrée	la entrada
exit	la sortie	la salida
give way/yield	céder le passage	ceda el paso
hire	louer	alquiler
(international) driving licence	un permis de conduire (international)	el carnet de conducir (internacional)
motorbike/moped	la moto/le vélomoteur	la moto/el ciclomotor
no parking	stationnement interdit	estacionamento prohibido
petrol (unleaded)	l'essence (sans plomb)	la gasolina (sin plombo)
road	la route	la carretera
road works	les travaux	las obras
This doesn't work	Ça ne marche pas	Este no funciona
Is the road good?	Est-ce que la route est bonne?	¿Es buena la carretera?
Days		
Monday	lundi	lunes
Tuesday	mardi	martes
Wednesday	mercredi	miércoles
Thursday	jeudi	jueves
Friday	vendredi	viernes
Saturday	samedi	sábado
Sunday	dimanche	domingo

English	French	Spanish
Months		
January	*janvier*	*enero*
February	*février*	*febrero*
March	*mars*	*marzo*
April	*avril*	*abril*
May	*mai*	*mayo*
June	*juin*	*junio*
July	*juillet*	*julio*
August	*août*	*agosto*
September	*septembre*	*septiembre*
October	*octobre*	*octubre*
November	*novembre*	*noviembre*
December	*décembre*	*diciembre*
Numbers		
one	*un*	*uno*
two	*deux*	*dos*
three	*trois*	*tres*
four	*quatre*	*cuatro*
five	*cinq*	*cinco*
six	*six*	*seis*
seven	*sept*	*siete*
eight	*huit*	*ocho*
nine	*neuf*	*nueve*
ten	*dix*	*diez*
eleven	*onze*	*once*
twelve	*douze*	*doce*
thirteen	*treize*	*trece*
fourteen	*quatorze*	*catorce*
fifteen	*quinze*	*quince*
sixteen	*seize*	*dieciséis*
seventeen	*dix-sept*	*diecisiete*
eighteen	*dix-huit*	*dieciocho*
nineteen	*dix-neuf*	*diecinueve*
twenty	*vingt*	*veinte*
twenty-one	*vingt et un*	*veintiuno*
twenty-two	*vingt-deux*	*veintidós*
thirty	*trente*	*treinta*
forty	*quarante*	*cuarenta*
fifty	*cinquante*	*cincuenta*
sixty	*soixante*	*sesenta*
seventy	*soixante-dix*	*setenta*
seventy-one	*soixante et onze*	*setenta y uno*
eighty	*quatre-vingts*	*ochenta*
eighty-one	*quatre-vingt-un*	*ochenta y uno*
ninety	*quatre-vingt-dix*	*noventa*
one hundred	*cent*	*cien*
two hundred	*deux cents*	*doscientos*
one thousand	*mille*	*mil*

English	French	Spanish
Time		
What time is it?	*Quelle heure est-il?*	*¿Qué hora es?*
It's 2 o'clock (am/pm)	*Il est deux heures (du matin/de l'après-midi)*	*Son las dos (de la mañana/de la tarde*
... half past 2	*...deux heures et demie*	*... las dos y media*
... a quarter past 2	*...deux heures et quart*	*... las dos y cuarto*
... a quarter to 3	*...trois heures moins le quart*	*... las tres menos cuarto*
it is early	*il est tôt*	*es temprano*
it is late	*il est tard*	*es tarde*
month	*un mois*	*un mes*
week	*une semaine*	*una semana*
day	*un jour/une journée*	*un día*
morning	*le matin*	*la mañana*
afternoon	*l'après-midi*	*la tarde*
evening	*le soir*	*el anochecer*
night	*la nuit*	*la noche*
today	*aujourd'hui*	*hoy*
yesterday	*hier*	*ayer*
tomorrow	*demain*	*mañana*
day before yesterday	*avant-hier*	*antes de ayer*
day after tomorrow	*après-demain*	*pasado manaña*
soon	*bientôt*	*pronto*

Glossary

abbaye abbey

arènes bullring

auberge inn

ayuntamiento city/town hall

baserri/borda Basque farmhouse

bastide a medieval new town, usually rectangular, with a grid of streets and an arcaded central square

Batua Standard Basque language

bodega winery

borda see *baserri*

cave cellar

cesta punta *pelota* played with long wicker baskets; also known as *jaï-alaï*

château mansion, manor house or castle

chemin path

churrigueresque florid Baroque style of the late 17th and early 18th centuries

cloître cloister

col mountain pass

cortes Spanish parliament

couvent convent or monastery

dolmen Neolithic funerary monument shaped like a table

DO Denominación de Origen, the Spanish equivalent of AOC for wine credentials

église church

encierro running of the bulls

estación train station (Renfe)

Euskal Herria the Basque country

Euskera the Basque language

extea Basque house

frontón pelota court

fueros exemptions or privileges of a region under medieval Spanish law

gare train station (SNCF)

gaztelulaks earthen hilltop forts

grange farm

halles covered market

hôtel originally the town residence of the nobility; by the 18th century used for any large, private residence

iglesia church

lauburu the 'Basque cross'

mairie town hall

marché/mercado market

mirador a scenic view point or belvedere

Modernista Art Nouveau

Mudéjar Moorish-influenced architecture; Spain's 'National style' in the 12th to the 16th centuries

oppidum pre-Roman town

pais/pays region or village

parlement a French juridical body, with members appointed by the king; by the late Ancien Régime, parlements exercised a great deal of influence over political affairs

Plateresque 16th-century style; heavily ornamented Gothic

plage/playa beach

plaza de toros bullring

port mountain pass

pronunciamiento military coup

quartier a division of land in a *commune*; each *commune* had 6–12 *quartiers*

retablo carved or painted altarpiece, often consisting of a number of scenes or sculptural ensembles

tour tower

trinquete indoor *pelota* court

Chronology

Denbora badoa eta gu harekin. (Time goes by, and we go with it.)

old Basque proverb

56 BC Caesar's lieutenant Crassus takes over Aquitania, including Vasconia, which subsequently becomes Novempopulani.

AD 448 Visigoths control most of Iberia and try to subdue Basque resistance.

711–13 Moors sweep across Iberia and over the Pyrenees.

778 Charlemagne attempts to take Zaragoza from the Moors and destroys Pamplona. His rearguard is ambushed by the Basques near Roncesvalles.

824 Birth of the Basque kingdom in Pamplona under Iñigo de Aritza.

892 St Leon, attempting to convert the heathens, is decapitated in Bayonne under Norman occupation. The Normans are finally pushed back by the duke of Vasconia.

950 The French bishop of Le Puy blazes the pilgrimage route to Santiago.

1004 The Basque king of Navarra, Sancho the Great, reigns over the Basque regions as well as Gascony, Aragón, Castile and the County of Toulouse.

1023 Sancho the Great creates the title of viscount of Labourd for his cousin Loup Sanche in Bayonne, and gives Soule to the Viscount Guillaume Fort.

1179 The French Church calls for the excommunication of Basques and Navarrese, based on the horror stories told in the *Codex Calixtus*, which contained a guide to the Compostela pilgrimage.

1193 Henry Plantagenet, king of England and duke of Aquitaine, takes the French Basque country.

1200 Álava is taken by Castile. Basques recognize the king of Castile on the condition that he recognize their *fueros* (municipal charters/laws).

1234 The Basque dynasty of Navarra dies with Sancho the Strong and the crown falls into the hands of Thibault, a Franco-Basque relative of the French royal family.

1332 Álava is forced to recognize the king of Castile as its lord.

1379 Juan de Haro, the lord of Vizcaya, becomes king of Castile.

1450 Treaty of Ayherre: Labourd acquiesces to the king of France's authority in exchange for its independence.

1471 After riding roughshod over Basque *fueros*, Henry IV of Castile is disqualified by the *junta general* and replaced by his sister Isabella. He sends an army to crush Viscaya; instead the Basques thrash him soundly at Mungia.

1483 Catherine d'Albret of the Béarn inherits the kingdom of Navarra.

1492 Ferdinand and Isabella complete the Reconquista and expel all Jews from Spain; Basques accompany Columbus to the New World.

1514 The armies of Ferdinand and Isabella take Pamplona and occupy all of Navarra.

1522 Juan Sebastián Elcano (Magellan's lieutenant) from Getaria, tours around the world.

1534 Ignatius of Loyola founds the Company of Jesus (Jesuits).

1589 Henri III of Navarre becomes king of France under the name of Henri IV.

1609 Pierre de Lancre leads witch trials in Labourd.

1659 The Treaty of the Pyrenees sets the international frontier through the Basque country; Louis XIV renounces his rights to southern Navarra.

1713 The Treaty of Utrecht ends the War of the Spanish Succession and bars Basque cod fleets from the Grand Bank.

1765 The Treaty of Elizondo officially splits Navarre between France and Spain, but the treaty is not applied because of protests from the citizens of Navarre.

1789 The French Revolutionary government overrules the autonomy of Soule, Labourd and Basse-Navarre.

1790 Creation of the French *département* of Pyrénées-Atlantiques.

1813 Peninsular War; Wellington decisively defeats the French at Vitoria, then burns down San Sebastián.

1833–9 First Carlist War.

1835 Church properties across Spain are confiscated by Madrid and auctioned off.

1841 The Spanish customs office is transferred from the Ebro to the French frontier. Álava, Vizcaya and Guipúzcoa lose most of their *fueros*.

1845 Basques emigrate en masse to South America.

1856 The Franco-Spanish Convention splits Navarre once and for all.

1872–6 Second Carlist War.

1877 Vizcaya and Guipúzcoa are the poorest provinces in Spain.

1887 Vizcaya and Guipúzcoa are the richest provinces in Spain.

1890 Workers in Bilbao lead the first general strike in Spanish history.

1895 Sabino Arana founds the Basque Nationalist Party (PNV).

1898 Spanish-American War; Spain loses last remnants of its overseas empire.

1913 Founding of the Basque Academy to create a Standard Basque language.

1936–9 Spanish Civil War.

1936 José Antonio de Aguirre forms the first government of Euskadi.

1937 The Nazis bomb Gernika for Franco, 26 April.

1959 ETA (Euskadi Ta Askatsuna – Basque Homeland and Liberty) is founded.

1970 Trial in Burgos of alleged ETA-ists.

1973 ETA blows up the Spanish prime minister Carrero Blanco in Madrid.

1975 EHAS (Basque Socialist Party) is founded. Franco dies.

1980 Creation of the Autonomous Government of Euskadi in Vitoria for Álava, Vizcaya and Guipúzcoa, and the Autonomous Government of Navarra in Pamplona.

1981 President Mitterrand begins regionalization in France.

1986 The Herri Batasuna party is legalized.

1997 Opening of the Guggenheim Museum Bilbao.

2000 ETA assasinates the popular ex-minister Ernest Lluch in Barcelona; this is followed by a street protest with over 900,000 participants.

2002 The euro replaces the peseta as the currency in Spain and France. Spanish government passes a law to ban Batasuna, the political wing of ETA.

2004 After the Madrid bombings on 11 March, the hard-line Partido Popular are ousted in the Spanish general election. Zapatero's new Socialist government promises to negotiate with ETA if they lay down their arms.

2006 ETA declares a 'permanent' ceasefire and talks look set to begun, until a bomb is detonated in Madrid airport on 30 December, killing two men.

2007 ETA announces end of ceasefire; Zapatero's government suspends talks.

2008 The Socialists, still led by Zapatero, are returned to power in Spanish general elections.

2010 ETA declares a third ceasefire, promising (in a statement made Jan 2011) that it will be 'permanent, general and verifiable'.

12

Chronology

Further Reading

Astrain, Luis Nuñez, *The Basques: Their Struggle for Independence* (Welsh Academic Press, 1997). Concise and well-balanced argument from the non-violent nationalist point of view.

Atxaga, Bernardo, *Obabakoak* (Pantheon, 1993). Collection of stories by the best-known living Basque author, the first to be translated into English.

Barrenechea, Teresa, *The Basque Table: Passionate Home Cooking From Spain's Most Celebrated Cuisine* (Harvard Common Press, 2006). 130 recipes by an expert on Basque regional cuisine.

Beevor, Antony, *The Battle for Spain* (Phoenix, 2007). Possibly the definitive book on the Spanish Civil War.

Boling, Dave, *Guernica* (Picador, 2009). An epic family saga which takes place in Guernica at the time of the savage bombing.

Carr, Raymond (editor), *Spain: A History* (OUP, 2000). Probably the best concise history of Spain available.

Collins, Roger, *The Basques* (Blackwell, 1990). A good general introduction to the Basques.

Conversi, Daniele, *The Basques, The Catalans and Spain: Alternative Routes to Nationalist Mobilisation* (Hurst and Co, 1997). An interesting comparison of two nations and their search for legitimacy in the New Spain.

Epton, Nina, *Navarre: the Flea between Two Monkeys* (1993). A good read but out of print, available only in libraries.

Forster, Kurt W., Arnold Hadley Soutter and Francesco Dal Co, *Frank O. Gehry: The Complete Works* (Monacelli Press, 1998). Great overview of the career of the architect of El Goog.

Foster, Nelson, and Linda S. Cordell (ed), *Chilies to Chocolate: Food the Americas Gave the World* (University of Arizona Press, 1992).

Gallop, Rodney, *A Book of the Basques* (published in 1930 and reissued in 1998). During his boyhood, Gallop, an Englishman, spent his summers in St-Jean-de-Luz, and his book has a great feel for the history and often peculiar customs of the Basques.

Hamilton, Carrie, *Women and ETA: The Gender Politics of Radical Basque Nationalism* (Manchester University Press, 2007). A feminist perspective.

Hemingway, Ernest, *The Sun Also Rises*, (1926, *Fiesta* in the UK). The book that put Pamplona on the map.

Hooper, John, *The New Spaniards* (Penguin, 2006). A comprehensive and enjoyable account of contemporary Spanish life and politics.

King, Alan, *The Basque Language* (University of Nevada Press, 1994). Probably the most comprehensive learn-Basque book, with lots of grammar.

King, Alan and Begotxu Olaizola Elordi, *Colloquial Basque* (Routledge, 1996). Shorter learn-Basque book, complete with cassettes.

Kurlansky, Mark, *The Basque History of the World* (Penguin Books, 2001). Wonderful, wide-ranging and *simpatico* account of the Basques; history, cuisine and much more.

Lacambra-Loizu, José Maria , *The Lords of Navarre: A Basque Family Saga* (iUniverse.com, 2004)

Lecours, Andre, *Basque Nationalism and the Spanish State* (University of Nevada Press, 2007).

Lojendio, Louis, *Navarre Romaine* (Zodiaque, 1967). One of the excellent illustrated volumes in the French Zodiaque series on medieval art.

Minta, Stephen, *Aguirre* (Henry Holt and Company, 1994). The adventures of Lope de

Aguirre, the mad Basque *conquistador*, with lots about the Amazon and Basques, too.

Peñín, *Peñín Guide to Spanish Wine* (Peñín, 2010). Good introduction to Spanish wines.

Richardson, Paul, *Our Lady of the Sewers* (Abacus, 1999). An engaging collection of stories about almost forgotten corners and customs of Spain, including a description of Lekeitio's gruesome goose rodeo.

Sevilla, María José, *Life and Food in the Basque Country* (New Amsterdam, 1990). Cooking, culture and culinary traditions, with recipes.

Thomas, Hugh, *The Spanish Civil War* (Penguin, 2003). An excellent, if rather dated, general work.

Trask, Robert L.,*The History of Basque* (Routledge, 1996). The authority on an intriguing subject.

Tremlett, Giles, *Ghosts of Spain* (Faber and Faber, 2007). A fascinating and entertaining travelogue, by a British journalist long resident in Spain.

Van Bruggen, Coosje, *Frank O.Gehry: Guggenheim Museum, Bilbao* (Harry N. Abrams, 1998). An in-depth look at the design process of the great museum, aimed at students and professionals alike. The text is accompanied by colour photographs of the building and reproductions of Gehry's drawings and models.

Woodworth, Paddy, *The Basque Country: A Cultural History* (Signal, 2007). Engaging general history and background.

Zulaika, Joseba, and William Douglas, *Terror and Taboo: the Follies, Fables and Faces of Terrorism* (Routledge, 1996). In-depth study on ETA.

14

Further Reading

Index

Main page references are in **bold**. Page references to maps are in *italics*.

About the Updaters

Luciano di Giordana was born in Italy, and migrated with his family to Melbourne, Australia in his teens. Now he divides his time between Australia and Europe. A travel writer, journalist and teacher, he has published guidebooks and articles on destinations around the world.

Mary-Ann Gallagher is a British editor and travel journalist who has written extensively on Spain for numerous magazines, newspapers and guidebook publishers, including Cadogan. Although based in Barcelona, she spends as much time as she can in the Basque Lands.

5th American edition published 2012 by

CADOGAN GUIDES USA
An imprint of Interlink Publishing Group, Inc
46 Crosby Street, Northampton, Massachusetts 01060
www.interlinkbooks.com
www.cadoganguidesusa.com

Text copyright © Dana Facaros and Michael Pauls 1996, 1999. 2001, 2003, 2006, 2008, 2012
Copyright © 2012 New Holland Publishers (UK) Ltd

Cover photographs. Front: The Guggenheim, Bilbao © Art Kowalsky / Alamy. Back: San Sebastian panorama © istockphoto.com
Photo essay photographs: © istockphoto.com except p.13 (bottom) and p.15 (top) © Shutterstock.
Maps © Cadogan Guides, drawn by Maidenhead Cartographic Services Ltd
Publisher: Guy Hobbs
Cover design: Jason Hopper
Photo essay design: Sarah Gardner
Editor: Mary-Ann Gallagher
Proofreading: Linda McQueen
Indexing: Isobel McLean

Printed in India by Replika Press Pvt Ltd
Library of Congress Cataloging-in-Publication Data available
ISBN: 978 1 56656 880 7

The author and publishers have made every effort to ensure the accuracy of the information in this book at the time of going to press. However, they cannot accept any responsibility for any loss, injury or inconvenience resulting from the use of information contained in this guide.

Please help us to keep this guide up to date. Although we have done our best to ensure that the information in this guide is correct at the time of going to press, laws and regulations are constantly changing and standards and prices fluctuate. We would be delighted to receive any comments concerning existing entries or omissions.

All rights reserved. No part of this publication may be reproduced, stored in a retrieval system, or transmitted, in any form or by any means, electronic or mechanical, including photocopying and recording, or by any information storage and retrieval system except as may be expressly permitted by the USA 1976 Copyright Act or in writing from the publisher. Requests for permission should be addressed to Cadogan Guides USA, Interlink Publishing, 46 Crosby Street, Northampton MA 01060, USA.

To request our complete full-color catalog, please call use toll free at 1-800-238-LINK, visit our website at www.interlinkbooks.com, or send us an email: info@interlinkbooks.com.

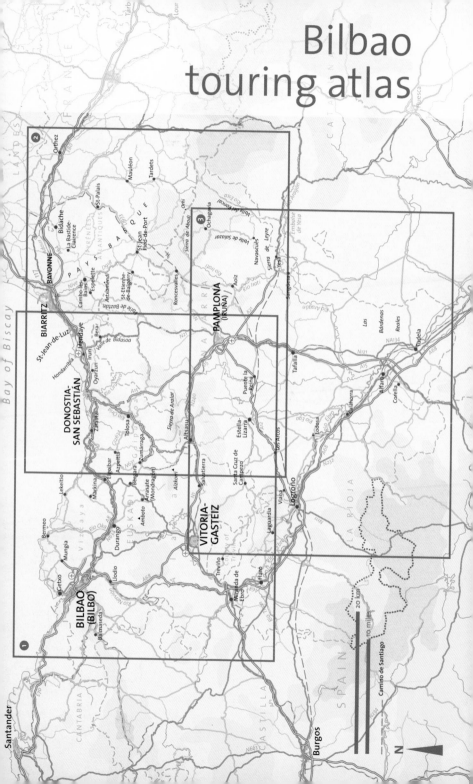

Bilbao
touring atlas

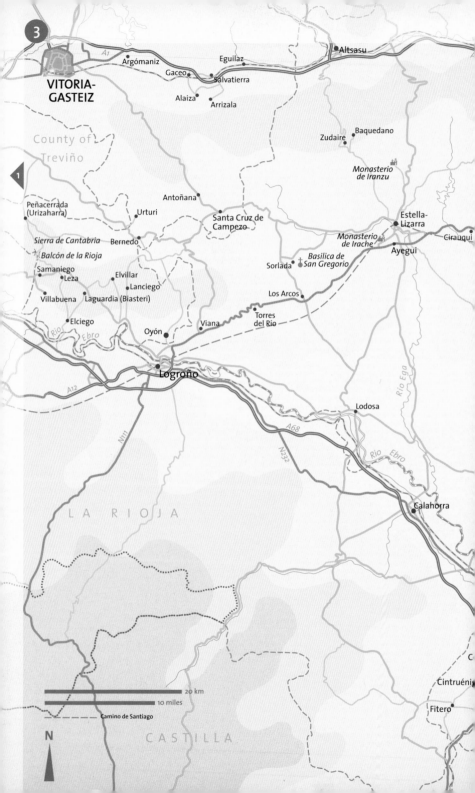

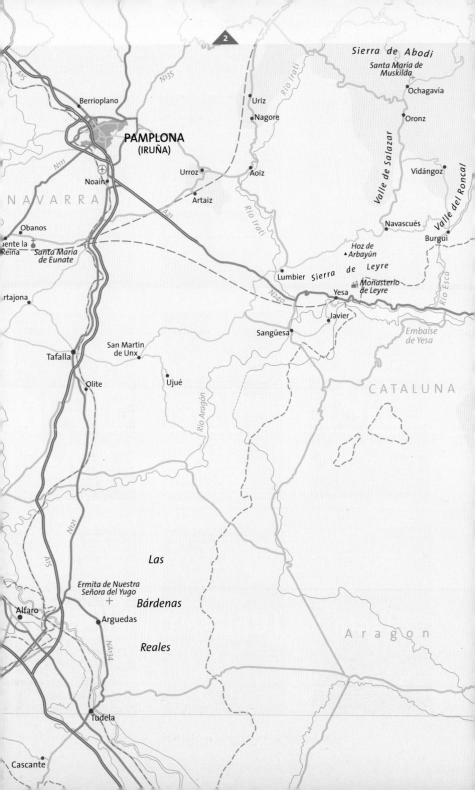

If you are interested in the art, architecture, history or culture of the regions you visit in Europe and the Mediterranean basin, try the wonderfully readable **Cadogan Guides**

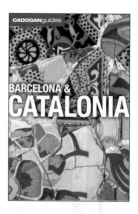

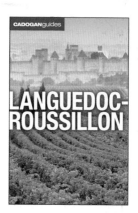

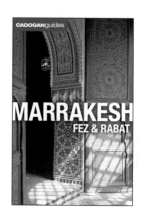

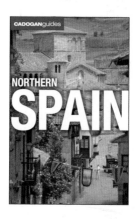

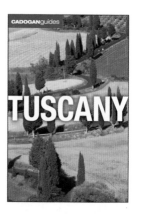

www.newhollandpublishers.com